1 YEAR DAILY DEVOTIONAL

FOR TEENS & ADULTS

Word of Life.
Youth Ministries

1 YEAR DAILY DEVOTIONAL

FOR TEENS & ADULTS

Word of Life Local Church Ministries

A division of Word of Life Fellowship, Inc.
Dr. Don Lough Jr. – President & CEO
Jack Wyrtzen & Harry Bollback - Founders
John Collins – Director, Local Church Ministries

USA
P.O. Box 600
Schroon Lake, NY 12870
youthministry@wol.org
518-494-6000

Canada
RR#8/Owen Sound
ON, Canada N4K 5W4
lcm@wol.ca
1-800-461-3503

Web Address: www.wol.org

Publisher's Acknowledgements:

Writers and Contributors: Dr. Tom Davis, Gary Ingersoll, David Livingston, Doug Reider, Cindy Skeffington, Chris Selby, Greg Stier, Mark Strout
Editor: Mark Strout
Curriculum Manager: Don Reichard
Cover and Page Design: Edwin Cruz, Ottoman Creative Group

Prayer, Care, Share is adapted from Mission America Coalition. The content in sections 2-5 of the Mobilize guide is adapted and used by permission from Dare 2 Share Ministries, Inc., www.dare2share.org.

Printed in the United States of America

HELPFUL HINTS FOR A DAILY QUIET TIME

The Quiet Time with Commentary was created to encourage and facilitate spiritual growth in the lives of Christians as they conduct their own personal investigation into the Bible. Consider the following helpful hints:

1 Prioritize your time with God. Morning is often best, but choose the time that works for you.

2 As you read the daily passage in God's Word, look at it from God's point of view. Meditate on what you have read. (In one sentence, write the main thought).

■ Apply the truth to your life. (Use first person pronouns: I, me, my, mine). If you have difficulty finding an application for your life, think of yourself as a Bible SPECTator and ask yourself the following questions:

S – Is there any **SIN** for me to forsake?
P – Is there any **PROMISE** for me to claim?
E – Is there any **EXAMPLE** for me to follow?
C – Is there any **COMMAND** for me to obey?
T – Is there a **TRUTH** for me to embrace?

3   Read the commentary portion only after you have read the daily passage. This should provide additional insight into the passage.

4   Be sure to fill out your Quiet Time sheets. This will really help you remember the things the Lord brings to your mind and establish action steps to take.

5   Organizing and documenting your prayer time will help you stay faithful in prayer and rejoice as you see God at work. There are several pages in this book for you to use or you can create your own.

6   Each day, purpose to share something you gained from your quiet time with another person. Whether it's face to face, through a phone call, text, or on social media, communicating what you have learned from God's Word encourages others and solidifies its truth in your own heart.

MY PERSONAL PRAYER JOURNAL

The Cause Circle is a simple tool that will help you be more intentional about sharing Jesus' message, the Gospel, with your friends. It is built around three simple priorities: **Prayer. Care. Share.**

Prayer. Jesus knew how important it was to talk to God about people, before He talked to people about God…and the same is true for us. When we start by praying for the people we are seeking to reach with the gospel, it prepares their hearts to hear the good news of Jesus.

Care. Jesus often healed the sick, fed the hungry, and helped the hurting. In the same way, we must show love to those we are trying to reach. We do this by listening to them and caring for them.

Share. We must lovingly share the gospel message clearly and confidently. A restored relationship with God is the absolute best news on the planet, so don't be afraid to ask them to put their trust in Jesus! If they say "No," or "Not now," continue the Prayer, Care, Share process. And if they say "Yes," celebrate! Then get them plugged into a good church, help them grow deeper in the faith, and challenge them to begin their own Cause Circle of Prayer, Care, Share with their own friends.

Below, under **PRAYER**, write the names of friends and family members that you desire to reach with the Gospel.

Each week, think of ways you can **CARE** for those you are seeking to reach and make a plan to carry them out.

When you are ready to **SHARE** the gospel with your friend, think through how you will do this and then write the details of where, when, and how.

PRAYER

DATE / REQUEST

DATE / ANSWER

DARE 2 SHARE CAUSE CIRCLE STRATEGY

PRAYER: Asking God to prepare my friend's heart to hear the good news of Jesus.

CARE: Asking God to help me love my friend by listening to them and caring for them.

SHARE: Asking God to help me lovingly share the gospel message clearly and confidently with my friend.

DATE / REQUEST **DATE / ANSWER**

DARE 2 SHARE CAUSE CIRCLE STRATEGY

PRAYER: Asking God to prepare my friend's heart to hear the good news of Jesus.

CARE: Asking God to help me love my friend by listening to them and caring for them.

SHARE: Asking God to help me lovingly share the gospel message clearly and confidently with my friend.

DATE / REQUEST   **DATE / ANSWER**

DARE 2 SHARE CAUSE CIRCLE STRATEGY

PRAYER: Asking God to prepare my friend's heart to hear the good news of Jesus.
CARE: Asking God to help me love my friend by listening to them and caring for them.
SHARE: Asking God to help me lovingly share the gospel message clearly and confidently with my friend.

DATE / REQUEST   **DATE / ANSWER**

DARE 2 SHARE CAUSE CIRCLE STRATEGY

PRAYER: Asking God to prepare my friend's heart to hear the good news of Jesus.

CARE: Asking God to help me love my friend by listening to them and caring for them.

SHARE: Asking God to help me lovingly share the gospel message clearly and confidently with my friend.

DATE / REQUEST   **DATE / ANSWER**

DARE 2 SHARE CAUSE CIRCLE STRATEGY

PRAYER: Asking God to prepare my friend's heart to hear the good news of Jesus.

CARE: Asking God to help me love my friend by listening to them and caring for them.

SHARE: Asking God to help me lovingly share the gospel message clearly and confidently with my friend.

DATE / REQUEST   **DATE / ANSWER**

DARE 2 SHARE CAUSE CIRCLE STRATEGY

PRAYER: Asking God to prepare my friend's heart to hear the good news of Jesus.

CARE: Asking God to help me love my friend by listening to them and caring for them.

SHARE: Asking God to help me lovingly share the gospel message clearly and confidently with my friend.

DATE / REQUEST　　　　　　　　**DATE / ANSWER**

DARE 2 SHARE CAUSE CIRCLE STRATEGY

PRAYER: Asking God to prepare my friend's heart to hear the good news of Jesus.

CARE: Asking God to help me love my friend by listening to them and caring for them.

SHARE: Asking God to help me lovingly share the gospel message clearly and confidently with my friend.

DATE / REQUEST   **DATE / ANSWER**

DARE 2 SHARE CAUSE CIRCLE STRATEGY

PRAYER: Asking God to prepare my friend's heart to hear the good news of Jesus.

CARE: Asking God to help me love my friend by listening to them and caring for them.

SHARE: Asking God to help me lovingly share the gospel message clearly and confidently with my friend.

Some people just can't get enough! That is why we have several dimensions in the Word of Life Quiet Time. Along with the daily reading, content and application questions for each day, two reading programs are given to help you understand the Bible better. Choose one or both.

Reading Through the New Testament Four Times In One Year

Turn the page and discover a schedule that takes you through the New Testament four times in one year. This is a great method to help you see the correlation of the Gospels and other New Testament books.

Reading Through the Whole Bible In One Year

Turn another page and find a program of several pages that will guide you through a chronological reading of the entire Bible. Follow this schedule and you will move from Genesis through Revelation in one year.

The Choice is Up to You

Whether you have a short quiet time, a quiet time with more scripture reading or one with a mini-Bible study each day, we trust your time with God will draw you closer to Him in every area of your life.

Read through the New Testament four times in one year

Weeks 1-13

- ❏ Matthew 1-3
- ❏ Matthew 4-6
- ❏ Matthew 7-9
- ❏ Matt. 10-12
- ❏ Matt. 13-15
- ❏ Matt. 16-18
- ❏ Matt. 19-21
- ❏ Matt. 22-24
- ❏ Matt. 25-26
- ❏ Matt. 27-28
- ❏ Mark 1-3
- ❏ Mark 4-5
- ❏ Mark 6-8
- ❏ Mark 9-11
- ❏ Mark 12-14
- ❏ Mark 15-16
- ❏ Luke 1-2
- ❏ Luke 3-5
- ❏ Luke 6-7
- ❏ Luke 8-9
- ❏ Luke 10-11
- ❏ Luke 12-14
- ❏ Luke 15-17
- ❏ Luke 18-20
- ❏ Luke 21-22
- ❏ Luke 23-24
- ❏ John 1-3
- ❏ John 4-5
- ❏ John 6-7
- ❏ John 8-10
- ❏ John 11-12
- ❏ John 13-15
- ❏ John 16-18
- ❏ John 19-21
- ❏ Acts 1-3
- ❏ Acts 4-6
- ❏ Acts 7-8
- ❏ Acts 9-11
- ❏ Acts 12-15
- ❏ Acts 16-18
- ❏ Acts 19-21
- ❏ Acts 22-24
- ❏ Acts 25-26
- ❏ Acts 27-28
- ❏ Romans 1-3

- ❏ Romans 4-6
- ❏ Romans 7-9
- ❏ Romans 10-12
- ❏ Romans 13-16
- ❏ 1 Cor. 1-4
- ❏ 1 Cor. 5-9
- ❏ 1 Cor. 10-12
- ❏ 1 Cor. 13-16
- ❏ 2 Cor. 1-4
- ❏ 2 Cor. 5-8
- ❏ 2 Cor. 9-13
- ❏ Galatians 1-3
- ❏ Galatians 4-6
- ❏ Ephesians 1-3
- ❏ Ephesians 4-6
- ❏ Philippians 1-4
- ❏ Colossians 1-4
- ❏ 1 Thes. 1-3
- ❏ 1 Thes. 4-5
- ❏ 2 Thes. 1-3
- ❏ 1 Timothy 1-3
- ❏ 1 Timothy 4-6
- ❏ 2 Timothy 1-4
- ❏ Titus 1-3
- ❏ Philemon
- ❏ Hebrews 1
- ❏ Hebrews 2-4
- ❏ Hebrews 5-7
- ❏ Hebrews 8-10
- ❏ Hebrews 11-13
- ❏ James 1-3
- ❏ James 4-5
- ❏ 1 Peter 1-3
- ❏ 1 Peter 4-5
- ❏ 2 Peter 1-3
- ❏ 1 John 1-3
- ❏ 1 John 4-5
- ❏ 2 Jn, 3 Jn, Jude
- ❏ Revelation 1-3
- ❏ Revelation 4-6
- ❏ Revelation 7-9
- ❏ Rev. 10-12
- ❏ Rev. 13-15
- ❏ Rev. 16-18
- ❏ Rev. 19-22

Weeks 14-26

- ❏ Matthew 1-3
- ❏ Matthew 4-6
- ❏ Matthew 7-9
- ❏ Matt. 10-12
- ❏ Matt. 13-15
- ❏ Matt. 16-18
- ❏ Matt. 19-21
- ❏ Matt. 22-24
- ❏ Matt. 25-26
- ❏ Matt. 27-28
- ❏ Mark 1-3
- ❏ Mark 4-5
- ❏ Mark 6-8
- ❏ Mark 9-11
- ❏ Mark 12-14
- ❏ Mark 15-16
- ❏ Luke 1-2
- ❏ Luke 3-5
- ❏ Luke 6-7
- ❏ Luke 8-9
- ❏ Luke 10-11
- ❏ Luke 12-14
- ❏ Luke 15-17
- ❏ Luke 18-20
- ❏ Luke 21-22
- ❏ Luke 23-24
- ❏ John 1-3
- ❏ John 4-5
- ❏ John 6-7
- ❏ John 8-10
- ❏ John 11-12
- ❏ John 13-15
- ❏ John 16-18
- ❏ John 19-21
- ❏ Acts 1-3
- ❏ Acts 4-6
- ❏ Acts 7-8
- ❏ Acts 9-11
- ❏ Acts 12-15
- ❏ Acts 16-18
- ❏ Acts 19-21
- ❏ Acts 22-24
- ❏ Acts 25-26
- ❏ Acts 27-28
- ❏ Romans 1-3

- ❏ Romans 4-6
- ❏ Romans 7-9
- ❏ Romans 10-12
- ❏ Romans 13-16
- ❏ 1 Cor. 1-4
- ❏ 1 Cor. 5-9
- ❏ 1 Cor. 10-12
- ❏ 1 Cor. 13-16
- ❏ 2 Cor. 1-4
- ❏ 2 Cor. 5-8
- ❏ 2 Cor. 9-13
- ❏ Galatians 1-3
- ❏ Galatians 4-6
- ❏ Ephesians 1-3
- ❏ Ephesians 4-6
- ❏ Philippians 1-4
- ❏ Colossians 1-4
- ❏ 1 Thes. 1-3
- ❏ 1 Thes. 4-5
- ❏ 2 Thes. 1-3
- ❏ 1 Timothy 1-3
- ❏ 1 Timothy 4-6
- ❏ 2 Timothy 1-4
- ❏ Titus 1-3
- ❏ Philemon
- ❏ Hebrews 1
- ❏ Hebrews 2-4
- ❏ Hebrews 5-7
- ❏ Hebrews 8-10
- ❏ Hebrews 11-13
- ❏ James 1-3
- ❏ James 4-5
- ❏ 1 Peter 1-3
- ❏ 1 Peter 4-5
- ❏ 2 Peter 1-3
- ❏ 1 John 1-3
- ❏ 1 John 4-5
- ❏ 2 Jn, 3 Jn, Jude
- ❏ Revelation 1-3
- ❏ Revelation 4-6
- ❏ Revelation 7-9
- ❏ Rev. 10-12
- ❏ Rev. 13-15
- ❏ Rev. 16-18
- ❏ Rev. 19-22

Read through the New Testament four times in one year

Weeks 27-39

- ❏ Matthew 1-3
- ❏ Matthew 4-6
- ❏ Matthew 7-9
- ❏ Matt. 10-12
- ❏ Matt. 13-15
- ❏ Matt. 16-18
- ❏ Matt. 19-21
- ❏ Matt. 22-24
- ❏ Matt. 25-26
- ❏ Matt. 27-28
- ❏ Mark 1-3
- ❏ Mark 4-5
- ❏ Mark 6-8
- ❏ Mark 9-11
- ❏ Mark 12-14
- ❏ Mark 15-16
- ❏ Luke 1-2
- ❏ Luke 3-5
- ❏ Luke 6-7
- ❏ Luke 8-9
- ❏ Luke 10-11
- ❏ Luke 12-14
- ❏ Luke 15-17
- ❏ Luke 18-20
- ❏ Luke 21-22
- ❏ Luke 23-24
- ❏ John 1-3
- ❏ John 4-5
- ❏ John 6-7
- ❏ John 8-10
- ❏ John 11-12
- ❏ John 13-15
- ❏ John 16-18
- ❏ John 19-21
- ❏ Acts 1-3
- ❏ Acts 4-6
- ❏ Acts 7-8
- ❏ Acts 9-11
- ❏ Acts 12-15
- ❏ Acts 16-18
- ❏ Acts 19-21
- ❏ Acts 22-24
- ❏ Acts 25-26
- ❏ Acts 27-28
- ❏ Romans 1-3

- ❏ Romans 4-6
- ❏ Romans 7-9
- ❏ Romans 10-12
- ❏ Romans 13-16
- ❏ 1 Cor. 1-4
- ❏ 1 Cor. 5-9
- ❏ 1 Cor. 10-12
- ❏ 1 Cor. 13-16
- ❏ 2 Cor. 1-4
- ❏ 2 Cor. 5-8
- ❏ 2 Cor. 9-13
- ❏ Galatians 1-3
- ❏ Galatians 4-6
- ❏ Ephesians 1-3
- ❏ Ephesians 4-6
- ❏ Phil. 1-4
- ❏ Colossians 1-4
- ❏ 1 Thes. 1-3
- ❏ 1 Thes. 4-5
- ❏ 2 Thes. 1-3
- ❏ 1 Timothy 1-3
- ❏ 1 Timothy 4-6
- ❏ 2 Timothy 1-4
- ❏ Titus 1-3
- ❏ Philemon
- ❏ Hebrews 1
- ❏ Hebrews 2-4
- ❏ Hebrews 5-7
- ❏ Hebrews 8-10
- ❏ Hebrews 11-13
- ❏ James 1-3
- ❏ James 4-5
- ❏ 1 Peter 1-3
- ❏ 1 Peter 4-5
- ❏ 2 Peter 1-3
- ❏ 1 John 1-3
- ❏ 1 John 4-5
- ❏ 2 Jn, 3 Jn, Jude
- ❏ Revelation 1-3
- ❏ Revelation 4-6
- ❏ Revelation 7-9
- ❏ Rev. 10-12
- ❏ Rev. 13-15
- ❏ Rev. 16-18
- ❏ Rev. 19-22

Weeks 40-52

- ❏ Matthew 1-3
- ❏ Matthew 4-6
- ❏ Matthew 7-9
- ❏ Matt. 10-12
- ❏ Matt. 13-15
- ❏ Matt. 16-18
- ❏ Matt. 19-21
- ❏ Matt. 22-24
- ❏ Matt. 25-26
- ❏ Matt. 27-28
- ❏ Mark 1-3
- ❏ Mark 4-5
- ❏ Mark 6-8
- ❏ Mark 9-11
- ❏ Mark 12-14
- ❏ Mark 15-16
- ❏ Luke 1-2
- ❏ Luke 3-5
- ❏ Luke 6-7
- ❏ Luke 8-9
- ❏ Luke 10-11
- ❏ Luke 12-14
- ❏ Luke 15-17
- ❏ Luke 18-20
- ❏ Luke 21-22
- ❏ Luke 23-24
- ❏ John 1-3
- ❏ John 4-5
- ❏ John 6-7
- ❏ John 8-10
- ❏ John 11-12
- ❏ John 13-15
- ❏ John 16-18
- ❏ John 19-21
- ❏ Acts 1-3
- ❏ Acts 4-6
- ❏ Acts 7-8
- ❏ Acts 9-11
- ❏ Acts 12-15
- ❏ Acts 16-18
- ❏ Acts 19-21
- ❏ Acts 22-24
- ❏ Acts 25-26
- ❏ Acts 27-28
- ❏ Romans 1-3

- ❏ Romans 4-6
- ❏ Romans 7-9
- ❏ Romans 10-12
- ❏ Romans 13-16
- ❏ 1 Cor. 1-4
- ❏ 1 Cor. 5-9
- ❏ 1 Cor. 10-12
- ❏ 1 Cor. 13-16
- ❏ 2 Cor. 1-4
- ❏ 2 Cor. 5-8
- ❏ 2 Cor. 9-13
- ❏ Galatians 1-3
- ❏ Galatians 4-6
- ❏ Ephesians 1-3
- ❏ Ephesians 4-6
- ❏ Phil. 1-4
- ❏ Colossians 1-4
- ❏ 1 Thes. 1-3
- ❏ 1 Thes. 4-5
- ❏ 2 Thes. 1-3
- ❏ 1 Timothy 1-3
- ❏ 1 Timothy 4-6
- ❏ 2 Timothy 1-4
- ❏ Titus 1-3
- ❏ Philemon
- ❏ Hebrews 1
- ❏ Hebrews 2-4
- ❏ Hebrews 5-7
- ❏ Hebrews 8-10
- ❏ Hebrews 11-13
- ❏ James 1-3
- ❏ James 4-5
- ❏ 1 Peter 1-3
- ❏ 1 Peter 4-5
- ❏ 2 Peter 1-3
- ❏ 1 John 1-3
- ❏ 1 John 4-5
- ❏ 2 Jn, 3 Jn, Jude
- ❏ Revelation 1-3
- ❏ Revelation 4-6
- ❏ Revelation 7-9
- ❏ Rev. 10-12
- ❏ Rev. 13-15
- ❏ Rev. 16-18
- ❏ Rev. 19-22

Bible Reading Schedule

Read through the Bible chronologically in one year!

- ❏ 1 Genesis 1-3
- ❏ 2 Genesis 4:1-6:8
- ❏ 3 Genesis 6:9-9:29
- ❏ 4 Genesis 10-11
- ❏ 5 Genesis 12-14
- ❏ 6 Genesis 15-17
- ❏ 7 Genesis 18-19
- ❏ 8 Genesis 20-22
- ❏ 9 Genesis 23-24
- ❏ 10 Genesis 25-26
- ❏ 11 Genesis 27-28
- ❏ 12 Genesis 29-30
- ❏ 13 Genesis 31-32
- ❏ 14 Genesis 33-35
- ❏ 15 Genesis 36-37
- ❏ 16 Genesis 38-40
- ❏ 17 Genesis 41-42
- ❏ 18 Genesis 43-45
- ❏ 19 Genesis 46-47
- ❏ 20 Genesis 48-50
- ❏ 21 Job 1-3
- ❏ 22 Job 4-7
- ❏ 23 Job 8-11
- ❏ 24 Job 12-15
- ❏ 25 Job 16-19
- ❏ 26 Job 20-22
- ❏ 27 Job 23-28
- ❏ 28 Job 29-31
- ❏ 29 Job 32-34
- ❏ 30 Job 35-37
- ❏ 31 Job 38-42
- ❏ 32 Exodus 1-4
- ❏ 33 Exodus 5-8
- ❏ 34 Exodus 9-11
- ❏ 35 Exodus 12-13
- ❏ 36 Exodus 14-15
- ❏ 37 Exodus 16-18
- ❏ 38 Exodus 19-21
- ❏ 39 Exodus 22-24
- ❏ 40 Exodus 25-27
- ❏ 41 Exodus 28-29
- ❏ 42 Exodus 30-31
- ❏ 43 Exodus 32-34
- ❏ 44 Exodus 35-36
- ❏ 45 Exodus 37-38
- ❏ 46 Exodus 39-40
- ❏ 47 Leviticus 1:1-5:13
- ❏ 48 Leviticus 5:14-7:38
- ❏ 49 Leviticus 8-10
- ❏ 50 Leviticus 11-12
- ❏ 51 Leviticus 13-14
- ❏ 52 Leviticus 15-17
- ❏ 53 Leviticus 18-20
- ❏ 54 Leviticus 21-23
- ❏ 55 Leviticus 24-25
- ❏ 56 Leviticus 26-27
- ❏ 57 Numbers 1-2
- ❏ 58 Numbers 3-4
- ❏ 59 Numbers 5-6
- ❏ 60 Numbers 7
- ❏ 61 Numbers 8-10
- ❏ 62 Numbers 11-13
- ❏ 63 Numbers 14-15
- ❏ 64 Numbers 16-18
- ❏ 65 Numbers 19-21
- ❏ 66 Numbers 22-24
- ❏ 67 Numbers 25-26
- ❏ 68 Numbers 27-29
- ❏ 69 Numbers 30-31
- ❏ 70 Numbers 32-33
- ❏ 71 Numbers 34-36
- ❏ 72 Deuteronomy 1-2
- ❏ 73 Deuteronomy 3-4
- ❏ 74 Deuteronomy 5-7
- ❏ 75 Deuteronomy 8-10
- ❏ 76 Deuteronomy 11-13
- ❏ 77 Deuteronomy 14-17
- ❏ 78 Deuteronomy 18-21
- ❏ 79 Deuteronomy 22-25
- ❏ 80 Deuteronomy 26-28
- ❏ 81 Deuteronomy 29:1-31:29
- ❏ 82 Deuteronomy 31:30-34:12
- ❏ 83 Joshua 1-4
- ❏ 84 Joshua 5-8
- ❏ 85 Joshua 9-11
- ❏ 86 Joshua 12-14
- ❏ 87 Joshua 15-17
- ❏ 88 Joshua 18-19
- ❏ 89 Joshua 20-22
- ❏ 90 Joshua 23 - Judges 1
- ❏ 91 Judges 2-5
- ❏ 92 Judges 6-8
- ❏ 93 Judges 9
- ❏ 94 Judges 10-12
- ❏ 95 Judges 13-16
- ❏ 96 Judges 17-19
- ❏ 97 Judges 20-21
- ❏ 98 Ruth
- ❏ 99 1 Samuel 1-3
- ❏ 100 1 Samuel 4-7
- ❏ 101 1 Samuel 8-10
- ❏ 102 1 Samuel 11-13
- ❏ 103 1 Samuel 14-15
- ❏ 104 1 Samuel 16-17

Bible Reading Schedule
Day 105 - 197

- 105 1 Samuel 18-19; Psalm 59
- 106 1 Samuel 20-21; Psalm 56; 34
- 107 1 Samuel 22-23; 1 Chronicles 12:8-18; Psalm 52; 54; 63; 142
- 108 1 Samuel 24; Psalm 57; 1 Samuel 25
- 109 1 Samuel 26-29; 1 Chronicles 12:1-7, 19-22
- 110 1 Samuel 30-31; 1 Chronicles 10; 2 Samuel 1
- 111 2 Samuel 2-4
- 112 2 Samuel 5:1-6:11; 1 Chronicles 11:1-9; 2:23-40; 13:1-14:17
- 113 2 Samuel 22; Psalm 18
- 114 1 Chronicles 15-16; 2 Samuel 6:12-23; Psalm 96
- 115 Psalm 105; 2 Samuel 7; 1 Chronicles 17
- 116 2 Samuel 8-10; 1 Chronicles 18-19; Psalm 60
- 117 2 Samuel 11-12; 1 Chronicles 20:1-3; Psalm 51
- 118 2 Samuel 13-14
- 119 2 Samuel 15-17
- 120 Psalm 3; 2 Samuel 18-19
- 121 2 Samuel 20-21; 23:8-23; 1 Chronicles 20:4-8; 11:10-25
- 122 2 Samuel 23:24-24:25;
- 123 1 Chronicles 11:26-47; 21:1-30, 1 Chronicles 22-24
- 124 Psalm 30; 1 Chronicles 25-26
- 125 1 Chronicles 27-29
- 126 Psalms 5-7; 10; 11; 13; 17
- 127 Psalms 23; 26; 28; 31; 35
- 128 Psalms 41; 43; 46; 55; 61; 62; 64
- 129 Psalms 69-71; 77
- 130 Psalms 83; 86; 88; 91; 95
- 131 Psalms 108-9; 120-21; 140; 143-44
- 132 Psalms 1; 14-15; 36-37; 39
- 133 Psalms 40; 49-50; 73
- 134 Psalms 76; 82; 84; 90; 92; 112; 115
- 135 Psalms 8-9; 16; 19; 21; 24; 29
- 136 Psalms 33; 65-68
- 137 Psalms 75; 93-94; 97-100
- 138 Psalms 103-4; 113-14; 117
- 139 Psalm 119:1-88
- 140 Psalm 119:89-176
- 141 Psalms 122; 124; 133-36
- 142 Psalms 138-39; 145; 148; 150
- 143 Psalms 4; 12; 20; 25; 32; 38
- 144 Psalms 42; 53; 58; 81; 101; 111; 130-31;141;146
- 145 Psalms 2; 22; 27
- 146 Psalms 45; 47-48; 87; 110
- 147 1 Kings 1:1-2:12; 2 Samuel 23:1-7
- 148 1 Kings 2:13-3:28; 2 Chronicles 1:1-13

- 149 1 Kings 5-6; 2 Chronicles 2-3
- 150 1 Kings 7; 2 Chronicles 4
- 151 1 Kings 8; 2 Chronicles 5:1-7:10
- 152 1 Kings 9:1-10:13; 2 Chronicles 7:11-9:12
- 153 1 Kings 4; 10:14-29; 2 Chronicles 1:14-17; 9:13-28; Psalm 72
- 154 Proverbs 1-3
- 155 Proverbs 4-6
- 156 Proverbs 7-9
- 157 Proverbs 10-12
- 158 Proverbs 13-15
- 159 Proverbs 16-18
- 160 Proverbs 19-21
- 161 Proverbs 22-24
- 162 Proverbs 25-27
- 163 Proverbs 28-29
- 164 Proverbs 30-31; Psalm 127
- 165 Song of Solomon
- 166 1 Kings 11:1-40; Ecclesiastes 1-2
- 167 Ecclesiastes 3-7
- 168 Ecclesiastes 8-12; 1 Kings 11:41-43; 2 Chronicles 9:29-31
- 169 1 Kings 12; 2 Chronicles 10:1-11:17
- 170 1 Kings 13-14; 2 Chronicles 11:18-12:16
- 171 1 Kings 15:1-24; 2 Chronicles 13-16
- 172 1 Kings 15:25-16:34; 2 Chronicles 17; 1 Kings 17
- 173 1 Kings 18-19
- 174 1 Kings 20-21
- 175 1 Kings 22:1-40; 2 Chronicles 18
- 176 1 Kings 22:41-53; 2 Kings 1; 2 Chronicles 19:1-21:3
- 177 2 Kings 2-4
- 178 2 Kings 5-7
- 179 2 Kings 8-9; 2 Chronicles 21:4-22:9
- 180 2 Kings 10-11; 2 Chronicles 22:10-23:21
- 181 Joel
- 182 2 Kings 12-13; 2 Chronicles 24
- 183 2 Kings 14; 2 Chronicles 25; Jonah
- 184 Hosea 1-7
- 185 Hosea 8-14
- 186 2 Kings 15:1-7; 2 Chronicles 26; Amos 1-4
- 187 Amos 5-9; 2 Kings 15:8-18
- 188 Isaiah 1-4
- 189 2 Kings 15:19-38; 2 Chronicles 27; Isaiah 5-6
- 190 Micah
- 191 2 Kings 16; 2 Chronicles 28; Isaiah 7-8
- 192 Isaiah 9-12
- 193 Isaiah 13-16
- 194 Isaiah 17-22
- 195 Isaiah 23-27
- 196 Isaiah 28-30
- 197 Isaiah 31-35

Bible Reading Schedule

Day 198 - 287

- ❏ 198 2 Kings 18:1-8; 2 Chronicles 29-31
- ❏ 199 2 Kings 17; 18:9-37; 2 Chronicles 32:1-19; Isaiah 36
- ❏ 200 2 Kings 19; 2 Chronicles 32:20-23; Isaiah 37
- ❏ 201 2 Kings 20; 2 Chronicles 32:24-33; Isaiah 38-39
- ❏ 202 2 Kings 21:1-18; 2 Chronicles 33:1-20; Isaiah 40
- ❏ 203 Isaiah 41-43
- ❏ 204 Isaiah 44-47
- ❏ 205 Isaiah 48-51
- ❏ 206 Isaiah 52-57
- ❏ 207 Isaiah 58-62
- ❏ 208 Isaiah 63-66
- ❏ 209 2 Kings 21:19-26; 2 Chronicles 33:21-34:7; Zephaniah
- ❏ 210 Jeremiah 1-3
- ❏ 211 Jeremiah 4-6
- ❏ 212 Jeremiah 7-9
- ❏ 213 Jeremiah 10-13
- ❏ 214 Jeremiah 14-16
- ❏ 215 Jeremiah 17-20
- ❏ 216 2 Kings 22:1-23:28; 2 Chronicles 34:8-35:19
- ❏ 217 Nahum; 2 Kings 23:29-37; 2 Chronicles 35:20-36:5; Jeremiah 22:10-17
- ❏ 218 Jeremiah 26; Habakkuk
- ❏ 219 Jeremiah 46-47; 2 Kings 24:1-4, 7; 2 Chronicles 36:6-7; Jeremiah 25, 35
- ❏ 220 Jeremiah 36, 45, 48
- ❏ 221 Jeremiah 49:1-33; Daniel 1-2
- ❏ 222 Jeremiah 22:18-30; 2 Kings 24:5-20; 2 Chronicles 36:8-12; Jeremiah 37:1-2; 52:1-3; 24; 29
- ❏ 223 Jeremiah 27-28, 23
- ❏ 224 Jeremiah 50-51
- ❏ 225 Jeremiah 49:34-39; 34:1-22; Ezekiel 1-3
- ❏ 226 Ezekiel 4-7
- ❏ 227 Ezekiel 8-11
- ❏ 228 Ezekiel 12-14
- ❏ 229 Ezekiel 15-17
- ❏ 230 Ezekiel 18-20
- ❏ 231 Ezekiel 21-23
- ❏ 232 2 Kings 25:1; 2 Chronicles 36:13-16; Jeremiah 39:1; 52:4; Ezekiel 24; Jeremiah 21:1-22:9; 32:1-44
- ❏ 233 Jeremiah 30-31, 33
- ❏ 234 Ezekiel 25; 29:1-16; 30; 31
- ❏ 235 Ezekiel 26-28
- ❏ 236 Jeremiah 37:3-39:10; 52:5-30; 2 Kings 25:2-21; 2 Chronicles 36:17-21
- ❏ 237 2 Kings 25:22; Jeremiah 39:11-40:6; Lamentations 1-3
- ❏ 238 Lamentations 4-5; Obadiah
- ❏ 239 Jeremiah 40:7-44:30; 2 Kings 25:23-26
- ❏ 240 Ezekiel 33:21-36:38
- ❏ 241 Ezekiel 37-39
- ❏ 242 Ezekiel 32:1-33:20; Daniel 3
- ❏ 243 Ezekiel 40-42
- ❏ 244 Ezekiel 43-45
- ❏ 245 Ezekiel 46-48
- ❏ 246 Ezekiel 29:17-21; Daniel 4; Jeremiah 52:31-34; 2 Kings 25:27-30; Psalm 44
- ❏ 247 Psalms 74; 79-80; 89
- ❏ 248 Psalms 85; 102; 106; 123; 137
- ❏ 249 Daniel 7-8; 5
- ❏ 250 Daniel 9; 6
- ❏ 251 2 Chronicles 36:22-23; Ezra 1:1-4:5
- ❏ 252 Daniel 10-12
- ❏ 253 Ezra 4:6-6:13; Haggai
- ❏ 254 Zechariah 1-6
- ❏ 255 Zechariah 7-8; Ezra 6:14-22; Psalm 78
- ❏ 256 Psalms 107; 116; 118
- ❏ 257 Psalms 125-26; 128-29; 132; 147; 149
- ❏ 258 Zechariah 9-14
- ❏ 259 Esther 1-4
- ❏ 260 Esther 5-10
- ❏ 261 Ezra 7-8
- ❏ 262 Ezra 9-10
- ❏ 263 Nehemiah 1-5
- ❏ 264 Nehemiah 6-7
- ❏ 265 Nehemiah 8-10
- ❏ 266 Nehemiah 11-13
- ❏ 267 Malachi
- ❏ 268 1 Chronicles 1-2
- ❏ 269 1 Chronicles 3-5
- ❏ 270 1 Chronicles 6
- ❏ 271 1 Chronicles 7:1-8:27
- ❏ 272 1 Chronicles 8:28-9:44
- ❏ 273 John 1:1-18; Mark 1:1; Luke 1:1-4; 3:23-38; Matthew 1:1-17
- ❏ 274 Luke 1:5-80
- ❏ 275 Matthew 1:18-2:23; Luke 2
- ❏ 276 Matthew 3:1-4:11; Mark 1:2-13; Luke 3:1-23; 4:1-13; John 1:19-34
- ❏ 277 John 1:35-3:36
- ❏ 278 John 4; Matthew 4:12-17; Mark 1:14-15; Luke 4:14-30
- ❏ 279 Mark 1:16-45; Matthew 4:18-25; 8:2-4, 14-17; Luke 4:31-5:16
- ❏ 280 Matthew 9:1-17; Mark 2:1-22; Luke 5:17-39
- ❏ 281 John 5; Matthew 12:1-21; Mark 2:23-3:12; Luke 6:1-11
- ❏ 282 Matthew 5; Mark 3:13-19; Luke 6:12-36
- ❏ 283 Matthew 6-7; Luke 6:37-49
- ❏ 284 Luke 7; Matthew 8:1, 5-13; 11:2-30
- ❏ 285 Matthew 12:22-50; Mark 3:20-35; Luke 8:1-21
- ❏ 286 Mark 4:1-34; Matthew 13:1-53
- ❏ 287 Mark 4:35-5:43; Matthew 8:18, 23-34; 9:18-34; Luke 8:22-56

Bible Reading Schedule
Day 288 - 365

- 288 Mark 6:1-30; Matthew 13:54-58; 9:35-11:1; 14:1-12; Luke 9:1-10
- 289 Matthew 14:13-36; Mark 6:31-56; Luke 9:11-17; John 6:1-21
- 290 John 6:22-7:1; Matthew 15:1-20; Mark 7:1-23
- 291 Matthew 15:21-16:20; Mark 7:24-8:30; Luke 9:18-21
- 292 Matthew 16:21-17:27; Mark 8:31-9:32; Luke 9:22-45
- 293 Matthew 18; 8:19-22; Mark 9:33-50; Luke 9:46-62; John 7:2-10
- 294 John 7:11-8:59
- 295 Luke 10:1-11:36
- 296 Luke 11:37-13:21
- 297 John 9-10
- 298 Luke 13:22-15:32
- 299 Luke 16:1-17:10; John 11:1-54
- 300 Luke 17:11-18:17; Matthew 19:1-15; Mark 10:1-16
- 301 Matthew 19:16-20:28; Mark 10:17-45; Luke 18:18-34
- 302 Matthew 20:29-34; 26:6-13; Mark 10:46-52; 14:3-9; Luke 18:35-19:28; John 11:55-12:11
- 303 Matthew 21:1-22; Mark 11:1-26; Luke 19:29-48; John 12:12-50
- 304 Matthew 21:23-22:14; Mark 11:27-12:12; Luke 20:1-19
- 305 Matthew 22:15-46; Mark 12:13-37; Luke 20:20-44
- 306 Matthew 23; Mark 12:38-44; Luke 20:45-21:4
- 307 Matthew 24:1-31; Mark 13:1-27; Luke 21:5-27
- 308 Matthew 24:32-26:5, 14-16; Mark 13:28-14:2, 10-11; Luke 21:28-22:6
- 309 Matthew 26:17-29; Mark 14:12-25; Luke 22:7-38; John 13
- 310 John 14-16
- 311 John 17:1-18:1; Matthew 26:30-46; Mark 14:26-42; Luke 22:39-46
- 312 Matthew 26:47-75; Mark 14:43-72; Luke 22:47-65; John 18:2-27
- 313 Matthew 27:1-26; Mark 15:1-15; Luke 22:66-23:25; John 18:28-19:16
- 314 Matthew 27:27-56; Mark 15:16-41; Luke 23:26-49; John 19:17-30
- 315 Matthew 27:57-28:8; Mark 15:42-16:8; Luke 23:50-24:12; John 19:31-20:10
- 316 Matthew 28:9-20; Mark 16:9-20; Luke 24:13-53; John 20:11-21:25
- 317 Acts 1-2
- 318 Acts 3-5
- 319 Acts 6:1-8:1
- 320 Acts 8:2-9:43
- 321 Acts 10-11
- 322 Acts 12-13
- 323 Acts 14-15
- 324 Galatians 1-3
- 325 Galatians 4-6
- 326 James
- 327 Acts 16:1-18:11
- 328 1 Thessalonians
- 329 2 Thessalonians; Acts 18:12-19:22
- 330 1 Corinthians 1-4
- 331 1 Corinthians 5-8
- 332 1 Corinthians 9-11
- 333 1 Corinthians 12-14
- 334 1 Corinthians 15-16
- 335 Acts 19:23-20:1; 2 Corinthians 1-4
- 336 2 Corinthians 5-9
- 337 2 Corinthians 10-13
- 338 Romans 1-3
- 339 Romans 4-6
- 340 Romans 7-8
- 341 Romans 9-11
- 342 Romans 12-15
- 343 Romans 16; Acts 20:2-21:16
- 344 Acts 21:17-23:35
- 345 Acts 24-26
- 346 Acts 27-28
- 347 Ephesians 1-3
- 348 Ephesians 4-6
- 349 Colossians
- 350 Philippians
- 351 Philemon; 1 Timothy 1-3
- 352 1 Timothy 4-6; Titus
- 353 2 Timothy
- 354 1 Peter
- 355 Jude; 2 Peter
- 356 Hebrews 1:1-5:10
- 357 Hebrews 5:11-9:28
- 358 Hebrews 10-11
- 359 Hebrews 12-13; 2 John; 3 John
- 360 1 John
- 361 Revelation 1-3
- 362 Revelation 4-9
- 363 Revelation 10-14
- 364 Revelation 15-18
- 365 Revelation 19-22

From the Liberty Bible, King James Version.
Copyright ©1975, Thomas Nelson, Inc. Publishers
Used by permission.

What is the writer saying?

How can I apply this to my life?

PRAY   Slovakia – For the church planting to be successful in bringing the Good News to many unbelievers.

There are few words that provoke as strong a reaction as the word "submission." It usually conjures up negative thoughts and emotions for most people who instinctively link the concept with a person's value or worth. Authority is then associated with power and privilege while submission is seen as degrading and even abusive. Though this is how popular culture may view it, as far as the Bible is concerned, such a perspective could not be further from the truth. Headship and submission as taught in God's Word have nothing to do with value or worth but rather with roles and responsibilities. The fact is no one is exempt from functioning in a submissive role to some form of leadership. Even those in authority must live in submission ultimately to God Who holds them responsible for the welfare of those they are called to lead. Another way of saying this is that no one is ever "over" without also being "under" (see Matthew 8:8-9)! Furthermore, we are all to submit to the needs of others regardless of what our role may be (Ephesians 5:21). In these verses, Paul highlights several types of relationships where a submissive attitude is to be evident. Not only are wives, children, and servants to function in submission but so also are husbands, fathers, and masters as they self-sacrificially serve those they are called to lead. As biblical headship and submission are lived out the way God intends (Matthew 20:25-28), it brings blessing, and glorifies God by putting Him on display since the Father and the Son also function in a beautiful headship/submission relationship (1 Corinthians 11:3).

LIFE STEP   *Are you in a position of authority? Identify one way you can fulfill that role today through self-sacrificial service to those you lead. Are you called to submit to someone else? Identify one way you can bless them by making it easier for them to lead you well. Finally, how can you demonstrate your submission to God through your submission to others?*

What is the writer saying?

How can I apply this to my life?

PRAY

Jamaica – Pray for repentance and deeper commitment from the predominantly Christian population.

What is the common denominator in the instructions given in these verses? Our speech! The Apostle James reminds us that our tongue, though a very small part of the body, is extremely powerful (James 3:1-12). It can set the entire course of our life on fire, or it can be the source of profound blessing. Controlled speech is an indication of mature character. In today's passage, we're reminded that Christ's supremacy must be reflected in how I use this little member. My tongue should first be used to speak earnestly to God (vv. 2-3a) about others. Note that prayer is hard work. It requires steadfast perseverance and needs to be characterized by thanksgiving, not complaints or bitterness. Then our tongues are to be used to speak to others about God (vv. 3b-4). It's amazing to think that what we say can be used by the Lord to change the lives of fellow believers and the eternal destiny of those who do not yet know Him! Paul's ultimate concern in today's passage was that his own proclamation of the truth would be crystal clear and understandable. As one wise preacher puts it, "Be clear, be clear, be clear!" We need to be alert to every opportunity that comes our way to tell others of Christ and then take full advantage of it. Finally, our words are to be gracious and tasteful (v. 6) as were the words of Christ (Luke 4:22). Notice that there is a right and a wrong way to respond to others. Furthermore, the way one responds needs to be fitted to the person to whom one is responding. This requires sensitivity and discernment. Our words are to be marked by gentleness and respect (1 Peter 3:15) and should minister grace to others (Ephesians 4:29) rather than harshness or unkindness.

LIFE STEP

Ask the Lord to help you to honestly review how you're using your tongue. Do you talk to God about others? Do you talk to others about God? Is your speech gentle or harsh? Bitter or tasty? Gracious or demanding? Respond to whatever the Holy Spirit brings to mind.

What is the writer saying?

How can I apply this to my life?

PRAY Sweden – Pray for Christian leaders and educators to be strong apologists for the biblical worldview.

In yesterday's passage we noted the importance of gracious speech. As Paul concluded his epistle, notice how this characterizes the way he spoke of five companions and his appreciation of them. Tychicus is the one who brought this letter to the Colossians, just as he did with Paul's letter to the Ephesians (Ephesians 6:21). These were important assignments, and Paul knew he could trust this man who was also a gifted encourager. Onesimus was an unbelieving servant who had escaped from his master Philemon, who lived in Colossae. In God's providence, Onesimus ended up meeting Paul, who led him to the Lord. Now Paul was sending him back with a letter asking Philemon to forgive him (see Philemon in the New Testament). Aristarchus was a faithful companion during Paul's imprisonment, a great example of Proverbs 17:17. Mark was another recipient of grace. He had abandoned Paul and Barnabas on their first missionary journey (Acts 13:13) and Paul later refused to bring him on his second trip because of this failure (Acts 15:36-41). But here we see that Paul had forgiven Mark and now counted him among his faithful companions (2 Timothy 4:11). Paul also mentions Jesus, called Justus. These last three were the only believing Jews among Paul's fellow workers (v. 11).

LIFE STEP

What is your view of the importance of fellow believers to your spiritual growth and ministry? Too often we adopt a "Lone Ranger" mentality as though we need no one. To have such a perspective is to fail to live in a way that is worthy of our calling (Philippians 1:27). Take time today to express your appreciation to at least three believers and let them know how their fellowship in the Gospel is a blessing to you. Don't wait for them to "deserve" this. Instead, be known for your gracious words.

What is the writer saying?

How can I apply this to my life?

Paul concluded by passing along greetings from three other companions and then addressing comments to two people in Colossae. Epaphras was a true prayer warrior (vv.12-13). The Greek word used in reference to the intensity of his prayers means to agonize and is also used of Christ's prayer in the garden of Gethsemane (Luke 22:44). Epaphras' deepest concern was that the Colossians would know and do God's entire will for them, not just part of it. This matches what Paul was also praying for them (see comments from Colossians 1:9-14 commentary). God's will for us encompasses the gifts and abilities which He gives to us. Luke, the physician, was doing God's will by caring for Paul (v. 14).

God's will can be ignored and eventually abandoned after a season of obedience. This happened to Demas who is mentioned here as one of Paul's companions (v. 14) but who later abandoned him because his love for the world overtook his love for the Lord (2 Timothy 4:10). God's will includes using what we own to serve Him as in the case of Nympha who made her house available for the church to use (v.15). Finally, God's will requires focused attention on our part. Archippus needed to be reminded that He had received a specific assignment from the Lord which he was responsible for carefully fulfilling. It is God's will for us to know and to do God's will (Ephesians 5:17).

LIFE STEP

God does have a plan for us that includes specific things which He wants us to accomplish (Ephesians 2:10). It's easy to miss this by becoming distracted with many other things. Write a short paragraph that includes two things. First, include a brief description of what you believe to be the main thing God wants you to pursue in terms of a life calling. Whether you can write a lot or a little, begin asking Him to help you bring focus to this in the long-term. Second, make a short list of specific things which you already know God wants you to do. Pursue these in the short-term starting today! Remember that Christ in you is sufficient for all of these.

What is the writer saying?

How can I apply this to my life?

Ruth, the Moabite woman who is the central figure in the book that bears her name, lived during the time when judges ruled over Israel. It was a time when every man did what was right in his own eyes (Judges 21:25). Israel's general disobedience and rebellion led to periods of judgment from God, followed by restoration and a period of security and prosperity under the leadership of one of Israel's judges. We follow a very brief narrative of a family from Bethlehem in Judah, whose patriarch (Elimelech) took his wife (Naomi) and two sons to the heathen land of Moab to escape a famine in Israel. Shortly after resettlement in Moab, Elimelech died, and his two sons took Moabite wives. After ten years, the two sons also died, leaving the widow Naomi, along with her two widowed daughters-in-law, Orpah and Ruth. Childless and widowed women in those days were a particularly vulnerable group, and this trio of widows found themselves in a crisis.

Without someone to support them, they would be forced to rely almost entirely on the generosity of strangers or, at best, other family members. Hearing that conditions in Israel had improved, Naomi determined to return to her homeland in Judah. She wisely assessed the likelihood that her two daughters-in-law could find new husbands and better chances of prosperity by staying behind in their homeland of Moab and urged them to remain (vv. 7-8). When the daughters-in-law objected and pledged their loyalty to Naomi, she pointed to the hopelessness of her plight. Even if she were able to bear more sons through a new marriage, waiting for those sons to grow up to marry the two widowed Moabite women would be impractical (vv. 12-13). Verse 13 shows us that Naomi saw God's divine hand as "against me" in her current situation. Orpah reluctantly agreed to remain behind, but Ruth "clung" to her mother-in-law.

LIFE STEP

Do you think God was really against Naomi because her husband and sons had died? There is a hint of bitterness in her statement that God's hand was against her, as if she were being punished by an unjust God. If only she knew what God had in store for her and Ruth! If she could only see the joy she would share at the end of this story! You may be like Naomi at times. Don't look at trials and difficulties as the unjust treatment of an angry God. Learn to trust Him—even during trials. Read and meditate on Isaiah 26:3 before you write out your prayer to God today.

What is the writer saying?

How can I apply this to my life?

Although Naomi persisted in her efforts to convince Ruth to stay behind, Ruth would not agree. She had a deep sense of love and commitment to her mother-in-law, expressed beautifully in verses 16-18. Not only did Ruth intend to leave her homeland, but she also pledged to adopt Naomi's people as her own and Naomi's God as her God—even to the end of her days. We should remember that Moab was a pagan land in which the people worshiped and sacrificed to idols. Perhaps Naomi's worship of the One True God had made a lasting impact on Ruth. Whatever the case, Ruth attached her fortunes to her mother-in-law and determined to accompany her to Bethlehem.

Upon their arrival in Bethlehem, the women there recognized Naomi despite her extended absence. Naomi replied to their greeting by urging them to call her *Mara*, meaning "*bitter*," because of the way things had fallen out for her. Her given name, *Naomi*, (meaning "pleasant") was no longer appropriate, she contended, because she considered herself emptied of God's blessings (v. 21). More distressing still was her opinion that God the Almighty had brought this calamity upon her. She struggled to see God's goodness and protection considering her current circumstances. She could not see that her plight was about to take a favorable turn through God's divine intervention. Though she left Moab in famine, she was now among her own people with a harvest of food just starting to come in.

LIFE STEP

Without a doubt, you will experience valleys in your life. To admit that you don't like what is happening right now isn't a sin. Recall that some of David's Psalms were laments to God about the distress he was facing. But despite these moments of difficulty you may be dealing with, you can find hope in God, just as the psalmist did. Read Psalm 13, focusing on verses 5-6. Praise God for the truth that David discovered about God's trustworthiness.

What is the writer saying?

How can I apply this to my life?

God takes notice of good deeds done and rewards those who show compassion for others. Boaz, one of Naomi's close relatives, certainly believed this general principle. As we are introduced to Boaz in today's passage, we see several ways in which God took care of Naomi and Ruth. Verses 1-3 give us a view of Ruth's intention to work for the food she and Naomi would need. She would exercise the customary privileges of the needy by gleaning from the fields of local farmers. "Gleaning" was part of the Law of Moses that established a safety net for the needy. Instead of picking every morsel of grain within their fields, farmers were to leave the corners of their fields unreaped, thereby leaving food for the poor and widowed of the land (Leviticus 19:9-10). But how did Ruth "happen" upon the field of Boaz, who was a wealthy man and a relative of Elimelech, Naomi's dead husband? God's intervention in the life of Naomi and Ruth is becoming evident.

Ruth worked diligently in the fields and gained Boaz's attention when he came out to inspect the work. When he inquired about the young woman in his field, Boaz learned of Ruth and how she had come to Bethlehem from Moab, leaving behind her homeland and her family to stay with her mother-in-law. He instructed Ruth to stay with his servants in his fields under the protection of his overseers. She, in turn, bowed in humility after being shown such kindness. Boaz showed his deep devotion to the Lord by pronouncing God's blessings on Ruth on account of her sacrifice for Naomi (v. 12).

LIFE STEP

People who have no relationship with the Lord typically don't consider good outcomes to be anything more than "luck." Even some Christians fail to recognize that God is working in all things, including the "good fortune" we may enjoy at just the right moment. Take a lesson from Ruth's situation here. God was working behind the scenes, directing her to the field of Boaz rather than any of the other fields she might have chosen. It was so much more than just luck. Make a commitment to God that you will look for ways He has blessed you and give thanks to Him. Eliminate "luck" and "lucky" from your vocabulary if you're a believer.

What is the writer saying?

How can I apply this to my life?

Boaz showed more than a casual interest in Ruth in their first meeting in his fields. In today's passage, we see that Ruth was genuinely gracious and humble in expressing her gratitude to Boaz for his favor, noting that she had no right or standing to deserve such treatment (v. 13). Boaz invited her to the privileges of his servants at mealtime, encouraging her personally to refresh herself with something to eat and drink. He instructed his overseers to give special attention to Ruth's progress in gleaning their produce, even to the point of purposefully dropping handfuls of barley stalks in her path to assure an abundance of food for Ruth and Naomi. At the end of the day, Ruth had managed to collect approximately a half-bushel of grain—enough to provide meals for several days. When Naomi saw the results of Ruth's efforts, she asked where Ruth had managed to glean. Hearing the mention of Boaz, Naomi praised God for His continued provision in bringing them to one of their close relatives (v. 20).

Ruth also reported the kindness of Boaz in instructing her to remain with his servants in his fields to the exclusion of all others. Naomi's delight was magnified again, as she saw how God was blessing her and Ruth through Boaz, her close relative. It is likely that Naomi saw more in Boaz's kindness than simple hospitality and generosity. She knew that he was a "kinsman-redeemer." He had the legal right to fulfill the levirate law which required a brother of a deceased man to marry his widow and raise up a son to his name (Deuteronomy 25:5-10). Naomi encouraged Ruth to stay with Boaz' young women in his fields for the remaining months of the harvest.

LIFE STEP

Just when things seem to be going from bad to worse, God steps in! It may be that you've felt the weight of disagreeable or even unbearable burdens, just as Naomi and Ruth did when they were suddenly forced to scavenge for food. Know this: God knows your circumstances. He isn't blind to your condition. There is hope when you trust Him and turn to Him. If you're His child, He will never leave you or forsake you (Hebrews 13:5). Give God your burden and keep doing your best to honor Him. Make that commitment right now.

What is the writer saying?

How can I apply this to my life?

Naomi finally got around to explaining the levirate marriage custom to Ruth (see Deuteronomy 25). This is not unique to Jewish culture, but the details would have been different enough that Ruth would need guidance. "*Security*," or "*rest*" (v. 1) refers to marriage and can be traced to Naomi's words in Ruth 1:9. How did Naomi know that Boaz would be threshing barley that night? Either the farming schedule was very specific, or Naomi had been out gathering intelligence (she has her sources). What follows sounds strange and some have turned it into a risqué episode. However, both parties are known for their integrity, and a sexual interpretation is demeaning.

Boaz had given every indication of his willingness to be the kinsman-redeemer. Due to his age, perhaps he felt it awkward to make a direct offer. Up to this point in the narrative, Boaz had seen Ruth only in her work clothes, but in preparation for this meeting, Ruth followed Naomi's advice to "dress up" a bit (v. 3). There are meaningful cultural norms at play here. Even though Boaz had addressed her in public, it would have been inappropriate for a poor woman to initiate a social conversation or ask for a private audience. Naomi's planned meeting was designed as a formal request for marriage in a private setting. While Boaz and his servants were asleep, Ruth approached him and uncovered his feet to gradually awaken him. The startling realization of her presence and the simultaneous realization of what she would ask added to the importance of the moment. "*Take your maidservant under your wing*" (v. 9) is a request for protection (see Ezekiel 16:8). Boaz praised her for not desiring a younger man. He protected her reputation and virtue by having her leave early in the morning before anyone could see that she had been there. Boaz had a plan to try to redeem Ruth as his wife.

LIFE STEP

Ruth followed Naomi's advice because she loved and trusted her mother-in-law in every way. What a beautiful picture of family love and trust! When you need to know how to navigate through a difficult or awkward situation, do you turn to mature, godly people? Or do you turn to your peers? Yes, your peers may qualify as "mature and godly," but be sure of that before you settle on your course of action. Go to God first with your questions. Then, when you're still not sure, seek out somebody you trust who is faithful to pray and seek God's direction.　41

What is the writer saying?

How can I apply this to my life?

PRAY Sweden – Pray for a national spiritual awakening and for the re-evangelization of Sweden.

Boaz is a man of his word and a man of action. After pledging to Ruth that he would take steps to try to marry her (Ruth 3:12-13), our passage today starts with a civil proceeding initiated by Boaz to make things happen. The custom in that day was to decide on legal matters at the city gates through hearings and testimony among the city elders. Boaz waited at the gate for the nearest kinsman to pass by—the one who had the first right of redemption under the Law. After inviting this unnamed relative to sit down, Boaz also asked ten other elders to sit and hear the proceedings.

Boaz then laid out the case for all to hear, carefully putting the option to the nearest kinsman to purchase Naomi's parcel of land that she intended to sell. He made it clear that, next to this man, he (Boaz) was the next in line and would purchase the land if the man declined. Initially, the man agreed to make the purchase as the "redeemer." But then Boaz reminded him of the rest of the deal. "When you buy Naomi's land, you also are obligated to take Ruth as a wife to raise up a son to her dead husband." This is the essence of the levirate marriage and the role of the kinsman-redeemer. The man, fearing that taking on a new wife would jeopardize his existing family and inheritance, then declined to buy Naomi's land and deferred to Boaz as the rightful kinsman-redeemer. Without hesitation, Boaz called all the witnesses to note that the transaction was made fairly and in keeping with their customs. He would marry Ruth and they would raise children to perpetuate the inheritance of her dead husband. God's hand moved the course of events in a miraculous way to rescue Naomi and Ruth.

LIFE STEP

Boaz was careful to do what was right both morally and legally in arranging to take Ruth as his wife. It's an amazing illustration of trust in God. After all, though Boaz wanted to marry Ruth, he approached the first-in-line kinsman redeemer and gave him the option. He couldn't be sure how this issue would turn out. Boaz did what was right, and it turned out for the best. Is that the way it always turns out? No. But as a believer in God's goodness, and trusting Him for all things, you can do what is right all the time. Whatever the circumstances, commit to doing the right thing.

What is the writer saying?

How can I apply this to my life?

We don't know how long Ruth had been married to Mahlon but obviously God had prevented them from having children. Now God, the author and giver of life, gave Ruth and Boaz a son. The people of Bethlehem were very kind to Naomi. They saw in her life a tremendous reversal of fortune. Instead of *Bitter*, she could now really enjoy her name, *Pleasant* (see Ruth 1:20). She had financial protection, she had a grandson to enjoy, she had the joy of knowing that her husband and son would live on in her grandson, and most importantly, she knew true love— Ruth's love. In the Bible, seven is the number of perfection. To have seven sons (a quiver full) would have been the ultimate mark of God's blessing on the family. But the women of Bethlehem stated that this Moabite woman, Ruth, was even better (v. 15).

Notice that the women of the neighborhood, rather than Boaz and Ruth, gave the child the name, Obed ("*Worshiper*"). The joy experienced by the larger community at the turnaround in Naomi and Ruth's fortunes by the hand of God led the people to look for great things in this child. And, indeed, Obed became the grandfather of Israel's King David. Boaz became the redeemer for Ruth, but the ultimate Redeemer, Jesus Christ the Messiah, would come from the house of David as described by the Apostle Matthew (Matthew 15:22). The sovereign hand of God turned this story of sadness and distress into the beautiful story of redemption for all mankind through Jesus Christ.

LIFE STEP

Knowing Ruth's story should remind you that God has a plan, and He will bring it to pass. Who would have expected that a Moabite woman like Ruth would be in the Messiah's bloodline? Trust God for the unknown, the unexpected, and even the "impossible." Express your confidence in a prayer to God and ask Him to remind you of His power and authority over every circumstance you will ever encounter.

What is the writer saying?

How can I apply this to my life?

PRAY Papua New Guinea – Effectiveness of literacy ministries that enable nationals to study God's Word.

Are you experiencing such a close relationship with Jesus that you are filled with joy regardless of what's happening? Are you confident that you are a beloved child of God, or a little nervous about meeting Him? These questions reflect the concerns John had when he wrote this epistle. It gives us a glimpse into the struggle of the early church with false teaching about Christ's identity and what He promises to those who believe in Him.

Today's verses reveal John's purpose. It wasn't about helping his readers determine if they were saved or not. He knew that they were (2:12-14; 3:1-2)! It was about maintaining and deepening their fellowship with Him to experience fullness of joy. Note the sensory words: *heard, seen, looked upon, handled.* John was referring to Christ Whom he and the other apostles had seen with their own eyes (John 19:34-35). John had enjoyed an exceptionally close relationship with Him (John 13:23; 19:26-

27; 20:2; 21:20, 24). He was the one who had been reclining on Jesus at the Last Supper and to whom Christ confided the care of His mother when He was on the cross. So, John was well qualified to speak about fellowship with Jesus. He wanted his saved readers to know Christ the way he did so their joy would be full.

Fullness of joy was a favorite theme for John (see John 3:29; 15:11; 16:24; 17:13; 2 John 1:12). Such joy is not the same as happiness. Happiness is the feeling we get when we like what is happening to us. It depends on our circumstances. Biblical joy is a settled contentment and a peaceful confidence in *any* circumstance. It is only possible when we are living in fellowship with God and His people. If we aren't, we will lose the joy of God's salvation like David did when he continued in sin for a time (Psalm 51:7-13). In this epistle, John discussed obstacles (1:5-2:27), pathways (2:28-4:21), and benefits of fellowship (5:1-21).

LIFE STEP

The word translated fellowship means to share something in common. It refers to close companionship rather than casual acquaintance. Does this word describe the relationship you enjoy with Christ? Do you have such a strong awareness of His personal love, favor, care, and forgiveness that you are content and confident regardless of what's happening to you? Reflect deeply on these questions and you will set the stage to better understand this epistle.

What is the writer saying?

How can I apply this to my life?

PRAY   Egypt – Pray for the Church to continue to overcome evil with divine forgiveness and love.

The biggest obstacle to fellowship with God is what John called walking in darkness. Just as walking involves intentionally and continuously taking steps in a certain direction, *walking in darkness* is to intentionally and continuously yield to the desires of the flesh. Who is capable of doing this? Notice the sixteen appearances of the word we in this chapter! Who was John referring to? At first, he was referring to himself and the other apostles, but beginning in verse 6, he clearly included his saved readers. Believers are capable of walking in darkness, including the apostles. Peter did so for a time when he denied the Lord and so did David when he committed adultery and murder. As long as we knowingly continue in sin, we cannot enjoy fellowship with God because He is light and can have no communion with darkness. Those who say that believers can't do this are denying that sin is still a present reality that can enslave them; they have deceived themselves (v. 8). In contrast to this, when we walk in the light, we enjoy fellowship with God and Christ's blood continuously cleanses us from sin that we may not be aware of or that we quickly turn away from (v. 7).

When believers have been *walking in darkness,* fellowship can be restored through confession (v. 9) the way David did (Psalm 51). Confession means to say the same thing as another. Notice the plural form of the word sins. To confess our sins means to agree with God that specific sins that we've been continuing in are wrong because we want to abandon them and restore fellowship. The forgiveness we then experience does not refer to the canceling of our sin debt since that's already been done. It refers to the restoration of fellowship. The story of the prodigal son illustrates this (Luke 15). As long as the son walked in darkness, he could not enjoy fellowship with his father, even though he never lost sonship. His confession quickly restored the relationship.

LIFE STEP

Satan wants to keep us out of fellowship with God by convincing us that it will be very difficult to restore once it is broken. This is NOT true. Christ has already paid the price for our sin, and we are no longer under any condemnation (Romans 8:1). Fellowship is never more than an agreement away. Is there any sin that you are refusing to acknowledge before God? Agree with Him about it, turn from it, and draw near to Him. He will draw near to you (James 4:8)!

What is the writer saying?

How can I apply this to my life?

PRAY Poland – For God to protect missionaries and ministry equipment from criminal activity.

John continued on the subject of walking in darkness versus walking in the light. Having assured his saved readers that they always have a pathway to restoration whenever they do sin (1:9), he did not want this to be taken as an encouragement to yield to sin. A lack of obedience to God's commands, particularly the one about loving others, prevents us from truly getting to know our Father and finding deep joy by abiding in Him and experiencing His love. Verses 3-6 are about fellowship, NOT salvation. The phrase *come to know Him* does not mean *been saved,* though we often use it this way. Notice that John was still using the word *we* as in all of the previous verses to speak of the apostles and his saved readers. He was talking about children of God really getting to know their Heavenly Father. When we walk in darkness while claiming to know Him well, we are lying and the truth is not in us.

John had already mentioned how this can be true of a believer (1:6, 8). King David also noted how truth can be absent from our hearts (Psalm 51:6).

It's possible to be saved and to not really know God very well. If a deep knowledge of God were automatic for believers, then why the references to growing in our knowledge of Him (Colossians 1:10; 2 Peter 3:17-18)? Obedience shows that we're truly getting to know our Father because this knowledge leads to loving Him, which leads to obeying Him (see also John 14:15; 15:10). When this happens, God's great love for us is achieving its intended effect (v. 5). John would later return to the idea of God's love being perfected in believers (4:12, 17-18). The words *in Him* (v. 5) are not referring to salvation but rather to abiding in Him (see the very next verse). This too is not an automatic reality for believers (John 15:14-15).

LIFE STEP

Believers don't have to sin. They have the option to refuse the lusts of the flesh. We should not take God's readiness to forgive and to restore as an invitation to sin! When we do, we've been deceived into thinking that sin will bring us something desirable when in fact it will always bring us some form of death. God's great love can prevent further sin by interrupting the sin spiral in which we fail, flee, fear, and then continue to fail because we're certain that God will not have us back. Do you need to return to your loving Heavenly Father?

What is the writer saying?

How can I apply this to my life?

The final verses in today's passage show us that John was still discussing the idea of believers walking in darkness and how this breaks fellowship with God. He had just affirmed that obedience to God shows we really know Him and that His love is having its desired effect in our lives (vv. 3-6). Given how important obedience is to enjoying fellowship with God, John turned his attention to one specific command that he had in mind: the command to love one another. His emphasis on this command should serve to highlight just how important it is and why failure to obey it is one of the primary ways that we can walk in darkness.

This command was one they had known *from the beginning* (see also 2 John 1:5-6). It wasn't a new idea, and yet John went on to say that it was a new one. Why this seeming contradiction? Because it was both old and new. The command to love others had been included in the Law of Moses (Leviticus 19:18), but Jesus had updated it and called it *new* by saying that we should love one another *as I have loved you* (John 13:34-35). Believers who are walking in the light will walk just as He did (v. 6).

On the other hand, if we hate a fellow believer, it shows that we're walking in darkness (vv. 9-11). These were strong words. Some say that John was talking about an unsaved person hating a saved person. If this were true, then the word *brother* in verse 9 would have to be taken in a generic rather than a spiritual sense. But that's clearly not how John was using the word in verse 10! The only sense that fits both verses is to understand *brother* in the "spiritual family" sense. Saved people can hate fellow believers just as they can be led by their flesh into every type of sin and wickedness (1 Peter 4:15). John was simply restating what he had already said in 1:6.

LIFE STEP

Are you nursing a strong distaste or even hatred of another believer? If so, you are walking in darkness. The results will be broken fellowship with God, bewildered living, and a growing blindness to truth (v. 11). Make this a prayer focus today. Ask the Lord to fill your heart with His sacrificial love for this person and to reveal to you at least one way you can love them the way Christ does. Then commit to doing that one thing today.

What is the writer saying?

How can I apply this to my life?

PRAY North Korea – Pray for the Church to persevere and multiply amid horrific persecution.

John had warned his readers of the perils of *walking in darkness.* His language had been direct and could imply that he was unsure of their salvation! So, before going further, he affimed his conviction that they were children of God (vv. 12-14). It's unlikely that John was referring here to different age groups. After all, he called all of them *little children* elsewhere (2:18, 28; 3:7, 18; 4:4; 5:21). Furthermore, the sequence is out of order (children, *fathers*, young men), and both little children and fathers are said to know God. Instead, John was likely referring to all of them and affirming that they were spiritually mature and had already experienced forgiveness of sins, victory over evil, and a deep knowledge of God.

John then addressed a second obstacle which prevents fellowship with God: love for the world. The word *world* does not refer to unsaved people. After all, we are to love them the way God does (John 3:16). Here John used the Greek word *kosmos* which means an ordered system. He was referring

to a satanic system of affections, activities, and assets that stands against God. If we are attached to this, then God's love is not in us. The phrase "the love of the Father is not in him" does not mean that his readers were unsaved. He had just affirmed that they were! Rather, he meant that a believer's love for God can be snuffed out by a love for the world. If it weren't possible for saved people to love the world, why would John warn them not to?! It's impossible to love the world and God at the same time (Mark 4:19; Luke 16:13) because such affection breaks our fellowship with Him.

Satan uses three pathways to draw our affection away from God and attach it to the world (v. 16). These are the lust of the flesh (physical appetites), the lust of the eyes (the appeal of beauty), and the pride of life (the desire for power and recognition). He used these three to tempt Eve in the Garden (Genesis 3:6) and Jesus in the wilderness (Matthew 4:1-11). The world is passing away, which is why it can never ultimately satisfy.

LIFE STEP

What dominates your life? Is it love for God or love for the affections, activities, and assets of the world? Which of the driving forces mentioned in verse 16 does Satan use most successfully in your life to draw you away from loving God toward loving the world? How can you best arm yourself against his attacks in this area?

What is the writer saying?

How can I apply this to my life?

PRAY

Bulgaria – Pray for generations-long racism to be healed through believers who demonstrate the love of Christ.

John now addressed a third obstacle that can prevent fellowship with God: wayward belief. The word *antichrist* can speak of the individual who will lead the world against Christ in the end times, the one whom Paul calls the "*man of lawlessness*" (2 Thessalonians 2:3-4). But the term can also refer to anyone who stands against Christ or who denies who He is. In that sense, there are many antichrists. They are a characteristic of this age *(last hour)* since no one could have explicitly stood against Christ in the Old Testament. Such false teachers were present in John's day. They not only denied who Jesus was, they also denied what would happen to those who simply believed in Him (1 John 2:25-26; 4:1-3; 5:1), namely that they would receive eternal life in return.

The word *us* appears five times in verse 19. If this is referring to all believers, then John was saying that these false teachers had left the church. But they had not! In fact, John's concern was that such false teachers were circulating among the churches and deceiving believers (v. 26)! Instead, John was likely referring to the apostles when using the word *us*. These false teachers had been associated with the apostles but had abandoned them, and their false teaching proved that they were fraudulent. This makes sense when we note how John then went on to say, "but you …" (v. 20). He reminded them that they had an anointing which taught them truth (v. 27). This is a clear reference to the Holy Spirit who leads believers into all truth (John 14:16-17, 26). They were to be careful to listen to what the Holy Spirit taught them, not what they heard from the antichrists (4:1-6).

One of Satan's most successful strategies is to infiltrate the church with false teachers who sound spiritual but who deny the simple message of salvation through faith in the Son of God and who add to this requirement. Many such *antichrists* can be found in churches today. They claim to preach the Gospel, but have really corrupted it.

LIFE STEP

How seriously do you take the Bible's warnings about false teachers and the possibility of being misled by them? Is your understanding of the Gospel of salvation through faith in Christ influenced more by what you hear from men, or by what you read in God's Word? Ask the Holy Spirit to help you to rest in Christ's promise of eternal life (v. 25) and in what He did for you, not in yourself and in your works.

What is the writer saying?

How can I apply this to my life?

The word *abide* shows up five times in these verses. It was one of John's favorite words. In fact, he used it over sixty-five times in his writings which represents 58% of the times it appears in the New Testament. The basic meaning of the word is to remain, stay, or reside. It is used in a two-fold direction: we can abide in something, or we can allow something to abide in us. A simple comparison helps to grasp the idea: as meat abides in a marinating sauce, the sauce ends up abiding in the meat and changing its taste, hopefully for the better!

What were John's readers to let abide in them (v. 24)? It was something that they had heard from the beginning. John often emphasized the importance of sticking with what they had first heard (2:7, 13-14; 3:11; 2 John 1:5-6). So, what was the truth that they were to remain in? It is the truth that Jesus, God's Son, promises eternal life if we believe in Him (v. 25). They were to let that simple truth reside and have the last word in their hearts. They were to soak in it and let it soak into them. As a result, they would find themselves abiding in the Son and in the Father and enjoying fellowship with them. Intimate fellowship with God is impossible when we are doubting Christ's promise of eternal life. To doubt our salvation when we've believed in Jesus Christ is to not believe His promise. It destroys fellowship because we're saying He's a liar (5:10). The Holy Spirit teaches only truth. To abide in His teaching is to abide in God.

LIFE STEP

Truth is a precious gift from God. It is powerful but fragile: powerful in that it has the ability to set people free from the bondage of sin (John 8:31-32), fragile in that it doesn't have to be changed much in order to become a lie and lead a person back into bondage! Satan is an expert in error and lies (John 8:44), which is why we must be diligent to guard the truth that has been entrusted to us in God's Word. What can you do to let God's Truth abide in you today, especially the truth of the Gospel?

What is the writer saying?

How can I apply this to my life?

Verse 28 launches a new section. It's not about testing the readers to see if they're believers. John had affirmed that they were (see 2:7,12-14). It's about being a confident believer (3:21; 4:17; 5:14) who is looking forward to Christ's return rather than being nervous about meeting Him. The key is to abide in Christ. John had already spoken of this (2:6, 24-27), but now he began unpacking it in practical terms, laying out four pathways to confident fellowship with God. First, we abide in Christ and enjoy confidence before God by understanding and embracing our true identity as born-again children of God.

Verse 29 introduces the idea of being born of God. This is the basic truth which sets the stage for understanding what follows. It refers to the fact that our death, burial, and resurrection with Christ removed us from Adam's family and placed us into God's family (2 Corinthians 5:17). John was astounded by this. God's love isn't just seen in the way He forgave us. He went further and adopted us into His family! By first birth, we had entered Adam's family. Now, by second birth, we have been joined to God's family. It's not that we are children of God in name only (v. 1); it's that we actually are (v. 2)! God has made us partakers of His very nature (2 Peter 1:4) and given us His Son's righteousness (2 Corinthians 5:21)!

The fact that we have this clarifies what John meant in verses 2-3. He wasn't saying that we must work hard to purify ourselves before Christ returns or else we will be ashamed. If this were so, it would be impossible to enjoy confidence at His coming (2:28) since we are unable to purify ourselves just as He is pure! Rather, we have already done this by abandoning our own righteousness and receiving Christ's (vv. 3, 5). Though we don't always see this purity in practice now, we have it in Him and will see it fully when He appears. This alone provides confidence!

LIFE STEP

Satan desperately wants us to forget who we are in Christ. Spiritual amnesia has far more profound consequences than natural amnesia. It complicates the Christian life and destroys the assurance of our salvation. If you have trusted Christ for salvation, remind yourself that you are, right now, a child of God. Though you struggle with sin and impurity, these do not reflect who you really are. Take your stand on the truth and ask the Lord to help you to understand and embrace your new family identity.

What is the writer saying?

How can I apply this to my life?

PRAY Argentina – Increased scholarship funding to enable foreign students to attend Bible colleges.

Some teach sinless perfection from this text, but this can't be accurate based on what John said earlier (1:8-10). It's obvious that no one can claim to never sin but how can this be reconciled with verses 6 and 9?!

Jesus came to save us from the penalty of sin and from its power to hold us captive. This required more than forgiveness. Our main problem was not that we had sinned but that we were, by nature, sinners (Ephesians 2:3). We received this nature the way any living thing receives its nature: by birth! Just as an apple tree becomes one by "birth" into the family of apple trees, we became sinners by birth into the family of sinners: into Adam's family! Therefore, when we sinned, it was as natural as an apple tree bearing apples. Just as the source of apples is the tree because of what it is, the source of sins is the sinner because of what he or she is.

When we were saved, what we were by first birth was crucified with Christ, and we received a new, righteous nature by second birth (2 Corinthians 5:17). It cannot be the source of sin any more than an apple tree could continue generating apples if it had been changed into a banana tree! John is saying that sin cannot find its source in a born-again believer because of what they now are.

However, because of the power of the flesh which we still struggle against (Romans 7:15-23; Galatians 5:16-17), a believer can yield their will to sin and experience its bondage. Believers can avoid experiencing sin by abiding in Christ (v. 6). If abiding in Christ were something that we always did, the Scriptures would not need to exhort us to do so!

LIFE STEP

We must understand what happened when we were born again. It was not merely a change of our destination; it was also a change of our origins. We were once in Adam; we are now in Christ. The new birth is a description, not an illustration of salvation. Refuse at all times to tie your identity to the lusts of your flesh. They no longer represent who you are. When we tie our identity to the lusts of the flesh, we soon capitulate our wills to its power. This is what is happening all around us. Instead, take your stand on who you now are in Christ, stay in constant fellowship with (abide in) Him, and you will live up to who you now are. That's true freedom!

What is the writer saying?

How can I apply this to my life?

If you don't love others, are you really saved? These verses might lead you to this conclusion, but is this what John was saying? He was writing to born-again people (2:7, 12-14), and yet he did not assume they would love one another even though they should (3:11,16; 4:7,11, 21). His purpose wasn't to urge his readers to verify their salvation. Instead, he described how fellowship with God can be experienced more deeply by sacrificially loving one another in deeds, not mere words.

Abiding and possessing aren't the same. It's possible to possess something without abiding in it or having it abide in us. For example, we have God's love, but failure to act in love shows that it's not abiding in us (3:17; 4:12) and we can fail to abide in it (John 15:9). The disciples had a relationship with Christ, but He still told them to abide in Him (John 15:4-5). In essence, abiding is staying close to Christ and His Truth so that these in turn permeate our thoughts, attitudes, and actions.

The word *know* in verse 14 is used 113 times in John's writings. It refers to a knowledge that comes from experiencing something. I can be a pilot and yet fail to experience the joy of being one if I don't go flying! In the same way, it's possible to possess salvation and yet miss the joy of new life in Christ because we're not abiding in love. John's readers had passed from death to life, but to experience the joy of this they needed to love one another. In contrast to this, a failure to love would keep them from experiencing their new life because they would be abiding in death. Verse 15 does not say that *anyone* who hates does not have eternal life, but that *believers* who hate are not allowing their new life in Christ to be reflected in their actions. A child of God can yield to hatred and allow it to abide in their heart. They can even murder someone in thought (Matthew 5:21-22) or in action like David did (2 Samuel 11; 1 Peter 4:15), but they can't experience or reflect the joy of their salvation when operating this way.

LIFE STEP *A second pathway to confident fellowship with God is to love one another. Most of us can quote John 3:16. How about 1 John 3:16? Both verses provide us with the correct definition of love. True love is the sacrifice of oneself for the good of another. How can your love for fellow believers reflect this today?*

What is the writer saying?

How can I apply this to my life?

PRAY   Venezuela – Pray for all 30 Amerindian tribes to be transformed by the Word of God despite government opposition.

Notice again John's concern that his saved readers experience assurance and confidence before God (vv. 19-20). Why is this? Because these are not automatic commodities. It's possible to be saved and yet to struggle with an inward sense of shame before the Lord. John's desire for his saved readers was that they experience the joy and confidence that come through fellowship with Christ (1:1-4; 2:8) by sacrifically loving other believers.

Christ's actions are the ultimate example of genuine love (v. 16). It focuses on the well-being of others and is demonstrated in sacrificial actions. It seeks to give rather than receive. Christ gave all that He had even when we did not deserve it. True love is an act of the will, not of the emotions. Christ did not wait to feel like dying for us or wait until we deserved it. Instead, He chose to love us and did whatever it took to save us. That is the kind of love we are called to show one another. When we do, we not only possess God's love, we are possessed by it. When we don't, we still possess God's love, but it is not abiding in us.

Choosing to live this way results in a greater confidence before God (vv. 19-21) because our actions are aligned with truth rather than with error (1:6; 2:4). We are walking in light rather than in darkness and will experience the reality of the new life we have in Christ. Continuing yesterday's illustration, we're not just pilots who can fly, we're experiencing the joy of being one by actually flying. John reminds us that salvation does not depend on how we feel about it. Even in moments when we struggle with the assurance of our salvation, God knows we are His children. An added benefit of living in fellowship with God is answered prayer. Why? Because abiding in Christ results in our desires becoming narrowly aligned with His!

LIFE STEP

We all have moments when we struggle with the assurance of our salvation. Most of the time we equate it with a feeling to be felt rather than a truth to be known. When this happens, it's an opportunity to review what we are basing our assurance upon, our feelings or God's promises? Selfish living never results in a confident walk with the Lord. However, if we will begin to love our brothers and sisters in action and not just in word, we will find our hearts aligning themselves with the truth that all who trust in Christ alone are saved, permanently!

What is the writer saying?

How can I apply this to my life?

John had already discussed how believing error can break our fellowship with God (2:18-27). He now returned to this topic and pointed the importance of listening to the indwelling Holy Spirit. This is a third pathway to deeper fellowship with God and confidence before Him.

The word *spirit* occurs eight times in these verses and can refer to the human spirit, a supernatural spirit, or a disposition. These verses are about supernatural spirits conveying ideas through human teachers. Error is communicated through false prophets (v. 1) who are characterized by an anti-Christ message. Truth is communicated through the teaching of Christ's apostles (v. 6) who were alive at the time. John wanted his readers to listen to the right spirit. We are NOT to listen to every spirit but to test them to see if they really do come from God by examining what they say about Christ. The word *confess* means to say the same thing as someone else. Here it is referring to agreeing with what God has said about Christ. The identity and work of Christ is the central issue that separates false spirits and their teaching from the Holy Spirit and His teaching. Notice how verses 4-6 begin with *you, they, and we* respectively. Verse 5 (they) refers to the false prophets in the world and those who listen to them and believe their lies about Christ. Verse 4 (you) refers to the readers who have overcome them by listening to the Holy Spirit and believing what He says about Jesus. Simple faith in Christ overcomes the most powerful voices of error (5:4-5). Satan wants to lead our minds away from this (2 Corinthians 11:3)! Verse 6 (we) refers to the apostles and their witness about Christ (1:1-3). We must listen to the Holy Spirit speaking through them, otherwise we will find ourselves walking in darkness, out of fellowship with Christ. If it weren't possible for believers to listen to the wrong spirit, John wouldn't warn us about this!

LIFE STEP *We all listen to voices. Which do we choose to believe? This determines the entire course of our daily lives. Christians who listen to false teachers will find themselves struggling more and more in their walk as their confidence before God is undermined. But as we listen to the Holy Spirit and His teaching through the apostles, we abide in Christ, our fellowship with Him deepens, and we enjoy confidence before the Father. Are you listening more to false spirits in the world or to the true Spirit who leads us into all truth (John 16:13)?*

What is the writer saying?

How can I apply this to my life?

Do you have such a strong sense of God's loving favor that you instinctively draw near to Him, or do you tend to fear His disfavor and keep your distance? Fear is the enemy of fellowship. This is precisely what John wanted to correct (look ahead to verses 17-18). Once again, we see that he wanted his readers to have confidence before God and to live without fear of punishment. In these verses, he repeated many things he'd already said, weaving them together to show his readers a fourth pathway into deeper fellowship with God: growing in our understanding of our Father's love for us and resting in it.

The defining statement of this section is that "God is love." This is the second of two great affirmations in this epistle concerning the very nature of God (see also 1:5). Love isn't just something that God does, it is central to who He is. He is love personified. The members of the Trinity function in a love relationship and were doing so even before the foundation of the world (John 17:24).

God's love didn't ignore sin, it prompted Him to deal with it at great personal expense to restore fellowship with fallen mankind (vv. 9-10).

Verses 7-8 are not saying that a failure to love others proves that we're not saved. If loving others were an automatic fruit of salvation, there would be no need for John to exhort his saved readers to love one another (3:11,16; 4:11, 21)! He was simply making the point that if we love others as God does, we are BOTH born of God and know Him (v. 7). If we don't love as He does, it shows that we don't really know our Father very well even though we are born of Him (v. 8). This parallels John's earlier teaching about believers who don't really know God the way they should (2:3-4). Why the reference to the invisibility of God in these verses? Because it is precisely when God's love abides in us and is expressed through us that others can "see" the invisible God who is love (John 13:34-35).

When you think about God's character, what comes immediately to mind? If it is not that He is love, your perspective likely doesn't match John's view of his Savior. Spend at least ten minutes reflecting on the concept that God IS love, not merely that He DOES loving things. How does this change your desire to spend time with Him? How will this change the way you love others today?

What is the writer saying?

How can I apply this to my life?

Notice the four references to perfection in these verses (vv. 12, 17, 18). The same thought is also expressed in 2:5. What is meant by God's love being perfected in us? It can't mean that God's love is somehow imperfect in itself. God's love is already perfect because it is a reflection of God Himself who is perfect in all His ways (Deuteronomy 32:4; Psalm 18:30). Instead, it refers to God's love achieving what it should in our lives. The Greek word used here for *perfected* refers to something being completed or accomplishing its objective. The apostles who had personally seen the Lord Jesus and spent considerable time with him had really come to know and rest in His love (v. 16). Now John was expressing his desire to see God's amazing love reach its goal (be perfected) in them as well. This is a pathway to deeper fellowship with Christ. The result will be happy obedience to Him (2:5), sacrificial love for others (4:12), and confidence before God (4:18). When we truly understand our Father's love for us and rest in it, it banishes all fear of facing Him someday and prompts us to love and obey Him in return. We often view obedience as being restrictive, but God knows that it is incredibly liberating (John 8:31-32). As God's love is perfected in us, we will instinctively love Him in return. We will also naturally love our fellow believers. Once again, the fact that we are commanded to love one another shows that it's possible for a true believer to fail to do so. When this happens, it is evidence that they are not abiding in Christ, not that they are unsaved.

LIFE STEP

The application is pretty simple: If we want to enjoy confidence and assurance in our walk with Christ, we must abide in Christ. One pathway to this deeper fellowship with Him is to stop yielding to the flesh that constantly pressures us to live for ourselves and to begin loving our brothers and sisters in Christ in tangible ways. How can you step that up in your life today?

What is the writer saying?

How can I apply this to my life?

PRAY Libya – Pray for the tiny Libyan Church to be united and established despite intense persecution.

John had discussed both obstacles and pathways to deeper fellowship with Christ. He now highlighted the benefits of fellowship. The first is that we enjoy the confidence of knowing that we have eternal life because we have believed in Jesus. Look ahead to verse 13 and notice the words "these *things* I have written to you." Today's verses are the *things* that John was referring to. The readers had eternal life, but John wanted them to enjoy the certainty of it. Many say that we can only have assurance later, after we've demonstrated that we have *behaved*. John says we can have it now by affirming what we've *believed*.

A person is born of God by believing that Jesus is the Christ (v. 1), the Son of God (v. 5) sent to save us (4:14). What about believing in His death, burial, and resurrection? These are included in this belief. No one can truly believe in Christ while denying what He did to save us. Many distort the gospel by claiming that it can't be this easy. According to them, one must commit to doing certain things in order to be saved. All such objections are grounded in pride and self-righteousness. They are based on the idea that we have something of value to bring to God without which He will not grant us eternal life. The truth is, we are all spiritually bankrupt. This precisely why Jesus came to save us!

This simple belief "overcomes the world" (vv. 4-5). This refers primarily to the false teaching of the world expressed by the antichrists (see 4:1-5). They were denying that Christ would give eternal life to those who believed in Him. Simple faith in what God has said about His Son is what overcomes all the confusing, doubt-inducing error of the antichrists.

LIFE STEP

The power of faith does not lie in faith itself; it always lies in whatever faith is placed in. Great faith in something that is false or in someone who is not true will lead to nothing at best or disaster at worst. But faith placed in God's Word cannot fail to accomplish much. Take a moment to review your own faith in Christ. What are you believing exactly? If you have believed what the Father has said about His Son, you have been born again; it's that simple. That is the power of the Gospel. Paul was not ashamed of it (Romans 1:16) even though many accused him of teaching "cheap grace" (Romans 6:1, 15) and considered it foolishness (1 Corinthians 1:18). What about you?

What is the writer saying?

How can I apply this to my life?

Variations of the words *witness* and *testimony* appear nine times in these verses. It reminds us of what happens in a court of law. John's point is that we readily believe human testimony based on two or three witnesses. How much more should we believe God's testimony about Jesus Christ based on three witnesses. Witnesses support a specific claim (testimony). What is God the Father's testimony (claim) about Jesus? That those who believe in His Son have eternal life (vv.11-12). Period. We either accept and believe this testimony, or we don't. If we don't, we are treating God as though He were a liar (v. 10). How do we know if we have believed what God has said about His Son? This is where many go wrong with the Gospel by making a false distinction between *head* and *heart* belief. The Bible makes no such distinction. We either believe something or we don't. It's really quite simple.

Notice verse 10. Where do we find the evidence that we have believed? We find it within ourselves. We know what we believe and what we don't. There is no need for external evidence to prove salvation. Internal belief is the evidence of salvation. Why? Because internal belief is the only requirement for salvation! It's simple: "I believe God's testimony about Jesus; therefore, I have eternal life!" Simply put, how can we be assured of eternal life? By believing God's testimony about Jesus! This is what John was reminding his saved readers of. The words "that you may know" (v.13) were not implying a need to test to see if they were saved. John had already affirmed many times that they were. They merely reflect what John had been desiring all along for his readers: confidence and assurance rather than shame and fear (2:28; 3:19-21).

LIFE STEP

Today's verses do not say, "Believe in Jesus and then wait to see how your life changes and you'll be sure of heaven then." It says, "Believe in Jesus and you can be sure of heaven now." Assurance does NOT come from examining what we do for Jesus but what we believe about Jesus. It comes when we believe God the Father's witness about Him and trust His promise of eternal life (2:25). Nothing can prevent you from doing this now. Why wait?

What is the writer saying?

How can I apply this to my life?

PRAY Panama – Pray for strong Christian impact on the multitude of nationalities passing through the Canal Zone.

John concludes with two other benefits we enjoy when we walk in fellowship with Christ. The first is confidence that our prayers will be answered because they will be according to His will (see vv. 14-15). For reasons we likely cannot know, John spoke about prayer for a believer caught in visible sin and urged his readers to pray that they would repent and be spared sin's deadly earthside consequences (1:5-10); the costliest being physical death. How do we know that he was not referring to spiritual death (eternal separation from God)? Because he also refers to sin that *doesn't* lead to death. That would be a false concept if he meant spiritual death.

The final benefit we enjoy is the confidence of knowing that sin and Satan can never change who we are and what we have in Christ. The Greek word translated *touch* (v. 18) refers to the kind which leaves a lasting mark. Most of the times it's used, it refers to Jesus' healing touch (Matthew 8:3; Mark 6:56; Luke 6:19). Though Satan *can* tempt, mislead, and oppress a born-again person, he *cannot* affect them in any permanent way. This is because their new birth has fundamentally changed who they are, and this cannot be reversed. The phrase "he who has been born of God keeps himself" is like saying, "an apple tree always stays an apple tree regardless of what you do to it." Salvation is an irreversible change of identity. In contrast to this, those who are not born again are under the sway of Satan who blinds (2 Corinthians 4:4), binds (Ephesians 2:1-3), deceives (2 Corinthians 11:14), and controls them (James 3:14-16). John concludes with what he started with—Jesus, God's Son, is eternal life (see 1:1-2). Those who have Him have eternal life because the two go together (John 14:6). We must avoid anything that takes the place of Christ in our hearts. To look for confidence and assurance in anything other than Him is idolatry.

LIFE STEP

Where do you look for confidence that you are a beloved child of God? If the answer has anything to do with your own attitudes or actions, you have replaced Christ with yourself and are committing idolatry. It's time to repent of such self-sufficiency and reaffirm that you are His child because you have simply believed that Christ is the Son of God who died for your sins and rose again from the dead. There are no other grounds for joyful, confident fellowship with God. Stop looking elsewhere. That's what this epistle has been all about!

What is the writer saying?

How can I apply this to my life?

PRAY Peru – Pray for humble pastors trained in biblical theology who reflect Jesus to a watching culture.

Second and Third John were most likely written prior to their larger companion, 1 John. Trouble had arisen in some of the smaller assemblies in and around Ephesus. John may have been partly responsible for these flocks. Unable to visit each one, he sent out a quick letter to at least two of them giving them some advice until he would be able to bring a more complete response to the false teachers who had risen from within. This false teaching was producing errors of doctrine and practice.

This short letter appears to have been written to a woman (vv. 1, 12-13) whose home may have been used as a place for believers to gather. The fact that her husband was not addressed would imply that either he was not saved or that she was single or a widow. The fact that no pastor or church leader is mentioned may be an indication that they too were involved with these false teachings.

John began by expressing his delight that some were walking in the truth. He then pleaded with her that she should also walk in love. This would not be easy as false teachers were trying to influence this group of believers and this would require firm, deliberate action. She was not to allow them into her house and was not even to greet them (vv. 7-11)! Truth and love are not mutually exclusive; in fact, they are mutually dependent upon one another. If the greatest commandment is to love God and to love one another, and if the whole of the Law and the prophets is devoted to this endeavor, it surely follows that all truth by its very nature will promote genuine love. False doctrine always produces corrupt and selfish behavior and such behavior is the antithesis of love.

LIFE STEP

Unfortunately, many people associate truth with divisiveness. They claim that anything which offends or contradicts can't be loving and may be a display of hatred. This shows an incorrect understanding of what love really is. True love "does not rejoice in unrighteousness but rejoices with the truth" (1 Corinthians 13:6). That's because truth is the friend of all who want to know freedom and success in life. Truth is simply a description of the way things really are. It's not loving to mislead and help people to walk away from reality into illusion and error. Love always does what is best for the person loved even if it hurts. Are you being truthful with those you love?

What is the writer saying?

How can I apply this to my life?

The second half of this little epistle establishes a very important principle: any claim to spiritual life must be evaluated based on a person's doctrine as well as their behavior. Many deceivers have gone out into the world. They talk right, dress right, and hang out with the right people, but what they teach is a lie. There are those who preach tolerance in these situations. However, false teachers are not well-meaning souls who need a little encouragement and consolation; they are emissaries of Satan whose only desire is to divide and destroy the sheep (see 2 Corinthians 11:13-15). We should beware of them because their message can be very persuasive.

Some have asked how verses 6 and 10 could have been written by the same author. Love cannot embrace that which is not true. When we tolerate false doctrine under the guise of *love*, we destroy the very ones we claim to love. Truth and love are inseparably linked. One cannot exist without the other. It would be a crime to feed our children to a starving wolf because we don't want to impose our views on them or because we want to be tolerant toward the wolf! Not only does it destroy the ones we claim to love, but it emboldens the wolf as well and results in its being more likely to attack others and ultimately be killed.

LIFE STEP

Love hates evil (Psalm 119:104; Amos 5:15; 1 Corinthians 13:6). Love does not mean compromise; it means a compassionate commitment to God's way of living. Where there is no commitment, there is no love. Love can only exist where there is a covenant with truth. Is there someone that you should part ways with out of love for them and for others that they are harming?

What is the writer saying?

How can I apply this to my life?

PRAY   Slovakia – Pray for the Slovak church to embrace a vision for planting churches, discipleship, and evangelism.

Just like 2 John, this epistle was written to an individual. Whereas 2 John had prohibited fellowship with false teachers, this epistle was written to encourage practical fellowship with those who teach the truth. It is one of the key New Testament passages dealing with the responsibility of believers to provide material support for those who serve the Lord in full-time, vocational ministry. The people that John was describing were clearly itinerant servants of God, similar to missionaries today. It's possible that John had even sent some of them out himself.

The Bible teaches the concept of supporting recognized servants of God. Several details are worth noting. First, at least some of the servants described in these verses were not known to Gaius

(v. 5). This implies that they didn't come from his church. The phrase "send them on their way" (v. 6) implies that they were moving on after being with Gaius. They "went forth" and were not receiving any material support from unbelievers (v. 7), which indicates that ministry was now their main activity rather than a secular job or trade. John made it clear that such servants should be supported "in a manner worthy of God" (v. 6). This is a stunning statement when one considers how poorly many of God's servants are encouraged and supported today, particularly those who are serving in remote locations. The old adage, "out of sight, out of mind," often applies in such cases. John reminded Gaius that to support such servants was the equivalent of partnering with them in ministry (v. 8).

LIFE STEP

How much priority do you give to encouraging missionaries and supporting them financially? Do such men and women have your highest respect? Far too often, because they are out of sight, they can easily be neglected. Find a way to encourage a missionary today in a tangible way and sincerely ask the Lord to show you how He wants you to become involved in supporting His full-time servants. You will literally become a partner in what God is doing through their ministry.

What is the writer saying?

How can I apply this to my life?

PRAY   Albania – Pray for spiritual maturity in Christians who come from a long history of communism, atheism, or Islam.

We see in today's passage a little of the struggle that was taking place in this local church. Diotrephes, who appears to have been a church leader with great influence, was refusing to receive John and others who were associated with him.

Demetrius (v. 12) may have been a lesser leader who had opposed Diotrephes and had himself been put out of the church. Gaius, to whom the letter was written, was likely torn between loyalty to the local church and its leadership and loyalty to John and his teaching. John made it clear that it was right to denounce Diotrephes, even though he was a leader, because of his clear rejection of God's truth as proclaimed by the apostle. His actions were based in pride and a desire to "have the preeminence." Such an attitude should never characterize a church leader and should be withstood in love.

LIFE STEP

Taking a biblical stand against a leader in a local church who is not living according to the truth is one of the most difficult things that a believer can be called upon to do. However, sometimes it becomes necessary in the interests of love and truth. When a church leader rejects the clear teaching of God's Word, silences the voice of truth, and begins to act as though the church belongs to them, we need to be ready to lovingly stand against them and call them to repentance. In the most extreme cases, it may require leaving the church that they are claiming to shepherd. Such decisions should never be taken lightly.

What is the writer saying?

How can I apply this to my life?

As we open the Book of Joshua, it is helpful to recall the context of this historical record of Israel's march into the Promised Land following the death of Moses. The writer is thought to be Joshua himself, with some help from other sources who chronicled the events that followed Joshua's death. God had selected Joshua to be Moses' successor (Numbers 27:5-23) and credited him as a man "in whom is the Spirit" (v. 18). Notice the frequent references to courage and encouragement in this passage, along with the repetition of God's promise to fulfill all that had been promised to Moses (vv. 2-7). Although God had promised the Israelites this beautiful, bountiful land, He required that they fight for it. Thus, it would take a leader filled with reverence for God and the courage to take on hard things, like driving out the pagan inhabitants of this land.

Verse 8 is an amazingly positive statement of God's provision as a promise to the obedient leader. Consider that God chose to give Joshua the recipe for success, not only on the battlefields he would encounter but also in all of life's pursuits. Given the size and scope of the task ahead of Joshua, one might have expected God's advice on military or logistical strategy. Instead, God focused on "this Book of the Law," which was the Word of God available to Joshua at that time. Joshua was told to talk about it, think about it, and obey its every command. This was the key to Joshua's success as a leader. Verse 11 affirms Joshua's faith in what God had promised. He told his officers to ready the people to go in to take possession of the land that God had promised.

LIFE STEP

You will likely never face a challenge like the one faced by Joshua, but your life will certainly bring its share of difficulties and hardships. What will be your strategy? Take Joshua 1:8 as the key to success in every battle, no matter the size or the source of that battle. It is no oversimplification of the Christian experience to reflect on this verse as your key to success. Do your best to memorize this verse in the week ahead. Recite it often. Hide it in your heart. Let it be your guide to every decision you make.

What is the writer saying?

How can I apply this to my life?

Before sending the troops against the heathen inhabitants of the land, Joshua discreetly commissioned two spies to go into the land to find out about the fortifications and the morale of the people they were planning to invade. Joshua directed them to report specifically on the walled city of Jericho. It is likely that Joshua's desire for secrecy in this matter stemmed from the incident of forty years prior when the ten spies returned from their reconnaissance mission in the same area and eight of these men gave a bad report, leading to the Israelites' wilderness wanderings of an entire generation (Numbers 13).

The spies, apparently attempting to blend in with the inhabitants of Jericho, made their way to the house of a prostitute named Rahab. Their arrival did not go unnoticed by the alert inhabitants of the city, though. Someone reported the two spies to the king, and agents were dispatched to Rahab's house to investigate. At this moment, Rahab risked her life by lying to the king's men, telling them that the two men who checked in had already exited the city. She urged them to hurry outside the city gates to pursue the spies. When alone again, Rahab went up to her rooftop where she had hidden the spies and declared her faith and confidence in the God of the Israelites. The entire city was in fear of God, she informed the spies, because of what God had done in bringing the Jews out of Egypt and the victories He had granted them thus far. She professed her belief that "...the Lord your God, He is God in heaven above and on earth beneath" (v. 11).

Today's passage underscores a central truth about God's unlimited mercy and grace towards sinners. Rahab was a harlot. She was also a liar. But her profession of faith in God was enough to bring salvation to her house and give us a beautiful picture of God's desire to save all who will turn to Him in faith.

LIFE STEP

What do you think about a prostitute being chosen in God's sovereign plan as a sinner to be saved? Can you see through this historical account that God is no respecter of persons, and that He desires that all would come to faith? Can you meditate on this truth and let it remind you that no person—no matter how vile or evil or sinful—is outside the range of God's mercy and grace. Nothing you have done or will ever do invalidates God's desire to bring you to Himself. Write a prayer of joyful acceptance and thanksgiving for this wonderful truth.

What is the writer saying?

How can I apply this to my life?

Our passage today provides clear evidence that Rahab saw her future and the safety of her family as tied up entirely in identification with the God of the Israelites. Having just risked her life to save the two Hebrew spies, she pleaded for the life of her loved ones by asking the spies to take an oath to spare her family when they returned as victors over Jericho. They agreed to do as she requested but conditioned their promise on four points: First, she must remain silent about what had transpired. Second, she must mark out her dwelling place by placing a scarlet cord in the window to enable the attackers to locate her and her family. Third, all her family must be brought within her home in order to be saved. Finally, they must all remain in her home or risk their lives at the hands of the invaders.

Rahab gave the spies sound advice to go in the opposite direction to the mountains to hide out for three days while their pursuers hunted toward the Jordan River. She wasted no time in preparing for the coming day of judgment. Immediately after letting the spies down from her window, she placed the scarlet cord in the window. One can guess that she also quickly collected her family members into her home, since she had no idea when the Israelites would attack. Following Rahab's advice, the spies ultimately made their way back to their Israelite camp on the other side of the Jordan River and reported to Joshua what had happened. Though they could provide little intelligence regarding Jericho's fortifications, they were able to report with confidence that the inhabitants of Jericho trembled with fear and dread over the prospects of the Jewish advance. "Truly the Lord has delivered all the land into our hands" (v. 24).

LIFE STEP

Rahab's commitment to the God of the Hebrews was not partial, but total. She took action to secure her own salvation and that of her loved ones. Isn't that how we should respond to our eternal salvation? Shouldn't we take steps to gather others into our circle of faith under God's direction and leadership? Remember, everyone who believes in Jesus Christ is not condemned, but those who do not believe are condemned already (John 3:18). Write out a "next step" you can commit to take that could bring a loved one to saving faith in Jesus Christ. Pray for boldness to act on this next step.

What is the writer saying?

How can I apply this to my life?

Joshua acted decisively and confidently upon hearing the report of the two spies, ordering the movement of the children of Israel from their encampment to the edges of the Jordan River, about seven miles distant. One can only imagine the building anticipation and excitement felt by the approximately two million Israelites who had been wandering for years, waiting to go into the land that God had promised generations before. Imagine the anxiety they may have felt when they arrived at the river, now out of its banks and flowing rapidly with the influx of snowmelt from nearby mountains, as is so common in that season. Joshua ordered a three-day rest, and then called upon all the people to sanctify themselves for the next day "for tomorrow the Lord will do wonders among you" (v. 5). Through divine communication,

God instructed Joshua how to proceed. The priests were to take the ark of the covenant before the people into the Jordan. When their feet hit the water, the waters of the Jordan would be cut off from upstream, allowing the people to cross over against Jericho on dry ground within the riverbed. God chose to exalt Joshua in the sight of all Israel through this mighty miracle (v. 7), but Joshua exalted the Lord when he explained what was about to happen. He told the children of Israel that what they were about to witness would affirm in their sight that God was with them and would surely drive out the inhabitants of the land (v. 10). God not only made the way for the people to cross over into the Promised Land, but He also gave Joshua the place of prominence as Moses' capable and God-ordained replacement as the leader of the Israelites.

LIFE STEP

Put yourself in the place of these Israelites as they were assembled to cross a vast floodplain with no apparent way to cross over with their families, possessions, and livestock. Rather than quake with fear or rebel against their leader, the Israelites used their eyes of faith to envision more than what they could see or do. When you come to that place in your life, will you leave it to God? Discipline yourself to make this kind of trust a reality by doing as the Israelites did in their preparation for crossing the Jordan. Take time to set yourself apart unto God—sanctify the moment by drawing close to Him. Then, trust Him to act.

What is the writer saying?

How can I apply this to my life?

PRAY Pakistan – Pray for the spiritually oppressed in remote areas to encounter the Gospel.

God wanted the Israelites to remember the miraculous crossing of the Jordan River and to pass on to future generations the significance of this great day. He instructed Joshua to have twelve men chosen, one from every tribe of the children of Israel, who would each gather a large stone from the riverbed of the Jordan and erect it at their encampment on the other side. Verses 6-7 provide the intended results of this memorial: the visible sign of the stones would prompt conversation between fathers and their children about the meaning of the stones. The stones were to be an eternal memorial to the Israelites in all their future generations.

On his own initiative, Joshua also erected twelve stones in the Jordan where the priests had stood, apparently to mark out the place where the people had crossed. Those stones, possibly hidden under the waters except during dry periods, remained "to this day" (v. 9), which would suggest at least during Joshua's lifetime. Once everyone had passed over and the memorial stones were in place, the priests crossed and joined the people on the other side toward Jericho. The tribes of Reuben, Gad, and half the tribe of Manasseh followed the priests, sending an army of men across to take part in the battle for Jericho. Recall that these "Transjordan" tribes had elected to settle their families on the east side of the Jordan but had committed to engage their fighting forces in battling for the land along with the rest of their Israelite brethren (Numbers 32:16-32; Joshua 1:12-18). As a result of God's intervention and Joshua's leadership, the people revered Joshua as they had Moses in his day.

LIFE STEP *What big event in your Christian journey have you memorialized with an outward sign or private observance? Many Christians rarely stop long enough in their coming and going to reflect on God's goodness, provision, and protection. Yet, that is precisely why the stone memorials were erected in our reading today. You have similar markers to remind you of God's marvelous work on your behalf, "lest you forget the Lord..." (Deuteronomy 6:12). The Lord's Supper, or Communion, is an observance of the Christian church that serves to remind believers of Jesus' shed blood and broken body that serves as our redemption. Make it a meaningful moment to reflect on what God has done for you. Read 1 Corinthians 11:23-29 to understand the significance of the Lord's Supper as a memorial service.*

What is the writer saying?

How can I apply this to my life?

PRAY   Ukraine – Pray for followers of Jesus to arise as messengers of His hope to the hopeless and the oppressed.

God instructed Joshua to have the priests who bore the ark to come up out of the water. Remember, they had been standing in the water the entire time that the people crossed and the stone memorials were set up. Imagine the scene as approximately two million people, along with their baggage and animals, made their way in a wide path across the now-dry riverbed. Imagine watching as the waters of the Jordan returned to their normal flow at flood level immediately after the priests, bearing the ark, stepped foot on the other side. The text doesn't say if it was a sudden rush (as with a dam burst) or a relatively slow rise. Either way, the timing was miraculous and was clearly impressive! Just over forty years before, in the living memory of the oldest people, they had seen something similar when leaving Egypt, crossing the Red Sea (v. 23). Once again, Joshua instructed the people to pass down to their children and future generations the importance of this great day (vv. 21-24). All the people of the earth would know that the Lord was mighty.

Verse 1 of chapter 5 tells us that the Israelites weren't the only ones impacted by the miracle God brought about in the crossing of the Jordan. Simply hearing of it caused the kings of the Canaanites and all the people on the west side of the Jordan to lose heart. It was clear now that God would fight for His people, the Israelites.

LIFE STEP

God performed miracles to bring His people into the Promised Land, and He is still a miracle-working God! Don't ever forget that God is bigger than your problems and challenges. Right now, offer Him a prayer of gratefulness for the victories He has allowed in your life. If you're at the bottom of a valley right now and struggling to see your way out of the pit you're in, talk to God about what you see and ask for the vision to see His way through the trial. Let today serve as a marker for a new way of thinking and trusting.

What is the writer saying?

How can I apply this to my life?

God's ways are not like man's ways (Isaiah 55:9). This truth is played out in dramatic fashion in today's reading, as we see the Israelites on the west side of the Jordan River, in Canaan, poised to take on the multitude of Canaanites who stood between them and the Promised Land. So, what's the next step? God instructed Joshua to circumcise all the males who were uncircumcised! Doing as God commanded left the Israelites in a medically fragile state, unable to attack and probably unable even to defend themselves. Circumcision for the Israelites dates to Abraham, when God told him that every male child was to be circumcised. Failure to do so meant that they weren't under God's covenant (Genesis 17:10-14). At the time of the first Passover, the night before leaving Egypt, all the male Israelites and any non-ethnic male Israelites desiring to stay with them were circumcised (Exodus 12:43-51). What happened during the forty years of wandering in the wilderness? Apparently, the males born during the wilderness wanderings were not circumcised (v. 5). Verse 6 informs us that this was because the generation that left Egypt didn't obey God's command.

The people remained encamped while the healing of their males was completed. The restoration of God's covenant sign with His people resulted in God taking away "the reproach of Egypt" (v. 9) from the Israelites. Having restored their covenant relationship with God, the people kept the Passover and ate from the produce of the land. The following day, the manna ceased to fall on the ground. Later, Joshua encountered a man along the route while scouting out the city of Jericho. The man stood before Joshua with a sword in his hand, prompting Joshua to question whether he was a friend or a foe. The man identified himself as "the Commander of the army of the Lord" (v. 14). He told Joshua to remove his sandals, for the place he stood was holy ground.

LIFE STEP

God is serious about the issue of obedience. Do a bit of self-inspection. Ask yourself if there is any area of your life in which you have only partially obeyed the Lord, or maybe even openly defied His clear direction for your life. In your own words, consider asking God to reveal to you any act of disobedience or partial obedience that you may be unaware of. Then, make a commitment to change. Remember that the pathway to a solid relationship with God is a solid commitment to obedience.

What is the writer saying?

How can I apply this to my life?

PRAY Pray that God will bless the ministry and outreach of your local Christian radio station.

God spoke again with Joshua, assuring him that the city of Jericho would fall to the Israelites (v. 2). But God didn't stop with encouragement. He also gave Joshua the specific strategy to employ to take the city and conquer its inhabitants. It quickly became apparent to Joshua, no doubt, that God's focus was not on the military strategy, but rather on magnifying His glory. Here is the plan of action laid out by God:

• Joshua and the armed Israelites were to march around the city once a day for six consecutive days (v. 3).

• Seven priests were to join the march, probably behind the armed men, blowing trumpets (ram's horns) continuously (v. 4).

• The ark of the covenant, carried by priests, would follow the trumpet-blowing priests (v. 6).

• On day seven, the men and priests were to make their march not just one time, but seven times around the city.

• Following the seventh circuit around the city walls on the seventh day, the priests were to make a loud blast on the trumpets and all the people were to give a loud shout. Then, the walls of the city would fall flat, and the Israelites were to advance and take the city (v. 5).

Verse 10 includes one final instruction from Joshua. The people were commanded to maintain complete silence during each trip around the walls until given the signal on the final day to shout. One can only imagine how the Israelite's tactics must have affected the inhabitants of Jericho, particularly the defenders on the wall who watched in amazement as their attackers merely circled the city while blaring their trumpets, then returned to their camps. The entire exercise, given the size of the city (estimated at six to nine acres within the walls), could easily have been accomplished within an hour, even with an army of forty thousand men.

LIFE STEP

Never dictate to God how to meet a need or bring a victory! The account of the battle of Jericho surely serves to assure the believer that God can do whatever He chooses in whatever way He chooses. Give God the glory for this truth. Though we must recognize that God is not obligated to bring about a miracle, we surely can see that He is not limited to conventional ways of accomplishing His will. Offer your word of thanksgiving in light of this truth.

What is the writer saying?

How can I apply this to my life?

In these verses we see Joshua's obedience in commanding the priests and the armed men, just as God had instructed. Verse 12 picks up with day two of their seven-day march around Jericho's walls. The details of day seven are given in verses 15-17. Notice that Joshua gave all the credit for the pending victory to God (v. 16). Notice, too, that Joshua's personal instructions to his forces included protection for Rahab and all who were in her house, in keeping with the promise of the spies (Joshua 2:8,13).

God's promises of victories often come wrapped in expectations placed upon His people. Here, Joshua prescribed a critical restriction for his forces. The city had already been declared as "dedicated unto the Lord." The Hebrew word, devoted, or dedicated (such as in v. 17) carries the idea of accursed, or under the ban, or devoted/set apart for destruction. Essentially, the city and everything in it belonged to the Lord. Nothing could be used for any other purpose, and therefore would need to be destroyed. In verse 19 we also see that the gold, silver, bronze, and iron vessels were to be confiscated and placed in the Lord's treasury. Again, the idea was that these were devoted to the Lord.

The destruction of Jericho and the curse pronounced by Joshua in verse 26 underscores the importance of obedience to God's plan. This was the Israelite's first engagement with Canaanite inhabitants in the land that God had determined would be theirs. God did not intend to let His people experience the defilement of the pagan peoples of those lands, nor to take for themselves the spoils that He had devoted to destruction.

LIFE STEP

Don't ignore the clear instructions of God and attempt to do God's work your way. That's the lesson we may derive from the things "doomed by the Lord to destruction" (v. 17) that the Israelites were to destroy. There is plenty of room for you to utilize your unique giftedness and talents to bring glory to the Lord, but the most important asset you have to offer is your full attention and obedience to His instructions. Make a commitment today to do it (whatever it is) the Lord's way.

What is the writer saying?

How can I apply this to my life?

PRAY Cuba – Pray for evangelism and discipleship of Cuban expatriates around the world.

The account of Israel's defeat at the hands of the small enemy outpost at Ai illustrates how devastating and far-reaching a "little sin" can be. We see in verse 1 that, despite Joshua's decree that there could be no plunder taken from Jericho for personal gain, one man of the tribe of Judah, Achan by name, disobeyed and brought on the fierce anger of God. Notice that God's wrath was not limited to the one who sinned. God's anger burned against all the children of Israel, and the consequences of this sin by one man led to the deaths of thirty-six Israelite soldiers who were routed by the defenders of Ai (v. 5). Was Achan's sin the only reason for the defeat of the Israelites? Could it be that Joshua's decision to send a force of only three thousand soldiers without consulting the Lord was also a factor leading to this defeat? It seems reasonable to believe that God would

have intervened if, after the Jericho victory, Joshua and his leaders had prayed earnestly for direction and the favor of God in their next battle.

God did not seem pleased with Joshua's reaction when he learned of the defeat at Ai. Verses 6-9 give us a picture of a leader who questioned God rather than seeking answers. Though Joshua seemed to convey concern over God's reputation among the heathen nations surrounding them, his overriding fear was over the possibility of defeat at the hands of the Canaanites. God would have none of it! He told Joshua, "Get up!" and informed Joshua that there was sin in the camp. In verses 12-13, God instructed Joshua to prepare the people for the revelation, the uncovering, of the sinful actions by Achan. He promised, "You cannot stand before your enemies until you take away the accursed thing from among you."

LIFE STEP

Never let Satan or anyone else convince you that disobedience to God hurts only the sinner. Be honest enough to inspect your life and acknowledge where your sinful actions caused hurt or harm to another person. Maybe you've been dealing with the consequences of someone else's sin. If that is the case, you need no convincing. The impact of sin travels further than sin itself. Ask God to help you avoid the path that leads to disobedience and sin.

What is the writer saying?

How can I apply this to my life?

God's wrath against the people of Israel would be turned away only by holding the sinner responsible for his transgression. Following God's directions, Joshua assembled the people the next day and had them pass before him clan by clan and family by family. As this exercise progressed by the casting of lots (like drawing straws), the vast number of Israelites was narrowed down to one man—Achan (vv. 16-18). When confronted, Achan acknowledged his sin before God and the rest of the people. It was a classic case of the progression of temptation to sinful action as recorded in James 1:14-15. Achan saw the prohibited valuables; he was enticed by his own desires; then he fueled that lust by moving to action and giving birth to sin. The result was condemnation and death. We see this in the next few verses.

When the search of Achan's tent was complete and the prohibited items were discovered where he had hidden them, Joshua had Achan and his belongings, along with his family, brought outside the camp. There, Achan was stoned. They then burned "them" with fire and heaped up a great pile of stones to mark the spot where this sin was laid to rest. We cannot be sure whether "them" referred to Achan's family members or simply the prohibited items he had taken from Jericho. Since Deuteronomy 24:16 specifically states that children could not be executed for the sins of their father, we can assume either that they were spared, or that they were in on the sinful actions and were also killed. It seems unlikely that Achan could have hidden all these prohibited items within his tent without the knowledge of his family.

LIFE STEP

Do you think Achan rested well at night knowing he had deliberately violated the commands of his leader, Joshua, in taking things that were devoted to the Lord for destruction? Can you imagine how he must have felt when the news of the Israelite's stunning defeat came down after the battle at Ai? Numbers 32:23 tells us, "Be sure, your sins will find you out!" Take time this week to memorize 1 John 1:9 as a reminder to keep close accounts with God about sin.

What is the writer saying?

How can I apply this to my life?

PRAY China – Pray for continued Church growth and pure biblical teaching amid ongoing persecution.

In today's reading, we see the Gentile ruler of Jerusalem (v. 1) forming a coalition of pagan armies to attack the Gibeonites because of their defection to the Israelites (Joshua 9). This king knew that the larger forces of five Canaanite cities, gathered as one to attack Gibeon, would pit them in battle against Joshua and Israel. In desperation, the Gibeonites appealed to Joshua for military protection, prompting Joshua's immediate decision to march his forces during the night to make war with the five Canaanite kings. He had God's assurance (Joshua 10:8) that there was nothing to fear, as the Lord had determined to bring a decisive and total victory to the Israelites. As God promised, the Canaanites were routed, as the Lord caused a sense of panic amongst their forces. As this vast army ran from the Israelites, God brought a supernatural weapon against the Canaanites in the form of giant hailstones. In fact, more were killed by the hailstones than the Israelites killed with the sword (vv. 11-12).

Seeing that his military advantage over these five Canaanite kings was slipping away as the day progressed toward nightfall, Joshua confidently petitioned the Lord for help. All he needed was more time to take out his adversaries, so he asked that the Lord stop the sun and moon from progressing toward the horizon (vv. 12-13). God miraculously extended the day, providing enough light and time for a total victory of the Israelites against the Canaanites. Does this mean the earth's rotation was stopped or slowed? Science will claim that an event like this is not possible, but taking God at His word means believing that He can do whatever He chooses. This is just one of God's many miracles performed to bring about His divine plan. Remember, one definition of "miracle" is an event that occurs that cannot be explained by the laws of science and physics.

LIFE STEP

Joshua headed off to battle against the five Canaanite kings with confidence, having God's assurance that He would bring victory. Do you have confidence in God's ultimate victory over evil, sin, and death? We, as believers, have the promise of eternal life that starts now and lasts forever. We have the promise that He who is in us is greater than he who is in the world (1 John 4:4). Exercise your faith by praising God right now for the ultimate victory that is already yours in Jesus Christ.

What is the writer saying?

How can I apply this to my life?

PRAY   Chile – Pray for zeal within the Church to evangelize the Mapuche people in the South.

In today's brief passage, we read a summary of the long conquest of Joshua and the Israelites over the remaining Canaanite enemies. In contrast to the defeat of the five Canaanite kings we read about in chapter 10, this condensed description of Israel's conquest lists no miracles of God. We can assume, then, that this was a series of hard-fought, bloody battles that raged city by city and one king after another, until all were overtaken or killed. Verse 18 provides this insight: "Joshua made war a long time with all those kings."

The inspired writer also tells us that not one city, aside from Gibeon, chose to make peace with Israel. If the Gibeonites had the foresight to give themselves up to save themselves, why not others? It was because God gave them up to follow their own hearts, which they had hardened against the idea of aligning with Israel in peace (v. 20). God is not responsible for the direction of anyone's heart, but He will enable an already settled hatred for God's people to end His offer of grace and mercy. It happened that way in Pharoah's refusal to let the Jews leave Egypt, too (see Exodus 7:3 and 8:15). It was God's plan to devote to destruction, with no provision of mercy, those who would not accept His sovereign plan to show favor to the Israelites.

Joshua also took out the cities inhabited by the giants in the land, known as the Anakim. These were the same giants who were so intimidating to Israel's ten spies that the majority gave a bad report, leading to forty more years of wandering in the desert (Numbers 13:33). Only a handful of cities still contained such giants, which later became a problem for Israel. The final word on Joshua's leadership in these battles is in verse 23: "Then the land rested from war."

LIFE STEP

The value of persistence and perseverance cannot be overstated. Just as Joshua stayed "on mission" a long time to defeat the Canaanites, we must press on in the battle. Take a moment to read 2 Corinthians 5:20 several times to see what your mission should be all about. Then, write out a prayer to God, asking for strength and renewed commitment to persevere as a faithful ambassador for Christ.

What is the writer saying?

How can I apply this to my life?

PRAY Philippines – Funding for the staff and supplies needed to continue Bible correspondence courses.

We are re-introduced in today's passage to Caleb, one of the ten spies sent out to spy out the land in the early days of the Israelite Exodus from Egypt (Numbers 13:6-20). When eight of the ten gave a bad report and sowed seeds of fear and doubt, only Caleb and Joshua expressed confidence in God's ability to give Israel victory over all the Canaanites in the land. Now, after forty years of wandering in the desert and five years of battling the inhabitants of the land, Caleb stepped forward to claim his portion. He reminded Joshua of Moses' words in that day when Caleb fully followed the Lord while his brethren were unwilling to trust God (v. 9). Notice that Caleb, now age eighty-five, had not lost his edge physically or emotionally.

In fact, he said, "I am as strong this day as on the day that Moses sent me" (v. 11). Caleb then boldly proclaimed, "Give me this mountain of which the Lord spoke" (v. 12) One might expect such an old man to seek an easy place to settle, but that did not interest Caleb. Knowing there were still giants in the land he requested did not dissuade him. Rather, he expressed willingness to take on the inhabitants of the area he chose, declaring, "It may be that the Lord will be with me, and I shall be able to drive them out as the Lord said" (v. 12). From Joshua 15:13-19, we see that Caleb succeeded in driving out the Anakim (giants) and possessing the land he had requested.

LIFE STEP

Caleb was fearless in his pursuit of God's best! Even when he was advanced in age, he expressed full confidence that what God intended for him was not just possible, but as good as done. Can you see yourself fearlessly facing "giants" in your Christian walk? Perhaps you could use some encouragement from Paul's letter to Timothy when Timothy was facing the unknown. Learn to quote 2 Timothy 1:7 whenever you are feeling fearful. "For God has not given us a spirit of fear, but of power and of love and of a sound mind." Put your confidence in God.

What is the writer saying?

How can I apply this to my life?

PRAY
Pray for those serving in your local government.

God established a system of justice within the ranks of the Israelites that recognized the difference between a murder and an unintentional killing that was charged as murder. In this short chapter, we are given the details of the cities of refuge that, by God's design and directive, were set aside by Joshua and his people to serve as a haven for anyone who killed another person, but without malice or hatred. In today's legal system, we call such cases "manslaughter." We can trace the origins of this concept back to Numbers 35:9-34 and Deuteronomy 19:1-9, where God first prescribed to Moses the setting aside of six cities, three on either side of the Jordan River. Essentially, if a person was accused of murder, he could flee to one of the cities of refuge to remain protected from retribution by the deceased man's kinsmen. The elders of the city of refuge were to guarantee his safety for delivery to trial (v. 5), normally in his home city before the people. Someone could only be executed for premeditated murder on sufficient evidence—specifically more than one eyewitness (Numbers 35:30).

If it was determined that the accused had killed the man, but not in a premeditated fashion, he was permitted to dwell without fear of retribution in the city of refuge until the death of the sitting high priest. Then, he was permitted to return to his home with protection against retribution from the dead man's family. If he left earlier, he was open to execution by the kinsmen of the dead man. If there was insufficient evidence to call the killing a murder, or if the accused was found not guilty, he was free to go.

LIFE STEP

God's plan for man includes consequences for wrong actions, even when those actions were not planned (accidents) or could be described simply as carelessness. Think of what our society would be like if God's plan were ignored, and everyone was subject to vigilante justice—where kinsmen could take a life to avenge even an accidental killing. Romans 13:1 is a good reference point for every child of God. Thank God right now for instituting government over us to provide a system of justice. Even if you don't agree with every judgment or every law, God intends for Christians to be good citizens.

MONDAY - WEEK 09

What is the writer saying?

How can I apply this to my life?

PRAY Italy – Pray for Italians enslaved by tradition or disillusioned with church structures to encounter the living Christ.

Though God had dealt severely with the stubborn Israelites during their forty years of wandering (Joshua 5:6), His faithfulness in bringing the people into the Promised Land and driving out their enemies is on display in the final verses of chapter 21. Everything He promised to Israel's forefathers He delivered (v. 43). Every enemy that withstood them in their conquest He delivered into their hands. God gave them rest all around (v. 44).

Joshua then called the Reubenites, the Gadites, and half of the tribe of Manasseh to meet with him. He commended them for fulfilling their commitment to Moses to stand with their brothers in fighting against the Canaanites. Recall that these Israelite tribes were intent on settling on the east side of the Jordan River and petitioned Moses for permission (Numbers 32) to settle there instead of crossing over to the west side of the river. Moses granted their request, but only after securing their pledge to fight with and for the remaining Israelite tribes as they drove out the Canaanites (Numbers 32:16-19) west of the Jordan River.

Now, Joshua released these tribes from their commitment and urged them to return to their families on the other side of the Jordan. Notice in Joshua 22:5 the concern of Joshua for the spiritual well-being of his kinsmen who were about to depart. Most likely he realized that their separation from the rest of their brothers and their proximity to pagan peoples to the east could pose a problem. He challenged them to love God with a whole-hearted devotion, serving Him with all diligence. Here is clear evidence that Joshua's interests went beyond simply occupying the land that God had promised. As Israel's leader, he wanted all his brothers to follow the Lord faithfully.

LIFE STEP

Joshua's final warning to the two-and-a-half tribes is an example of spiritual leadership that is worthy of imitation. God desires your faithfulness above all else. Even if you don't find yourself leading others, your willingness to obey God and His leadership is important. Read Joshua 22:5 again and speak these words to yourself. Close with a prayer of commitment to walk in God's ways and to serve Him with all your heart and all your soul.

TUESDAY - WEEK 09

What is the writer saying?

How can I apply this to my life?

PRAY Lebanon – Pray for Christians to commit to staying in the land in order to spread the Gospel to their neighbors.

Sensing the reality of his advancing age and the certainty of his passing, Joshua began to address the elders and the rest of Israel's leaders to issue his final charge and encouragement. The message here is similar to Moses' message in Deuteronomy 31, both in the content of his words and the structure of his address.

First, he reminded the Israelites of all that God had done on their behalf, reminded them that it was God's prerogative to fight for them (v. 3). Then Joshua pointed to the reality that there were still Canaanite peoples yet to be conquered, adding his confident assurance that the Lord would expel these pagan people and give the land to the Israelite tribes (vv. 5-6). The remainder of this passage is Joshua's encouragement to the Israelites in two distinct areas of concern. The people were challenged to:

• Remain very courageous
• Live in obedience to God's Word as written in the book of the Law of Moses. This is a reference to the first five books of our Old Testament, a collection of writings that Moses recorded under the inspiration of the Holy Spirit.

The results of this kind of devotion and obedience to God's Word included the nation of Israel's consistency in refraining from intermarriage with pagan nations or adopting their pagan gods. Joshua's primary encouragement is in verse 8. "Hold fast to the Lord your God, as you have done to this day."

LIFE STEP

It's no coincidence that Moses and Joshua had the same message to those who would remain after their passing from the scene. Take a moment to read Joshua 23:8 and Deuteronomy 32:45-47. Use these words of encouragement from Israel's leaders to renew your commitment to the Lord to live in obedience to His Word. Close your quiet time with a prayer of commitment to study and obey God's voice as revealed in His Word.

What is the writer saying?

How can I apply this to my life?

PRAY

Turkey – Pray for a radical change in deep-seated prejudices and biases against Christianity.

Joshua's concern for his people is evident in today's passage. Verse 11 fairly summarizes his overriding concern about their continued faithfulness to the Lord when he is no longer their leader. His message is simple: "Love the Lord your God."

Joshua also balanced his message with a clear warning of the consequences the Israelites would face if they turned from God and assimilated with the pagan nations that remained in the land. God would not go before them and drive out these people. Rather, they would become a trap to the Israelites, like thorns that prick the skin (v. 13). Furthermore, rather than delivering all the good things He had promised, God would bring on the Israelites harmful things (v. 15). God's wrath would burn hot against them if they turned to the pagan gods of the Canaanites (v. 16). Their disobedience would lead to their destruction, Joshua warned.

Every believer must come to terms with the same message that Joshua tried to impress on his people. If you want God's blessings, you must "take careful heed to yourself" (v. 11) and follow God's leadership. This is the essence of loving God. In John 14:15, we see that Jesus gave us the same basic message that Joshua gave the Israelites. He told His disciples, "If you love me, keep my commandments." Today, just as it was in Joshua's day, we pay the price for our disobedience to the Lord.

LIFE STEP

A sign of your maturity as a child of God is your desire to love God supremely. Think of the ultimate demonstration of such love not in terms of how sincerely you worship at church, or how emotionally connected you feel with God. Rather, think of Jesus' words in John 14:15 and focus on your submission to Him through obedience. That is the ultimate demonstration of your love for God. Pray today for a growing, loving commitment to your Savior.

What is the writer saying?

How can I apply this to my life?

PRAY

Cameroon – Pray for a gentle transfer of spiritual leadership from Western organizations to national believers.

Joshua assembled the people at Shechem to renew their covenant with God. This covenant renewal was necessary because the Mosaic Covenant at Sinai (Exodus 24) was not an everlasting covenant. Rather, it was a binding agreement between parties that called for a renewal of the covenant with each generation. The format of this covenant renewal is typical of ancient treaties between a ruler (God) and his subjects (the people). As with the ancient secular treaties, there is a preamble (vv. 1-2a), historical prologue (vv. 2b-13), stipulations for the covenant (vv. 14-24) with curses if it is broken, and the official recording of the agreement (vv. 25-28). Shechem was where God first appeared to Abraham, the place where Abraham first built an altar to the Lord (Genesis 12:6, 7). Also there, Jacob built an altar (Genesis 33:18-20) and buried all foreign idols (Genesis 35:2-4). Shechem was in the valley between Mt. Ebal and Mt. Gerizim, where Israel had assembled for the re-reading of the covenant following the defeat of Ai (Joshua 8:30-35).

These verses (vv. 2-13) are mainly the historical background to the treaty. As Joshua spoke the words of God to the elders and leaders, he recalled the many instances in which God had intervened for Israel.

- Though their ancestors worshiped other gods, the Lord chose Abraham, led him, and blessed him (Genesis 12-50).
- When Egypt oppressed Israel, God sent Moses and the plagues and brought Israel out of Egypt (Exodus 1-14).
- God gave them victory over the eastern Amorites (Numbers 21) and protected them from their relatives, the Moabites (Numbers 22-24).
- Then in their own times, they crossed into the land and took possession, as the previous chapters of Joshua tell.

Verse 13 reminded the Israelites of the blessings God brought to them as he fought for them, giving them land and cities to dwell in and vineyards and groves to enjoy.

LIFE STEP

Every gift from God is to be celebrated with thanksgiving! But how many of God's blessings do you find yourself taking for granted? Don't do that. Make a list right now of ten blessings you enjoy because of what God has done for you and use the list as a reminder of God's goodness. Start with the very breath you are breathing right now. If you're a believer, you certainly can be grateful for the gift of eternal life offered through faith in Jesus Christ (John 3:16-18).

What is the writer saying?

How can I apply this to my life?

PRAY   Nigeria – Pray for increasingly persecuted Christians in Islamicized northern states to be characterized by supernatural love and forgiveness.

Continuing the reestablishment of their covenant relationship with God, Joshua came to the point of decision with the Israelites in which he pressed in on their conviction and their commitment to God. He boldly challenged them to serve the Lord "in sincerity and in truth" (v. 14) by putting false gods away from them—whether the false deities their forefathers served years before or the many idols worshiped by the Canaanites in whose lands they now dwelt. Verse 15 is Joshua's firm statement of commitment to lead by example: "As for me and my house, we will serve the Lord!"

Three times in this passage the people responded to Joshua's demand that they make a choice about whom they would serve. Each time they cried, "We will serve the Lord!" (See vv. 18, 21, and 24) Their initial response (vv. 16-18) even included a tone of shock that there would be any doubt as to their faithfulness. But Joshua seemed to know his people well. Perhaps the fact that there were "secret" idol-worshipers in their midst was widely known. Whatever the case, Joshua pressed against their affirmation of faith (v. 19). God will not put up with compromise. God will not overlook sin. Turning away from God in unbelief to serve other gods, or worse, to blend true worship with false, will bring God's discipline. God is holy and His people must be holy, too.

Joshua called them out as witnesses against themselves should they depart from this commitment, and the people again professed their unyielding devotion to the Lord. He then challenged them to action (v. 24) by calling on them to put away the foreign gods that were in their midst.

Just as it was in Joshua's day, God wants your whole-hearted devotion today. How would your life be different if you committed to this kind of relationship with Him? Would you need to put away any "foreign gods" from your life? Is there something you hold to more dearly than your relationship with God? Recall that an idol can be anything that takes priority over God in your life. Spend time in prayer today seeking God's help in becoming totally committed to Him.

What is the writer saying?

How can I apply this to my life?

This part of the covenant renewal between God and the children of Israel deals with the official recording of the agreement (vv. 25-28). We are told that Joshua wrote the words of the covenant in a document which was then kept with the Law. He also set up a memorial stone as a testimony of the promises made, to serve as a visual reminder of their commitment to God should they be tempted to turn from Him.

The book ends with an historical appendix, the only part that wouldn't have been written by Joshua. Joshua's death at the age of 110 was recorded with a description of his burial (vv. 29, 30). We are told also that the generation present in Joshua's time remembered what God had done and served the Lord as long as they lived. The final verses give the reader the details of the burial of Joseph's remains at Shechem, having been transported by Moses out of Egypt during the Exodus from slavery (Genesis 50:25-26). The account of the burial of Phineas, the son of Aaron, who served as high priest following his father's death, is included as this chapter in Israel's history ends.

LIFE STEP

How do you feel about renewing a commitment you've made? Do you think it might be a good idea, particularly for a challenging commitment, to rehearse your promises from time to time and reestablish your commitment? Walking with God in faith is one such commitment. Consider right now whether you've maintained your path toward holiness and godliness that once seemed so important to you. If you sense that you've strayed or lost your way, renew your commitment to follow the Lord with all your heart.

What is the writer saying?

How can I apply this to my life?

PRAY   Pray for those who teach in your church to be faithful to the Word.

In today's passage, Peter reveals two of the several points that he is going to make in his introduction. After a brief greeting (vv. 1-2), he wants believers to grasp the plan of grace (vv. 3-5) and the permanence of grace (vv. 6-9). Given that we enjoy a "by grace" salvation, Peter knows that it is imperative for us to understand how such a grace should affect our worldview. In verses 3-5, he emphasizes God's design in salvation. In the past, God saved us and freely gave us the incredible gift of justification (v. 3). In the present, we are being prepared (the process of sanctification) for an inheritance that cannot be taken away or even tarnished. Earthly citizenship may be lost but not our home in heaven (v. 4). In the future, the exact nature of this salvation is going to be revealed in all its glory (glorification). It cannot be fully understood until we experience it (v. 5).

We cannot allow present troubles to rob us of the joy that God has given to us through this salvation. It cannot be taken from us, but we can surrender our joy. Troubles or trials are designed to improve our faith and, thereby, the quality of our lives. "Under-the-sun" living (see Ecclesiastes) is the result of a wrong response to trials. "In-the-Son" living is what comes from a right response to trials. If our focus is on Jesus Christ and the salvation that He has provided, we will have the ability to rejoice no matter what the trial. We must not focus on ourselves or our present circumstances. The Old Testament prophets clearly prophesied that such a salvation would come and that its details would be clarified by the Savior who brought it. We now understand what Old Testament saints longed to see. They looked forward by faith to the coming Messiah. We must live with that same "looking-forwardness" that they had.

Faith is the answer to all of life's turbulence. Grace requires faith to be enjoyed. Abundant grace is always available, but without faith it can be sidelined in a person's life. What specific truth do you need to reaffirm today in order to receive God's grace?

What is the writer saying?

How can I apply this to my life?

PRAY   Poland – Pray for hearts open to the message of salvation among the materialistic youth.

Verses 9-12 make it seem that the Old Testament prophets and even the angels did not understand salvation. That is not the case. They understood the basics of a "by grace through faith" salvation. What they did not understand was how God would accomplish this incredible feat. There was even among the angels a desire to understand exactly how God would work this out. Beginning in verse 13, Peter initiates his first major point. He tells his readers to fix their hope completely on the grace they will experience when Christ is revealed. The emphasis in this section is on their intellectual knowledge of the gracious salvation that God has provided for them. If the believer is to correctly interpret and respond to his present situation, he must have a clear understanding of the nature of this salvation. He then tells them to avoid conforming to their former lusts and to be holy. Holiness needs to be understood in this case in the same way that it is used in the passage that Peter quotes (Leviticus 11:44). In that passage, it is referring to non-moral issues such as food. It is not addressing the purity issues we often associate with holiness. Thus, Peter is not merely speaking of purity in conduct but of a distinct or separate perspective than that of the world. The believer, because of his salvation, cannot look at the circumstances that surround him in the same way that an unbeliever does. God wants the believer to see life the same way that He does. This is the distinctiveness (holiness) that Peter deems crucial for sanctification.

LIFE STEP

No matter how dark the hour, the believer is always commanded to format his worldview (gird his mind) based on the fundamental dynamics of salvation, namely, God's grace! How should the awareness of God's gracious salvation change the way you're perceiving some challenging circumstance in your life?

What is the writer saying?

How can I apply this to my life?

PRAY   Israel – Pray or the peace of Jerusalem in obedience to Psalm 122:6.

Peter wants the believer to live in such a way that his behavior accurately reflects the kind of salvation that he enjoys. It is more precious than silver or gold. Those early believers were being robbed of the ability to accumulate wealth. Their citizenship on earth was being taken from them. Peter points out that silver and gold cannot help the one who possesses it in any permanent way. Quality of life is fundamentally determined by only one thing: the quality of a person's relationship to God. Our salvation is in a category all by itself. It is not just of future value. It is the only thing that can rescue a person from the tyranny of this present evil age. Given this understanding of "be holy," John's reference to obeying the truth is likely referring to worldviews. Peter is commanding that believers adopt a biblical worldview. This worldview is communicated through the Word. This new worldview is driven by a sincere "love of the brethren." It starts with a proper understanding of our salvation and matures with an appropriate commitment to the body of Christ. The only way that believers can master this new way of living is to have their souls purged of the old way of thinking and living. The Word of God gives a replacement model so that the believer is no longer conformed to the former loves (lusts). There can be no mixing of the old and new. We have been born again through the eternal and unchanging Word of God. Salvation is not renovation; it is transformation into a completely new person. Therefore, we are to abandon our old ways, including those habits which do not reflect who we now are in Christ. Our salvation must penetrate to the very foundations of our thinking so that it transforms our actions.

LIFE STEP

Salvation works from the inside out. Merely changing our outward behavior is an insufficient response to the awesome salvation God has provided for us. We must embrace the reality of our new birth and be renewed in our thinking. A renewed mind lies at the heart of transformation (Romans 12:2). Ask God to change your thinking in one key area today.

What is the writer saying?

How can I apply this to my life?

Too often we view the analogy of "newborn babes" as referring to the eagerness of the infant rather than the submissiveness of the infant. Peter is arguing that believers must put aside the lusts and perspectives of the flesh and, as a totally empty vessel, be refilled with the biblical worldview. Newborns have no ulterior motives and are totally dependent upon and trusting of the one who feeds them. The milk of the Word enables the believer to appreciate the kindness of the Lord. The kindness of the Lord cannot be experienced in this life if the believer continues to hold to his former worldview. Life must be understood according to the message of Scripture in order to be fully appreciated. The Lord's kindness is an anticipated reward for those who worship successfully in the age in which they find themselves, whether Old Testament Israel or the New Testament church.

Present grace is clearly available, but it only gives salvation to those who believe. Beginning with verse 4, Peter begins a series of metaphors from the Old Testament to highlight the special distinctives of the church. He moves from the rejected Christ to the "by-faith" Christians, to the new spiritual household, which is the church. It is interesting that Peter is clearly making a strong statement in favor of the church but never uses the word "church." Christ is certainly the "Cornerstone," but He was also the stone upon which the nation of Israel stumbled. They stumbled because they chose works over faith and their own worldview over that of Scripture. The one who believes is the one who experiences blessing. Blessing has always been available; it is faith that has been lacking. Church-age saints must not stumble here.

LIFE STEP

Is your desire for the Word of God similar to the instinctive desire of a newborn baby for milk? If not, your spiritual growth will be greatly affected. Find a way to remind yourself of verses 9-10 throughout your entire day today.

What is the writer saying?

How can I apply this to my life?

PRAY

Pray that your pastor will have God's wisdom and guidance in the area of counseling.

Peter uses the descriptors "beloved" and "strangers and pilgrims" to mark verse 11 as the beginning of a new section. Clearly the believers in Asia Minor feel ostracized from someone or something. Based upon the larger discourse, it may be that they had been excommunicated from the synagogue which had previously provided legal protection. Without the protection of the synagogue, they were now experiencing civil rejection and persecution as an illegal religion. This rejection has provided a new opportunity for witness. Just as the early persecution in Jerusalem propelled missionaries throughout Judea, Samaria, and the world, so this rejection was providing an opportunity for believers to shine before their Gentile neighbors and authorities.

Beginning with verse 13, Peter suggests that the believers can do this if they continue to respect and show loyalty toward secular authorities. These were the very authorities that were persecuting the churches. We have no way of knowing exactly how intense the persecution may have been, but historical accounts of the period would certainly lead us to believe that it was brutal. Still, Peter is clear about the believer's need to recognize that all authorities are put in place by God and are to be respected as such. The reason that we do this is because of the opportunity that it will provide. True freedom only exists when we are totally submitted to God and His all-encompassing purposes.

LIFE STEP

Persecution is never pleasant, especially when it is unfair. And yet, it is often in these kinds of situations that the believer is given the greatest opportunity to be a light in this darkened world. Pray today for your civil leaders and look for ways to serve unbelievers around you.

What is the writer saying?

How can I apply this to my life?

Government is not the only authority that exists for the believer. In today's passage, Peter suggests two additional "authorities" to which believers must show deference if they are to live excellently among the Gentiles. In verses 18-20, he speaks of economic authorities, and in verses 21-25, he refers to unjust circumstances as an "authority." The economic authorities of that day would be the "masters." Times have changed, but, whether the relationship is employer/employee or master/slave, the mandate is the same. If we react as the world would react, we will not advance the cause of Christ.

In verse 21, Peter lays out the heart of the matter: believers are called to follow Christ's example when suffering injustice (see also 3:9).

Unfair treatment can be interpreted in many ways. We can view it as the enemy of our spiritual life, or we can view it as a friend. Peter points to Christ and His acceptance of such treatment as a model to follow. Christ provided more than salvation to heaven; He provided an example of how we ought to walk in this life on earth. He did not view His mission here as a minor inconvenience to be endured until His glorification. He lived His life just as we should live ours and He gave His life just as we should give ours, as living sacrifices. He kept entrusting Himself to the Father. Christ lived a life of total dependence upon the Father, and He expects us to live similar lives. It is not enough to submit to the authorities that God has placed in our lives, we must also accept the unfair circumstances that may swirl around us. Left to our own resources we will always stray like sheep and wander from the path that God would have us walk.

LIFE STEP

Only by entrusting our welfare to our Shepherd and Guardian can we ever hope to experience the quality of life that God would have us experience. How are you reacting to some unfair circumstance in life? Consider how Jesus responded and ask the Holy Spirit to empower you to imitate Him today.

What is the writer saying?

How can I apply this to my life?

Another area in which the believer must practice submission is the family. Wives are to willingly submit to their husband's leadership, even when husbands are not entirely behaving the way that they should. This certainly requires discernment since the believer is also called to avoid enabling evil (Ephesians 5:8-14). Note that when speaking to women about hairstyles, jewelry, and nice clothing, Peter's exhortation is not to forbid these entirely but to exhort women not to make these the primary way they pursue beauty. Instead, their focus should be the cultivation of the inner beauty of godliness. Humans tend to focus on outward beauty and to neglect those heart traits that are most precious to God. This is in keeping with the emphasis on worldview change seen throughout the epistle. We must keep in mind that the wife finds contentment by being in a right relationship with her husband. When we step outside of the divinely provided forms, we become estranged from the blessings with which God wants to flood our lives.

Husbands are exhorted to live with their wives in an understanding way, respecting and honoring them as being of equal worth and standing before God. They are to submit themselves to whatever sacrifices are necessary in order to love their wives as Christ loved the Church (Ephesians 5:21, 25-31). Only when husband and wife both accept their God-ordained roles and responsibilities can the family know the kind of blessing that God wants for His children. Each partner in the husband/wife relationship is expected to enthusiastically carry out his/her responsibility regardless of his/her partner's compliance.

LIFE STEP   *Love is not a two-way street. Peter does not want us to have a conditional commitment to the family. Each one of us must act in response to God's love, not our spouse's. Identify one way you can put this text into practice today. Then, do it!*

What is the writer saying?

How can I apply this to my life?

PRAY   Canada – Pray for a revival that would stir the Canadian people to give God His rightful place in their culture yet again.

The larger section here opens with a paragraph exhorting brotherly love (3:8) and closes with a similar exhortation (4:8). When we live this way, we not only are a blessing to others, but we also receive a blessing. We are debtors as Paul mentioned in Romans 1:14. This deep obligation must be based on God's treatment of us, but it is always shown by extending similar grace to others. We shouldn't return evil for evil or good for good; we should always treat others the way God has treated us. We are truly blessed only when we are a living and contributing member of the household that God is building on earth.

Peter is clearly talking about the church, not as an institution of salvation but as an institution of fellowship. Love God. Love one another. That's all there is. We were called for this very purpose. We were not called to be miserable. True, we were called to experience difficult circumstances, but difficult circumstances have no power to diminish blessing. If God sends them, then they are to be welcomed. We will then inherit a blessing. The believers in Asia Minor were taking an escapist attitude and banking entirely on the return of the Lord to soothe their hurts. Peter tells them that blessings are available here and now, no matter how dark the trial may appear.

LIFE STEP   *Never give up on the present. Never throw in the towel. Life only has value when it is given in the service of others. How will you specifically serve others today in the midst of whatever trial you may find yourself in?*

What is the writer saying?

How can I apply this to my life?

Unfortunately, our worldviews are seldom shaped by faith. They are more likely to be shaped by experience. That is why many believers continually stray like sheep from the pastures that God has chosen for them. It goes against our nature to be happy when we suffer, but God does not want us to be intimidated by our nature and the fears of this life. We are intimidated by the world when we let the people or circumstances that we encounter shape our worldview. We fail to experience the full joy of this life because we have neglected a vital part of our great salvation. What controls our feelings and decisions is ultimately what we worship. If we fear our friends' opinions, we worship our friends. We are told to "sanctify the Lord" in our hearts. Christ must dwell alone in this central part of the believer's heart. All others must pale in His presence. Christ, and Christ alone, must be feared and worshiped.

If we rejoice in hardship, we are sure to get questions about our behavior. These questions will give an opportunity for the believer to share his faith with those who slander him as an evildoer. The issue is never the nature of the circumstance that one faces; the issue must always be the source of the circumstance. Should one despise a trial as an independent entity, or should one esteem it in the larger perspective of God's providence? The trial that Christ experienced was certainly undeserved; it occurred, not for Christ's benefit but for ours. Since His suffering took care of the sin problem, all present trials are corrective and beneficial, not punitive.

LIFE STEP

No matter how dark the hour, the proper response is always to trust the Lord and to demonstrate this trust by our response to the trials. James tells us to consider them a source of joy (James 1:2). Take time to thank the Lord right now for the trials you are experiencing.

What is the writer saying?

How can I apply this to my life?

PRAY Spain – Pray for Jesus to be made known among the millions of immigrants, many of whom are Muslim.

When Peter states that Christ has "suffered in the flesh," he is referring to the previous verses and is speaking of His death. The believer must arm himself to combat temptation with the same mindset that Jesus had toward the struggles that He faced. Because we died with Christ, we are to factor this reality into all of decision making when facing the continuing lusts of the flesh (Romans 6:11-14). This is essential for dealing with sinful responses to trials and temptations. Dead people are immune to the influences around them. In the same way, the believer must reckon the old worldview to be dead and must accept a new worldview.

Believers have a choice about the quality of life that they experience in this world. Outside influences can only control us to the degree that we welcome and accommodate them. The time has come to offer our lives fully and permanently to God for His use. The choice is simple. The believer can accept God's will for his life, or he can yield to anger, bitterness, and a hardened heart, which inevitably lead to indulging the corrupt desires of his old flesh. The believer cannot escape the pull of the lusts of his old flesh. But this does not mean that he must yield to them. The first step in arming ourselves to gain victory is to correctly position our thinking. The Bible teaches that we have died to sin. We must count this to be a fact and reason from there.

LIFE STEP *Make a short list of the most powerful temptations that you face. Then cross them out and write, "These are not me." If it will help, put the list in a place where you can see it regularly.*

What is the writer saying?

How can I apply this to my life?

PRAY
France – Pray for compelling Christlikeness among both foreign and indigenous believers.

The believer must understand that the "end of all things is at hand." All physical things related to this present creation will end. The suffering and eventual death of the body are not tragedies. The believer must understand that they are part of God's will. Since this is true, we need to choose to function from the right perspective. We must be serious about the decisions we make. We must pray in a way that demonstrates a measured understanding that God is in control and that all circumstances are under His providential supervision. Finally, we must see our purpose in life from a body (church) perspective rather than from an individual one. Suffering in my life may be permitted to prepare me to minister help and comfort to others. We must be good stewards of the manifold grace of God. By this, Peter is referring to the spiritual gifting which every believer receives from God. These are unmerited abilities and are given to us for the benefit of those around us. We need to be good stewards of these precious abilities which God has entrusted to us.

LIFE STEP

One day, we will all give an account of how we have stewarded our opportunities and gifting. Have you considered how the trials you face are equipping you to minister uniquely to others who are going through the same thing? How can you put your trials to a useful end by taking what they've taught you and using this experience to fervently love others? It's the best way to bring value to your losses and to exchange the seeming uselessness of trials for great benefit!

What is the writer saying?

How can I apply this to my life?

PRAY

Pray for the salvation and protection of those serving in the military around the world.

Peter has yet to fully address what he considers to be the appropriate response to fiery ordeals. He does so in this section. Our response to trials is a measure of our relationship with Christ. There is no doubt that his readers were facing an intense ordeal. Peter is not talking about some personal inconveniences. It was severe testing. They were concerned that they were becoming strangers and aliens in their own country. Peter says, "Praise the Lord. That's exactly what you are!" They considered the trials as strangers and intruders, but they weren't. Trials are to be counted as normal and ultimately beneficial. Therefore, Peter tells believers to keep on rejoicing. They were not to rejoice despite trials but rather to rejoice because of trials! That being said, he makes it clear that those who suffer for their own evil behavior should not expect to rejoice.

As with the previous segments, Peter speaks of the return of Christ at the beginning of this, the third section. It must be counted as a blessing to rightly suffer for Christ today because of the tremendous joy such faithful suffering will bring in that coming day. In contrast to this, the judgment which awaits the ungodly in that day will cause the present suffering of the godly to pale in comparison.

LIFE STEP

In the final analysis what really counts is where one's trust is anchored. Blessing is available to those who trust God's grace and not their own understanding of how life should be. How can you commit yourself to the Lord in the middle of your trials today, leave the outcome to Him, and continue to faithfully do good?

What is the writer saying?

How can I apply this to my life?

PRAY   Puerto Rico – Pray for wise governance that works for the best interests of the islands' inhabitants.

Life was always meant to be shared, and that sharing begins with shepherding the flock or investing in the lives of other believers. This sounds a lot like the discussion that Jesus had with Peter in John 21. Left on our own, we believers will wander through a wide range of emotions when responding to the trials of life. We need shepherding. Believers are not born with a biblical worldview. We need to be taught and shepherded into right thinking. We need to be transformed by the renewing of our minds. Once we are strong enough to count trials as our friends, then we can begin to minister to others.

Younger men are exhorted to learn from those who have had more experience in the pastures of God's grace. This requires a humble heart and a willingness to serve and grow together. Remember, when Peter exhorts us to humble ourselves, the immediate context is trials. When we make grandiose proclamations about fairness and grudgingly accepting God's will, we fail miserably in our mission. God's grace should always be prized. It must be received with a grateful and humble heart in order to be maximized. The fiery ordeals of life are permitted and directed by the mighty, gracious hand of God. We are never victims of a mindless fate. Instead, Peter reminds us that God cares for us and that we should, therefore, bring all our cares directly to Him, rather than casting them onto others.

LIFE STEP

To whom do you tend to unburden your heart? There is no doubt that believers ought to help one another to carry burdens. But our first instinct must be to bring ALL our cares to the Lord and to cast them on Him. Spend a few moments right now "unloading" your cares to God in prayer. Deliberately reject the idea that He doesn't care to hear what you have to say. That's a lie!

What is the writer saying?

How can I apply this to my life?

PRAY France – For missionaries to integrate well into French culture and to persevere amidst slow results.

Before concluding, Peter takes a moment to put the adversary into proper perspective. Yes, the devil is real and yes, he seeks victims. However, he can be successfully resisted. Don't fall into his trap and begin to fear him or his minions. The only power with which he can harm us is the power that we give him when we yield to anger and bitterness. God is "the God of all grace." There is no ungracious part in Him. All His dealings with us are an expression of pure grace. He has called us to "His eternal glory." The question has never been whether we possess this glory, but rather if we will be submissive enough to experience it here and now. Will we let God change how we view life and what we should expect this side of heaven?

Peter wraps up the letter with a mention of "Silvanus, our faithful brother." This is Silas, Paul's former compatriot. He appears to be the scribe taking Peter's dictation. Peter concludes by restating his theme. This letter is about "the true grace of God" and how we are to "stand firm in it." God's grace in our lives does not mean that we will be free from the fiery ordeals of life, but rather that we can experience the joy that only God can provide in the midst of those trials.

LIFE STEP

When we understand God's grace, we can experience personal and present peace. Paul opens all his letters with "grace and peace." Peter spends the whole of this first letter telling us what grace and peace look like in the life of a believer. Grace is always available; it is our responsibility to receive it and experience peace. Consider regularly asking God to help you know His grace and peace in every circumstance of life.

What is the writer saying?

How can I apply this to my life?

PRAY

Canada – For the hundreds of reservations of Canadian indigenous people without an ongoing witness.

God cares deeply for the souls of all men, including those who live wicked lives marked by horrible brutality. This can be viewed as the primary message of the Book of Jonah. The Assyrian city of Nineveh was a center of wickedness in an empire noted for its horrible acts of depravity toward other nations. Yet, it was God's prerogative to instruct his servant, Jonah, to arise and go to Nineveh to cry out against it in an effort to draw them to repentance.

We also are given a picture of a rebellious, selfish servant of God in the person of Jonah, who deliberately refused God's instructions and headed in the opposite direction away from Nineveh. Why? Jonah would prefer to see the Assyrians suffer the consequences of their brutality than to see God's mercy granted to them as repentant sinners.

One would think that any person who identified himself as a God-fearer and recognized God's power as the creator of the earth and sea (v. 9) would know better than to try to run from God. God sees all and knows all. He can find you regardless of where you run! (See Psalm 139:7-12.) But for all of Jonah's self-proclaimed beliefs in God, he foolishly sought to get out of the assignment God had given him. The pagan sailors demonstrated more piety and respect for God than Jonah did, attempting to find ways to avoid sacrificing Jonah to the sea to atone for his transgression (vv. 11-16). Jonah chose to face the raging sea rather than obey God. That's how rebellious and stubborn he was! Ultimately, the sailors tossed him into the sea as a desperate attempt to appease God's anger, and immediately the sea calmed down.

God would not give up on Jonah despite his disobedience. He sent a "great fish" to swallow up Jonah and enabled Jonah a second chance at obedience.

LIFE STEP

When you decide to run from God's clear direction, you do so at your own peril. He will not always overlook your acts of rebellion or wink at your disobedience. Be honest with yourself by reviewing any area of your life which reflects disobedience to God. Pray for the boldness to turn around (repent) and get on the path of obedience, whatever it takes.

What is the writer saying?

How can I apply this to my life?

Jonah had a moment within the belly of the great fish when he came to his senses and reached out to his only source of hope—the Lord God. In the prayer he later recorded from the safety of dry ground (he obviously had no writing tools within the fish's belly), Jonah recalls God's faithfulness to hear his cries while he was in great distress (vv. 2-3). He makes the direct connection with his plight and God's hand of intervention. It wasn't the sailors whom Jonah saw as casting him into the sea but God Himself! Verse 4 indicates that more concerning to Jonah than the tossing of the waves was the sense that God had cast him out of His sight.

Jonah most likely sensed that his end was near as he sank beneath the waves, as indicated in verses 5 and 6. Wrapped in seaweed, enveloped by the crashing waters, he saw himself being closed off from God forever through death. Yet, God heard his prayer of desperation and brought deliverance from the pit to which Jonah was headed.

It appears that Jonah's experience in the fish's belly awakened in him the reality of God's presence and power, as he recalls in verses. 7-9 that moment when he uttered his plea to the God of second chances. Whereas before the storm he was intent on pursuing his own path, in his desperation he comes to himself in acknowledging God's worthiness and expressing his vow to worship God through his obedience. Notice the scope of his repentance in verse 9, when he praised God for saving him and pledged to fulfill his promises with a grateful heart.

LIFE STEP

Does it surprise you when you find yourself in a mess following an act of disobedience toward God? You may be feeling distress right now because of bad choices you've made. Although Jonah does not serve as a great example in general, at least in today's reading he realized where his help must come from. Will you do likewise? Cry out to God in humility and acknowledge that salvation and deliverance is from the Lord. He can do it. He can move any obstacle and make right any wrong. He can turn things around and put you on a good path again. Turn to him in heartfelt obedience.

What is the writer saying?

How can I apply this to my life?

PRAY — United Kingdom – For God to raise up a new generation of vibrant, doctrinally sound, Bible teachers.

God spoke to Jonah a second time following his release from the great fish, this time repeating His command that Jonah go to Nineveh to preach against that great city. This time, however, Jonah immediately obeyed and set out for Nineveh. We learn from Jonah's narrative that the city was huge (most likely including its surrounding suburbs), requiring three days to walk through it. Some experts theorize that the circumference of the city was about sixty miles. Others propose a less literal interpretation, suggesting that it would take three days to visit the city's various surrounding towns and settlements.

Jonah's message from God was simple and direct (v. 4). Destruction would surely come to the city and its inhabitants unless they turned to God in repentance. Amazingly, these hardened sinners responded by taking Jonah's prophecy as truth, believing that God would surely do what He threatened to do. Their turn-around was total, from the greatest to the least of their citizens, including the king of Nineveh, who put on sackcloth and sat in ashes as a show of his brokenness because of his sins (vv. 5-7). In verse 9, the king uttered his hope that God would stay his hand of punishment because of the sincerity of their repentance.

God graciously viewed the response of the Ninevites as a true sign of repentance and withheld the judgment He had promised to bring upon them (v. 10).

LIFE STEP

The king of Nineveh got it right. In verse 8, he challenged his people to join him in turning from their evil ways in heartfelt repentance. What about you? Do you need to make a turn in direction? That's really the definition of repentance—a change of mind or direction toward God and away from sin. What action do you need to take right now to start this turn-around?

What is the writer saying?

How can I apply this to my life?

PRAY   Germany – That believers will take advantage of every opportunity to share the Gospel with the unsaved.

We see in today's reading a man whose hatred for a wicked people has clouded his better judgment as a man of God. Rather than rejoice in God's mercy toward the Assyrians, Jonah reacts as a spoiled child who failed to get his way, angrily reminding God that this was just what he feared when he initially ran away from God's assignment. He claimed it would be better for him if he died right then and there, than to see his enemies receive God's mercy and grace (vv. 2-3).

God responded patiently, demanding that Jonah review his motivations in growing angry. "Is it right for you to be angry?" (v. 4) He asked. In verses. 5-7, we see how God mercifully provided for Jonah as he waited outside the city to see what would happen. First, God prepared a plant to grow up quickly to give shade to Jonah. Then, He had a worm infest the plant, causing it to wither. Suffering from the heat, Jonah once more pouted, "It is better for me to die than to live." Then, God gave Jonah an object lesson that surely would convict his heart of his selfishness (v. 10).

Jonah didn't deserve God's merciful provision of the plant's shade any more than the Assyrians deserved God's mercy. But just as He gave Jonah what he didn't deserve, God chose to show mercy toward the repentant Assyrians who numbered more than 120,000 souls. This is God's choice, and Jonah is left to think on the matter.

Why would God give us the Book of Jonah with its less than stellar example of a prophet? Paul provides a good answer to this question in Romans 15:4 when he tells us that these things from the former days were "written for our instruction." Jonah serves to instruct us in God's overwhelming desire to draw people to Himself through any means.

LIFE STEP

Do you have a bit of Jonah in you—willing and happy to receive God's mercy but unwilling to rejoice in the mercy God extends to people you don't love? Ask God right now to give you a heart for the lost so that you can see all people as God sees them. All people are unclean and undeserving. All are bound for either heaven or hell. Pray for God's intervention in the lives of the unsaved all over the world, since He desires that all might be saved (2 Peter 3:9).

What is the writer saying?

How can I apply this to my life?

PRAY
Ghana – Pray for God to send laborers to the 15,000 villages with no local body of believers.

The Prophet Haggai was God's chosen spokesperson to warn the Israelites in Jerusalem that their priorities were all out of order. His ministry is highlighted in four inspired messages to the Jews when they had returned to the city from their exile in Babylon in the reign of King Darius of Persia. Their original mission in returning to Jerusalem was the rebuilding of the city and its grand temple (see Ezra 3), but the work had ceased years before and was still delayed. In this context, God commissioned Haggai to speak directly to the governmental and spiritual leaders, as well as to the people in general.

The problem Haggai was to call to their attention was quite simple. God's house remained in disrepair while the people had found ample time and resources to build for themselves nice homes (vv. 2-4). God warns, "Consider your ways!" (vv. 5, 7) Though the people had sown much, their produce was limited and insufficient to satisfy their needs. Though they had basic necessities, they could not find enough clothing to stay warm in the cold winter (v. 6). In verse 9, God speaks of blowing away the foods they had gathered. Why? Because God's house remained in ruins while the people enjoyed fine houses. Even the normally reliable dew drops that watered their crops were absent, leading to drought and famine (vv. 10-11).

The solution to their dilemma? Verse 8 tells us plainly what God wanted. They were to go and gather the materials needed and start the work of rebuilding the temple, all to the glory of God!

LIFE STEP

Here we find a lesson in priorities that should remind us that God wants our best, not our leftovers—not our leftover time or our leftover resources. Read Matthew 6:33 and write down what you believe is God's desire for you when it comes to what matters most. As God spoke through Haggai to the inhabitants of Jerusalem, "Consider you ways!" Are you making God the priority in your life?

What is the writer saying?

How can I apply this to my life?

PRAY New Zealand – Pray for committed Christian leaders to be raised up from the Maori.

God now commanded Haggai to speak a second sermon, this time addressing the frustrations and fears of those who were discouraged by comparisons of the new temple construction with the glorious temple of Solomon's day. It had been more than sixty years since that temple was destroyed, and the crowd consisted of some who were present in the "old days." To them, this new temple seemed "as nothing."

God issued a three-fold command to be strong (courageous) and do the work. Those who were downcast because nothing (they thought) could ever match the previous temple in its glory and beauty needed to set aside the distraction of discouragement and get to work! They could move forward with confidence and enthusiasm because God is with them! Therefore, there is no reason to fear (vv. 4-5).

Verses 6-9 are futuristic, promising what is yet to come when the temple is rebuilt. The temple would once more be filled with God's glory—a greater manifestation of His glory even than in the days of the former temple. God pledged to "shake heaven and earth, the sea and dry land" once more—a reference to future divine judgment.

God also pledged the full benefit of His unlimited resources. Though the people thought they could never match Solomon's wealth in bringing the temple to its magnificent completion, God assured them that He controlled all the silver and gold in the universe (v. 8). The reference to the "Desire of All Nations" in verse 7 is either a prophecy of Jesus' return as Messiah, or may refer to treasures that will adorn the temple in the days of the millennial reign (see Zechariah 14:14). Both interpretations illustrate the fullness of God's glory associated with the temple-rebuilding project.

LIFE STEP

God wants His people to find their confidence not in themselves or their meager resources but in His power and riches. Ours are limited; His are infinite and unlimited. Let this be a reminder to you that nothing is too hard for God. Regardless of the challenge you are facing or will ever face, He is greater in both power and resources. Why don't you pray right now, affirming your trust in Him in every situation and thanking Him for His faithfulness. He is able!

What is the writer saying?

How can I apply this to my life?

PRAY

Honduras – Pray for unity and cooperation among various denominations within the growing evangelical community.

Haggai's third and fourth messages from God bring his prophecy to a close. In message three (vv. 10-19), he is told to ask the priests for a ruling on a question of ritualistic cleansing. What he hears in response affords the opportunity to condemn the people of Israel for their disobedience in the past. They had ignored God's warnings about true repentance and busied themselves with their own houses while neglecting the temple rebuilding (Haggai 1:2-4). The principal is this: Holiness is not contagious, but impurity is. Spiritual neglect cannot be overcome by mere rituals and ceremony (v. 14). Their offerings were considered unclean if their hearts were dirty. What they needed was to "carefully consider" their ways, from the days before temple reconstruction began, when God pointed out the decline in their living conditions (vv. 15-17) because of their sin. But this message provides hope, too. It is the hope of a new beginning that is tied to proper priorities, commencing with the current day's efforts to rebuild the temple (vv.18-19). Though they had neither the seed they needed nor the abundance of delicacies they desired (figs, pomegranates), things would be different. God would restore His blessings from this day forward because of their renewed commitment to put Him first. Obedience leads to blessings.

In verses 20-23, Haggai directs message four to Zerubbabel, the governor of Judah and political leader of the Israelites. God will fight for His people in a miraculous way and bring destruction and defeat to the Gentile nations that hate them. This section, most experts agree, speaks of end times events, paralleling Daniel 2. Verse 23 indicates that God has marked Zerubbabel for special honor by making him the channel for the coming of the Messiah. Zerubbabel is mentioned in the lineage of Jesus as recorded by Matthew (Matthew 1:12).

LIFE STEP

Like the Israelites, we need to carefully consider our past and our present obedience in light of God's revealed Word. When He speaks, do you listen? Are you seeking His will by staying in the Word? Are you walking in obedience? We often fail to pay close attention to the matter of our obedience. Don't neglect your spiritual health and leave yourself vulnerable to the consequences of sinful rebellion. Discipline yourself to "carefully consider" your ways. Read aloud Psalm 139:23-24 now as a prayer to God to help you in your obedience.

What is the writer saying?

How can I apply this to my life?

PRAY   India – For the 900 million who are blinded by Hinduism to find true spiritual fulfillment in Christ.

Luke wrote this material for Theophilus, likely a man of some rank who may have been supporting him financially. Luke appears to be the only gospel writer who had no firsthand, eyewitness knowledge of the earthly life of Christ. Rather than a weakness though, this turns out to be a strength. It becomes a perfect example of how the divine and the human constantly intersect and coexist in our everyday experience. Luke studied and researched his topic in the same way any scholar of that day would have. However, the result of his labor was still the Word of God because the Holy Spirit moved him. The relationship between the two was seamless and the results can be seen in that the text is both understandable and authoritative. Its human qualities give us the ability to know what it means, and its divine qualities guarantee that what it means is without error.

Luke's research into the life of Jesus Christ begins with the extended family, Zacharias and Elizabeth. They were an elderly couple and without children when the angel appeared to Zacharias as he performed his duties in the Holy Place. God spoke to Zacharias while he served in the Temple. Apparently, God had not communicated any fresh revelation to mankind since the last prophet of the Old Testament, Malachi. The last words of Malachi predicted the coming of a forerunner of the Messiah, and now Zacharias is told that his son would be that man.

LIFE STEP

It's easy to forget that long periods of time often passed without God communicating new things to His people. Though God doesn't communicate fresh revelation to us in our day, we can easily become discouraged when we feel that we haven't "heard from Him" in a long while. The truth is, we always have God's revelation available to us in His Word. Are we paying attention to it? Is there anything that He's already made clear that you've not yet followed through on? Commit to do so today!

107

What is the writer saying?

How can I apply this to my life?

PRAY   Nigeria – Pray that the churches in Nigeria would be more committed to ministering to their children and youth.

The interaction between Zacharias and the angel, who identified himself as Gabriel, is very instructive. One would think that the mere presence of an angel in the Holy Place would be enough "evidence" that the message was accurate. But Zacharias appeared unwilling or unable to accept that message, even when the angel demonstrated from Scripture that these things had been prophesied. The promise of God had remained unfulfilled for many years and this childless couple had no doubt experienced disappointments before. Thus, Zacharias felt he needed more to go on than the word of an angel, so he asked for a sign. The response to this request is enlightening. It did indeed demonstrate God's power, but it severely limited Zacharias' lifestyle and ministry. The lesson is that when men fail to believe God's initial word, any additional help often comes at a price. Consider King Ahaz in Isaiah 7. He lost the chance to be a physical ancestor of the Messiah. Verse 22 is almost humorous. Here is a man of God who has just been given the most incredible news both personally and for all mankind, but he cannot speak. God's plan marches forward. Elizabeth conceived and remained in seclusion for five months. There is no question that this family felt blessed - blessed to be with child and blessed to be a part of God's plan. This is true of all of us. Each one experiences and appreciates God's blessing to the degree that his faith allows.

This passage clearly shows that God wants to use us. His blessing does not depend entirely on our initial response, but it is certainly far better for us to believe Him immediately. When God makes something abundantly clear in His Word, don't look for signs before committing to believing it. Are you delaying obedience on any point that God has made clear?

What is the writer saying?

How can I apply this to my life?

Pray for those that work with the youth of your church to have love, wisdom, and perseverance.

What unfolds in these few verses is the greatest mystery that man has ever faced. The Almighty God, the Creator of the universe, the Holy One of Israel, stooped to earth and became a man. The Hebrew word used in Isaiah 7:14 would indicate that Mary was a young virgin girl who had just come of age to marry. Unlike Zacharias, she did not question the facts, only the method. She did not ask *if* this could happen but rather *how* this could happen. The simple faith found in Mary is the most elevated trait in Scripture. While Mary is not to be worshiped, she is still to be respected and admired.

Luke's choice of the Greek word *charis* (translated *favor* here but usually *grace*) is clearly to be understood in the way that Paul used the word. Correctly understood, the grace of God, acknowledged by faith, will produce peace in the most unusual circumstances. Mary had to know that few, if any, were going to believe her story. Not even Joseph believed her at first. Her purity would be questioned. Her life was about to change forever. Her childhood was past. But she had the peace to say, "Be it unto me according to thy word." Wow!

One other point to note is that the child in her womb was Jesus from day one. It was not an extension of her body that would eventually become Jesus. Children are persons from the moment of conception. The life that quivered in her womb was clearly Who He was from the moment she was overshadowed by the Highest.

LIFE STEP

This is truly a precious and well-known Christmas story, but it is more than that. It is the account of a person just like us, a young girl who was willing to put her whole future in the hands of the God she trusted. Do we have such faith? If not, ask the Lord to increase your faith and to come to the help of your unbelief (Luke 17:5; Mark 9:24).

What is the writer saying?

How can I apply this to my life?

Elizabeth was perhaps the only person who could understand how Mary felt. Both had come face to face with the grace of God and recognized it for what it was. Both were about to be the mother of a fulfillment of God's promises. Both were relentless in their acceptance and appreciation of God's will for their lives. The whole passage exudes an atmosphere of joy and not fear.

The words of Elizabeth to Mary are accurate but often misinterpreted. Blessing is something that God entrusts to mankind. It is never earned and never owned, always available but seldom seen. The world we live in and the very air we breathe are blessings. Mary was not blessed because she was a woman of faith; she was blessed because by faith she understood and accepted God's will for her life.

Mary's song is a simple psalm of praise. Its wording and structure are similar to the Psalms we find in the Old Testament. Mary truly understood her humble estate. She knew that the path before her was one of incredible blessing and that the hardships were but a pittance in comparison to the opportunity she had been given. The song has no self-pity, no hint of complaint, and no suggestion of an alternate future. The words reflect just a simple peace that only faith in God can bring.

LIFE STEP

The generation of people that left Egypt with Moses did not enter the Promised Land. They looked at things through the eyes of facts, figures, and grim reality. They should have looked through the eyes of faith as Mary and Elizabeth did. What kind of eyes do you have today? Do you see opportunity or opposition?

What is the writer saying?

How can I apply this to my life?

For nine months Zacharias has been silent, unable to speak. Imagine his frustration. For years he had heard his friends talk of their children. For years he had carried the desire to be a father and to hold his own child. And now, throughout the whole process, he is not much more than a silent bystander. But there is no resentment building in this man, as can be seen by his reaction to the birth.

The custom in those days was to name a child after the father or an honored relative. The officials at the circumcision, where this was usually done, assumed that the child would be named after his father and announced it as so. Elizabeth stopped the proceedings and declared that the child was to be named John. When Elizabeth announced this, the officials turned to Zacharias, who then confirmed it in writing. Suddenly, his mouth was opened and he began to praise God. He did not say, "Whew, glad that's over!" He had grown a bit since he had first spoken with Gabriel!

Interestingly, a name is really a sign used to identify a person. In the recent past, signs had been important to Zacharias, but not now. He knew his son would never follow in the family tradition; he was a special child with a special name because he had a special future. With joy, Zacharias recognized this and, as Abraham with Isaac, he put his son's future totally in the hands of the Holy One of Israel. As word of all this began to spread, many began to ask, "What kind of child will this be?"

LIFE STEP   *Children are a gift from the Lord. They are blessings on loan from their Maker. We love and cherish them, but we never own them. Their road of blessing may lead into the wilderness and as parents we need to be careful not to stand in the way. Have you surrendered your children to the Lord for Him to use as He sees fit?*

What is the writer saying?

How can I apply this to my life?

PRAY Uganda – Pray for a deep hunger for God and His Word in the Ugandan Church.

Zacharias' prophetic benediction had probably been in the making throughout his nine months of silence. Like Mary's song, this doxology is patterned after the poetry that we find in the Old Testament. It is a psalm of praise. The most common type of psalm we find in the Old Testament is the lament. Such poems start out with a call for help and end up with a faith resolution. But with both Mary and Zacharias, there is no call for help, just the simple recognition that the hope that was sought throughout the whole of the Old Testament had arrived.

Zacharias tied the birth of John to two key promises. In fact, these two promises are the central promises made to Israel: the Davidic covenant and the Abrahamic covenant. Both are unconditional covenants. We should never forget that the initial emphasis of God's salvation was directed toward Israel. God has not changed His mind about the elements within these covenants. Blessing is presently offered apart from the nation of Israel, but the restoration of the nation is indispensable to God in completing His program.

Verse 80 deserves special comment. By itself, it would raise little interest. However, when similar statements are made about Jesus a little later in the text (2:40, 52), we are left to wonder how a divine child could experience the same type of growth as a normal one. How is it possible for deity to mature in the same way that a normal human child does? Luke's comparison of the two children is designed to emphasize similarities as well as distinctions.

LIFE STEP

What makes us human? Why are we different from the animals? How could God literally become one of us? More importantly, why was it necessary for God to do such a thing? Take a bit of time today to reflect on the stunning fact of the incarnation. Then praise the Lord for it!

What is the writer saying?

How can I apply this to my life?

PRAY Bolivia – For youth outreach activities to the 53% of the population that is 19 or under.

The narrative now returns to the central figure in this gospel account. Mary was great with child, and the wheels of providence began to turn. Cyrenius, the governor of Syria, had no idea that he was playing a part in the unfolding drama. His decree was purely intended to collect more taxes, but it launched Mary and Joseph on a journey that would connect the prophetic dots laid out in the Old Testament. Micah 5:2 was clear about the fact that the Messiah would be born in Bethlehem, and it was to that city that Joseph returned with his young wife. The swaddling cloths and the manger are mentioned only by Luke. They have become a recurring element within the Christmas story partly because they are uncommon items in our culture. Swaddling an infant (wrapping tightly) with strips of cloth was thought to produce good posture and to keep the child from accidentally scratching himself. A manger was a wooden or stone bin designed to hold hay or water for animals. Nothing about this child was out of the ordinary to human eyes. He required the same motherly care as any other infant.

What was invisible to the human eye was announced by the heavenly host of angels. This very ordinary-looking child was in fact the promised Son of David, the Savior, the Messiah, the very Son of God! Peace was now available. The favor (grace) of God to Mary had opened the door so that all mankind could now experience real peace.

LIFE STEP

Familiarity often breeds apathy. We too often read Luke's telling of the Christmas story and miss the major emphasis. Anyone searching for the newborn Son of God would have expected to find Him anywhere else but where He was. Where do you expect God to show up? More often than not, He works through the simple and the ordinary, which is why we often fail to perceive His presence. Look for the Lord in the small things today.

What is the writer saying?

How can I apply this to my life?

Luke has obviously chosen to recount different details of the nativity than Matthew did. Matthew focused on the child as the true King of Israel and heir to David's throne. Luke took a different approach, presenting Him as the fully human Son of Man.

As the shepherds approached the stable, the spectacular was replaced by the common—no angels, no choirs, just a baby lying in a manger, bundled up like many other babies of that day. The story which the shepherds widely circulated was not based on what they had seen in the stable but what they had heard in the fields. This was indeed good tidings of great joy!

After eight days had passed, the child was circumcised as required. Thirty-three days later, he was brought to the temple so his parents could offer a sacrifice of dedication. A lamb was normally offered but, if people were poor, they could offer a pair of turtledoves or two young pigeons. This is a clear indication that, while still a part of the royal line, Jesus' family was not wealthy. Jesus was not treated any differently than any other, nor did He appear any different from His contemporaries. All of this emphasized His identification with common humanity. He grew up from his earliest days with the same kinds of physical limitations that we face.

LIFE STEP

The transition from the transcendent glory of Heaven to the cold reality of life on earth was, for Jesus Christ, a personal decision. He did not come because He was forced to do so. He came because He wanted to do so, because of His great love for each of us. If you struggle with feelings that no one cares, let the account of Christ's coming encourage your heart.

What is the writer saying?

How can I apply this to my life?

Just as the birth of Christ was accompanied by a divine announcement (by the angelic host), so was the sacrifice of dedication (by Simeon). Mary hid these things in her heart and perhaps rightly so. People would be tempted to dismiss her as an overzealous mother. But it was not Mary who spoke; God sent messengers. An angelic chorus appeared at Jesus' birth and then God sent Simeon and Anna. Later, He sent John the Baptist.

Simeon was an older saint who had been waiting for the Savior. He was privileged to see what every generation of faithful Israelites had longed for. He saw the Lord, not high and lifted up with His robe filling the temple as Isaiah had, but low and carried by a young girl out of a very different sanctuary. Simeon's message was one of exaltation and warning. He rejoiced in what was about to be accomplished but warned of the difficult road that would be traversed. Anna's exact words are not recorded in the text. We only know that she recognized the child for Who He was and gave thanks to God for Jesus' appearing. She spread word throughout Jerusalem that the Messiah had come.

Anna and Simeon were the exceptions. The message they proclaimed appears to have fallen on deaf ears. A short time after this, according to Matthew, wise men would come from the east, asking about this child, but nobody seemed to remember. How could such a thing happen? God was walking among His people and only a couple of elderly folks noticed! How easily the divine is overlooked in the day-to-day hectic pace of our busy lives.

LIFE STEP   *God was walking among His people. The vast majority just yawned and went on about their daily lives. Do we do the same? Ask God to make you sensitive to His presence and to the ways He is working in people's lives all around you.*

What is the writer saying?

How can I apply this to my life?

PRAY Senegal – Pray for indigenous churches to be planted among many unreached people groups.

We must remember that each Gospel presents a different (but not contradictory) view of Christ. Matthew presents Him as king, Mark as a servant, and John as the Son of God. Luke focuses on the humanity of Christ. Today's passage concludes what Luke shares about Jesus' early years. In this last passage, he draws his argument to a close, making what may be the most puzzling statement found anywhere in Scripture: Jesus "increased in wisdom and stature, and in favor with God and men."

The confusion lies not with the words but with the theology that accompanies them. How can an unchanging God grow or increase in any way? The very concept seems incompatible with God's attributes as described in the Scriptures.

Other passages deepen the mystery. Christ was tested in every way as we are, yet He did not sin (Hebrews 4:15). He emptied Himself and was made in the image of man (Philippians 2:5-9). Though He was rich, yet for our sakes He became poor (2 Corinthians 8:9). These verses describe but never explain the precise relationship between the human and the divine in the person of Jesus Christ. It almost certainly can't be explained in a way that we can fully understand, but we must not miss the amazing point: Jesus was 100% human!

LIFE STEP

The first lesson in theology is that God is God, and we are not! There are many mysteries surrounding His ways that we cannot fully grasp. If we could, then His thoughts would rise no higher than our own, but in fact they do (Isaiah 55:8-9)! We honor Him by admitting that our minds are not the final arbiter of all truth and humbly acknowledging our limitations. Is there something about God that you are waiting to understand before you'll trust Him?

What is the writer saying?

How can I apply this to my life?

PRAY

Pray that the youth of your church will know the Word, grow in Christ, and live out their faith.

At least eighteen years pass between the second and third chapters. We know next to nothing about those years. Then the voice of John the Baptist was heard, the forerunner of the Lord. His message was simple: repent for the remission of sins. It is not clear, given today's use of these words, exactly what John was asking them to do. The word used here to refer to repentance is *metanoieo*. It literally means to change one's mind. Based on a correct understanding of Matthew's Gospel and of Paul's teaching (Luke was an associate of Paul), it seems clear that John was asking them to change their minds about how they dealt with sin. The nation of Israel had fallen under the tyrannical expectations of a law-based self-righteousness that made salvation impossible and caused men to despise one another. John was preaching a new way: a way that depended upon being buried and resurrected to a new life. This was the same message Paul described in his preaching about being crucified and raised with Christ (Galatians 2:20; Ephesians 2:4-6).

Luke was building to a very special climax in his Gospel. His thesis was not new; it was the same message that appears all through Scripture: righteousness is only possible through faith. Baptism would be a symbol of what faith in the Son of God would accomplish. It would result in our being put to death with Him in order to rise with Him to a new life.

LIFE STEP

John did not ask for a change in the degree that men kept the Law; he called for them to abandon dead works in pursuit of genuine fruit that could only come from a changed heart. The nation of Israel needed to change their whole approach to becoming righteous. They needed faith in the One who had been sent to provide it, not more confidence in their own good works. Have you come to the end of measuring your standing before God by how much good you do or how much evil you avoid? Salvation is only available by trusting that Jesus died for your sins and was raised to life on your behalf so that you could have His righteousness. Trust in Him, not in yourself!

What is the writer saying?

How can I apply this to my life?

PRAY Botswana – Pray for more biblical training for indigenous church leaders to protect from syncretism.

While John's message was not new to Scripture, it was new to the people of Israel. They had not heard these words from their religious leaders. The message was so unique and so powerful that some began to suggest that John was the Messiah. John's answer was profound on several levels. First, it was a clear assertion that he was not the Messiah. Second, he communicated that his baptism was only a picture of spiritual realities and not a spiritual reality in and of itself. It was only water! The only meaningful baptism was the one that would result in receiving the Holy Spirit. The act of water baptism merely portrays our death, burial, and resurrection in Christ. We need to be very careful that we do not confuse the symbol with the reality it portrays. Water baptism cannot save us or make us holy. Instead, it is a public, visible statement that our life is now totally identified with the death, burial, and resurrection of Jesus Christ just as a piece of cloth takes on the color of the dye it is dipped into.

No doubt John knew his cousin by sight. He was likely aware of His deity, which explains his shock to receive Jesus' request for baptism. Why would Jesus need to be baptized given the fact that He was sinless?! Christ's baptism was a powerful indication of His willing identification with sinful mankind and marked the beginning of His public ministry, which would be done in the power of the Holy Spirit.

LIFE STEP *The humility of both John the Baptist and Jesus provides excellent food for thought. John did not hesitate to turn the spotlight away from himself and onto Christ. Jesus did not hesitate to humbly be baptized, even though He didn't need to be. How can you walk in humility, and divert attention away from yourself and toward Christ today?*

What is the writer saying?

How can I apply this to my life?

Modern readers do not enjoy genealogies. In fact, because the names are so obscure and hard to pronounce, we often just skip over them. But we do need to ask ourselves why they take up so much precious space in Scripture. God clearly considers them important. Genealogies are not included in Scripture because the nation of Israel thought them important; Israel esteemed them highly because God constantly included them in Scripture. They go back to the very beginning, when God promised that the seed of the woman would crush the head of the serpent (Genesis 3:15). From the time of that promise until the birth of Jesus Christ, men like Simeon waited and longed to see that Deliverer. Luke's genealogy is different from Matthew's in several ways. Luke would have been aware of Matthew's, so these differences were by design. Luke traced the family tree from Jesus back to Adam. Matthew, however, started at Abraham. Luke recorded the families in a traditional way, while Matthew arranged his genealogy in three groups of fourteen. The names in the two lists are different from David to Jesus. These differences are accounted for by the different purposes in writing. Matthew was proclaiming Jesus to be the true King of Israel and, therefore, traced Joseph's family, only going back to Abraham. Luke was interested in His humanity and, therefore, gave us Mary's family and went back to Adam. Luke showed that Jesus is related to us all, for we have all descended from that one original couple. The Greek grammar indicates that Luke knew that Heli was Joseph's father-in-law, not father (v. 23). This is important since Jesus' human genealogy did NOT run through a male father even though Jesus was fully human. Quite literally, the Deliverer was the descendant of a woman but not of a man just as it was expressed in the very first promise of His coming (Genesis 3:15)!

LIFE STEP

Luke knew how important it was to show that Jesus Christ was descended from Adam and, therefore, was one of us, yet without the fallen sin nature inherited by all other descendants of Adam. God's plan of salvation is absolutely ingenious (Romans 11:33-36)! Praise Him for it today.

What is the writer saying?

How can I apply this to my life?

The Greek word here translated *tempted* is in other places translated *tested*. Greek does not have different words for *tempt* and *test* as there are in English. This has created some confusion. We are left to decide with each occurrence of the word whether it should be translated *tempt* or *test*. Because it has been so often translated *tempt* in this passage, many have come to believe that Jesus could be tempted to sin. This is a wrong conclusion because God cannot be tempted by evil (James 1:13).

We always need to think in terms of a substitutionary salvation—of trading places. Jesus took our death so that we could have His life. In the Garden of Eden, Adam failed the test. He was in a perfect place, with perfect food, and a perfect companion, but he failed the test and so did we in him. Jesus, the last Adam, was forty days in a barren place, without any food, and without any company, but He passed the test and so did we in Him. The tests were along precisely the same lines: the lust of the flesh (feed yourself), the lust of the eyes (look at the kingdoms), and the pride of life (cast Yourself down so the world can see the angels and know who You are). Finally, it was the same tester—Satan—but, praise God, the outcome was not the same!

We should also note that Jesus did not use any resource when tested by Satan other than the one that we have: He simply quoted Scripture. He did not invoke His personal status as the Son of God or use His divine power to overcome. Instead, He fought His battles by faith in the Word of God. We must do the same.

LIFE STEP

Do you know the Scriptures well enough to use them against temptation? Identify three verses that can be used against your three most frequent temptations. Memorize them, post them where you can see them, and quote them as needed when taking your stand against Satan.

What is the writer saying?

How can I apply this to my life?

PRAY Finland – For believers to abandon church hopping and become committed church members.

This encounter in Nazareth is only recorded in Luke. Therefore, like the childhood incidents, it must have a special relationship to Luke's primary message. The correct focus of this passage is upon the reaction of the people of Jesus' hometown. These are people who would have known Him from childhood. Do they appear convinced that He is a special person? Have they been overwhelmed by His mere presence? Apparently not! In fact, it appears that He was held in disdain. When the crowd asked, "Is not this Joseph's son?" they were likely referring to the uncertainty associated with His conception. No one likely accepted Mary's accounting of what happened and probably considered Joseph a fool for believing her. They thought it was a cover-up of some kind. Jesus had been saddled with this stigma His whole life and nothing about His appearance or abilities seemed able to convince the townsfolk otherwise. To them, He was but a cruel joke played by Mary on Joseph. Because of this, they were offended that He would even suggest that He could be the Messiah, even though "they marveled at the gracious words which proceeded out of His mouth."

Some of the false gospel accounts recorded amazing miracles performed by Jesus in His childhood, but it would appear from this passage that there was nothing about Him that impressed His community. He was just Jesus, the kid next door, no different from all the other kids running around the streets of Nazareth. This was so embedded in the townsfolk that when He tried to convince them otherwise, they attempted to throw Him to His death!

LIFE STEP *Even as Jesus refused to use His divine power to His own advantage when He was tempted (vv. 1-13), Jesus clearly had not used His divine power to solidify His reputation as He grew up in Nazareth. How can you avoid using your abilities to exalt yourself today?*

121

What is the writer saying?

How can I apply this to my life?

Having been rejected in Nazareth, Jesus set up His headquarters in Capernaum. This was a much larger town about twenty-five miles northeast of Nazareth. Here His ministry began to flourish.

This is the first time that Luke described specific miracles for the reader. Jesus cast out a demon and healed Peter's mother-in-law. These were not the only miracles He performed (see vv. 40-41), but they are the ones that Luke chose to emphasize.

One important detail is that the demons knew who Jesus was (v. 41). It seems ironic that the demons acknowledged who He was, whereas the people of Nazareth refused to do so. Interestingly,

Jesus did not allow the demons to publicly proclaim this fact. There can be no alliance between God and Satan, even if Satan's minions appear to promote the same agenda as Christ!

This day in the life of the Lord was like many of His days. He traveled about doing good and meeting the needs of people, but He did not have limitless physical resources. Verse 42 says the next day, "He went into a deserted place." He needed solitude and time with His heavenly Father just as we do. Once again, Luke's account focused on the fact that Jesus labored within the same limitations that are common to all men.

LIFE STEP

One could argue that Jesus' cause would have been helped if He had permitted the demons to witness to His identity. But He did not allow that to happen. Do we form alliances with unbelievers in the pursuit of accomplishing God's work? Elsewhere, Paul teaches that we must be very careful in this area (2 Corinthians 6:14-18). The ends clearly do NOT justify the means.

What is the writer saying?

How can I apply this to my life?

PRAY Iraq – Pray for the Gospel message to break through hearts hardened by longstanding divisions and intense rivalries.

Lake Gennesaret is another name for the Sea of Galilee. Today's passage shows Christ using a fishing boat as a platform from which to teach! After the message, He told Simon Peter, the boat's owner, to launch out into the deep. Peter, who considered himself to be somewhat of an expert on everything, told Jesus that they had worked hard all night and caught nothing. Peter knew that night was the best time to fish because the fish would venture into shallower waters. Peter seemed to think that the Lord needed some advice on the science of fishing, but he finally obeyed. The result was such a huge catch that their net broke and the boat started to sink!

We need to remember that these men had been with Jesus prior to this point.

They were not new to His ministry or to His miracles. After all, Peter's mother-in-law had recently been healed. But the text says they were astonished at this specific miracle. This appears to be the moment when it all became very personal for Peter. This was no longer about a great prophet and the aspirations of the nation of Israel; it was about Jesus the Son of God and Peter a sinful man. Peter suddenly grasped the significance of the situation and fell to his knees. Like Isaiah when he saw the glory of God (Isaiah 6), Peter realized the precariousness of the moment—a sinful man in the presence of a holy God—and his confidence gave way to consternation.

LIFE STEP *There is often a gap between the objective and the personal. Many of us have a clear and clinical understanding of Christ's identity, but it has never become personal. A miracle is as meaningless as a magic trick if we don't come face to face with the God behind the miracle.*

What is the writer saying?

How can I apply this to my life?

PRAY Philippines – Pray for the church to stand firm on biblical truth and to be unified with one another.

In the previous miracles described by Luke, Jesus has shown mastery over physical weakness (fever), spiritual wickedness (demons), and natural laws (fish). The next two miracles shift the emphasis away from people and onto their sin. In the Old Testament, leprosy was an affliction designed by God to punish specific sins—a spiritual problem, not a physical one. When the leper approached Jesus and understood that He could heal him if He wanted to, he was in effect equating Jesus with God since leprosy was imposed by God and could only be removed by God. Jesus was doing far more than any prophet could do. He said simply, "I am willing," and thereby accepted the position of God with respect to the leper.

The next miracle is even clearer. Before Jesus healed the paralytic, He said, "Your sins are forgiven you." This statement was as much for the crowd as it was for the unfortunate invalid. They rightly thought in their hearts, "Who can forgive sins but God alone?" Jesus then healed the man as proof that His statements concerning forgiveness were true. This is the proper role of miracles in the New Testament. They were not designed to thrill the crowd. Christ and His apostles used them judiciously to authenticate their claims. Performing a miracle did not make Jesus God, but claiming to be God and then performing a miracle proved the point. If Jesus' purpose in performing miracles was merely to attract a crowd, why would He command the leper to not tell anyone about what had happened?

LIFE STEP

It's easy to be more interested in physical than spiritual healing. Christ clearly showed concern for the physical welfare of people, but His priority was their spiritual well-being. People offer praise when you care for the former but often ridicule when you give attention to the latter. As you minister in Christ's name, what is your highest priority? If all we do is meet physical needs, our mission doesn't fully match Christ's.

What is the writer saying?

How can I apply this to my life?

PRAY Brazil – Pray for missionaries to be sent to areas and roughly 130 tribes unreached by the Gospel.

Levi was a tax collector or publican (a public contractor who worked for the Roman government). As such, he belonged to one of the most unpopular professions in the land. Jesus did not despise him, however. In fact, Levi was another name for Matthew, who later wrote the gospel account that is named after him.

The feast and the resulting questions reintroduce John the Baptist into the narrative and mark this as a summary point in Luke's account. It allows Luke to reassert the message that had opened the section: repent for the remission of sins. Remission can never be accomplished by putting new wine into old skins. To save one's life, one must lose it. There is no salvation in our old skin; we need a new skin to hold the new life. The old man must be buried, as pictured in John's baptism, and resurrected in newness of life.

Levi gave up the old and embraced the new. Most of the religious crowd understood that he had to change, but they did not think that they themselves had to. After all, they were the righteous ones, not the publicans! Jesus' last words are ominous. As long as a person is satisfied with the old, they are never going to accept the new. Jesus was offering a new life, not an improved old life. The religious leadership enjoyed their elite status. They did not want to give up all that they had worked for and start anew with the likes of Levi. But that is exactly what Jesus did. Their self-righteous, spiritual pride locked them in darkness, and they refused to even taste the new wine.

LIFE STEP

The message, simply put, is that the only genuinely righteous person is one who has died to himself and his hopes of achieving righteousness and has put his faith in Christ. Paul beseeches us to be living sacrifices, to die daily in practice because we have already died with Christ in position. As long as we drink the old wine of self-righteous living, we will never truly live in the humility and Christ-dependence of our new life in Him.

What is the writer saying?

How can I apply this to my life?

This chapter marks a new emphasis in Luke's Gospel account. We now begin to see the opposition of those who were content with the "old wine." The Sabbath was established in the very beginning (Genesis 2) and was inserted as an integral part of the Mosaic Law as the fourth of the Ten Commandments. But it is also the only commandment that is not reaffirmed in the New Testament. This is certainly by divine design. It's a perfect test case because it involves no evil desires of the heart such as are associated with the other nine commandments. Keeping the Sabbath is merely outward conformity to God's command.

Luke had left the reader in a bit of a logical quandary as he closed the last section. If those who had lived and loved the old were doomed to stick with the old, how would anyone be made new? They would have to become convinced that the old was not as good as they thought it was. That is where Luke's focus is now directed. The religious crowd wanted to interact about the Sabbath. They wanted to fight the battle on their own terms. Jesus made it a battle of the human heart. The example of hungry David is perfect. Man, by nature, is a lawbreaker. Therefore, he was not made for the Law. The Law was made for him. But why was it made? A study of all related passages indicates that it was not designed to frustrate man but so that man could fully enjoy life here.

LIFE STEP

Legalism is a religion that seeks to gain God's favor and blessing based on a merit system. It's the most persistent spiritual disease in all of Scripture. When our focus is a person's outward conformity to a set of standards, it isn't long before compassion gives way to criticism, and it becomes impossible to rejoice in God's grace. If we can't tolerate the sight of grace poured out on the undeserving, then we don't understand what grace is. After all, a basic quality of grace is that it's unmerited! Do you gladly welcome grace?

What is the writer saying?

How can I apply this to my life?

There are nine occurrences of the Lord praying in Scripture (some have multiple mentions). Seven of the nine are unique to Luke. He alone emphasized this aspect of Jesus' life, such as in this passage where Jesus went to His Father in prayer before choosing the twelve disciples. The names of the twelve are not always listed in the same order, but it appears that Peter, Matthew, Phillip, and James had leadership roles within the administrative setup of the group. The message recorded in verses 20-49 is Luke's version of what we generally refer to as the Sermon on the Mount. Jesus almost certainly preached this sermon on numerous occasions. According to Matthew, it was the Gospel (Good News) of the Kingdom (Matthew 4:23). The Good News was that the kingdom was not for the so-called spiritual elite. It was for everyone and anyone who wanted to participate. That is why Jesus opened with a very profound statement: "Blessed are you poor." Matthew's account is a little less cryptic: "Blessed are the poor in spirit." Both versions communicate the exact same information. In order to participate in the new, one must break fellowship with the old. Those who seek righteousness find it, but those who think they have found righteousness never look for it. Therein is the enigma. For one to embrace the righteousness provided by God, one must let go of all earned righteousness. They must die to the old in order to benefit from the new.

LIFE STEP

Blessing comes via the strangest of routes. It requires that we let go of what was formerly counted as blessing and embrace a new life. Jesus' message was good news for the poor and the desperate soul but a warning to the rich and the self-confident. Take a close look at the four "blessed are you" and the four "woe to you" statements. In which category of people do you find yourself? This can be a source of great encouragement or of profound challenge!

What is the writer saying?

How can I apply this to my life?

PRAY   Albania – Pray for the continual growth and training of leadership in the young Albanian church.

The reporting of this sermon is much shorter in Luke than it is in Matthew. This was probably a different occasion, but there is no reason to believe that both Matthew and Luke did not condense the message for their gospel accounts. Luke's research would have brought him into contact with Matthew's account, so we may assume that he had a purpose for including this sermon in his book as well. Matthew used the sermon to emphasize the difference between the true intent of the Law and the Pharisees' use of the Law. Luke was more focused on the broader community. This message was not just for the Jews; it was for all mankind.

Just as the Pharisees had used the Law to promote their own status and agenda, men from all tribes and peoples use various laws in general as a means to righteousness. Jesus was offering a righteousness that came from outside of the universe—a righteousness from God Himself. This is an infinite righteousness that enables us to genuinely love our enemies, to authentically sacrifice for those who do not deserve it, and to be truly gracious to all without ever resenting it.

One may be tempted to ask as Paul did in 2 Corinthians 2:16, "Who is sufficient for these things?" The answer is simple: none but the Lord Jesus Christ. If we are to walk the walk and talk the talk, we must decrease so He can increase (John 3:30).

LIFE STEP

Today's passage contains numerous practical principles. Identify one that needs to be more fully applied in your life. Then ask the Lord to help you to live it out today. Share it with someone and ask them to pray for you in this area as well.

What is the writer saying?

How can I apply this to my life?

The lesson that began two days ago concludes in today's passage. If we look back at verse 20, we discover that Jesus was speaking these words to His disciples. He was asking them to live as He, their teacher, lived. The nature of fruit trees is to produce fruit, and it is not enough to simply accept salvation. Believers must become like their teacher in every way. Jesus took care of their sin and lived sinlessly in reality so that they could partake of this lifestyle by faith.

Ground zero for this new life is inside each one of us: our hearts. The way this message of a transformed life is proclaimed is from a transformed heart. Men who set aside the old and embraced the new, such as Matthew the tax collector and Simon the Zealot, proclaimed it.

Jesus' disciples were a band of fishermen and common laborers brought together by a carpenter from Nazareth. None of them were religious leaders. Jesus was relentless in communicating to them the simple but profound message of new life in new skins, and they appreciated the Good News because they knew they needed it.

LIFE STEP

We often postpone opportunities needlessly and think that being spiritual is a distant target. Jesus saw it differently. He called the disciples to immediate change. Are we calling Jesus "Lord" while not paying attention to what He says or, worse, refusing to do what He asks? If so, we are building our lives on a foundation that cannot last. It's only a matter of time before we will come to ruin.

What is the writer saying?

How can I apply this to my life?

PRAY Spain – For missionaries to be humble, loving, and culturally sensitive as they seek to minister.

After recounting this wonderful sermon, Luke followed up with several incidents that flesh out the principles he has been focusing on. Looking at the broader picture for a moment will be helpful. The word *faith* is used four times in the next two chapters. It has only been used once so far (5:20) and will not be used again until 12:28. In these two chapters, Luke points to three examples of exceptional faith and one example of questionable faith. What is remarkable is that the exceptional faith comes from the least likely sources: a centurion (7:9); a sinful woman who was likely a prostitute (7:50); and another woman considered unclean according to the Law because of a bleeding issue (8:48). While these three people demonstrated faith, the faith of the disciples is questioned. Jesus' "blessed are you poor" principle is clearly exhibited. Those with nothing to lose embrace what is a challenge to those who perceive themselves to be blessed already.

The centurion was a friend of the Jewish population and perhaps already a God-fearer, but he would still be considered a Gentile and outside of the family. He was permitted to watch from the perimeter but never really allowed into the congregation. For the Jews, he was spiritually invisible. Yet, Jesus commends him as having greater faith than anyone in Israel. His faith was so great that Jesus marveled at him.

LIFE STEP

Sometimes, we equate giftedness and confidence with faith. We expect great faith to come from strength. But truly great faith can only come from weakness since it is essentially a dependence on God, not a dependence on our abilities, logic, or perceptions. This centurion was acutely aware of his inability and thus put his entire confidence in Christ. For what do you need to abandon all hope in yourself and place your hope fully on the Lord?

What is the writer saying?

How can I apply this to my life?

PRAY For safety, salvation decisions, and consecration commitments during Word of Life Snow Camp weekends.

Today's passage contains two incidents: the raising of the widow's son and the question sent by John the Baptist via his disciples. Widows in that ancient world were generally objects of pity. They were seen as non-contributing members of the community and, like the centurion, were spiritually invisible. Widows were most often viewed as an opportunity for the more affluent members of the community to publicly demonstrate their righteousness with alms. James remarked, however, in his epistle that true and undefiled religion was "to visit orphans and widows in their trouble" (James 1:27).

In verses 16-17, the crowds were calling Jesus a great prophet. When John was told of these things, he sent two men to Jesus to ask Him if He was indeed the Messiah or just another prophet.

Here we find another case of the weak and the strong. More than anyone, John should have been convinced that Jesus was indeed the Messiah, but even he had moments of doubt. John himself had much to lose since he had preached about the coming Savior. He had baptized Jesus and declared him to be the Messiah. But now John was no longer certain.

Jesus' response was to point to the authenticating miracles that He had performed. Even with these highly visible evidences in play, John still needed to exercise faith. Faith is not merely the doorway to a new life; it is essential in order to live the new life. Whether one is a widow who has just lost her only son, or the greatest prophet born of a woman (v. 28), we are all equally in need of, and can only please God by, faith (Hebrews 11:6).

LIFE STEP

We often feel that walking with Christ and living the Christian life would be so much easier if we could see great and mighty miracles happening on a regular basis. Today's passage and others such as Luke 16:29-31 highlight the fact that such spectacular evidence will not make up for a lack of faith in what God has said. What has God said in His Word that seems to be contradicted by your circumstances? He calls you to believe Him despite all appearances. Will you trust Him today?

What is the writer saying?

How can I apply this to my life?

Jesus uses John's question as an opportunity to ask the crowd about John. He uses the same question - "What did you go out to see?" - three times, showing the importance of the issue. The people did not go out to see healings and miracles, or a well-dressed man, or an important official. They went out to hear a very special message; a message of hope, of change, and of salvation. And yet this simple man, with a simple lifestyle and a non-miraculous ministry, drew great crowds. He was as great as any prophet that ever lived. What John said defined his ministry.

But the crowds following John, then Jesus, missed the message. People were attracted to Jesus' miracles rather than to His message: repent and change your mind about what it means to be blessed. Those who rejected John said he was a strange person who lived in the wilderness. The same leaders said that Jesus was a party animal who didn't understand true spirituality (Matthew 11:19). Their objections were about the outward things, but, in fact, it was always the message they couldn't handle. They would not admit to being poor. They would not repent. The truly wise man is the one who can see through the spectacle, discern the message behind the miracle, and then respond to it.

LIFE STEP

Evaluating our own accomplishments as nothing, and letting go of our hopes and dreams, is not easy, but it is essential. We need to accept Jesus' accomplishments and embrace His hopes and dreams for us. That is the pathway to true and lasting blessing, both now and all through eternity.

What is the writer saying?

How can I apply this to my life?

Today, we are introduced to the second of the three people commended for their faith (v. 50): a woman who had the reputation of being a *sinner*. The episode begins with a prominent Pharisee who invited Jesus to dine with him. During the meal, the woman approached Jesus and began to wash His feet with her tears and wipe them with her hair. Notice the reaction of the host. He questioned whether Jesus was anything more than a regular man and noted the disreputable kind of woman who had approached Him. In contrast to this, the woman knew who Jesus was and humbly came to Him, not to be healed but to receive forgiveness for her sins. Neither the Pharisee nor those seated at his table realized that they were just as needy as she was!

Notice Christ's words to Simon. Jesus was not complaining about how He had been welcomed into his home. Instead, He emphasized how one's love for the Lord is directly proportional to one's awareness of their guilt before God and of how much they have been forgiven. We can appreciate Christ as a wonderful teacher, a great prophet, or even as the Son of God. But if we stop there, we will never love Him the way we should. Jesus came to save sinners and the sinful woman was the only one who got it. She understood that the grace of God was walking in their midst and her affection for Christ knew no bounds.

LIFE STEP　　*We should be living our lives at Jesus' feet with hearts full of love for Him. But this will never truly happen until we come to grips with the depth of our sin and the tremendous debt that Christ paid on our behalf. Take time to reflect on all that God has graciously forgiven you. Then express your love and appreciation to Him.*

133

What is the writer saying?

How can I apply this to my life?

PRAY   Germany – Pray for a spiritual awakening among the predominantly lost youth.

As with many of the sermons and illustrations used by Christ, there is no reason to think they were only spoken on one occasion or that they were always used for the same purpose. The parable of the sower is also recounted in Matthew in a somewhat different context but with a very similar application. The point emphasized in Luke is that the impact of the seed is determined by the nature of the soil. Not every person will respond to the Gospel in the same way. The centurion (7:1-10) and the sinful woman (7:36-50) were examples of good soil, whereas the religious leaders and the crowds who followed them were examples of unproductive soil. The seed is the same, the absolute and eternally unchanging Word of God. But it will only germinate and produce fruit when it falls on the right kind of soil.

Parables are a unique form of communication. Jesus used them intentionally so that those who rejected His teaching would not understand it: "That seeing they may not see and hearing they may not understand" (v. 10). This is explained more extensively in Matthew 13:11-17. Parables are illustrations of the truth, not the truth themselves. Unless one is willing to accept the truth being illustrated, the parable may accomplish nothing of value. For the one willing to accept the truth, a parable makes the truth clearer. For the one unwilling to accept the truth, it provides an occasion to reject truth or to claim an alternate truth.

LIFE STEP

The sower sowed the seed indiscriminately. He didn't worry about the type of soil in which he was throwing it. This is how it should be with us. We should never restrict our sowing only to soil that we believe will produce results. We should leave that with the Lord. How can you spread the seed of God's Word all around you today, even in places where you doubt that it will produce a result?

What is the writer saying?

How can I apply this to my life?

The disciples had spent time with the Lord and had seen Him heal the centurion's servant, raise the widow's son, and forgive the sinful woman. They had witnessed the miraculous power of Christ and the critical role that faith had played in these events. They had been instructed in the meaning of the parable of the sower, seed, and soils and had been challenged with the critical importance of believing and acting on God's Word.

Yet, when faced with a situation that they couldn't handle on their own, they reverted to their old instinctive ways of dealing with the unknown and were gripped with fear. They forgot Who it was that was sleeping aboard the boat and began to panic instead of trusting the One who is greater than the storm. One would think that, given all they had heard and seen, the disciples would be the most likely to pass the faith test. But they failed where a centurion and a sinful woman had succeeded. Note also that they were still uncertain as to Christ's identity.

LIFE STEP

Faith does not come to us naturally and it never emerges from strength. Faith can only flourish in weakness since it involves surrendering our dependence on self and trusting in whatever God's Word has to say about any given situation. Whenever faith is operating, there will always be something in the mix that we can't perceive, reason out, or otherwise control. If we could, faith would not be required! Identify the biggest faith challenge that you're currently facing. What specific situation has you cornered? What truths from God's Word apply to this, and how will you respond differently than you would if you didn't know them?

What is the writer saying?

How can I apply this to my life?

PRAY For missionaries who will be separated from family and friends this Christmas season.

The demon-possessed man generally receives most of the attention in this story, but it's helpful to observe the other characters as well. The people in the region not only dismissed this miracle, they resented it. They may have reacted this way because of the loss of livestock when the pigs ran into the lake and were drowned. If that was the case, then they put their financial security ahead of a human life.

As terrible as the loss of their personal property may appear, remember that it was unlawful for Jews to eat pork or any part of the pig. These farmers were promoting and enabling the people of the area to break the Law. Even if they were selling the product to Gentiles, they were still compromising their status as Law-abiding members of the Jewish community.

The demons reacted in a similar way to the crowd. They wanted to get away from Jesus as fast as possible. Only the demoniac wanted to associate himself with Jesus. The demoniac cannot be put in the same category as the centurion and the sinful woman because he was not healed in response to his faith. Being possessed by demons, his will was bound. Still, he clearly responded properly to Jesus' intervention. The more important theme, life through death, is advanced. He was a man who had nothing, and yet he was the only person that Jesus was able to help.

LIFE STEP

Do you see a pattern here? The religious crowds with all their supposed righteousness were fighting Jesus at every turn. Only the helpless and the hopeless clung to Him. Self-sufficiency will always keep us from an essential dependence on the Lord and will stunt our spiritual growth. Ask the Lord today to show you areas of your life where you need to abandon your self-sufficiency and ask Him to teach you how to do that.

What is the writer saying?

How can I apply this to my life?

PRAY Namibia – Pray for reformation among Christians who cling to unbiblical beliefs.

Many wonder why the primary miracle in this passage, the raising of Jairus' daughter, is interrupted by what appears to be a lesser miracle, the healing of an issue of blood. Besides the fact that the events unfolded this way, Luke likely intended to highlight the differences. Jairus was part of the religious crowd, the ruler of the synagogue. We cannot discern what he believed about Jesus, but he did recognize His ability to perform miracles.

The sick woman, on the other hand, was afflicted with an issue of blood that made her legally unclean. She wouldn't have been able to participate in most social gatherings such as attending synagogue. She became the third person commended for her faith in this section of Luke, and Jesus told her to "go in peace."

In contrast to this woman's faith stood the situation with Jairus' daughter. The girl had now died. Jesus still wanted to see her, but Luke tells us that everyone ridiculed Jesus when He said that she was not dead. How the parents responded is not clear, but Jairus apparently did not rebuke the crowd. After Jesus raised the daughter from the dead, He told Jairus and his wife that they should tell no one. The fact that they were astonished by what was done seems to put them in the same category as the disciples, who marveled when Jesus calmed the sea. Again, the weak understood, and the strong missed the true meaning of what was happening.

LIFE STEP

Once again, we see that faith can only be exercised from a position of weakness that has been acknowledged and which prompts us to reach out to the Lord for help, not just because it's the right thing to do but because it's the only thing we can do! The application of these passages to our lives continues to be the same: surrender and reach out to the Lord in faith. Just like the woman in this story, He will not miss you in the crowd!

What is the writer saying?

How can I apply this to my life?

PRAY Ukraine – Wisdom and courage for full-time workers hampered by restrictions that limit growth.

Jesus had just told Jairus and his wife to "tell no one what had happened." Now He sent out His disciples to preach and to perform similar miracles. Their faith appeared to be growing, and they could now be entrusted with greater tasks.

The principle that to whom much is given, much will be required (Luke 12:48) is seen in two ways in today's passage. First, the disciples were given a great privilege when they were chosen to walk with the Lord. That privilege was quickly converted into responsibility. They were sent out as authorized representatives to share the same message Jesus had been proclaiming. Second, the villages where the disciples ministered were also given a special opportunity. Very few humans have been privileged to see the kinds of miracles that were being performed by Jesus and His disciples in their sight. Therefore, their rejection was dealt with harshly.

Note also that Judas was one of those sent out. Every gospel writer, upon the first mention of his name, proclaimed him as the traitor (Luke 6:16). Surprisingly, he too was enabled to do miraculous works. Clearly, this empowerment was not related to salvation or to spirituality. It was a delegated responsibility.

LIFE STEP

The fact that Judas received power and authority from Christ over demons and illness is a compelling reminder that any gifting we have comes from the Lord and is never granted because we deserve it. Evaluate your use of the abilities God has given you. To whom much is given, much is required. Are you stewarding them for His glory or for your own cause? We must beware of pride and the tendency to misuse our spiritual gifts (see 1 Corinthians 4:7).

What is the writer saying?

How can I apply this to my life?

PRAY   North Korea – For the message of the Gospel to penetrate North Korea's isolation from the modern world.

The feeding of the five thousand is the only miracle mentioned in all four Gospel accounts. Although it may not be the most dramatic miracle (Jesus once fed seven thousand), it is still very pivotal. The disciples had just returned from an awesome experience and a season of powerful, miraculous ministry together. Now they were faced with a somewhat common problem: a shortage of food. Immediately, they reverted to "old wine" thinking and suggested an obvious course of action: "Send the multitude away." Perhaps their focus was on their own comfort, and they just couldn't be bothered. More likely, they weren't attracted to the idea of responding to such a mundane, unimpressive need. They had been casting out demons and healing sick people; now that's cool! Who wants to serve a large crowd a bunch of food? That's for servants, not superstars! But that's exactly what Jesus now asked them to do.

Here we see a critically important truth: serving the Lord is just that—serving Him: doing what He asks us to do, not what we choose to do. Faith cannot act independently; it can only exist in conjunction with an instruction from God (Romans 10:17) which we then obey. Our will must be disabled so His will can flourish.

Shortly after these events, Jesus asked them a ministry-defining question: "Who do you say that I am?" Earlier, they had not been clear on this issue (8:25), but now they were ready to draw a better conclusion. Now they understood who He really was.

LIFE STEP

Often, a time of ministry can move our focus away from simple faith in God toward looking instead at the results or impact of certain types of ministry compared to others. Whatever God asks us to do, we need to remain focused on Who He is and the fact that we serve at His pleasure. Is the Lord asking you to accept some assignment that you'd rather not step up to? It's at moments like these that we discover whom we are really serving.

139

What is the writer saying?

How can I apply this to my life?

What has been stated about the pursuit of righteousness (justification) is now stated with respect to spiritual growth (sanctification). The foundational concept behind justification is an exchange of places (Christ takes our judgment and we inherit His righteousness), and the same is true of sanctification (Christ lives, not me). Paul, Luke's mentor, clearly described this principle in his epistle to the Galatians (Galatians 2:20).

To deny ourselves means exactly that: we deny ourselves. It does not mean to deny ourselves some legitimate pleasure in life; it means to deny that we ourselves have any power or ability to become righteous or to live righteously. Instead, we yield control to Christ Who lives within us. To deny ourselves is to accept being crucified, buried, and raised again with Christ. Only then can Christ live within and empower us to do God's will.

To carry our cross does not mean that we must "suck it up" and endure pain. It means that we must leave behind the flesh-driven approach to life and choose the Spirit-driven way of living. The cross that the disciples had to bear was, essentially, to forego justice and accept grace. After all, in a just world, all would end up in hell since none are righteous. The solution is not to carry a bigger load or to do a better job. The answer is to embrace a *grace* world, where we do not need to carry that load. In this world, the burden is easy, and the yoke is light (Matthew 11:30) because Christ carries the weight.

LIFE STEP

Even if we do all that can be done in our own strength, we will still fail. Jesus calls us to give up this dependence on self, to die to it, and to accept His abundant grace. Take a few moments to think deeply about Galatians 2:20 and its implications. It will be time well spent!

What is the writer saying?

How can I apply this to my life?

PRAY　　Japan – For the Holy Spirit to help believers overcome ancestral influences by the study of God's Word.

Men can only see what the heart is prepared to see. As the disciples' hearts began to change, they were prepared to see an even clearer picture of Who Jesus was. They believed He was the Christ and now they had just seen that He certainly was as He was transfigured before them. It was a stunning spectacle. The way Peter referred to it in his second epistle (2 Peter 1:16-18) makes it clear that it was the most powerful confirmation of Christ's identity ever to be witnessed during His earthly life. Yet Peter went on to say that we have an even more powerful witness than what could be seen by the naked eye: the testimony of God's Word written by holy men of God who were led by the Holy Spirit (2 Peter 1:19-21).

The disciples had correctly perceived what took place during the transfiguration: Christ glorified standing with Moses and Elijah. But they were clearly not expecting a far different moment that would soon occur: Christ betrayed, hanging on a cross between two thieves. Jesus spoke to them about this and urged them to allow it to sink into their ears. But they still didn't understand, nor could they even imagine it!

Rather than deal with the harsh reality of Jesus' words, they chose instead to squabble over their positions in the kingdom. So, Jesus reminded them again of the message He had been constantly preaching: he who is least will be greatest in the kingdom of God.

LIFE STEP　　*Paul says, "Let this mind be in you which was also in Christ Jesus…" (Philippians 2:5). We need a new mind to understand this new life. How can you decrease today and allow Christ to increase in your life?*

What is the writer saying?

How can I apply this to my life?

PRAY   Kyrgyzstan – Pray for the small church to mature in faith and stand strong against evil.

A shift in tone becomes obvious in today's text. The crowds were shrinking and the specter of the cross now loomed large over Jesus. When the passage talks of Jesus setting His face to go to Jerusalem, it is speaking primarily of His determination to head to Calvary. Rejection was rising and a positive outcome of Christ's ministry was not evident to those following Him. Whereas many had initially jumped at the chance to follow Him, excuses were now being offered (vv. 57-62).

As the crowds gathered early in Christ's ministry, they cheered the miracles as well as the message. But they were now beginning to grasp more clearly the implications of what Jesus was teaching, that to follow Him and ultimately save their lives first meant losing them. They were not up to that level of commitment. Luke is not trying to tell us that it is wrong to own a house, or to bury one's father, or to bid farewell to loved ones. Rather, he is saying that these kinds of present life responsibilities must be considered as nothing in comparison to the responsibility of following Christ. In another place (Luke 14:26), Jesus said, "If anyone comes to Me and does not hate his father and mother, wife and children, brothers and sisters, yes, and his own life also, he cannot be My disciple." All earthly relationships, even good ones, must pale in comparison to our commitment to Christ.

LIFE STEP

The meaning here is not to despise or reject important family responsibilities (1 Timothy 5:4,8); rather, they must be secondary to our relationship with Jesus Christ. The word translated hate in the Greek language is a comparative term that means to consider less important. Is there some human relationship, even a legitimate one, that is somehow keeping you from fully following Christ wherever He leads? Bring this before the Lord and ask Him to give you the faith to trust and obey Him above all.

What is the writer saying?

How can I apply this to my life?

This is the second time that Jesus sent out disciples to proclaim a message. In chapter 9, He had sent the twelve; now, He sends out seventy others. This second "witnessing trip" probably took place in a different region than the first.

Luke alone recorded this event and spent more time on it than he did the first. The content is very similar, but this commissioning is much more detailed. In this exchange, Jesus also gave them power over demons and illness. This would be very much in keeping with biblical tradition. In the Old Testament, prophets generally had a group of associates (sons of the prophets) who would be sent throughout the countryside to proclaim any revelatory message that the primary prophet had received. These associates would also be given the ability to prophesy, but not in the same sense as the primary prophet. This ability to send disciples out with power was the sign of a primary truth-giver. When such a person spoke or wrote, there could be no questioning his words. Jesus would later give this ability to the apostles so that their writings would be confirmed as Scripture.

The negative consequences of rejection are now emphasized more clearly. Christ's early ministry had focused on "blessed are those who..." Now the message was that Sodom would find it more tolerable in the day of judgment than would those who rejected the message.

Today's passage is a sobering one. The primary emphasis of the Gospel is life. Jesus came that we would have life and have it more abundantly (John 10:10). But we must never forget that the alternative is not neutral; it is an eternal existence in the lake of fire, a situation far worse than what happened to Sodom and Gomorrah. The most important issue for all of us is what we have done with Christ. Have you trusted Him to save you from the eternal consequences of your sin? He stands ready to do so if you will receive Him by faith.

What is the writer saying?

How can I apply this to my life?

The life of Christ is generally considered in three distinct phases. Phase one is the period of obscurity, which covers the time from His birth to His baptism. Phase two is the period of popularity, from His baptism until His transfiguration. Phase three is the period of rejection, covering His transfiguration until His crucifixion. Luke spends much less time on the second phase than Matthew does. He moves through it quickly because his primary concern is the humanity, or the self-imposed limitations, of Christ. The rest of the Gospel of Luke is dominated by conflict and how Jesus taught the disciples to handle it.

Luke now recounts one of the many woes that Jesus pronounced on the cities of that day. This is a common prophetic device going all the way back to the blessings and the cursings contained in the Law (Deuteronomy 29). These pronouncements sometimes seem harsh to our postmodern ears, but the curses described in Scripture are always made with the intent to move people back toward blessing, not to exclude them from it. That element can be seen in this passage when the seventy returned. There had been opposition to their ministry, but there had also been victories.

Jesus' words about seeing Satan falling from heaven remind us of Revelation 12:9 where we are told that Satan will be cast out of heaven shortly before the Messianic Kingdom is established on earth. The effect of the ministry of these seventy disciples was a foretaste of that future event.

LIFE STEP

Today's passage is one of the few places that records Jesus rejoicing over something specific. In this case, it was the fact that the Father had revealed truth to the simple and hidden it from the worldly wise. He also told us what we should rejoice in. It's not the impact of our ministry or even spectacular manifestations of God's power on earth. Rather, it should be the fact that our name is written in heaven (Revelation 21:27). Think of that! Are you certain that yours is? You can be if you've placed your faith in Jesus Christ.

What is the writer saying?

How can I apply this to my life?

PRAY

Pray for your pastor and the leadership of your local church.

The kingdom did not come. It came close, but it did not happen then (see 10:11). In today's passage, we get a glimpse of the reasons why. The lawyer who asked the question was not trying to gain information but rather to test Jesus. He had no desire to learn, only a desire to dismiss. Jesus immediately turned the tables and asked the lawyer what the Law says one must do to inherit eternal life. The lawyer clearly thought that what Jesus was teaching was opposed to the Law of Moses. When Jesus agreed with the lawyer's answer, the lawyer was left in an awkward situation and tried to reverse the tables once again.

Jesus answered with a parable that creates a clear contrast between Jesus' understanding of the Law and the lawyers. The priest and the Levite were following the letter of the Law, but the Samaritan followed the intent of the Law. If a priest or a Levite touched a dead body, they would be made unclean and could not carry out their religious responsibilities until they offered a sacrifice and were made clean. The traveler was left for dead, and they could not be sure that he was alive or would survive. Therefore, they used an individual law to defy the purpose of the Law just as they would use the letter of the Law to crucify the Lord of the Law. The lawyer would have understood this perfectly. It would have been his responsibility as a lawyer to defend the behavior of the priest and the Levite. But in this context, he was forced to concede to Christ and recognize his own faulty reasoning.

LIFE STEP

As we study Scripture, we should determine the intent of God's teachings and seek to ensure that it is honored, not just seek to obey the letter of the law for its own sake. The Bible does not provide direct answers for every single situation. But it does provide us with the principles which can guide us to the most excellent choice in any situation, for God's glory and for our own good. It's right to seek to observe what is clearly laid out, but we also need discernment in applying truth in situations where the path is not as plain. In all cases, grace and patience are essential.

What is the writer saying?

How can I apply this to my life?

PRAY Paraguay – For pastors to actively model the disciplines of prayer, Bible study, and witnessing.

The following account of Christ's visit with Mary and Martha reinforces what Christ taught the lawyer who questioned Him. Martha was trying to impress Christ with her diligent service, and by human standards, she should have been commended for it. But in the "grace world," one is not rewarded for works but rather for faith.

Jesus had just demonstrated that the Mosaic Law could be used to frustrate the truth of God's Word. In this case, He was demonstrating that the very concept of choosing behavior (works) over grace is equally futile. Martha did not cite any law. She simply invoked what she felt was common to the human experience, that is, that certain behaviors ought to be rewarded, and other behaviors ought to be judged. This is a law that is written on the human conscience. But it too fails the test.

We ought not choose to live rightly because we want to be rewarded, but rather because we love God and our neighbor. Martha's attempt to be a servant was commendable until she started to judge her sister and to judge Christ. When she called Jesus out for letting Mary be lazy, she revealed the true motives of her heart. If they had been pure, she would have rejoiced that her efforts were providing opportunity for Mary to spend quality time with Jesus. Instead, she complained. This is a hard lesson, but one that we must learn. We cannot compare ourselves with others; we must always look to Christ.

LIFE STEP

The concept of "fairness" is often one of the devil's greatest weapons. Once we become convinced that our ideas of justice must be honored, we forfeit grace. What would be most fair would be if everyone paid for their own sins. Jesus offers an alternative: grace. We cannot accept grace, all the while expecting others to live by the Law. Do you resemble Mary or Martha? Spend time at Jesus' feet today rather than running around trying to please Him, all the while ignoring Him.

What is the writer saying?

How can I apply this to my life?

Many portions of Christ's teaching were given in more than one context. The so-called "Lord's Prayer" was first recorded as a part of the Gospel of the kingdom in the Sermon on the Mount. Here Jesus taught it in a different context, in response to the disciples' request. Jesus is not offering this as a prayer to be mindlessly repeated verbatim (see Matthew 6:7). What He is offering is a pattern to be followed when we pray.

First, we need to acknowledge God and His relationship to every event that occurs on earth. His purposes and His plans must be honored in every request that we make. We cannot always know what God's plans are. Therefore, we are likely to make requests, at times, which conflict with those plans. For this reason, we acknowledge from the start that we submit our desires to His will.

Second, we acknowledge His authority over the physical world and the fact that we depend on Him for our daily bread.

Finally, we acknowledge His authority over the spiritual realm. He forgives sins and, having received it, we are obligated to then extend forgiveness to others. The one who receives grace ought to be gracious (Matthew 18:23-35). God even has authority over the evil one (Job 1:12; Ephesians 1:20-21). Though God Himself never leads us into temptation (James 1:13), He has control over Satan who does. We know that God will not allow us to be tempted beyond what we can endure (1 Corinthians 10:13), but He does leave the enemy room to test us (Luke 22:31-32). This petition expresses the correct posture we should have. Our desire should be that we are not brought into temptation.

LIFE STEP

What is your position with respect to temptation? We should desire to avoid it as much as possible. Beyond expressing to the Lord your desire to be spared temptation, what steps can you take to minimize your exposure to it today and in the days ahead? It's far better to stay away from the edge of a dangerous precipice than to deliberately walk along the edge (see Proverbs 7:6-23)!

What is the writer saying?

How can I apply this to my life?

PRAY Belarus – Pray for a biblical expression of Christianity authentic to their culture and context.

Two messages were competing for the hearts and minds of Jesus' listeners. The first was what they had been taught all their lives. The other message was not only new, but the Messenger was also performing many impressive miracles to go along with it. However, miracles without a message are meaningless, so Jesus ultimately brought the discussion back to the correct message.

The old-school religious crowd hated the message and felt they needed to discredit the miracles that accompanied it. Therefore, they made a completely ridiculous and contradictory claim: Satan was fighting against himself! Others asked Jesus to prove that His miracles were truly from heaven. Christ first exposed the folly of their claim and then undermined their fundamental belief by showing the utter worthlessness of self-reformation.

He spoke of an unclean spirit that had left but then returned, making the situation worse than it initially was. What was needed was not reformation, but new life - not a heart cleaned up, but a new heart. The religious crowd thought they could use the Law to clean up a person's life, but little did they know, in so doing they were breaking the greater commandment of truly loving God and others as themselves. The Law always denied that righteousness could be obtained through human effort. It demonstrated that righteousness could only come from God. This is what Christ meant when He proclaimed, "Blessed are those who hear the Word of God and keep it" (v. 28).

LIFE STEP

Have you ever shaken a Bible speaker's hand and told him/her that his/her message was a blessing to you? The sentiment is understandable, but the truth is that the blessing doesn't come with the hearing of truth but with the doing of it (v. 28). In that sense, the true blessing of any Bible teaching can only begin after the message has been delivered (see James 1:22-25). Don't be cheated out of the blessing by being satisfied with the hearing only. Go further and put what you've heard into practice.

What is the writer saying?

How can I apply this to my life?

PRAY Papua New Guinea – For Christian youth camps to see significant salvation and consecration decisions.

Regardless how many miracles Jesus performed, there were never enough to please the doubters because those who sought the signs were not seeking the truth but rather personal affirmation. Christ had already given enough signs to verify His words, but these people were not interested in listening; they only wanted the perks that came from the miracles, such as the fish and the bread. Therefore, Jesus offered them only one more sign: the prophet Jonah (v. 29). The sign was not the preaching of Jonah but, rather, the fact that he spent three days and three nights in the belly of the great fish. This sign corresponded to the message that both Jesus and John the Baptist had been preaching about Christ's role and His fulfillment of prophecy.

Jesus pointed to the example of the Queen of Sheba. This raises the question as to what these two incidents have in common. The answer appears to be Gentile participation. Sheba was an ancient country in northern Africa, and Jonah went to Nineveh even though he despised the Assyrians with the result being a great revival. Israel had witnessed miracle after miracle throughout its history and yet failed to grasp the real treasure: the message of the prophets. They were focused on the signs, but signs have no intrinsic value. Instead, they have but one simple purpose: to be a sign! Israel wanted the signs without accepting what these signs pointed to. If more signs would have helped these people, Jesus would have given them more, but He understood that any signs that He performed from that point on would only cause them to think that this was their rightful reward.

LIFE STEP

The reason for signs and their use has not changed. Where there is no divine messenger and a corresponding message, there is no need for signs. Signs were never intended to serve as proof of salvation or spirituality. When used that way, they always lead to downplaying and ultimately ignoring or rejecting the message. Beware of the tendency to focus on the spectacular and the unusual. Fireworks always draw attention, but, after a brief flash, they leave nothing but smoke behind. It's the teaching of God's Word and its application by faith in our lives that should be our focus. We are called to walk by faith, not by sight (2 Corinthians 5:7).

149

What is the writer saying?

How can I apply this to my life?

PRAY   Switzerland – Pray for the barriers of apathy, wealth, and vague religiosity to be overcome by a deep hunger for God.

Just as the signs were an external component of a much more spiritual concept, the external observation of the Law, or lack thereof, was meant to reveal the spiritual condition of one's internal life. Jesus had no problem with the Law of Moses, but He did have a serious problem with how the Pharisees and lawyers were using it to promote external obedience without internal change. Repentance has always been about the inside, about having a changed mind and adopting God's worldview. The religious leaders of Jesus' day were using the Law to advance their own devious agenda. The more of the Law they obeyed, the more in awe of their own significance they became. But what outraged Christ the most was that they were using the Law to enslave and destroy those whom they were entrusted to lead spiritually. Jesus preached a message that empowered only the poor in spirit. He offered a righteousness that was there for those who asked, for the outcasts and the sinners who recognized their true condition. He let a sinful woman wash his feet and ate with people that the religious crowd would cross the street to avoid. To the religious elite, Jesus' message was shocking and offensive.

The "woe" passages in the Old Testament are very helpful in understanding Jesus' words. When used in a list by the prophets, they were mostly reserved for those who had distorted God's truth for personal gain (Isaiah 5:8-22; Habakkuk 2:6-19). The leadership in Israel knew better than to behave this way, but they were willing to twist the truth in order to keep their own personal position and prestige. They not only embraced a graceless system but encouraged others to do likewise.

LIFE STEP

Jesus quite literally blasted the religious leaders for seeking to look good on the outside while neglecting the inside (vv. 39-30). In His rebuke, He did not deny the importance of our outward behavior but affirmed that it must match the heart. The claim that it doesn't matter what we do outwardly because God only looks on the heart does not match with this. It's not a case of "either/or" but of "both/and" (see v. 42). We should be concerned with doing what is right in the eyes of both God and man (2 Corinthians 8:18-21). Are you more concerned about your outward behavior or the inward condition of your heart?

What is the writer saying?

How can I apply this to my life?

PRAY South Africa – Pray for reconciliation among all people groups.

Jesus now shifted His focus and spoke mainly to the disciples, warning them not to be intimidated by the religious establishment. The Pharisees had accumulated an incredible amount of power in the Jewish community. In many instances, they held what amounted to life-and-death control over the people. They believed that they answered to no one except Moses. But even then, it was a Moses that had been recreated in the image of themselves, not the Moses of Exodus who knew God.

Given that the Pharisees held so much power, it is not surprising that the Lord addressed the subject of fear. He said, "Do not be afraid" (v. 4) of any earthly power but "fear Him who… has power to cast into hell." (v. 5) Centuries later, Martin Luther said, "Fear God and you will have no one else to fear." Jesus was saying that earthly power, prestige, and position—all of which the Pharisees had—are the enemies of a genuine, faith relationship with God. They must be forsaken in favor of the eternal. Eternal life is not an extension of our present life; it is an alien life, a gift from Almighty God to anyone who requests it. Despite the emphasis on the eternal, God still looks after us right now. God orchestrates life's events for the benefit of His creation, not its demise. He even watches out for the sparrows (v. 6).

LIFE STEP

Verse 15 provides excellent food for thought and practical application. When we lose sight of the eternal and the pursuit of what really matters in the light of it, then the only thing left to pursue is "earthside stuff." We become enamored with what this world has to offer, and we measure our own worth by the things that we own. Where do you find meaning and purpose? If it's in the things you possess, ask God to begin a deep work of transformation in your heart so that you will begin to value what He values. You are of far greater worth to the Father than the earthly goods you possess for an infinitely brief speck of time!

What is the writer saying?

How can I apply this to my life?

In today's passage, the Lord continued to teach the disciples about the folly of valuing present possessions and power. He offered a parable concerning the subject in verses 16-21. The individual here was a productive member of his community. He worked hard and was rewarded with prosperity. But he made one fatal mistake: he interpreted the eternal in light of the external, not the other way around. He strove for present significance and ignored his eternal soul, choosing the fruit of his labors over the fruit of the Spirit.

The Lord continued with some positive illustrations. Having already referred to the sparrows, He now added the ravens, lilies, and grass of the field. In general, people are not discontented because they do not have enough of this world's goods but because they do not have as much as other people do. Even starvation, which does occur in some parts of the world, is often due to human greed more than natural shortages. Jesus presents a higher calling than acquiring material possessions. What you value the most will reveal the nature of your heart. Do not make the same mistake the rich man did. Value the things that Jesus valued, and you will live a life that is honoring to Him.

LIFE STEP

The greatest danger that we face in this present world is substituting the external for the eternal. Don't pursue the wrong kind of fruit. If heaven provided a quarterly statement of your eternal investment portfolio, how would it compare to the investments you've made down here? As we all know, our earthly investments, though an important part of our stewardship, will be consumed, whereas our eternal ones will literally last forever.

What is the writer saying?

How can I apply this to my life?

We live in a dangerous world, but not because of war, crime, and natural disasters. This world is dangerous because it lulls men into a false sense of security. Insignificant amounts of time are perceived to be extraordinarily long. But, in fact, what are the two thousand years that have passed since the Lord walked on this earth? They are a mere pittance, an indiscernible speck on the dial of eternity. Still, we begin to wonder where the Lord is and why He has not returned. Some treat the promise of His return as legend or fairy tale. Rather than questioning why Christ has not yet returned, people need to grasp the incredible opportunity to lead more souls to Him as each day is added to our calendars. Jesus warned His disciples of the danger of becoming complacent while waiting for His return. That day really is coming!

In this present world, the truly righteous may die young and are often ignored and unappreciated while the wicked and rebellious are esteemed and rewarded. This really isn't fair from earth's perspective. There is indeed little justice here. But Jesus' message is that justice is highly overrated; grace is to be desired. Those who most vehemently demand justice may risk finding it in the Lake of Fire because none are righteous (Romans 3:10). But those who love mercy will find it as they walk humbly with their God (Micah 6:8).

LIFE STEP   *As believers, we stand before a great chasm. We call out to those who are about to perish, "Repent and turn back!" Some do turn, but many don't. We need to stay on task. Don't cave into the pressure and begin to think that we aren't making a difference. That's the big lie. The less we are concerned with our lives and the pressures around us, the more our lives will matter for others.*

What is the writer saying?

How can I apply this to my life?

PRAY   Slovakia – For believers to overcome apathy and be consumed by a passion to please Christ.

This passage makes it unequivocally clear that the world is not a friend of grace. Sometimes, we are led to believe that the world is tolerant of all religions, and that in this pluralistic world, we will be accepted in the same way that other religions are. This is not the case. In fact, to claim that Christ is the only way to heaven brings immediate rebuke and rejection. People consider declarations of absolute truth to be the worst of sins. In today's passage, the Lord makes it clear that He is the great divider. True Christianity will always bring division and tension with the world and its views because the goals and aspirations of the world are different than those of the believer.

The last part of our passage deals with the reason Christ is rejected as the one and only way. Man is interested in man, not God. While intelligent in the ways of the world, such as discerning the weather (v. 54), he is unable to discern the essential truths necessary for life, such as the signs of the times (v. 56). What man needs is a new heart that is totally different from his current nature, not an improved heart. We need transformation, not reformation. It is not good enough to be all that we can be; we need to be all that Christ is. If we go before the Judge in our own strength, we will fail; yet Jesus can defeat our greatest enemy, death, and provide us with God's own righteousness. Many of us who have chosen Christ are going through difficult times with relatives and friends, and some may be experiencing scorn from those they love about their new life and motives in following Christ. Let this passage be an encouragement to you. Remember that your Lord was hated and despised even though He was without fault.

LIFE STEP

Knowing that Christ is the one true way does not mean we should be deliberately disagreeable, nor does it give us an excuse to react with a bad attitude when opposed. Instead, when misunderstood or mistreated, pray that you will respond as the Lord did, with love and kindness.

What is the writer saying?

How can I apply this to my life?

PRAY Peru – Apathy, doctrinal error, and cults are crippling churches. Pray for more trained Bible teachers.

It would be nice to blame all the dangers we face in this world on some huge satanic plot. But there is so much suffering caused by natural phenomena that it's obvious that life is ultimately under the control of our sovereign Creator. Two events are mentioned here that must be considered. One is the act of a Gentile ruler and the other is the result of human error and the forces of nature. How should believers assess such events? Did these people reap what they sowed? Do the righteous suffer and the guilty go free? How should we see this world from a faith perspective? Does every event have some hidden meaning and reflect some hidden justice? If God is in control, how do we account for the fickleness and uncertainties of life?

Jesus' answer is as profound as it is simple: we must not judge. It is not our place in this world to determine guilt; judgment should be left to God. But we should also remember that God is actively at work in each one of our lives to mature and develop us. For the believer, His goal is never to punish us since Jesus took our punishment in our place (Romans 8:1). But He does discipline His children for the purpose of correction and training (Hebrews 12:6).

The formula that Christ uses here is not clearly definitive. It only gives us the broadest of outlines by which to function, asserting divine sovereignty and human responsibility with equal force. Rather than trying to answer these kinds of questions, we should instead place a priority on faith in the Lord and His ways and avoid judging such situations ourselves.

LIFE STEP

Not all that feels good is good, and not all that feels bad is bad. Our hearts and minds are not good judges of these things. The solutions that seem right to a man often lead to destruction (Proverbs 14:12). We must humbly seek to live and learn, keeping in mind what we do know about both God's sovereignty and our responsibility. When we try to interpret everything around us through a purely human grid of fair versus unfair, it isn't long before bitterness sets in. Keep your focus on turning away from your own understanding in favor of acknowledging Him in all your ways.

155

What is the writer saying?

How can I apply this to my life?

This section in Luke opened with a controversy about the Sabbath (6:1-5), and Luke now returns to this topic. Examining Jesus' treatment of the Sabbath is an important point in each of the gospel accounts because Jesus was never guilty of breaking a single law. He only interpreted the Law differently than the leadership of Israel. They saw the Law as a way to earn favor with God; Jesus saw it as a way to maximize the benefits of God's grace, in this case by providing a day of rest for man's enjoyment.

Left to his own resources, man would never figure out the best recipe for a meaningful life. But through the Law, God had provided a skillful manual for living. In it, He told man how to enjoy all the good He had built into this creation. Man chose, however, to use these guides as a means of death, allowing these standards to condemn him rather than tapping into them as a way to maximize life. Man chose to use the Law to try to *get* life as opposed to using it as a way to *live* life. The contrast between these perspectives could not be more evident than in today's passage. The woman was so afflicted that she was unable to enjoy even the most routine pleasures of life. With no request on her part, Jesus intervened and healed her, which resulted in her glorifying God (v. 13). Immediately, the legalists showed their hypocrisy by becoming incensed because this miracle was done on the Sabbath. In the context of the attitude displayed by these leaders of Israel who resembled the barren fig tree in the prior parable (vv. 6-9), the Lord gave two parables that made similar points: the small and seemingly insignificant (mustard seed and leaven) ultimately grow to have an all-pervasive impact. In the same way the Kingdom of God will not arise from the rich and powerful but from the poor and lowly.

LIFE STEP

While the future may seem bleak, our confidence is this: God will not leave us orphaned in this self-serving world! He will come to rescue us. Embrace humility and what may seem like insignificance as you walk with the Lord. It's better to be a "mustard seed" living by faith in Christ than a "mighty oak tree" standing tall in your own accomplishments.

What is the writer saying?

How can I apply this to my life?

PRAY   Cuba – For God to save and call to service many of the 1,000,000 Cuban refugees living in the United States.

The sad truth in today's passage is not that there are so few who find the right path but that so many walk in the ways of darkness, convinced that they are the true servants of the living God. They call out, "Lord, Lord," but the Lord does not know them. They claim to be followers because they walked in the same streets and were born in the same communities as those who do know God, but Jesus quickly dismisses their claims. Israel was betting its eternal future on an external relationship with the Messiah. They claimed to be a part of the same physical household and of the same community. But when judgment day comes, the external will have no value whatsoever. In Matthew 7:22-23, similar claims are mentioned, claims of having done mighty works and miracles worthy of reward, but they are also rejected. There is only one criterion by which men will be considered worthy to enter the Kingdom of God—whether or not Christ knows them. The word translated *know* has a much wider range of meaning in both Greek and Hebrew than it does in English. It speaks of an intimate relationship with another person. Unless we have a personal and intimate faith relationship with Jesus Christ, nothing else matters. This passage also makes it clear that failure to have such a relationship is never due to a shortcoming on Jesus' part. In fact, He wept because they would not come to Him. He longed to gather them together as a hen gathers her chicks, but they would not come.

LIFE STEP

What a sad day it will be when people realize that they never really trusted Christ for salvation. It will be made even sadder because there will be no one to blame but themselves. No one will utter the words, "But Jesus, I didn't know." They did know, yet they chose their own righteousness over the righteousness provided freely by God. Are you known to Christ because your name is written in His Book of Life? 157

What is the writer saying?

How can I apply this to my life?

PRAY | Pray for the elderly and those who are shut-ins in your church.

In stark contrast to the way the religious leadership treated Jesus, He was always willing to take the opportunity to sit and talk with them if invited. Here the passage seems to indicate that this event may have been an intentional trap since it was the Sabbath, and all eyes were on Jesus. In the middle of the crowd was a man with dropsy, a disease related to liver or kidney malfunction. Jesus discerned the situation immediately. He knew the religious leaders' hearts. They had placed the sick man in His presence to see what He would do on the Sabbath.

After Jesus healed the man, He confronted these leaders about their motives. The situation really had nothing to do with Jesus or the Sabbath; it had everything to do with the status of these "leaders" within the system. Jesus demanded that they become as little children, humbling themselves and associating with the unworthy. He demanded that they give up all they had acquired in order to attain what could not be bought. They needed to be poor in spirit, but they could not accept a kingdom in which they were not the center of attention. They would rather have no kingdom than to have a kingdom in which they were just as needy as the next person. They needed to discredit Jesus in order to make themselves look good. But the more they tried, the worse they looked. They never considered that they might be wrong, and their hatred grew with each failed trap.

LIFE STEP

Christ knows the motives of our hearts and whether we are truly seeking Him. Examine yourself today to see if you are poor in spirit and looking for His heavenly kingdom, or whether your lifestyle is working toward a self-centered kingdom here on earth.

What is the writer saying?

How can I apply this to my life?

One can only begin to imagine the heartache Jesus must have felt as He shared this parable. It's not just a story about a grand banquet; it is an analogy about the people of Israel. These are people that Jesus had known most of His life, people that filled the streets of His hometown, and people He had played with as a child. What is most distressing about this parable is that almost everyone found some excuse to avoid the banquet. The excuses were not frivolous or silly. They were the types of situations that conscientious people face every day. But in the final analysis, they were still excuses.

We must always remember that Jesus is an inconvenient reality. There will never be a "good" time to be crucified with Christ or to be publicly identified with Him. Our hearts will always see to it that there is something else that must be done first. The only right time to do God's will is now. We always think there will be plenty of time to follow Christ, but the door of opportunity is not always open. In this parable, after those invited had made their excuses, the servant began to comb the highways and byways for those who wanted to come. The Gospel marches forward with or without us. The nation of Israel thought that God could not bless the Gentiles without them, but He did. Step out for God today while you hear His call. Don't wait for tomorrow.

LIFE STEP *Life sometimes seems so long and filled with so many opportunities. But do not be fooled. As James 4:14 says that life is like "a vapor that appears for a little time and then vanishes away." Use your time wisely today.*

What is the writer saying?

How can I apply this to my life?

PRAY Yemen – Pray for the Gospel to go forth in power despite current legal restrictions.

The first time we read this passage, it probably comes as a great shock to our preconceived ideas of biblical living. We have been taught to love our parents, siblings, and spouse. Part of the shock we feel is cultural because, in our postmodern world, most everyone views love as an emotional response. In the ancient world where marriages were arranged, love was a proactive choice. It was based on covenant loyalty. Jesus is not asking us to feel animosity toward any of these people; He is asking us to prioritize our commitments in such a way that He always comes first. Only when we do this can we truly love our families. Love built on any other foundation than the truth of Jesus' words will fail.

Understand what Jesus is saying when He calls the crowd to count the cost. He is not asking for payment of any kind. Luke has already made it perfectly clear that salvation (justification and sanctification) cannot be earned or deserved. Jesus is saying that either we are *all in*, or we are *all out*. Half a building is no building at all. This passage makes us wonder what God really wants from us. The answer is simple: faith, faith, and more faith. We may be tempted to think that this is no cost at all, and we are right because salvation is entirely free. We must give up our failed righteousness, receive His divine righteousness, and exchange our dying lives to accept His eternal life.

LIFE STEP

The burden of self-righteousness that we bear is real and deadly. Only by getting rid of it can we begin to truly live. Yet we have grown attached to it. Lay down your old ways of assuring acceptance before God and a place in heaven in order to accept the new way of faith in Jesus Christ alone.

What is the writer saying?

How can I apply this to my life?

Some criticize the "faith alone" Gospel as cheap grace. They think believers should somehow earn their status in the invisible world of spirituality and fellowship with God. Never mind that grace, by definition, must be totally free and without merit. There is always pressure from the human heart to base it all or partially on works. But even partial works destroy grace (Romans 11:6)! Fruit is a sign of spiritual life; it is not the cause. Trees don't produce fruit to *become* fruit-bearing trees. They produce fruit because they *are* fruit-bearing trees!

In today's passage, we encounter the first of three parables that Jesus used to emphasize God's heart for lost people and the joy that is experienced when they are found. Notice that the shepherd seeks relentlessly until He finds that one sheep. Once He does, He takes the extra step and puts it on His shoulders—a place of safety and security, where the sheep is as strong and as safe as the shepherd. The shepherd does all of this while rejoicing. He finds his fulfillment, not in what the sheep has done or failed to do, but in the fact that the lost sheep has been found and is now safe.

In each of these three parables, rejoicing is the end response. Jesus did not go to the cross because it made Him look good or because it was easy. Death was so alien and repulsive to Him that as He anticipated the cross, He sweat, as it were, drops of blood and asked the Father if there was any other way (Luke 22:44). Our need and His love for us are what motivated Christ. He endured the cross for the joy it would bring to be reconciled to us.

LIFE STEP *There is great rejoicing to be found in partnering with God in His quest to find lost people and to bring them home to Him. When was the last time you experienced this type of joy? It can never be known in a "works world," but it bubbles up in a "grace world." Ask the Lord to fill your heart with a gracious love for lost people today.*

What is the writer saying?

How can I apply this to my life?

PRAY

United States – Pray for an outpouring of the Holy Spirit on the Church, bringing another Great Awakening.

The parables in this chapter have one main theme: The Lord finds great joy in seeking and saving the lost. Yesterday, we saw the lost sheep and the lost coin. Today's parable is well-known and is generally called the parable of the prodigal son. The prodigal is portrayed as a selfish child who squandered his inheritance until he found himself looking after pigs and wishing he could eat their food. He then came to his senses and returned home where his father welcomed him with a lavish feast.

But wait, this is a parable about two sons! The older son had stayed at home and done all that his father requested. He was incensed by his father's gracious reaction to the return of his younger brother. He resented that he had played by the rules and served his father many years while his younger brother was off squandering his portion of the inheritance. Now this younger, irresponsible brother was treated to all the favors which he believed that he was entitled to.

This elder brother wanted fair treatment in a grace world, a world where the Father provides opportunity for those who are lost. The younger son merely accepted the favor while the older son sank into anger and bitterness. Never complain when another sinner is welcomed into fellowship or resent the rejoicing that occurs. Life in the family is its own reward; it is the only real life there is.

LIFE STEP

Considering what prompted the Lord to tell this parable (v. 2), it's obvious that its intended focus was actually the elder brother who stayed home and diligently served his father. He resembled the religious leaders that Jesus was speaking to. Their fastidious observance of the Law made them feel entitled to the Father's blessing and caused them to despise "sinners." The irony of the story is that the most obedient son was the one who ended up out of fellowship with the father while the disobedient son enjoyed the grace party! How scandalous is this?! We do well to ask ourselves which of the two brothers resembles us the most?

What is the writer saying?

How can I apply this to my life?

Today's parable has raised many eyebrows. It appears that Jesus is commending dishonesty when in fact He is commending a principle as opposed to a practice. We may ask why Jesus would use a parable that could be so easily misinterpreted. The answer may be that He wanted to shock His listeners into thinking deeply about what they had just heard.

He described an unjust man (v. 8) who was about to be fired because he had been accused of wasting his master's goods. Being afraid of becoming destitute, he decided to add sin to sin by "fixing the books" and discounting the amounts that were owed to his boss by his debtors. Even this was done unfairly since the discounts were not all equal. His logic seemed to be that by becoming a friend to these debtors now, they would help him out when he lost his job.

His behavior was wrong, but the overall concern that motivated it was correct. Jesus was commending his astuteness, not his sin. The man realized that his present actions would have future consequences. He would be unable to take care of his future needs if he did not do something to prepare in the present. If he didn't act while he could, then he would never be able to do it later. Jesus then drove the point home by stating that sometimes the unsaved are wiser than the saved in this regard!

The principle of acting right now, while the opportunity is available, is what Jesus commends. We must decide now, or our future will be decided for us forever. There are no second chances. We must choose Jesus in this life because we won't have the opportunity to do it later.

LIFE STEP

God has entrusted us with the present. The past is gone and cannot be changed, and the future is not yet a reality. The incredible thing about this present moment is that we can make choices today that will affect our entire future, for all eternity. What decisions do you need to make NOW before it's too late?

What is the writer saying?

How can I apply this to my life?

PRAY Turkey – Pray for the Gospel to advance in power amid increased hostilities and persecution.

Many in the world today are claiming that everyone will get another opportunity to get things right with God. They suggest that we can change the future once we get there. They say that today is not the final day of salvation; it is just one of many opportunities, and there will always be more. This passage presents the horrible error of such beliefs.

Two men who have lived very different lives are described. The first was a rich man. Wealth in that culture suggested more than just material fortune; it was also perceived as evidence of divine approval and blessing. The second was a poor man who had to beg for food from the rich man. His poverty supposedly marked him as rejected and cursed by God. The spiritual realities, however, were very different. In the end, the poor man went to Paradise while the rich man ended up in a place of torment in Hades.

These are presented as real places where real people go when they die. Note also that there is no opportunity to trade places or cross over from one place to another once there. The key point here is that all opportunity for change evaporates after death; there are no second chances. The rich man became intensely missionary-minded once he realized his mistake and became very concerned for his five brothers who had not yet died. He was now aware that they could only repent while living. He begged Abraham to send Lazarus back to warn his brothers. His assumption is one that many easily make: that something miraculous is far more convincing than reading the warnings in God's Word. Abraham's answer is powerful: if people won't believe God's written warnings, even a resurrection won't convince them!

LIFE STEP

Man does not have an information deficit; he has a faith deficit. Heaven and hell are real places. The decisions we make in this life determine in which of the two places we will end up, and this cannot be changed once we die. Don't put off until tomorrow decisions that need to be made today. Similarly, don't put off sharing the Gospel while you have opportunity to do it now. Choose wisely!

What is the writer saying?

How can I apply this to my life?

As the disciples watched Jesus' ministry, they must have been acutely aware that the people who were coming to Him were not the social and spiritual elite. In fact, in many cases, these people were the outcasts and rejects of that society. They were people who often had serious sin problems. It appears that the disciples were wondering when it was appropriate to turn someone away because of their sin. They must have been thinking, "Surely, we cannot just go on forgiving these people." Many would have been very weak in their faith. But Jesus welcomed them and surrounded them with love and acceptance. The disciples were not so accommodating.

When Jesus told the disciples that they needed to keep on forgiving a brother who had sinned repeatedly, they felt that they needed a stronger faith. Somehow, they needed to believe more ardently the things that Jesus had taught them. Christ's answer must have been a shock. The mustard seed was the smallest seed used in the ancient world. But even that small amount of faith could move mountains according to Jesus. The problem is never the size of our faith; it is the object of our faith. Faith is not a belief in just anything or anyone. It is believing what God has said about what we cannot see and then ordering our priorities and actions based on that, not on our logic, feelings, or perceptions. The disciples didn't need to drum up a stronger *feeling* of belief about what Jesus said. All they really needed to do was choose to *act* on what Jesus said regardless of their feelings.

LIFE STEP

Many of the problems of the Christian life arise from the fact that we are trying to walk by sight when only faith will do. Faith is not a mystical power that produces whatever results we wish. Exercising faith is to trust in what God has said about what we cannot see. When God calls us to trust Him, we need to make sure we are placing our faith in His plans and promises, not in something abstract. Examine your faith today. Are you trusting what He has said about His forgiveness of your sins? How about what He has said about forgiving others?

What is the writer saying?

How can I apply this to my life?

Many have misunderstood today's passage. Jesus clearly could not have been saying that the Kingdom was in the hearts of these Pharisees or that they were somehow already themselves present in the Kingdom! The Pharisees' request was, as usual, an attempt to trip Jesus up. They were trying to question His claim of being the Messiah because there was no evidence that the Kingdom was launching. Their observation was half right.

The Old Testament *did* promise a literal, physical kingdom in which the Messiah would deliver the nation of Israel and establish Himself as the ruler of the entire world. Indeed, this was clearly not happening at that moment. However, the Old Testament had also spoken of a suffering Savior Who would bear the sins of His people (Isaiah 53). The common element in all these prophecies was the Messiah Himself. That is what Jesus was referring to when He spoke about the Kingdom being "within you" (v. 21). The Greek word can also be rendered "in your midst." The promised King was standing right in front of them! They were focused on finding the Kingdom in signs and wonders while rejecting the King who was right there! As a result, they would miss it. This leads naturally into what Jesus said next.

Be careful that you don't read the Rapture of the Church into these verses. Note that the ones taken away will be taken away to judgment, not blessing! They are compared to those who missed being saved in Noah's day or who faced the judgment of Sodom. These verses are referring to the second coming of Christ when He will establish His Kingdom on the earth. At that time, those who are removed will be taken away to judgment while those who remain will enter into the joys of the kingdom. The context shows that those left behind are the ones who will be saved and blessed.

LIFE STEP   *Let's not make the same mistake that these people did. They thought they could have the Kingdom without the King. Eternal life can't be had apart from Christ. Are we more interested in His miraculous signs or in Him and His righteousness?*

What is the writer saying?

How can I apply this to my life?

As events continued to unfold, the disciples must have had many questions about how it all related to their hopes and prayers. They did not want Jesus to die, and they wanted the Kingdom to come as soon as possible. Perhaps they wondered if there was any reason to pray since God's plan seemed to unfold in God's way regardless of how they prayed. We can sometimes feel the same way. Perhaps this is why Jesus told this parable: to encourage steadfastness in prayer.

The ruthless judge Jesus described was more likely to base his rulings on what was in it for him than on any sense of justice. The widow, by interrupting his sleep on a regular basis, was able to get him to rule in her favor because it was in his own self-interest. The lesson is seen by way of contrast. If a heartless, selfish judge could be swayed through persistent pestering, how much more would God answer the prayers of those He loves, albeit in His way and in His time. A second parable concerned the attitude a person should have when he/she prays. The Pharisee prayed as if God's response was guaranteed by his human righteousness. Such is never the case. In contrast to this, the tax collector prayed with an awareness that any answer would be pure grace because he clearly did not deserve it.

LIFE STEP

What are your expectations with respect to prayer? Taking to heart the lessons of these parables can help reinvigorate our prayer life. We should first expect that God is not reluctant to hear and answer the prayers of His people, but that He will do so in His perfect way and time. Second, we should not expect God to hear and answer prayer based on our own merit. When He does answer, it will be yet another demonstration of His amazing grace because we don't deserve to even be heard at all!

167

What is the writer saying?

How can I apply this to my life?

PRAY Serbia – Pray for a strong Christian presence among the many humanitarian aid groups.

The events found in today's passage are recounted together in the same order in all three synoptic Gospels (Matthew, Mark, Luke). They are kept together because they can only be understood when viewed as a single unit. At issue is what a person must do to inherit eternal life.

We first see the children whom the disciples attempted to send away thinking that they were incapable of benefiting from Jesus' teaching. Jesus rebuked the disciples, telling them that the opposite was true. Unless adults embrace childlike faith, they will not be saved and will not enter the kingdom of God.

We then see a rich ruler who appeared to be a perfect candidate for salvation. He had kept the Law from childhood and saw himself as a good person. When he called Jesus *good*, Christ picked up on this point and remarked that only God is truly good. However, the young man continued to make his case for salvation based on good works. Jesus then suggested that if he wanted to earn salvation this way, he should sell all that he had and give it to the poor. The point was not that he could really be saved this way. It was to get him to see that he could never be good enough; that he needed to become like a child and abandon his belief in his own goodness. Unfortunately, he was unwilling to abandon that illusion, so he left empty-handed and sorrowful.

The problem with riches making it difficult to enter the Kingdom (v. 25) lies not with the riches themselves but in the way riches easily cause a person to trust in themselves rather than embracing childlike faith and dependence.

LIFE STEP

When Jesus asked the rich ruler to sell all that he had and give it to the poor, He was not saying that this was how a person could be saved. He was trying to show him that he was not as good and righteous as he thought he was. Think of little children who are close to you, how unpretentious they are and how easily they trust in the provision of others. Ask the Lord to grant you the same kind of childlike faith to rest in God's care and provision.

What is the writer saying?

How can I apply this to my life?

PRAY For safety, salvation decisions, and consecration commitments during Christian winter camps.

In verses 28-30, Luke wraps up the discussion that has been taking place over the last few chapters. The disciples still had a very limited grasp of what Jesus had been teaching and were still focused on the physical rather than the spiritual implications of His teaching. Peter commented, "We have left all and followed You." Jesus answered that those who leave all, gain all, and those who cling to what they have, like the rich ruler, forfeit all. What they lose is not just in the next world but also the more abundant life Christ promised here.

Verse 31 marks the beginning of a new section. Jesus' announcement that He was heading to Jerusalem to die, as well as the disciples' failure to grasp the significance of this, form a literary divider used to alert the reader to a shift in emphasis. The previous section ended with the rich ruler. This section opens with a blind beggar and, as we will see tomorrow, a wealthy tax collector. Notice that the beggar received his sight from Jesus along with the commendation that his faith had saved him. This put him in the same category as the centurion, the sinful woman, and the unclean woman. This beggar believed that Jesus was the answer for all his needs. His faith was simple and childlike, not based on a life of Law-keeping. His faith came from a broken and contrite heart, which found hope in Jesus Christ.

LIFE STEP

One of the most difficult challenges we have as believers is to integrate our faith into our everyday lives. Salvation is not just about our eternal destiny in either heaven or hell. It is about real life in the real world. Faith needs to be exercised in the here and now in order to be set free from all that Christ desires to save us from. Jesus' question to the blind man in verse 41 seems odd. Wasn't it obvious that the man would want to regain his sight? In the ultimate sense, yes. But would he ask for something impossible or for something less such as alms? The first would require faith, the second would not. Do you only ever ask the Lord for the possible or do you trust Him for greater things? What we ask for is an indicator of the depth of our faith in what the Lord has said He will do.

169

What is the writer saying?

How can I apply this to my life?

PRAY

Japan – For more men to choose active church ministry over an obsession with career advancement.

Like many of the lives that Jesus touched, Zacchaeus was not on the "spiritual radar" in his community. He was a tax collector, the most hated of all people among the Jews. Apparently, he was a rich man, having tax jurisdiction over Jericho, a major area of commerce. But with all his wealth and success, he was a very unhappy man. We read that "he sought to see who Jesus was" and that to do so, he had run ahead and climbed into a sycamore tree. He was determined to see Christ! We do not know what Zacchaeus was expecting, but it seems clear that he was surprised and joyful when the Lord spoke to him and invited Himself for dinner. The reaction of the others was not joy but scorn. Zacchaeus was not the kind of person with whom *spiritual* people associated.

It's interesting to compare Zacchaeus with the rich young ruler. One would think that a greedy sinner such as Zacchaeus would cling to his money, but Jesus did not have to ask Zacchaeus to give away anything. Zacchaeus brought the subject up himself. He understood what the rich ruler had failed to grasp, that in comparison to eternal life, riches are meaningless. Zacchaeus chose to really live. He knew that Jesus could give him what no amount of money ever could. The rich ruler was only looking for Jesus to affirm his own righteousness; Zacchaeus was willing for Jesus to grant him a righteousness that was not his own.

LIFE STEP

We are often afraid to trust Christ because we think we are going to have to give up the things we love. We need to realize that Jesus only takes away the things that are neutralizing His blessing. An empty cup can hold a lot more than a full one. How attached are you to your earthly possessions? What steps can you take to ensure that your heart does not become so tied to them that you would never give them up? Regular, sacrificial giving can help keep our hands open rather than tightly closed.

What is the writer saying?

How can I apply this to my life?

Today's parable follows on the heels of the accounts of Zacchaeus and the blind beggar and explains them more fully. Note the introduction to the parable: "They thought the kingdom of God would appear immediately." (v. 11) The crowd and perhaps the disciples thought Jesus was going to Jerusalem to receive something. Nothing could be further from the truth. He was going to do what He'd told the rich ruler to do, to give up everything for the sake of the poor. In Jesus' case, it was not material wealth but rather His own life so that those who were poor in spirit could receive life.

The parable depicts two types of servants: those who recognize and accept the opportunities placed before them and those who simply squander them. Each servant is given the same opportunity. One reaches out by faith and experiences results. The other just sticks with the status quo. But the status quo is death; to reject this opportunity is to reject life itself. Some, like Zacchaeus and the blind beggar, accepted the salvation Jesus offered. But some, like the rich ruler, left convinced that they were all right just the way they were. This is perhaps the saddest of outcomes—people who had been given the greatest of opportunities, who had been striving to keep the Law without success, and yet were so convinced of their own righteousness that they wrapped the treasure of God in a napkin and set it aside indefinitely.

LIFE STEP *Opportunity ignored is opportunity squandered. Whether it is an opportunity to accept Christ or an opportunity to serve Christ, it is an opportunity lost. There is no guarantee that the opportunity will come again. Don't miss it!*

What is the writer saying?

How can I apply this to my life?

The wait was over. Jesus had been steadily heading toward Jerusalem and toward a final confrontation with Israel's leadership. Though He had been to Jerusalem several times before, this arrival was unprecedented.

The events that were about to unfold were not unexpected; they had been predicted! As Christ sent two disciples to get a colt, He was keenly aware of the significance of what was happening. This was to be a fulfillment of Zechariah 9:9: "Behold, your King is coming to you; He is just and having salvation, lowly and riding on a donkey, a colt, the foal of a donkey." The crowd reinforced this by singing the words of a prominent psalm of praise (118:26a). There was excitement and tears of joy, but the crowd walked away from the opportunity uncommitted. Perhaps many of this same crowd later cried out to Pilate, "Crucify Him."

There is a great difference between acknowledgement and commitment. Many people in the land of Israel acknowledged that Jesus was someone special. They cheered and applauded His healings, exorcisms, and raisings of the dead. They were vocal in their applause when He fed the five thousand. They came to Him for spiritual advice. But ultimately, the interest of the majority was self-motivated, and their only righteousness was self-righteousness. They were not interested in a salvation that involved giving up anything that they already had. When supporting Jesus became a liability, they switched sides.

LIFE STEP

Note that Christ wept on this day because the generation that had witnessed His miracles and heard His teaching had missed the greatest opportunity of all, the chance to receive their Messiah and be part of the establishment of His Kingdom. That would now be taken away and granted to a future generation because they had failed to recognize the time that their Messiah had come to them (v. 44). Few things are more tragic than missed opportunities that cannot be recovered. It's possible to miss what God is doing right around us and to forfeit the chance to be a part of it. Take some time to reflect on this in your own situation. Are you alert to God's presence and the way He is working?

WEDNESDAY - WEEK 22

What is the writer saying?

How can I apply this to my life?

PRAY   Angola – Pray for reconciliation through Christ's love after 40 years of civil war.

Amid this huge celebration, the seeds of rejection now began to bear fruit. The episode in which Christ cast out the moneychangers would be a message to the religious leaders that He was both a *spiritual* and a *political* leader. As the legal King of the Jews, His actions were what the temple authorities ought to have done long ago. The response of the chief priests and the scribes indicates that they may have had a vested interest in these financial dealings. Every year Jews would come to Jerusalem and would need to buy animals to offer. They had to buy from the Jewish vendors so the sacrifice would be without blemish. Taking advantage of this, these vendors boosted the price. Foreign money was also likely exchanged into the accepted currency at exorbitant rates. All this happened on Monday of the week Christ died.

On Tuesday, the Lord taught in the temple and preached the Gospel. The same chief priests and scribes attempted to demean Him by asking about His authority (credentials) to preach. Christ turned the tables on them by asking a question that they could not answer without backing themselves into a corner.

LIFE STEP

Dishonesty and the rejection of truth always back us into a corner from which we cannot escape without admitting our error. That's because truth is simply a description of the way things really are. Therefore, to deny truth is to deny the way things really are. When we do this, we can only end up being fools. That's where the religious leaders found themselves. The tragedy is that such folly has lasting consequences. Consider where the denial of truth in your life may need to give way to acceptance of it in order to avoid the consequences of foolishness.   173

What is the writer saying?

How can I apply this to my life?

PRAY Argentina – Funding for children and teens to attend camp and trust Christ as their Savior.

After the leadership in Jerusalem rejected the clear and simple message Jesus preached in the temple on Tuesday, He returned to speaking in parables. This parable was a scathing rebuke of the religious leaders in Jerusalem. They even recognized this themselves (v. 19)! A man planted a vineyard, leased it, and went into a far country. Servants who were sent back were all rejected by the tenants. Finally, the man sent his son, who was rejected and killed. The son, obviously, was Christ Himself, rejected by Israel's leaders. Now that the oppressors had gone so far as to kill the son, what would happen to them? They would be destroyed, and the vineyard given to others. This is precisely what happened as those who rejected Christ faced eternal judgment and Rome later conquered Jerusalem. Jesus quoted from Psalm 118:22: "The stone which the builders rejected has become the chief cornerstone." Even today, Jesus is a stumbling stone to those who do not believe but a precious cornerstone to those who do (1 Peter 2:3-8).

The reaction of the religious leaders was predictable. They sent spies in disguise to catch Jesus in His words. Then they openly attacked Him by asking whether they should pay taxes to Caesar or not. Christ's ingenious answer was simple yet devastating.

LIFE STEP

There is an interesting parallel to be drawn from this passage. Even as the image of Caesar was stamped on coins and provided the basis for Jesus to say that what belongs to Caesar should be rendered to him, the image of God has been stamped upon us (Genesis 1:26-27) and we ought to render to God what belongs to Him. This is true of all men and women but especially of those who have trusted Christ and been purchased with His blood (1 Corinthians 6:19-20). We pay our dues to our human government; are we rendering to God what belongs to Him?

What is the writer saying?

How can I apply this to my life?

PRAY   Nepal – Pray for Jesus to be made known among unreached peoples in hard-to-access locations.

By this time the chief priests and scribes were becoming frantic, and they asked a third question. This one came from the Sadducees who did not believe in a resurrection and often used this question to mock the Pharisees. Their question was based on a commandment found in the Law of Moses (Deuteronomy 25:5), which specified that if a man died, his brother was to marry the widow and care for her. But what if there were seven brothers and each of them died, leaving the wife to the other? Whose wife would she be after the resurrection? Christ's answer does not deny the resurrection nor the fact that we will know and recognize each other in heaven. What it does reveal is that marriage, as we know it in this life, will not exist in the next.

Much about the next life is unknown and we should avoid making arguments based on things about which we are unsure. But there is something we can know: Scripture. Jesus used them once again to turn the tables on his questioners. This time He invoked a well-known passage from the Old Testament. At the burning bush God had said to Moses, "I am… the God of Abraham." God had used the present tense. For that statement to be true, Abraham would have had to be living when it was said. Otherwise, God would have said, "I *was* the God of Abraham." This is not only a great argument for conscious existence after death, but it is also a clear indication that Jesus considered the very words of Scripture and their grammatical construction to be inspired truth, accurate and without error down to the verb tense!

LIFE STEP

How often do you think about the reality of life beyond the grave? Today's passage is a great reminder that death is not the end of life. We will continue to exist after this life is over. It's not a question of if but only of where. For the believer in Christ, there is so much to look forward to. Take some time to read Revelation 21-22 and use your imagination to carry you ahead to that day when all things will be renewed. It's essential that we nurture the certainty of this hope.

What is the writer saying?

How can I apply this to my life?

PRAY

For God to open the doors of foundations that would be compatible to the ministry of Word of Life.

Jesus had so deftly silenced His critics that no one wanted to ask Him another question. So, Jesus took this opportunity to ask a question of His own. The book of Psalms is the most quoted Old Testament book in the New Testament. Psalm 110 is the most quoted chapter and Psalm 110:1 is the most quoted verse. It's a very important passage that clearly establishes the priority of the Son of David (the Messiah) over His father David. The leadership was plotting to kill Jesus because He claimed to be God. They considered this to be blasphemy. They thought that this proved He was not the Messiah because the Messiah would not make such a false claim. Jesus refuted this again by appealing to the very wording of Scripture. He asked how the Messiah (Christ) could be the Lord over David and still be his son? Jesus was affirming his humanity as the descendant of David while also affirming His deity as Lord over David.

Looking up, Jesus saw the self-righteous and wealthy leaders of Israel putting huge amounts of money into the temple treasury. Standing before one of the chests was a poor widow casting in all she possessed: two mites, a very small amount. Jesus then made an important spiritual observation: God is not interested in how much people give but in how much they keep!

LIFE STEP

We often hear about giving to God in terms of the tithe, which is generally taken to mean 10% of our income. Regardless of one's view about tithing, the more significant number is the percentage that we keep! The story of the widow and her two mites should cause us to consider how much we are holding onto compared to how much we are giving to the Lord. Joyfully give today in a way that exceeds what you normally do.

What is the writer saying?

How can I apply this to my life?

PRAY Myanmar – Pray for effective evangelism that would penetrate the hearts of a staunchly Buddhist majority.

The temple of Jesus' day was a stunning sight to behold. As some commented on its beauty, Jesus pointed out that this very temple would be totally destroyed. This then prompted a discussion about the end times. This sermon is known as the Olivet Discourse and is also recorded in Matthew 24-25. Jesus draws on many portions of the Old Testament, but much of what He says is directly related to Daniel's prophecy about the seventieth week (Daniel 9:24-27). This final seven-year period will precede the setting up of the millennial kingdom and will be divided into two parts. The entire seven years is commonly referred to as the Tribulation and the last three and a half years as the Great Tribulation based on Jesus' words in Matthew 24:21.

Today's passage describes life in the first half of the Tribulation. Based on this passage and others that would be written later (1 Thessalonians 5; 2 Thessalonians 2; and Revelation 4-19), we know that the first half of the Tribulation, though a terrible time, will be mild compared to the second half. During the first half, the Antichrist will become the champion of the nation of Israel and defend her from surrounding enemies. Many will hail him as the Messiah. The period will be filled with war, famine, and death, but it will only be a taste of the horrors to come when the Antichrist breaks a covenant in the middle of the seven years and launches an unprecedented persecution of the nation of Israel.

LIFE STEP

These words were spoken before the Church Age was introduced. Believers living today, the Bride of Christ, do not need to fear the Tribulation because we will be taken away before it begins. Paul described this event, known as the Rapture, in 1 Thessalonians 4:13-18. No prophetic signs are given for the Rapture; all signs point to Christ's glorious Second Coming at the end of the Tribulation. If we see such signs in evidence today, this would indicate that the Rapture is very close. Don't be lulled into complacency just because many predictions of the Rapture have been wrong. It will happen!

What is the writer saying?

How can I apply this to my life?

This passage could potentially refer to either of two major destructions of Jerusalem. The first occurred in A.D. 70. However, Zechariah clearly prophesied a destruction of the city that will occur at the end of the Tribulation (Daniel's seventieth week), just prior to Christ's glorious Second Coming (Zechariah 14:2-4). Comparing today's passage with Zechariah as well as Matthew 24 makes it clear that it is this destruction which is in focus. The destruction of A.D. 70 was bad enough. According to the historian Josephus, when there were no more to plunder or slay after "incredible slaughter and miseries," Titus ordered the city to be "razed so completely as to look like a spot which had been never inhabited." In that first destruction of Jerusalem, an estimated 1.1 million Jews perished. Josephus tells us that 97,000 Jews were sent to various provinces and to the Egyptian mines. As horrible as that destruction was, it was but a foretaste of what will happen during the end times.

The "times of the Gentiles" mentioned in verse 24 is prophetically significant. This period is the primary focus of the Book of Daniel. Most of the Gentile world empires described in the Book of Daniel have already come and gone. Only some form of revived Roman empire is yet to appear with its head being the Antichrist. Until these Gentile kingdoms have finished having their day, the kingdom of God will not be instituted on the earth. The seventieth week ends with the physical return of Jesus Christ to the earth. This is not to be confused with the Rapture, which occurs seven years earlier during which believers will go to meet the Lord in the air. The reason the Rapture of the Church is not mentioned here is because the Church had not yet begun nor even been revealed. Paul said it was a mystery (Ephesians 3:1-12) until God revealed it through him. This explains why the Rapture was also called a mystery (1 Corinthians 15:51-52).

LIFE STEP *Sometimes, it seems that the world just keeps on spinning and that God's promises have failed. However, Peter warned us that the Lord is not slack about these promises; rather, He wants all people to have an opportunity to be saved (2 Peter 3:9). Who can you share the Gospel with today before it's too late?*

What is the writer saying?

How can I apply this to my life?

PRAY Austria – Pray for a renewal movement among the churches in Austria, most of which are experiencing grave decline.

The final week of Jesus' earthly life was rapidly winding down. As chapter 22 opens, it is now Thursday. Hate was blinding the hearts and minds of the chief priests and scribes, and Satan entered Judas. Luke briefly mentions these facts then quickly shifts his focus to Jesus and the disciples as they prepared for the Passover.

The Passover is an extremely important feast in the Jewish calendar. It looked back to the Exodus. But just as importantly, it looked forward to the final salvation that God had promised to His people. The lamb that was slain was a vivid picture of Jesus Christ: it was spotless; it was put to death in the place of another, and none of its bones were broken. Amazingly, in the first century the lambs used in Jerusalem came from Bethlehem! The exodus was but a picture of a future time when God

would bring His people into a permanent relationship with Him, a time when all the promises made to Abraham, Isaac, and Jacob would be fulfilled.

The event described in today's passage marks the institution of the Lord's Supper, often called communion. Later in the New Testament, the Apostle Paul referred back to this event when instituting the current Church practice (1 Corinthians 11). Much like the Passover, the Lord's Supper also looks both forward and backward. It is a table of *retrospection*, looking back to Calvary and understanding that Christ is our Passover. It is also a table of *introspection* as we examine ourselves (1 Corinthians 11:28). Finally, it is a table of *anticipation* as we partake of the Lord's Supper until He comes (1 Corinthians 11:26).

LIFE STEP *It's touching to note Jesus' earnest desire to share this final meal with His disciples before He faced the cross (v. 15). Later, Paul would reveal how Christ's use of the bread and the wine as symbols of His broken body and blood is something that Jesus also wants us to do to remember Him. We should place a high priority on participating in the Lord's Supper. It was among His very last requests!*

What is the writer saying?

How can I apply this to my life?

PRAY Chile – For future church leaders to be called from among those saved at evangelistic activities.

The intricate beauty of the picture before the disciples seemed to fall on blind eyes. They still didn't understand that Jesus was about to die. In fact, they were more concerned with their own position than they were with what Christ was telling them in words and symbols. So, they began arguing about which one of them would be greatest in the kingdom of God. Once again, this highlights a recurring theme in Luke's gospel account: the first shall be last and the last shall be first. The disciples had seen with their own eyes that the rich and the powerful rejected Jesus. They had also seen the weak and beggarly blessed. And yet they were still concerned with position. They still envisioned the kingdom in human terms, the way the kings of the Gentiles thought of kingdoms.

Jesus had consistently taught and illustrated for His disciples that life in the kingdom would be very different from life in this world. In the kingdom of God, weakness is of greatest value. Jesus Himself became weak so that He could provide salvation for us by becoming a babe in swaddling clothes and placing Himself under the leadership of the Holy Spirit. He was about to submit to the greatest injustice ever conceived: the Lord of Glory mocked and crucified by wicked men. What could be more humiliating? But that was the price of our salvation, and Jesus would willingly pay it.

LIFE STEP

If the Lord has placed you in a position of leadership, this passage is one of the best to get a sense of how God expects you to lead: not by lording it over people but by serving and being willing to sacrifice much in order to facilitate their service and ensure their success. What should that look like in your leadership responsibilities today?

What is the writer saying?

How can I apply this to my life?

After the meal, Jesus and the disciples headed out of the city to the Mount of Olives. In keeping with Luke's theme, we see Jesus in a very vulnerable position as He cried out to His Father in anguish and asked if there was another way. His prayer raises questions that are impossible to fully answer. Was this not the very reason that Jesus came into the world? How could He be in such emotional turmoil, given that He had been telling the disciples this was going to happen? One thing is clear: living by faith does not dismiss our emotions. To dread the necessary is human. A person may know that he needs surgery, but this doesn't prevent him from dreading the experience. Because Jesus was like us, He too faced those same emotions. He chose to live His life with the same limitations that men do (except without sin). This is perhaps one of the deepest mysteries in Scripture. Jesus felt life the same way we do. No one in their right mind would look forward to being crucified. Jesus counted it all joy, but He still agonized over the experience. It was not the physical pain that He feared most, however. It was the separation He was about to experience as He would be forsaken by His Father.

Luke alone mentions that an angel came from heaven to minister to Him. This further emphasizes Christ's human weakness. He was doing what only God could do, but He was doing it as a human. Any lesser man would have collapsed on the spot, and Jesus was close to that point. The angel came to support Him in the flesh so He could accomplish in the Spirit what needed to be done.

LIFE STEP

It is no dishonor to be weak. Jesus embraced weakness because it was the only way. Later, Paul experienced a thorn in the flesh that kept him in weakness as well. He also implored the Lord three times for it to be removed but the Lord did not do so (2 Corinthians 12:7-10). Instead, God reminded Paul that His strength would be made perfect in Paul's weakness. Thank God today for whatever weakness prevents you from depending on your own strength!

What is the writer saying?

How can I apply this to my life?

PRAY

Latvia – Pray for harvest workers to embrace the younger generation before they follow in the footsteps of their atheistic ancestors.

Jesus had clearly embraced weakness as essential to His mission, but the disciples were not so easily convinced, especially Peter. He had cut off the ear of the high priest's servant and had vowed never to deny Christ even if everyone else did (Mark 14:31). He was primed and ready for a fall!

The disciples who had just been arguing about who would be greatest in the Kingdom, now found themselves hiding from the temple police. Peter's denial is a very important element in the storyline. His self-sufficiency was exposed and proven totally ineffective. Peter needed a humble heart, and God delivered. Later he would write, "Humble yourselves under the mighty hand of God, that He may exalt you in due time." (1 Peter 5:6)

The morning after Christ was mocked and beaten (vv. 63-65), the religious leaders came together in council. This was called the Sanhedrin, an assembly of seventy people, which could pass judgment on religious and civil issues but could not authorize capital punishment under Roman law. They asked two questions as they sought cause to condemn Jesus. As soon as Christ affirmed that He was the Son of God, they needed nothing further!

LIFE STEP

Has the Lord been allowing you to fail in some area(s) where you were convinced that you would succeed? Though not easy, such experiences can be among the greatest steps forward in your walk with the Lord. Failure has been called the "back door to success". That's what it will be for you if you humbly accept it and ask the Lord to teach you through it. Praise God, Peter's failure was not the end of his usefulness to God. In fact, it truly was the starting point of a whole new era of effectiveness because he learned that his only hope was to depend on the Lord.

What is the writer saying?

How can I apply this to my life?

PRAY Pray for opportunities to witness to your unsaved friends and loved ones.

In today's passage, Christ appears before Pilate and Herod. The Sanhedrin had found itself in a rather precarious position. They wanted Jesus to be put to death, but they did not have the authority to do so without Roman permission. Not only that, they wanted Rome to take responsibility for it so they wouldn't be blamed by the masses, who may have remained favorable toward Christ. So, they went before Pilate, whom they hated, to ask him to grant permission. Notice how they modified the charges against Jesus. Instead of accusing him of blasphemy, which had been their concern, they claimed that he was trying to start an insurrection against Rome. It was pure manipulation.

Pilate could tell that Jesus was no threat to Roman rule, and he didn't like being manipulated by the Sanhedrin for religious purposes. So, he tried to get out of the predicament by sending Jesus to Herod who oversaw the region of Galilee. This is the same Herod who had John the Baptist beheaded. No doubt Pilate hoped that Herod would relieve him of all responsibility in this matter.

The Sanhedrin was acting purely out of rage and self-interest, Pilate was maneuvering to preserve any political advantage he could, and Herod was only interested in seeing Jesus do some miracles. When that didn't materialize, he and his men mistreated Him. Only Jesus acted out of love for others. It is not the power of the Sanhedrin, Pilate, or Herod that forced Jesus to submit to these atrocities. He did so willingly.

LIFE STEP

Imagine the scene: chaos and commotion motivated by rage, self-interest and pride frothing and foaming around the lone person acting out of pure love: Jesus Christ Himself. So, who came out ahead and ultimately won the day? You may be surrounded in a similar way by people clamoring for their own selfish agenda and perhaps even subjecting you to mistreatment. By the power of the Holy Spirit, you can stand strong in the middle of it all and humbly put love on display. Who will ultimately come out ahead? We all know the answer! This is part of our calling (2 Peter 2:21-23).

What is the writer saying?

How can I apply this to my life?

PRAY   China – For the failure of all government attempts to impose false doctrine on registered churches.

Pilate had likely assumed that he was done with Christ when he had sent Him to Herod. But now He was back, and Pilate was more confident than ever in his assessment that Jesus was not guilty of a capital crime. He wanted Jesus released. Pilate knew that the real reason they wanted Jesus dead was because of their own envy (Matthew 27:18). So, calling together the religious leaders, he also convened the crowds and pronounced him innocent. Note that he did not simply say this to the religious leaders. He added the crowd into the mix (v. 13), no doubt hoping that they would side with him in favor of releasing Christ. Most of them were likely in favor of this at first, but Matthew tells us in his gospel account that the religious leaders stirred up the crowd and persuaded them to ask for the release of Barabbas instead (Matthew 27:20).

A careful study of these events shows that Jesus was subjected to three Jewish and three Roman trials, none of which could establish any guilt. The overwhelming evidence of Jesus' innocence and the pressure that Pilate put on the religious leaders, only served to demonstrate how much they hated Jesus without cause.

LIFE STEP

Don't miss the irony here. These religious leaders were the ones who claimed to keep the Law since childhood. But, faced with their greatest opportunity to align themselves with what God was doing, their hatred and envy carried the day. Such is usually the case when we are pursuing our own righteousness through law observance. Let us examine our own hearts. Would we have welcomed the Lord of Glory, or would we have condemned Him because He didn't fit the mold of law-based religion?

What is the writer saying?

How can I apply this to my life?

Simon, a Cyrenian, was like so many of the people in Luke's Gospel. Like Zacchaeus or the centurion, he was not a person the Jewish population would respect since he was a foreigner. Suddenly, his life was changed as he was pressed into service bearing Christ's cross to Calvary. Like so many unforeseen situations in life, what seemed to be a sad circumstance may have turned out to be a great blessing. We are told in Mark 15:21 that Simon was the father of Alexander and Rufus. Why mention these names? Could it be because they all became followers of Christ and were known to the apostles and early believers? Paul mentions a Rufus along with his mother in Romans 16:13. Could it be the same man? It's an intriguing possibility!

The two thieves crucified along with Christ are mentioned briefly in Matthew and Mark, but Luke allots a significant amount of time to the conversation that took place between them and Jesus. Like the other converts we meet in the Book of Luke, these two were social outcasts, living at the bottom of the social ladder. No respectable chief priest or lawyer would be caught dead talking to the likes of them. The cultured people had too much to lose. How sad! Those who know they are poor in spirit have nothing to lose. Only the rich in spirit cling to their own righteousness.

LIFE STEP

The thief on the cross had not been baptized or lived a good life, yet he was saved. It was all of grace, not of works, and so it is with anyone. Jesus' words to the thief are reflected in Paul's words, that to be absent from the body is to be present with the Lord (2 Corinthians 5:8). Imagine that transition, stepping from the agony and shame of being hung on a cross right into Paradise! The certainty of this can be a great comfort to believers who face extreme suffering and possibly even persecution. Our afflictions here are light and momentary when compared to the eternal weight of glory that we'll experience (2 Corinthians 4:17). Hallelujah!

What is the writer saying?

How can I apply this to my life?

PRAY　Poland – For the salvation of many who are taking English classes taught by missionaries.

The sixth hour was noon according to the Jewish method of telling time. Yet there was darkness. We know from the other gospel accounts that other significant things happened between the sixth hour and the ninth hours, but Luke mentions only two. The first is the tearing of the temple veil, the curtain separating the Most Holy Place from the Holy Place (Exodus 26:33). Only the high priest was allowed to go behind the veil on the Day of Atonement each year (Leviticus 16:2). If there was an ultimate status symbol in Jewish society, it was having the honor of entering the Holy of Holies. But this veil was now torn from top to bottom, thereby abolishing the barrier between God and man (Hebrews 10:20). Note the direction in which it was torn—from heaven down to earth. Man could not tear it from earth up to heaven!

After Jesus gave up His spirit, Luke recounts the testimony of a Roman centurion who recognized that Jesus was a righteous man. Once again, the least likely and the despised were the ones who ultimately understood. But then, praise the Lord, a prominent leader finally stepped up, a secret believer from Arimathea named Joseph, who provided the tomb that would only be needed for three days.

LIFE STEP

The obvious faith of Joseph stood in stark contrast to the rest of his peers. It's encouraging to note the examples of a few prominent people who also believed in Jesus. They were the exception, but they do show that salvation was available to all. Take a moment today to pray for the salvation of people in powerful positions of earthly leadership (1 Timothy 2:1-4). Ask God to open their eyes to see who Jesus is.

What is the writer saying?

How can I apply this to my life?

PRAY   Argentina – For the salvation of the President and the stabilization of this country's economic and judicial systems.

Our journey through Luke has now come full circle. The book opened with great joy as angels proclaimed the birth of the Messiah. And so, it ends here in the resurrection chapter! The stone was rolled away, and angels stood in shining garments. Angels were present at Christ's birth, at His temptation, in the Garden of Gethsemane, and now at His resurrection. This time, however, they were not present to support Christ in His human frailty but rather to proclaim His victorious resurrection. New life had come, a new life that we as believers can share. His resurrection was the ultimate proof of His identity. Paul sums this up in Romans 1:3-4, "Concerning His Son Jesus Christ our Lord, who was born of the seed of David according to the flesh and declared to be the Son of God with power . . . by the resurrection from the dead."

The first witnesses of Christ's resurrection were not the chief priests or the princes of this age but rather a few humble women. They were ecstatic. They returned from the tomb and told the eleven and everyone with them. What appeared to be the greatest travesty ever committed had turned into an infinite, irreversible victory. Christ's victory is shared by all who place their faith in Him for salvation.

LIFE STEP

The resurrection is the historical anchor of our faith (1 Corinthians 15:12-20). Not only does it provide the proof that Christ was Who He claimed to be and validate His message of salvation, it also provides a sure hope to all who have placed their faith in Him that they too shall live again. Christ not only spoke of the fact that resurrection was possible, but He also experienced it Himself. Read Jesus' statement and question to Martha in John 11:25-26. Consider the profound implications of believing what Jesus said to her. How does that change the way you'll face life today?

What is the writer saying?

How can I apply this to my life?

PRAY   Pakistan – Pray for the government to have insight in how to deal with efforts to impose Sharia Law that appears impossible to root out.

This encounter, along with the other details with which Luke closed his book, wrap up the storyline concerning the disciples. At no point thus far have the disciples been presented in a consistently positive light. They were rebuked for having little faith. They were constantly squabbling over who would be greatest in the Kingdom. Their leader, Peter, had denied Jesus while He was on trial. One might be tempted to think that they were only fair-weather friends, but Jesus was preparing them for greater responsibility. As the conversation with these two disciples began, they were somehow prevented from recognizing Him (v. 16). But it was more than His appearance that they didn't recognize; they failed to grasp His mission as well. They had read the Scriptures through selective eyes, focusing on Messiah conquering Israel's enemies and ruling over the entire world but missing the suffering which would precede the glory to follow (1 Peter 1:10-11). In keeping with Luke's focus on faith, Jesus did not begin by revealing His identity to them. Instead, He started with the Scriptures and traced for them the necessity of the Messiah's humiliation and suffering, which would precede His glorious Kingdom. Even then, it was not until they broke bread with Him that their eyes were opened to recognize Him.

LIFE STEP

We can be tempted to think that experiencing Jesus in a visible, tactile sense would strengthen our faith. But it could never do this because faith is the evidence of things not seen (Hebrews 11:1) and is based solely on what God says (Romans 10:17). When we can see with our eyes, faith is no longer needed. These disciples didn't see until they had believed. The same is true for us. If we will not believe the Scriptures, we won't believe our eyes either. Today our fellowship with Jesus can be as real as theirs because we have the witness of the Scriptures.

What is the writer saying?

How can I apply this to my life?

PRAY   Guatemala – Pray for the church to commit herself to true discipleship rooted in the truths of the Bible.

The two disciples on the Emmaus road still did not know that they were with Jesus. They came to the village where they were planning to spend the night and asked Him to stay with them. When He broke the bread, they realized who He was, and He immediately vanished from their sight. There was no question-and-answer period. What Jesus had shared from the Scriptures was entirely sufficient. These disciples no doubt had many more questions, but Jesus left them with the greatest of all gifts, an understanding of God's Word.

Rushing back to Jerusalem, the two shared with the others what they had experienced. As they listened, Jesus suddenly appeared in their midst. They were terrified, thinking He was a spirit (ghost). Jesus then proceeded to assure them that He had a physical, tangible body with flesh and bones, even though He had just materialized in front of them! Even with hard evidence in view, they still did not believe (v. 41). Faith is not a sight-based activity; it is a Scripture-based activity. It comes by hearing and believing the Word of God in our hearts (Romans 10:17), not by seeing something with our eyes (Hebrews 11:1). To seek to live by sight is actually a pathway to unbelief and its terrible consequences. The Word of God is clear: "The just shall live by his faith" (Habakkuk 2:4) because "without faith it is impossible to please Him" (Hebrews 11:6).

LIFE STEP

Today's passage offers a fascinating glimpse into our own future. Jesus was the first human to be permanently raised from the dead with a glorified body. That's why He is called the "firstborn from the dead" (Colossians 1:18), even though others were raised back to life before Him. What is a glorified body like? It is clearly NOT ethereal and immaterial but real and tangible. Jesus could be seen, touched (He says He had flesh and bones), and could eat. Yet, He was able to do things that no unglorified body can do including appearing and disappearing, levitating, and leaving earth's atmosphere (Acts 1:9). One day we will be resurrected with a glorified body like His (Philippians 3:20-21). Do you envision heaven as a disembodied experience, floating in ethereal space? Buckle up; God is far more creative than that!

189

What is the writer saying?

How can I apply this to my life?

PRAY

Laos – Pray for Lao seekers to toss aside the social pressure to practice Buddhism and place their hope in the one true God.

Luke is about to "lay down his pen." He had diligently searched the records and listened to the eyewitness accounts so that Theophilus would know the certainty of these events. Certainty is a precious commodity. The disciples were there, they saw Jesus, they spoke with Jesus, they touched Jesus, yet they still did not believe. Their eyes were not opened until Jesus opened the Word of God and explained to them all the things that must be fulfilled. Once the disciples were willing to listen to the Scriptures, Jesus was able to explain to them the prime directive of His mission.

From the very beginning, the message had been simple: repentance (a change of mind) about how to deal with sin (Luke 3:3). It was John's message as well as Jesus'. The disciples had heard this message repeatedly. But now, perhaps for the first time, they understood that Jesus had to humble Himself, even to the point of dying on the cross in order to accomplish that which the Old Testament had predicted. They understood how they had read the Old Testament through the eyes of self-interest. They now understood how death was life and last was first.

They were now ready to go into the entire world and preach a new (repented) way of thinking that sees death as the path to life, weakness as better than strength, and last being ahead of first. The Good News was not about a righteousness that could be achieved or earned, but one that could only be humbly accepted by faith as a gift from God Himself. This righteousness could not be the basis for any pride or self-sufficiency, only wonder and gratitude.

LIFE STEP

We can read Luke's Gospel as the story of a Person who lived, died, and was resurrected two thousand years ago. This will only increase our knowledge. Or, by faith, we can grasp the meaning of this Person's life, death, and resurrection in our place and trust in Him. This will save us from our sin. Which will it be for you?

What is the writer saying?

How can I apply this to my life?

PRAY   Syria – Pray for the Church to be protected and expanded amid hostility.

Proverbs 7 is Solomon's warning to his son about sexual immorality. It starts out by elevating words of wisdom as life-giving and life-preserving tools in the hands and hearts of those who keep them. This wisdom comes from keeping God's words in obedience. In verse 5, Solomon got to the point of his warning—the enticements of an immoral woman, the adulterous woman— whose words have the potential to draw a man into sin.

In our reading today, Solomon told of looking out of his window and observing a young man falling into the trap of such a woman. He described the young man as "devoid of understanding" and emphasized his youthfulness twice in verse 7. He was not equipped with the experience to alert him to the risks ahead. He was filled with the confidence and passion typical of young men. Unwisely, he took the path that leads to her door, and there the immoral woman

met him. Notice the terms Solomon used to describe the temptress:
Dressed seductively *(like a harlot, or prostitute)*; with a crafty *(secretive)* heart (v. 10) Loud and rebellious; refusing to stay home (v. 11) Lurking at every corner *(on the prowl)* (v. 12) Sexually aggressive and unashamed *(kissed him; with a brazen, impudent face)* (v. 13) Religious, but uncommitted to righteousness (v. 14) Seeking sexual gratification from anyone she could entrap (v. 15) She proposed an unholy and immoral night of sexual gratification (vv. 16-20) while her husband was away, and the young man fell for it. Though she promised a night of pleasure, Solomon used vivid word pictures to describe what this liaison would cost the man (vv. 22-23). In the end, it would cost him his life! Solomon closed with a stern warning to his children: *Listen to me! Pay attention to the words of my mouth (v. 24).*

LIFE STEP

The way to keep temptation from turning into sin is to turn aside from the temptation without letting it take root in your heart or mind. Too many times it is the second thought, or the second look, that puts us on the path to sin and painful consequences. Paul urged his young protégé, Timothy, to flee youthful passions (2 Timothy 2:22). Read that passage right now and write down the things Paul urged Timothy to pursue. Pay attention to Solomon's words of wisdom and Paul's warning to Timothy.

What is the writer saying?

How can I apply this to my life?

PRAY

Mexico – For an end to the national media's portrayal of believers as enemies of Mexican culture.

This psalm is arranged in an acrostic pattern, with twenty-two units consisting of eight verses each. Each of the twenty-two sections is given a letter of the Hebrew alphabet, and each line in that section begins with that letter starting with the first Hebrew letter. The overall theme of this psalm is the glory of Scripture. The unknown writer (possibly David) uses various synonyms to refer to God's divine Word, such as "law," "testimonies," "judgments," "statutes," and several more.

Note that the reader is addressed in the first three verses. Here, the writer speaks of blessings that come to those who "walk" in the law of the Lord and in His ways, who "keep" His testimonies. The verbs "walk" (appearing four times) and "keep" (used twenty-four times in this psalm) suggest a diligent, consistent, and intentional series of actions that reflect obedience to God's Word as a way of life. One who lives in this manner also will succeed in avoiding sin (v. 3).

Throughout the balance of this section (through v. 8), the writer addresses Almighty God. He speaks of his commitments and intentions to honor God through obedience by following the path laid out through Scripture. Several word choices in this section speak to the dedication of the psalmist to live according to God's Word. Note the following:

• God has commanded us to do so (v. 4)
• The blessing is reserved for those who look to God's law (v. 6)
• Understanding and learning follow faithful searching (v. 7)

Perhaps the key to this passage is the emphasis on wholeness of heart, found in verse 2. Obedience that comes from an undivided heart truly is the way to God's blessings.

LIFE STEP

When you take an honest look at the way you respond to God's direction found in Scripture, do you find that you are normally obedient? Or is it that you don't really know what God expects from you? Remember that the Word of God does no good if it isn't searched out diligently. Let this be a day when you commit or recommit yourself to "walk" in the law of the Lord and "keep" His testimonies. Write out a prayer of commitment to the Lord.

What is the writer saying?

How can I apply this to my life?

The challenges faced by young men in living according to God's standards of holiness and purity are not new. How do we know this? The psalmist makes it plain that he, too, faced those challenges. They have been part of our world since the Fall of man and will continue until the end of times when all believers are gone from this world to live in Heaven's glory.

In the second section of this grand psalm, the author poses the question, "How can a young man cleanse his way?" He answers with three ways to put safeguards in place to ensure purity in life:

• By taking heed to God's Word (v. 9)
• By seeking God with a whole-hearted diligence (v. 10)
• By memorizing God's Word (v. 11)

As if he realizes his own shortcomings and powerlessness in following through with his commitments, the writer prays to the Lord with several specific requests:

• To be kept by God from straying or wandering from God's commandments (v. 10)
• For God to teach him in the Word (statutes) (v. 12)

He closes this section by boldly proclaiming his intentions to make good on his commitments (notice the "I will" statements in vv. 15-16):

• To meditate on God's precepts
• To contemplate God's ways
• To delight in God's statutes
• To never forget God's Word

Notice the joy that is his when he confidently follows God's law. In verse 13, he speaks of his verbal testimony to others of the depth of God's goodness as found in the Word. Verse 14 tells us of how he values God's divine directives—"as much as in all riches."

LIFE STEP

With God's great help, you are capable of walking in purity and holiness with the Lord—even in this sin-tainted world. But you must develop and maintain a learner's spirit and a dependence on God. As you close your time in the Word today, will you begin to pray as the psalmist prayed in verses 10 and 12? Ask the Lord to keep you from wandering from His commandments. Ask Him to teach you His statutes. Then, follow up by beginning to diligently search for His wisdom through His Word.

What is the writer saying?

How can I apply this to my life?

PRAY God's guidance for staff and candidates participating in the Word of Life Missionary in Training (MIT) program.

Talk about big requests! In this passage, the writer was not content to simply ask for God's blessings. No, he asked as one with big expectations that his all-powerful God would deal "bountifully" with him (v. 17). But there is much more behind this bold and simple request. Notice how he petitions God as a "humble servant," rightfully placing himself beneath the Master's grace. Notice, too, his motivation in making the request—that he may live and keep God's Word. This request is not just for survival, but also for the quality of life that comes only when one truly honors God.

He follows by asking for another gift—that God would open his eyes to see wonderful spiritual truths that lie hidden in God's precepts (v. 18). This points to the reality for us as modern-day readers that God's truths are ours for searching out through diligent effort, but understanding is granted by God. Throughout this psalm and others, you will notice the psalmist asking God to "teach me" or "give me understanding." We do well to pray the same way.

Most of the balance of this passage provides context for the prayer uttered by the writer—that of a man who knows firsthand the feelings of fear, hurt, and suffering. Verses 19-20 suggest periods of loneliness, rejection, and a sense of abandonment. Rather than falling from his love for God's Word, he longed even more for the comfort he found there. He has also experienced persecution (vv. 22-23). But even in those moments, he had held firm to God's commandments.

In the final verse, the writer speaks of the delight he holds for God's testimonies. He loves them, trusts them, and longs for them. Best of all, he learns from them as his counselors (v. 24).

LIFE STEP *Who are your "counselors"? Whom do you turn to when you want truth and guidance that can be trusted? For the believer, God's Word must rise to the top of the list in answering these questions. Make it your prayer, like the psalmist, that God would "open my eyes to see wondrous things from Your law." Believe God for big things as you commit yourself to Him and His Word.*

What is the writer saying?

How can I apply this to my life?

PRAY Benin – Pray for the church to be made pure, steeped in the power of prayer and having an uncompromising faith.

It appears that the author's context for this segment is the struggle between his flesh and the pursuit of godliness. He opens in verse 25 by declaring himself in the grips of deep despair and asking God for revival. To his credit, he lays bare his own faults (v. 26: "declared my ways"), even mentioning in his petition his strong desire to be freed from his deceitful ways (v. 29). In verses 26 and 27, he makes his plea to gain not just knowledge ("Teach me your statutes"), but also understanding to apply godly wisdom and knowledge.

His prayers can serve as a model for our own prayers today, for those who sincerely desire to walk in the path of godliness and obedience. For example, he rightly places his hopes for revival and strength in God's Word rather than any other source (vv. 25 and 28: "according to Your word"). Further, he positions himself mentally and emotionally to pursue what is right and good, pledging to meditate on God's wonderful works (v. 27), to choose to follow the way of truth that emanates from God's Word (v. 30), and to cling to God's testimonies (v. 31). Verse 32 reveals that, though he started in the dust in despair (v. 25), he did not stay there! One expositor noted, "He moved in a beautiful progression, from confessing to choosing to clinging to running!" Such is the great hope of all who focus on God's Word as their guide.

LIFE STEP

Did you notice in these verses how the psalmist looked to God for strength and revival while also pledging his own efforts to cling to God's direction? In truth, your progression from spiritual infant to mature believer depends on God (Philippians 1:6) but requires your effort, too (Philippians 2:12). While you must rely on the power of the Holy Spirit, you must also do the hard work of "exercising yourself toward godliness" (1 Timothy 4:7). What will you start doing today (or stop doing) that will help you grow in your walk with the Lord?

What is the writer saying?

How can I apply this to my life?

PRAY

Pray for God to show your church leaders creative ways to minister and to meet the needs of your community.

Here again, the writer seems to be inviting God Almighty to intervene in his life by "causing" or "making" the writer respond to the divine wisdom of the Word. He asks for God to

- Teach me (v. 33)
- Give me understanding (v. 34)
- Make me walk in obedience (v. 35)
- Incline my heart to your testimonies (v. 36)
- Turn my eyes from worthless things (v. 37)
- Revive me in Your way (v. 37)
- Plant (establish) your word within me (v. 38)

This is a picture of one who desires to remove his own hands from the day-to-day guidance of his life and place in God's hands the lifelong search for the path of righteousness. It is as if the writer recognizes how inadequate he is to bring about lasting change in himself, and, therefore, commits himself to total surrender to God! He recognizes how prone he is toward a divided heart (v. 36) and impurity (v. 37) and petitions God to make him different.

What the psalmist desires is as good as his when he follows the path God has for him. He expresses his delight in that path (v. 35), his devotion to the fear of God (v. 38), and his longing for God's precepts (v. 40). What motivates the psalmist to such devotion? He recognizes that God's judgments are altogether good (v. 39).

LIFE STEP

What portions of this passage would you consider adopting as your prayer to God for a changed life? There's nothing better than praying back to God the Scriptures. Do you need to pray for God to teach you? To give you understanding? How about the power to walk in His path, rather than your own? Maybe you need God's intervention in turning your eyes from worthless things. Think about it, and then pray about it with a sincere heart.

SATURDAY - WEEK 25

What is the writer saying?

How can I apply this to my life?

In the face of adversity, the psalmist leaned upon and trusted in God's Word (vv. 41-42). He saw that salvation and mercy are delivered to man through the Word of God, and only in the Word did he place his hope (vv. 4 and 49). Here lies a great lesson for modern readers (or readers of any era) to look only to God's Word to revive one's hope, for there is no other source of truth and hope that is eternal and unchanging. As a result of this truth, the psalmist pledged to keep God's law continually (v. 44).

Verses 45-48 reveal the writer's total and complete trust in the Word, as well as a summary of the benefits enjoyed by obedience to the Word. First, the psalmist walks in liberty because he loves the Word of God and seeks it constantly. Jesus spoke of the liberty gained by obedience to the Word when he said to the Pharisees, "You shall know the truth, and the truth shall set you free" (John 8:32). To the psalmist, this freedom meant the boldness to unashamedly give testimony of God's goodness before royalty (v. 46). Additionally, following God's ordinances and precepts brought him unmatched freedom in his loving expressions of worship and yearning for God's revealed truth in Scripture (v. 48). It is no wonder that he closed this segment with another pledge to meditate on God's statutes (v. 49).

LIFE STEP

The more you know the Word, the better you will know God. Do you believe that? Can you imagine having so much of the Bible within you that it just comes out of you whenever you are bumped or jostled by the world around you? That is the kind of liberty the psalmist was talking about. Unashamed. Bold. Free to worship and serve in every way without inhibitions or doubts. Pray for God to give you a hunger and thirst for His Word like never before.

197

What is the writer saying?

How can I apply this to my life?

This narrative starts with Elkanah, a Levite who was living in the territory of Ephraim with his two wives. One wife, Hannah, was unable to bear children, while the other wife, Peninnah, had given birth to children. Though such a polygamous marriage was never God's ideal (see Genesis 2:23-24), it was not uncommon in ancient civilizations, particularly among households in which the first wife was barren. In the Bible, polygamy is never portrayed favorably, as we see by the conflict that arose between Hannah and Peninnah (vv. 5-6).

As you read this passage, you see the faithfulness of Elkanah to worship the Lord in the proper ways. This is admirable in ordinary times but even more so when one considers that this period in Israel was characterized by ungodliness and disobedience. Roughly speaking, it is the same time frame as in the Book of Judges, when every man did what was right in his own eyes and there was no significant spiritual leadership in the nation. Even in these troubling times, Elkanah was consistent in traveling with his wives to Shiloh each year to worship and offer sacrifices to the Lord.

Hannah is noted also for her spiritual reaction to a very real problem. Having endured the taunts of Peninnah for years, she entered the temple in sorrow. This caused a bit of friction between her and Elkanah, who challenged her for her lack of contentment (vv. 7-8). She decided it was best to give the problem to the Lord! We see in the balance of this passage that Eli observed her in silent prayer within the temple (v. 13) and scolded her, thinking she was drunk. She very tactfully explained her situation and received a blessing from Eli. He urged her to go in peace "and the God of Israel grant your petition which you have asked of Him" (v. 17).

LIFE STEP

What's bothering you today? Will you make it your practice to go to God with your troubles and trials, as Hannah did? We all need to recognize that we will face troubles in this life. Isn't it better to settle now how you will handle the challenges you'll face? The more you learn to trust God with your difficulties, the closer you'll grow in your relationship with Him and the easier it will be to trust Him tomorrow when new challenges arise.

What is the writer saying?

How can I apply this to my life?

PRAY Mexico – For Bible schools to be characterized by doctrinal accuracy, depth, and personal integrity.

In our passage today, we see the faithfulness of God to grant Hannah's request, followed by her faithfulness to fulfill the vow she had made to the Lord. Soon after the family returned to their home, she conceived and bore Elkanah a son, whom she named *Samuel*, which we may translate, "heard of God." We see Hannah and Elkanah's commitment to bring Samuel to the Lord to present him for full-time service (vv. 21-23), but also Hannah's insistence that she first wean the boy so he could begin his full-time service without burdening Eli. According to the culture of that day, Samuel's weaning would likely end when he was about three years old. When the time came, Hannah took him to Shiloh to offer him to the Lord as a lifelong servant.

The prayer of Hannah (2:1-11) is a beautiful psalm of praise that exalts God in His power and holiness. Her joy was in the Lord, not the child Samuel, as He was the one Who brought her joy, not the happiness of motherhood. She contrasted the arrogance of those who trust in themselves against those who trust in the Lord (v. 3). She spoke of God's sovereign choice in giving children to the barren, raising up and taking down those whom He chooses, elevating the poor to places of prominence, and the like. It is through the Lord that one finds success, not by man's strength (v. 9). Her song of praise closes with a prophetic proclamation of God's judgment to come and His strengthening of His king (v. 10). Israel had no king when she offered this praise! And this king is called *the anointed*, which transliterated from Hebrew to English is "Messiah." This is fulfilled in David, but ultimately by the Messiah, Jesus.

LIFE STEP *Are you more like a reservoir, receiving God's blessings and holding them in like an "entitled" child of God, or do you live like a conduit of praise because of all the good God allows you to enjoy? Hannah's song of praise in 1 Samuel 2 reflects her heart of deep gratitude and love for her God. He had heard her request. He had granted her request. She could not help but express her gratitude in a heartfelt song of praise! Make your commitment today to actively praise and thank God for His favor and blessings. Write down a word of praise to God for at least one blessing you enjoy.*

199

What is the writer saying?

How can I apply this to my life?

PRAY   Pray that the Lord might lead someone from your church into short-term or full-time missions work.

As background for this passage, it is helpful to read 1 Samuel 2:12-36. We see here that Eli's two sons, Hophni and Phinehas, brought dishonor and shame to the role of the priesthood by their ungodly ways. Eli rebuked his sons, but they ignored his pleas and continued to live immoral lives while serving as priests. In contrast, we see that Samuel, as a boy, continued to serve faithfully while growing in favor both with the Lord and men (v. 27).

Chapter 3 gives us the launching point of Samuel's service as a man of God. By the time we get to this point, Samuel had been trained by Eli for a number of years and had served faithfully, though he had encountered no direct revelation from God. All of that changed one night when, while lying down to sleep, Samuel heard a voice call out his name. Thinking it was Eli

calling for him, Samuel dutifully arose and went to the prophet, only to be told to go back to bed. This occurred two more times in the same way, and on the third incident, Eli perceived that God was behind the voice speaking to Samuel (vv. 3-8). He told Samuel to lie down again and, if he heard the call again, to answer, "Speak, Lord, for Your servant hears." Upon hearing God's voice calling him the fourth time (v. 10), Samuel answered as Eli had instructed. God told Samuel of specific events He was about to bring to pass, including judgment on Eli's house because of the wickedness of his sons (v. 14). When pressed by Eli to divulge what the Lord had told him, Samuel reluctantly shared the news, holding nothing back. We see from this point on that Samuel became recognized by the people as God's prophet (vv. 19-21).

LIFE STEP

Eli's sons were born into a godly household but didn't catch their father's spiritual passion. Giving them the title of "priest" did nothing to change their spiritual trajectory. This illustrates the truth that your relationship with God is your responsibility. Being a true child of God requires that you be born into God's family (John 1:12). Don't take this for granted. Give thanks to God right now if you have been born into His family through faith in Jesus Christ. Don't rely on your heritage to get you to heaven. It won't! If your life is more like Eli's sons because you've never placed your faith in Christ, why not make that choice today?

WEDNESDAY - WEEK 26

What is the writer saying?

How can I apply this to my life?

PRAY

Sri Lanka – Pray for the freedom of religious expression without proposed anti-conversion laws.

The ark of the covenant was Israel's sacred symbol of God's blessings and presence, dating back to the days of Moses when he led the people out of Egypt and received instructions from God in the building of the ark (see Exodus 25:10-22). As such an important and sacred symbol, imagine the horror felt by the Israelites when their archenemies, the Philistines, captured the ark during a battle we read about in 1 Samuel 4. God used the ark to teach the Philistines that He alone is God. Wherever the Philistines stored or kept the ark, they faced troubles. In 1 Samuel 5, we read about tumors (generally believed to be horrible hemorrhoids) that broke out among the Philistines, finally forcing them to devise a plan to rid themselves of the ark. This is where Chapter 6 picks up the narrative. The Philistines had become so fearful of God's power, represented in the ark, that they decided to send it back with token gifts of gold to appease God. These gifts included rats fashioned from gold, suggesting to some scholars that the illness that came upon the Philistines (1 Samuel 5:6, 9, 12) may have been a form of the bubonic plague. The Philistines wanted to assure themselves that God approved of their plan, so they put the ark on a cart led by two milk cows and sent it down the road into a nearby border town of Israel. To make this a real test of God's favor, they removed the calves belonging to the cows and watched to see what they would do. The natural thing would be for the cows to return to the calves. If the cows led the ark out of Philistine territory, then they could rest assured it was the Lord who was in control. This is exactly what happened (v. 12).

LIFE STEP

We see several instances in Scripture where God supernaturally directed animals to accomplish His will. For example, He caused a donkey to talk (Numbers 22:28). In today's reading, He caused two cows with calves to move in the opposite direction from their calves to take the ark back into Israel. What does this teach you? God can use anything and anyone! Never minimize what God may choose to do with you and through you. Settle in your heart right now that you are available to Him for whatever He has in store. If He used donkeys and cows, He surely can use you!

What is the writer saying?

How can I apply this to my life?

PRAY Finland – For creative, committed believers willing to invest their lives in this country's youth.

This chapter illustrates the authority of Samuel as the judge over Israel. He is mysteriously absent from the narrative starting with the battle with Aphek, when the Philistines captured the ark (1 Samuel 4:1). It seems he wasn't consulted when the ark was returned to Israel and the men of Beth-Shemesh looked into the sacred ark, bringing upon themselves God's wrath and the death of more than fifty-thousand men (1 Samuel 6:18-19). But Samuel asserted himself as God's prophet and judge in 7:2-3, calling the people out for their ongoing idolatry and challenging them to whole-hearted repentance. Several observations from this chapter should be highlighted:

- Samuel called for inner change first (*heart change*) followed by outward change in their behavior (*put away the foreign gods*) to give evidence of their heart change (v. 3)
- Samuel called on a commitment to the one true God (v. 3) rather than simply including God in their worship, as had become the practice of the Israelites. (Notice "...*serve Him only.*")
- The preacher's words had the desired effect. The people responded obediently (v. 4).
- Samuel's arsenal for spiritual warfare in bringing about change featured intercessory prayer (v. 5).
- The people's real spiritual transformation included honest confession and repentance (v. 6).
- Just when they took a stand to honor God and God alone, the enemy was aroused to attack (v. 7).

In response to the pending attack by the Philistines, the Israelites urged Samuel to cry out to God for their protection, and the Lord answered him. The Lord thundered against the Philistines (v. 10) and their attack turned into a rout. Samuel set up a monument called *Ebenezer*, meaning "stone of help." The territory that the Philistines had conquered from Israel was recaptured and a strained peace remained in Israel for the rest of Samuel's life.

LIFE STEP

Modern-day believers often fall into the same sense of false security as the Israelites in Samuel's day, considering themselves all right with God because of their outward actions. Too often, we forget that what is in our heart is what God is concerned with most (Matthew 15:17-20). Make sure you are worshiping and serving God and Him only. He is not interested in sharing your devotion with other "gods," which could include anything you put before Him. What is one step you need to make today to avoid idolatry and follow the one true God?

What is the writer saying?

How can I apply this to my life?

Sadly, in today's reading we see the perversion of Samuel's sons, Abijah and Joel, whom Samuel had set up as judges over Israel. Because these men failed to assume the role of trusted and faithful leaders, and considering Samuel's advanced years, the elders came to Samuel to ask for a king—just like all the other nations around them. Samuel was not happy with their request and went to God in prayer, demonstrating once again his reliance on God's divine leadership. Though his parenting may not have proven effective, his prayer life was not open to criticism.

God pointed out that these elders and the rest of the people, in making a request for a king, were actually rejecting Him, not Samuel (v. 7). God's response was to give them what they wanted but required that Samuel warn them of the kinds of problems the people would encounter under the leadership of a king. In verses 11-17, Samuel dutifully warned the people as God had instructed. The king they desired would appropriate their sons and daughters to serve in his armies and as his servants; he would take for himself the very best of their fields and their produce to feed himself and his servants; and he would take a tenth of their livestock. One would think that these warnings would be enough to turn the people back to God instead of seeking relief from a king of human origin. But they saw other nations around them with their kings and quickly forgot the blessings and protection God provides to those who serve Him in obedience (vv. 19-20). When Samuel finished his warnings, the people were just as convinced as before and demanded, "We will have a king over us."

LIFE STEP

It is often difficult for believers to trust God when things around them aren't going well. The "human" instinct is to start coming up with solutions of our own making, just as the Israelites sought a king. Are you quick to start helping God when you face difficulties? Be careful that what you seek does not signal a loss of faith in God. If it's contrary to God's clear direction, it's a bad idea. He may let you have what you seek, but it may not be good for you. Better to wait on the Lord and follow His leadership all the way until He tells you otherwise.

What is the writer saying?

How can I apply this to my life?

PRAY Austria – Pray for Austrians to recognize their spiritual emptiness and to be drawn by the Holy Spirit into a genuine relationship with Jesus Christ.

Today, we are introduced to Saul, a physically impressive young man from the tribe of Benjamin whom God selected to be the first king over Israel. Upon reading the description of Saul (vv. 1-3), the reader may be inclined to agree that God had chosen just the right man for the job. After all, he was born into a family led by a "mighty man of power" (v. 1). He was noticeably handsome, and he stood head and shoulders taller than everyone else among his people. The life of Saul up to this point may have been a fairly normal life for a young Benjamite, but all of that was about to change. God had determined to change Saul's future and that of the nation of Israel by introducing him to the Prophet Samuel. It is worth noting that God used something as mundane as some lost donkeys to bring Saul and Samuel together (see 1 Samuel 9:3, 6-10).

Samuel received word of God's choice by direct revelation, which we read about in verses 15-16. When Saul showed up on the scene where Samuel was ministering, God told him in plain terms that Saul was the chosen one to reign over Israel. Samuel informed Saul that he intended to honor him by having Saul and his servant dine with him. Saul's response reveals a man of humble character—he knew his place in the culture and society as an ordinary man unworthy of such honor (v. 21). Throughout the banquet that followed, Samuel lavished upon Saul great hospitality and honor (vv. 22-24), and on the following day, carved out a private moment to speak to him about what God had in mind. What had started out as a search for his father's donkeys was about to take Saul on a journey that he never would have predicted.

LIFE STEP

What does God look for in a person destined for notoriety and leadership? In Saul's case, there is conflicting evidence about his spiritual qualifications, as we will read later. At least we can deduce that Saul did not have an entitlement attitude, as if his impressive physical traits warranted special honor. Let this be a lesson for you today. Seek God's help in developing the inner person as a humble servant and trust Him to take you where He chooses. Whether in a place of great notoriety or a position behind the scenes, seek to serve faithfully. Never seek to exalt your own position.

What is the writer saying?

How can I apply this to my life?

Try to put yourself in Saul's place. While simply fulfilling your obligations as a son, you encounter a man of God who informs you that you are to become your country's first king. It wasn't a position you had ever considered or even dreamed of, since there had never before been a king in your nation. To bring all of God's plans for Saul to pass, Samuel first performed a private ceremony in which he anointed Saul's head with oil—a symbolic way of demonstrating God's divine choice in setting Saul apart for this purpose (v. 1). Then, Samuel instructed Saul to expect three separate divine appointments that were filled with details to affirm this anointing of God upon the man, Saul. First, he would learn that his father's donkeys had been located, but his father was now worried about Saul (v. 2). Then, a group of men would meet him while he was on the road and would offer him three loaves of bread, which he would receive (vv. 3-4). Following that, Saul would join a group of prophets near a Phillistine outpost along the way. These prophets would be prophesying and playing musical instruments, and Saul would begin prophesying with them as the Spirit of God came upon him (v. 6). Upon being filled with the Spirit, Samuel said, "You will be turned into another man." Saul's duty when these things happened was to do as the situation demanded and to trust God's divine hand of leadership (v. 7). In addition, Saul was to travel to Gilgal and wait seven days for Samuel's arrival, where he would receive further instructions. The text tells us of the transformation that God brought about in Saul's life (v. 9), as God "gave him another heart." The meaning behind this miraculous transformation is centered on the trajectory of Saul's interests hereafter. Whereas before meeting with Samuel Saul was concerned about lost donkeys, he left Samuel's presence as a young man now prepared to prophesy with the prophets.

LIFE STEP

Saul became another man when he was filled with the Spirit of God. Do you realize that the Bible says the same thing about you as a child of God? Yes, if you've received God's gift of salvation through faith in Jesus Christ, you are a "new creation." We have the promise in 2 Corinthians 5:17 that old things are passed away and all things are made new! Rejoice in this truth. Write down one way that you sense the newness of the transformed life in Christ. If you've never made the choice to receive God's gift of salvation, now is the time.

What is the writer saying?

How can I apply this to my life?

Samuel is an example of selfless service as a prophet and judge. In this reading, Samuel put his track record as Israel's prophet and judge before the people and asked them to point out any deficiency, error, or wrongdoing he may have done. He reminded them that he even took his sons out of the priestly service because of the complaints of the people and the sons' obvious failure to represent God faithfully. Recall that it was the ungodly practices of his sons, coupled with the fact that Samuel had grown old, that led to the people's demand for a king (1 Samuel 8:1-5). The people responded to Samuel's speech by acknowledging his faithfulness. In their eyes, Samuel's conduct had been above reproach (v. 4). Verses 6-12 serve as a historical summary of Israel's history from Moses to the present time of the judges, culminating in verse 12 with the cry from the people for a king over them.

Samuel presented Saul to them as their king and challenged them about their future actions under the king. Obedience would lead to blessings, but disobedience (*rebellion*) would put them in opposition to God—His hand would be against them (vv. 14-15). To validate his prophetic message, Samuel called upon the Lord to send thunder and rain at a season (wheat harvest) that was normally extremely dry in Israel (vv. 17-18). When the Lord brought the rain and thunder that day, the people realized they had sinned against God in seeking a king and begged Samuel to intercede for them (v. 19). The people were concerned with what they had already done, while Samuel was cautioning them about the consequences of what they might do! If the people and their king continued to do wrong, they would be swept away. But the Lord would not reject His people (v. 22). Neither would Samuel refuse to pray for the people.

LIFE STEP

Like the Israelites who called for a king, maybe you realize you've messed up. Confess it and forsake it! If you've confessed your disobedience and sins, count on God to forgive those sins. Give thanks to the Lord that you, too, can make a fresh start today. Then, commit yourself to unwavering obedience in the moment and down the road. Recite the Apostle Paul's statement of commitment found in Philippians 3:13-14. Be consistent in pressing toward the goal of obedience to God's call as a follower of Christ.

What is the writer saying?

How can I apply this to my life?

PRAY For God to provide additional financial resources to meet the worldwide needs of the ministry of Word of Life.

Saul assumed his role as Israel's king in the face of threatening enemies like the Philistines. After a few years of leading the nation, he raised up a "professional" army of three thousand warriors which was the first such army in Israel's history (as opposed to the militia previously serving). His son, Jonathan, commanded a force of one thousand men against the Philistine garrison in Geba, arousing the interests of the larger Philistine army. Up to this point, Israel had been tolerated by the Philistines, who had for many years made subjects of the Israelites. They had even prevented Israel from manufacturing iron weapons (see 1 Samuel 13:19-22) lest they arm themselves with swords and spears. This explains why Israel's army, when faced with the much larger and better equipped army of the Philistines (vv. 5-7), hid themselves while trembling in fear.

Recall that during Samuel's anointing of Saul as the future king (1 Samuel 10:8) two years prior, Saul was told to wait for Samuel to join him at Gilgal to make sacrificial offerings and to show Saul what he must do. Faced with overwhelming odds against his army and the steady decline in morale while waiting at Gilgal, Saul faced a leadership crisis. Under the pressures of the moment, he chose to offer sacrifices to God, assuming the role of priest as well as king—a clear violation of God's standards and rejection of Samuel's instructions (vv. 8-9). Samuel arrived as the offering was completed. He immediately sought an explanation as to what Saul had done, and hearing Saul's efforts at rationalizing his sin, called him out. Because of his foolish actions, God would bring an end to Saul's reign and another man would take his place (vv. 13-14). Though he reigned another twenty years, God's stamp of approval on Saul was removed.

LIFE STEP

What does it take to put your faith on trial? Is it fear of loss of social standing with unsaved friends who may mock you and your God? Is it the first sign of trouble ahead that causes you to abandon godly wisdom while seeking a "better" way out of your trouble? Use Saul's example to learn a lesson. Obstacles and trials are opportunities to stand fast with God or to "cut and run" toward your own ways. Rationalizing your sin with the urgency of your trial is no excuse, just as it didn't hold water in Saul's situation. Take Moses' advice to Joshua as your rallying cry (Joshua 1:9). Stand firm.

What is the writer saying?

How can I apply this to my life?

Saul's leadership as Israel's king grew, as did his army. Verses 47-52 summarize the success God granted Saul in establishing his kingdom, including his ability to harass (but not conquer) the many enemies they faced and the family members that were part of his kingdom. Note that Saul had a knack for identifying and recruiting valiant men to join his army (v. 52).

Chapter 15 finds Samuel on the scene again, reminding Saul that God had sent him (Samuel) to anoint Saul as king. Thus, Saul was to heed the word of the Lord that Samuel was delivering. Saul was told to attack and utterly destroy the Amalekites, long-time enemies of the Israelites dating back to the days of their exodus from Egypt. God singled these people out for destruction because they had savagely attacked the Jewish ranks from the rear while they journeyed out of Egypt toward the Promised Land (Deuteronomy 25:17-19). Saul gathered his forces and attacked the Amalekites but failed to follow God's instructions to "utterly destroy" them. The rough translation of this term is *put under the ban*, signifying a thing especially devoted to God. Because of their savagery against His people more than four hundred years ago, God claimed the Amalekites as dedicated to destruction. By keeping the Amalekite King Agag alive along with the best of the sheep, oxen, and other livestock, Saul committed a grievous sin for which he would pay dearly (v. 9). God spoke to Samuel of His regrets over making Saul king. What Saul counted as partial obedience, God counted as rebellion. The burden Samuel felt over the word of the Lord caused him to weep all night (v. 11).

LIFE STEP

Look at your conduct in light of God's Word. Even if you haven't yet gained a thorough understanding of God's will for your life as a believer, you can obey what you know. This surely includes taking steps to get to know Him better by studying His Word (2 Timothy 2:15). Feed the habits that will help you grow in grace and in the knowledge of our Lord (2 Peter 3:17-18). Starve the habits that draw you away from obedience to God's direction for your life, found only in His Word. Don't try to rationalize partial obedience as "good enough."

What is the writer saying?

How can I apply this to my life?

In today's reading, we see the sad picture of a man whose pridefulness has blinded him to the truth about his sin. Saul had departed toward Gilgal and erected a monument to himself to draw attention to his leadership in defeating the Amalekites. Already, it is evident that Saul viewed himself as worthy of honor, rather than God. When Saul noticed Samuel's arrival, he greeted him with more self-deception, claiming to have obediently performed God's commandment concerning the Amalekites (v. 13). Samuel's response (v. 14) shows that the evidence of Saul's disobedience was plain as day—the sound (and probably smells) of livestock that were supposed to have been destroyed.

Rather than come clean with Samuel about his sin, Saul continued his blatant denials (v. 15). He offered the excuse that the people had spared these animals.

He tried to justify his actions (*spared the* best *of the sheep and oxen)* and his motivations as pure (*to sacrifice to the Lord your God).* The fact that Saul did not refer to the Lord as "my God" reveals how far his pride had taken him. In fact, it could be said that Saul viewed himself as his own god, even to the point of justifying his rejection of God's direct commands. Samuel responded with truth to counter Saul's deception. Having been anointed by God to a place of prominence when Saul viewed himself as nothing (v. 17), he now saw himself as bigger than God.

Samuel's reply is a classic lesson for Christians. God desires obedience, not sacrifice (v. 22). A heart of rebellion offends our holy God as much as wicked practices like witchcraft and idolatry (v. 23). As a result of Saul's rebellion, God would strip him of his leadership and give it to another (vv. 26-28).

LIFE STEP *Today's passage serves as a great reminder that obedience is better than sacrifice. Remember that true worship of God begins with surrender. It's not about what you do that justifies you before a holy God. It's about your heart. It's about your inward commitment to the King of kings. Is yours a heart of obedience, or a rebellious heart? Read Psalm 51:16-17 as a prayer to God. Speak to Him about developing a heart of obedience.*

What is the writer saying?

How can I apply this to my life?

PRAY South Africa – For believers within the government to apply biblical principles in solving problems.

Here we read of God's sovereign choice to anoint David, a lowly shepherd boy, as king over Israel. God instructed Samuel to travel to Bethlehem, to the house of Jesse, with anointing oil ready to honor one of Jesse's sons as the next king, whom God had chosen. As Jesse paraded seven of his sons before Samuel (vv. 6-10), God rejected each in turn. Recall that God had previously identified the key trait He wanted in Saul's replacement, declaring that He would take the kingdom from Saul and give it to a *man after His (God's) own heart* (1 Samuel 13:14). So it was that in the meeting with Jesse and his sons that God spoke to Samuel, reminding him not to look at the man's outward appearance as man normally sees. *"For man looks at the outward appearance, but the Lord looks at the heart" (v. 7).*

When, at Samuel's prompting, Jesse's youngest son, David, was brought into the picture, God told Samuel to anoint him, *for this is the one (v. 12)!* Without explaining his actions, Samuel anointed young David and the Spirit of the Lord came upon David (v. 13). Just as the Spirit of God came upon the young lad who would one day be king, Saul experienced the departure of God's Spirit (v. 13) and the distressing influence of an evil spirit. Since we know that God does not dispense evil (James 1:13 and 17), it is best to view the distressing spirit as a passive "allowance" from God. Absent God's indwelling influence on Saul, Saul became open territory for evil influences to captivate his heart and direct his actions. Saul's heart, unfortunately, had turned him away from the Lord and made him vulnerable to evil influences.

LIFE STEP

David is known as a man after God's own heart. Read Psalm 139:23-24 right now to get a glimpse of David's heart. He desired to have a clean heart. He knew that what was within his heart made all the difference in God's eyes. Pray Psalm 139:23-24 back to the Lord. Make it a regular habit to seek God's illumination of any evil or sin in your life. Remember that God looks on the heart of man, not on the outward appearance.

What is the writer saying?

How can I apply this to my life?

This is probably the best-known chapter from 1 Samuel. In verses 1-3, we see the opposing sides across a valley from each other, the valley being a strategic location allowing access to Israel's hill country. In those days, it was not uncommon for two warring armies to each select one man, a *champion*, to represent their side. Rather than exposing all the men to the risks of battle, the champions would fight it out, and the losing side would be subject to the will of the victorious side. Goliath, the champion of the Philistines, was almost ten feet tall, with his heavy coat of mail alone weighing 125 pounds or more. Recall that giants occupied portions of the land assigned by God to the Israelites. A race of giants known as the Anakin were still in the land when Joshua led the Israelites to their conquest of the land (Joshua 11:22). Goliath was likely a descendant of these giants. He hollered across the valley with taunts that brought great fear in the hearts of Saul and his army (vv. 8-11).

David, meanwhile, had been alternating between his place as Jesse's son, the shepherd boy, and the harpist for King Saul. At the same time, Jesse's three oldest sons were among Saul's warriors cowering in their places in the valley along with the rest of Israel's fighting force. We learn that the challenge from the Phillistine champion, Goliath, had gone on for forty days at this point (v. 16). The scene is now set for David to appear on the battlefront, where he would display his courage and his heart for God.

LIFE STEP

Does the "giant" confronting you seem too formidable for you? Do you find yourself trembling in fear and anxiety by this giant problem or challenge? Remember that nothing is too hard for God, and no enemy or obstacle you face is greater than God (Jeremiah 32:17; 1 John 4:4). Give your giant problem to the Lord and confront the problem, whatever it is, as He directs. There is an answer in His Word. Ask for direction. Ask for courage. Trust God.

211

What is the writer saying?

How can I apply this to my life?

PRAY South Korea – Pray for continued blessing on the Korean church and its remarkable commitment to fervent prayer and a broad missions vision.

In our passage today we catch a view of how the shepherd boy, David, differed from all the men who were on Israel's battle lines confronting Goliath. Jesse, David's father, instructed him to travel to the battlefield to check on his brothers and to bring them some provisions. Taking off the next morning after arranging for the care of his sheep (v. 20), David arrived just as the two armies gathered on either side of the great valley. Just as had been their practice for more than a month, the two armies hurled insults and threats at one another (v. 20). David left his provisions in the care of the supply keeper and ran to the army to greet his brothers. There, he heard Goliath yelling his insults and taunts against the army of Israel and saw Israel's army cowering in fear (vv. 23-24). He also heard that Saul was offering rewards for the man who would take on Goliath and bring him down in battle (v. 25).

David then stepped up with a bold question that revealed his heart for God (v. 26).
- While the army of Israel referred to Goliath as this man, David referred to him as this uncircumcised Phillistine.
- While they viewed Goliath as coming to defy Israel, David saw him as one who would defy the armies of the living God!
- When Israel's army talked of the reward for the man who kills him, David saw the spiritual value of killing Goliath to take away the reproach from Israel.

Even when David's brother, Eliab, accused him falsely of arrogance and pretense in posing these questions (v. 28), David held his ground and insisted, "*Is there not a cause?*" To David, the answer was obvious. God's honor must be protected, and he was prepared to silence the giant!

LIFE STEP

Notice that David was careful to put his sheep in the care of a substitute and to have a supply keeper in charge of the provisions he brought from home. He fulfilled his duties and assignments. He wasn't careless. What has God given you to protect and watch over? Even in the excitement and distractions of confronting your giants, be faithful as you carry out your responsibilities.

What is the writer saying?

How can I apply this to my life?

PRAY — Nigeria – For churches and youth ministries to reach the nearly 1,400,000 children orphaned by AIDS.

King Saul heard of this young man who had the boldness to make a plea for God's honor. For the first time in the narrative, David personally took on the responsibility of taking out this giant (v. 32). Imagine how Saul's countenance must have fallen when he sent for David and discovered that a mere teenager with no military experience and no real hope for success (v. 32-33) was the one who volunteered. It is clear that Saul was still viewing the situation through the lens of a man, while David saw things from God's perspective. David defended his role as the one to take out Goliath, telling Saul of his experience as a shepherd defending his sheep from both a bear and a lion. He had confidence that, just as God had delivered him from these dangerous animals, God would also give him victory over the Phillistine giant (v. 37).

Saul's efforts to enhance David's chances of success were futile, as David eventually laid aside the armor Saul had given him to use in the battle. Instead of the king's armor and a sword, David went out to meet Goliath armed with his staff, his sling, and five smooth stones. As Goliath saw David approach, he expressed his disgust at being challenged by a mere boy (v. 43) and his intentions to kill David. David's reply (vv. 45-47) demonstrated again his heart for God's glory as well as his firm belief that Goliath was as good as dead! The source of his confidence was clearly not his own strength or ability, but the secret weapon that only a follower of Almighty God could claim: *for the battle is the Lord's, and He will give you into our hands!*

LIFE STEP — *Two key factors point to David's success in this narrative, and both serve as reminders for Christians of all ages. Believe God and trust God. Regardless of the challenges you may face, God is able. No matter how badly you may want to "cut and run" in the face of hard decisions or circumstances, you cannot go wrong by trusting God. He will equip you for the battles you face when you trust Him.*

What is the writer saying?

How can I apply this to my life?

PRAY   Philippines – For effective outreach to youth through evangelistic sporting events.

As the giant started toward David, David ran to meet him. Reaching into his pouch, David calmly drew out a single stone, placed it into his sling, and let loose the stone toward the giant's unprotected head. The stone hit its mark, lodging in Goliath's forehead and causing his collapse, face down to the ground. Then, to finish the job, David ran to Goliath's body, pulled Goliath's sword out of its sheath, and killed the giant. He then cut off Goliath's head (vv. 49-51).

Seeing their champion defeated created chaos among the Phillistine army. They fled before the men of Israel and Judah, but the Israelites chased them along the way and defeated them before returning to the Phillistine camp to gather the plunder. Seeing David return to his own tent to remove his armor, Saul asked his army commander, Abner, of David's family lineage. Whether or not Saul recognized David at this point is uncertain. It is possible that David's role as a harpist in Saul's court (1 Samuel 16:17-23) had been fulfilled behind a veil, or that David's appearance had changed since he first started playing the harp for the king. The question Saul posed indicates a desire to know the identity of David's father. Since Saul had offered his daughter in marriage to the one who defeated the giant (1 Samuel 17:25), his question may be viewed as a natural step toward fulfilling that promise. Abner brought David before the king, where Saul asked him directly, "Whose son are you?"

LIFE STEP

Take note that David took Goliath down with the most basic of tools. A slingshot in that day was not the most technically advanced weaponry available, but it was what David knew, and he used it expertly. You, too, can be an effective servant of God by making use of what you've been given. Make your commitment now that you will trust God to empower you for what He calls you to. Then, use what you have to get to it! You don't need a miracle or something new if God is in it.

What is the writer saying?

How can I apply this to my life?

PRAY Macedonia – Pray for an end to racial and ethnic tensions through a vibrant and growing Church.

David's success over Goliath launched his rise to popularity and "stardom" in the eyes of the people of Israel. After David was made a permanent member of Saul's court (v. 2), he and Saul's son, Jonathan, became close friends (vv. 1, 3-4). Saul sent David out on raids of the Philistines, where he again proved himself a capable warrior—so capable in fact that the women of the cities of Israel lauded David as more successful than even King Saul (vv. 6-7). Unable to handle this blow to his ego and vexed by a distressing spirit because God had removed His Spirit's influence from Saul (1 Samuel 16:14), the king grew desperately jealous and began viewing David with eyes of suspicion (vv. 8-9). While David played his harp one day, Saul threw a spear at David but missed. Whether his aim was bad or God supernaturally protected David, we cannot be sure. But we know that David escaped from Saul while making no effort to defend himself or fight back, even when Saul tried twice to strike him down! Clearly, David was content to trust God's hand in this, again demonstrating his heart for God.

Verse 12 adds to the sad truth of Saul's spiritual decline and God's ongoing judgment of the king. David enjoyed the benefits of one who had the clear anointing of God, while Saul was sinking further into the pit of sin. Removing David from his court and sending him out as captain over his forces meant removing the best source of godly influence available to him (v. 13). David continued to grow in wisdom as the Lord blessed his efforts on every front, creating within Saul a sense of dread and fear of David. All the while, Saul was battling his feelings of fear, but the people loved David more and more.

LIFE STEP

Saul's decline as a spiritual leader came about as a result of his disobedience. He never recovered. Aren't you glad to know that God is gracious and forgiving toward those who come to Him? Thank God for second chances. Praise Him for His willingness to forgive your sins and for putting you on the right path again. If you sense that you're not there yet (on the right path), confess your sin to Him and trust Him to cleanse you of all unrighteousness (1 John 1:9).

215

What is the writer saying?

How can I apply this to my life?

PRAY Bulgaria – For freedom from the media and local government's constant attempts to obstruct any form of evangelical outreach or growth.

We see in today's passage how a word of truth spoken at the right time can help turn the tide of evil. Imagine the sense of horror Jonathan and Saul's servants must have felt when the king ordered them all to be complicit in killing David (v. 1). Recall that the servants loved David, as did Jonathan (1 Samuel 18:1-5). Jonathan went to David secretly, informing him of Saul's plot to take his life. He also proposed a plan to try to influence Saul to turn away from such thoughts (vv. 2-3). While standing out in the field with his father, Jonathan spoke truth to King Saul, reminding him that David was innocent of any evil. Furthermore, David had put his own life on the line in killing Goliath—a victory that Saul himself even celebrated at the time (vv. 4-5). Jonathan's words brought Saul back to his senses, and Saul promised to abandon his plans to kill David.

Unfortunately, Saul's sense of reason did not last. After David succeeded again in battles against the Philistines, Saul's jealousy got the better of him, and he tried once more to strike David with a spear (vv. 8-10). Again, David escaped and fled without being harmed. Still affected by jealous rage, Saul sent armed messengers to David's household where he lived with Michal, Saul's daughter. She refused to be part of her husband's murder and helped plan his getaway. Saul accused her of helping his enemy escape. Though she knew David was no threat to her father, Michal was compelled to lie to Saul, saying that David had threatened her life (vv. 13-17). David fled the area and went to Samuel at Ramah.

LIFE STEP — *Though Jonathan's influence was not long-lasting, he was nonetheless able to secure a change in direction from his father by bravely confronting the king with truth. Are you willing to step up and challenge someone with truth when they are about to do something evil or potentially harmful? Remember that we are accountable to our fellow believers to help keep one another from falling (Galatians 6:1).*

What is the writer saying?

How can I apply this to my life?

PRAY   Somalia – Pray for the believing minority who suffer great persecution and martyrdom.

Jonathan was unaware that his father had not kept his promise (1 Samuel 19:6) to stop trying to kill David. Imagine his surprise when David came to him and asked why Saul was still seeking his life! David proposed a reasonable test to see if Saul's intentions were good. He would stay away from the upcoming feast at the king's table (v. 5). Failure to come to this feast would be noticed and may be interpreted as a lack of support for the king. If Saul became upset, then they would know that Saul had evil plans. If it was not considered an issue to Saul, it would indicate his trust in David's loyalty, signaling to David that he need not fear. Having already pledged to support David (v. 4), Jonathan sought from David his assurance of favorable treatment for himself and his family in the future (vv. 13-15). Jonathan knew that David would be the king one day, and this was the Lord's doing.

Though he was the man in line to succeed King Saul, Jonathan didn't expect the kingship to be passed on to him. His life to this point had been marked by bravery (see 1 Samuel 14:12-14) and honorable conduct. He was the son of the king. But Jonathan brought his personal desires and expectations in line with what the Lord wanted. He would follow the Lord's agenda, not his own. If the Lord wanted David as king, so be it. His concern was that David, when he took the throne, would protect his family rather than eliminate all of Jonathan's sons, who may pose a threat to the new king. The two set up a method for Jonathan to signal David an "all-clear" or to show that there was a problem (vv. 19-23).

LIFE STEP

Jonathan's willingness to set aside his wants and expectations in favor of God's will is a trait worthy of imitation. Can you say this about yourself—that you are more concerned with following God's desires than your own? Are you ready to put your "yes" on the table and sincerely give God whatever He wants from you? Do that right now. If you sincerely want God to be glorified in your life, surrender your will to Him. Let Him give you direction and follow Him obediently.

What is the writer saying?

How can I apply this to my life?

PRAY   France – For American missionaries to overcome stereotypes and prejudices by reflecting Christ's love.

Saul overlooked David's absence on the first day of the feast, assuming that David may have become ceremoniously unclean in some way, requiring a waiting period for cleansing (Leviticus 17:19-21). On day two, however, he wanted an answer. When Jonathan covered for David with the pre-arranged story, Saul blew his top! He wasn't buying it. In a fit of rage, Saul accused Jonathan of conspiring with David (vv. 30-31), even going so far as to hurl derogatory words at Jonathan, suggesting shame to his mother. Saul's outlook on the entire matter was clouded by his overriding desire to continue his royal dynasty, so he reminded Jonathan that if David was in the way, Jonathan would never be king. When Jonathan attempted to defend David and questioned Saul's intentions, he found himself a target of Saul's wrath in the form of a spear (vv. 32-33).

Jonathan left the feast and grieved for David, as it was now obvious that the time had come to warn David to flee from Saul. The next morning, he arose and went out into the field with his bow and arrows and a young boy to help him. He delivered the news to David through the signal they had agreed upon (1 Samuel 20:20-22). After the young boy left, he and David secretly said their goodbyes. Verse 42 reflects Jonathan's hope that he and David and their households would again enjoy God's favor as they honored one another, now and even beyond their lifetimes.

LIFE STEP

It's a sad scene presented by the king trying to kill his own son, but that just shows how depraved our hearts can be when we aren't yielded to the Lord. The desire of our hearts must be to bring honor and glory to God, not to exalt ourselves or protect our status in the world we live in. Ask yourself this question: What is the driving force in my life? If it's anything other than to magnify God with your obedience and submission, some things need to change. Be honest with yourself and with God.

What is the writer saying?

How can I apply this to my life?

PRAY

Praise God for giving us a living hope through the resurrection of Jesus Christ.

Following Saul and Jonathan's death, Saul's son, Ishbosheth, began to reign over the northern tribes of Israel and David ruled over Judah. With the assassination of Ishbosheth (2 Samuel 4:5-8), we see another shake up of leadership that ultimately led to David's anointing for the third time as king, but this time as king over a united kingdom. Chapter 5 opens with the ten tribes of Israel *(representing the northern kingdom, formerly led by Ishbosheth)* coming to David at Hebron to ally themselves as one nation and to serve under David's leadership. They appealed to David based on their common kinship, his prior military expertise under King Saul, and God's calling as communicated by the prophet Samuel (vv. 1-2). Note that God's calling for David to be king happened when he was approximately age 15 (see 1 Samuel 16:11-13), so his preparation for leadership lasted 15 years before he became Israel's king. All in God's timing, the tribes of Israel were willing again to come under the same covenant of leadership.

Shortly after this, David decided to move his capital from Hebron to Jerusalem, which was still occupied by the Jebusites who were never conquered when Joshua brought the Israelites successfully into the land of Canaan (Joshua 15:63). Despite the overconfident taunts of the Jebusites (v. 6), David's army managed to take the city and he began to fortify the city with various construction projects (v. 9). The city, which was hereafter known as the *City of David*, was well-suited as Israel's capital because of its natural defenses and its geographic location. In addition, the city had no prior association with any of the tribal families of Israel, thus offering a neutral site to help unite all of Israel under a single banner of leadership. Verse 10 summarizes David's continued rise to greatness because of God's guiding presence.

LIFE STEP

Whatever God has in store for you, whether it be great or small, be patient and wait on Him. Like David, don't exalt yourself or try to push the timetable without asking God and following His direction. He'll bring things to pass according to His plan if you will simply remain faithful and patient. What changes might be appropriate in your life that would serve to help you in this area?

What is the writer saying?

How can I apply this to my life?

David's prosperity as Israel's king grew as he reigned in Jerusalem and strengthened the nation as God's ordained leader. As we get to Chapter 9, we see David's compassion toward Jonathan's lone surviving son, Mephibosheth, who was accidentally dropped by his caretaker at age 5 and, as a result, was lame in his legs (2 Samuel 4:4). Recall that David and Jonathan had a deep bond of friendship that was sealed with the promise we saw in 1 Samuel 20:14-17. There, as they tried to figure out how to handle Saul's efforts to kill David, Jonathan sought David's pledge to keep his household in mind and treat them with favor when he became king. This would not be the norm for kings and those involved in power shifts of that day, as the normal policy would be to kill all the male offspring of the deposed king to end all threats to the new king. Jonathan knew David would be king one day, and his unqualified request could be considered a call for mercy.

When David learned that Mephibosheth was alive, he called for him. When he arrived, Mephibosheth most likely expected to be executed. Instead, as he bowed on his face toward David, the king gave him reassuring words flowing from his love for Jonathan and his heart of compassion (v. 7). David arranged for Ziba, one of Saul's servants, to become caretaker over all of Saul's lands that should have fallen to Mephibosheth. Meanwhile, David had Mephibosheth, along with his young son, join him continually at his house to eat at the king's table like one of the king's sons (vv. 11-13).

LIFE STEP

David showed true leadership, compassion, and integrity as a promise-keeper. He was perfectly willing to honor the commitment made to Jonathan in showing kindness to Mephibosheth even when it was out of step with the culture and norms of the day. How about you and your commitments? Are you faithful to follow up with what you've pledged, promised, or committed to? Thank the Lord for being a promise-keeping God. Recommit yourself to keep your word, too.

What is the writer saying?

How can I apply this to my life?

PRAY Pray for opportunities to witness to your unsaved friends and loved ones.

Up to this point we have read of David's many good and godly traits, including the way in which God viewed him as *a man after His own heart* (1 Samuel 13:14). But today's reading shows us that even a godly, successful man can foolishly feed his fleshly desires rather than walking in step with God's desires for purity and righteousness. Over the years, David's desire to gratify his lust led him to have multiple wives *(eight wives are named in Scripture)* and numerous concubines (2 Samuel 5:13). In today's reading, we see a number of wrong choices that presented a perfect opportunity for the desires of his flesh to lead him from opportunity, to temptation, and to sin compounded by even more sin:

In verse 1 we're told it was a time when kings go off to war. David was not with his warriors, an expected duty, but was at home instead. He set himself up for temptation.

In verse 2, likely Bathsheba expected that she was in a secluded, private spot. David

didn't look away. He allowed his eyes to linger. He allowed temptation to gain a foothold and grow into lust in his heart.

In verse 3, David took an active step toward sin (rather than away from it) by inquiring about who this beautiful woman was and sending someone to fetch her. Obviously, David was not "falling" into sin. He was actively pursuing it.

In verse 4, David culminated his pursuit of sinful gratification by sleeping with Bathsheba. His un-checked lust led him to adultery.

Finding that Bathsheba was pregnant by him, David had Uriah called back from the front. He made a way for Uriah to sleep with his wife *(twice)*, hoping that everyone would conclude that the baby was Uriah's (vv. 5-8, 12-13).

David's departure from wisdom and obedience started with unrestrained desires and ended up with adultery and, as we will see tomorrow, murder of an innocent man.

LIFE STEP

David's example shows us that the battle for purity and righteousness is a moment-by-moment, day-to-day battle. Victory over temptation and sin today doesn't guarantee victory tomorrow. Don't enter the battle without arming yourself with a solid battle plan and God's full armor (Ephesians 6:13-17). Build a habit of turning away from temptations, rather than toward them. Write down one positive step you will take to help you avoid falling to temptation.

WEDNESDAY - WEEK 29

What is the writer saying?

How can I apply this to my life?

Now faced with the realization that he could not obtain cover for Bathsheba's pregnancy, David sent Uriah back to the battlefront with a sealed letter to Joab, the commander. In his letter, David effectively ordered Joab to have Uriah murdered by placing him at the hottest spot of the battle and then withdrawing from him (vv. 14-15). It's an amazing turnabout to see the king ordering the murder of one his most noble warriors, but that is in fact what we see. When he received the note delivered by the loyal servant, Uriah, Joab did as he was ordered, and Uriah died in the battle (v. 17). Joab then assigned a messenger to deliver the news to King David but prompted the messenger to be prepared for criticism from the king. Apparently, Joab had concerns that a man who would order the murder of another may also be unwilling to accept foolish military tactics as his own design (vv. 18-21).

David's response in verse 25 is, in effect, "Oh well, that's war, and these things happen," proclaiming coldly that such things are to be expected. Following the normal mourning period for a widow of one to four weeks, Bathsheba became David's wife and bore his son. David thought he had his bases covered. No one would know. There is no way to be sure, but it is likely that even Bathsheba did not know of David's role in her husband's death. But the final phrase of verse 27 is key: What David had done displeased the Lord. God always knows our actions and our motivations.

LIFE STEP

Galatians 6:7 tells us not to be deceived because God is not mocked—a man reaps what he sows. We can't knowingly and callously commit sin and expect that God is unaware or doesn't care. Confess your sin to God now. Don't wait until He chastens you or till someone else points it out to you.

What is the writer saying?

How can I apply this to my life?

While David had failed to heed the promptings of the Holy Spirit in his life that should have driven him from his temptations, he would not be able to avoid God's message through Nathan the prophet. The message came in the form of a story about a rich man who had many flocks but chose to take from another man his only little ewe lamb to offer as a meal for a traveler that had arrived (vv. 1-4). Nathan portrayed this transgression in vivid contrasts, highlighting how plentiful were the resources of the rich man, while the poor man had only this ewe lamb, which he loved as a daughter (v. 3). David became incensed at hearing this and demanded that the man who did such a thing should die and should be required to repay the poor man four times more than he took. David's reaction would have exceeded the normal punishment for such a sinful action in calling for the death of the rich man but matched precisely the fourfold requirement for taking the lamb (Exodus 22:1). Nathan blurted out, "You are the man!" As a result of his sin:

- David's house would be continually wrecked by violence within his family (v. 10)
- One of David's own sons would take his wives and do publicly what David had done secretly (vv. 11-12).
- The enemies of the Lord now had reason to blaspheme the Lord after seeing the evil David brought into his leadership, since he was no better than they were (v. 14).
- The child of David and Bathsheba would die (v. 14).

Unlike Saul, who explained away his sin (1 Samuel 15:24), David saw his sin as primarily against the Lord (Psalm 51:4). Psalm 51 records David's confession and Psalm 32 rejoices in His forgiveness.

LIFE STEP

"Be sure your sins will find you out." Those words from Moses to those whom he led into the land of Canaan (Numbers 32:23) are instructive for all believers. David's encounter with Nathan was the moment he was confronted with his sinfulness. Your unconfessed sin will find you out, too. Be sensitive to sin and confess it right away. Confess it, forsake it, and be restored in your fellowship with God (1 John 1:9).

What is the writer saying?

How can I apply this to my life?

PRAY Honduras – For God to provide the teaching staff and funding needed to keep Bible schools operating.

When David's son by Bathsheba was stricken with illness, David begged God for mercy. He fasted. He prayed. He laid himself out on the ground all night in humility before the Lord. Even David's closest of advisors *(elders)* could not convince him to get up and have some food (vv. 16-17). Hearing his servants' whispers as they conferred together about how to bring David the heartbreaking news of the child's death, David perceptively asked them directly if he had died (v. 19). Hearing their answer, David arose, washed himself, changed his clothes, and went to the house of the Lord to worship. Then he went home and requested that food be brought for him to eat. His servants were perplexed by his actions. They asked how it could be that David mourned and fasted while the child was alive but arose and ate when the child was dead (v. 21). His reply was simple. He threw himself on God's mercy in prayer and fasting while the life of his child was in the balance, hoping for a gracious change in God's intentions. When it became clear that God's decree would be fulfilled, David no longer saw the option of God's mercy in the matter. All he could do, and what he was committed to do, was worship God and long for the day when he would see his child again (v. 23).

Does this passage mean that children who die will go to heaven? Though the evidence may not be ironclad, this passage appears to offer real hope that, in the hereafter, born again parents will be able to be with their children who have died. It is best to look at God's sovereignty and grace as sufficient for our trust in His goodness in bringing into His eternal state those children who die before possessing the ability to know right from wrong. This "age of accountability," though a popular concept among Christians, is not specifically addressed in Scripture.

LIFE STEP

Even when faced with the prediction of God's judgment that would take his son's life, David remained hopeful. He did not have assurance that God would change His mind about his son, but he prayed and fasted anyway. It may be that you need David's attitude of prayer and total submission to God's will in the face of difficult circumstances. Even in the toughest of times—even when everyone says there's no use—you can ask God for mercy and grace.

What is the writer saying?

How can I apply this to my life?

The consequences of David's sin with Bathsheba now become reality in chapters 13-18. David's oldest son, Amnon, raped his younger half-sister, Tamar (Chapter 13). Tamar's full brother is Absolom, the third eldest of David's sons (2 Samuel 3:2-3). David failed to assertively reprove Amnon for his sin, and Absalom brought revenge upon Amnon two years later by having his half-brother killed (2 Samuel 13:28-29). As a result of his actions, Abasalom was banished from David's court. While he was exiled for three years, David continually mourned for Absalom every day, longing to see him again. Chapter 15 picks up with Absalom back in Jerusalem, thanks to intervention from Joab, the commander. David would not allow his son back into the court, but Absalom began secretly to build a following in hopes of taking the kingdom from David. He procured an entourage of 50 men to parade before him as he rode his chariot (v. 1). He curried favor among the visitors by offering to provide justice for their disputes, implying that David provided no resource for such justice (vv. 3-4). Verse 6 tells us of Absalom's success in stealing the hearts of the men of Israel.

When he felt the time was right, Absalom asked David for permission to go to Hebron under the pretense of a vow he'd made years before. David gave his consent. There, Absalom had invited two hundred guests, but these guests knew nothing of his plans. More significantly, he sent for Ahithophel, David's counsellor, who happened to be Bathsheba's grandfather (11:3 with 23:34). Absalom now felt as though everything was in place for him to be surrounded by prominent men of Israel, and to hear, "Absalom reigns in Hebron (v. 10)!" He planned for this to be viewed as a mere succession of leadership, rather than a rebellion.

LIFE STEP

Absalom's act of vengeance against his brother was just one step along a journey on the wrong path. Christians are called to be different from the rest of the world, and this is particularly true in the way we're to treat those who mistreat us. Though we may become angry at those who harm us or those we love, we aren't to seek vengeance. Rather, as the Apostle Paul says in Romans 15:19, we are to leave it to God. He has promised to provide the appropriate means of vengeance. Settle it now. Trust God to take care of avenging you in situations where you have been wronged.

What is the writer saying?

How can I apply this to my life?

PRAY Thailand – Pray for the Gospel to effectively permeate this culture of Buddhism, spiritism, and the occult.

David became a king on the run once Absalom's rebellion reached his ears (2 Samuel 15:13-17). Nathan's prophecies of 2 Samuel 12:11-12 were fulfilled as Absalom and his followers came into Jerusalem to occupy David's royal palace. However, Absalom made a great tactical mistake in rejecting Ahithophel's advice (2 Samuel 17:1-4) and taking the advice of another advisor who suggested he gather "all Israel" and attack David's camp later, rather than pursuing him right away (2 Samuel 17:7-14). This delay gave David's friends time to react to the rebellion (2 Samuel 18:1-4).

When Absalom's forces met up with David's in the forest of Ephraim (the location of which is unknown), Absalom was badly defeated, losing 20,000 men. In fact, more men died because of the forest terrain than by the sword (v. 8). Though we cannot be sure, this may have been due to the thick oaks, tangled brush, or other concealed hazards such as caverns or swamps. In his haste to escape, Absalom got stuck in the thick branches of a tree, possibly by the neck or his thick hair (v. 9). When one of Joab's men spotted Absalom dangling helplessly from the tree, he immediately reported this to Joab but refused to kill the king's son out of respect for David's instructions to "deal gently" with Absalom (v. 5). Joab, however, wasted no time arguing about his motives or even about the king's instructions. He killed Absalom and recalled the troops from fighting their brothers in Israel. Perhaps Joab reacted as he did out of regret for encouraging David to recall Absalom from exile in the first place (2 Samuel 14:19-21). More likely he reasoned that if he didn't kill the traitorous Absalom, many more innocent men would die.

LIFE STEP

Rather than honoring the God of David and of Israel, Absalom sought his own way and tried to exalt himself. His violent and dishonorable death seems a fitting end of a life devoted to selfish desires and rebellion against God and family. Take a moment to reflect on what may have happened had Absalom yielded himself to God's will rather than his own. Renew your commitment to following God's plan and path, rather than your own.

What is the writer saying?

How can I apply this to my life?

Joab was not always right in his actions, but in the aftermath of the defeat of Absalom's rebel forces Joab asserted himself effectively and appropriately by confronting the king about his lack of leadership. David had so much personal investment in his family and felt the loss of Absalom so deeply that he forgot about the sacrifices of the thousands of men who had fought for his kingdom. Verses 2-3 inform us that the people reentered the city in shame and mourning, rather than in celebration for their victory.

Such a scene called for prompt and forthright leadership, and Joab felt up to the task. He went to David and clarified the situation with words that surely stung the heart of the king. He reminded David that all his family would have likely perished if the rebellion of Absalom had not been put down (v. 5). Joab accused David of showing more love for his enemies than for all the loyal friends who had participated in David's defense. This kind of mourning and weeping was a disgrace to the people!

Joab's harsh words and the advice he rendered (v. 7) had the desired effect. David rose from his place and went out to the city gates, where he greeted the people who gathered to hear from him. While most of Israel's people thought of David's successes in the past (v. 9) and openly considered renewing their loyalty to him, the people of Judah were slower to respond. To pull his kingdom back together, David sent to the elders of Judah to appeal to their sense of kinship and to encourage their participation in restoring the king to his throne (vv. 11-12). Possibly some of the elders, due to their support of Absalom, feared reprisal from David.

LIFE STEP *Though David was the sovereign king over Israel and could have rejected Joab or even punished him for his words, he was at least humble enough to recognize the wisdom of Joab's counsel. Don't be like the fool, who thinks everything he does is right. Listen to advice (Proverbs 12:15). Ask God for guidance to know the wise way to handle your problems.*

What is the writer saying?

How can I apply this to my life?

PRAY   Pray for unity among the staff and the membership of your local church.

This passage demonstrates God's desire that promises made be kept. We must go back to the conquest of the Land, in the days of Joshua, to get the background. Joshua had led the Israelites to victories over Jericho and Ai and was advancing further into Canaan to take out other inhabitants of the land that God had given over to Israel (Joshua 8). The Gibeonites were among the people who were on the target list for Israel's conquest, and they heard what was coming. In desperation, the men of Gibeon disguised themselves as travelers from a faraway land and sought refuge among the Israelites (Joshua 9:3-15). God honored their desire for peaceful existence with Israel, and Joshua agreed to make them servants within their people instead of destroying them. For reasons unknown, king Saul in his day sent raiding parties to attack Gibeon, apparently to destroy them. We have nothing in Scripture to add more details to this event. Fast-forward to

the days of King David when a three-year famine arose in Israel, and we learn that God answered David's inquiry about the famine by pointing to Saul's treachery with the Gibeonites (2 Samuel 21:1).

David consulted the Gibeonites and agreed to their request for justice. Rather than "an eye for an eye" though, they sought a measured response that was considered gracious in those days. They did not ask for money or direct retribution. Instead, they asked that seven descendants of Saul be handed over to be hanged (vv. 4-6). When the executions were completed, Rizpah, the mother of two of the executed men, held a vigil over their hanging bodies. Hearing of this, David ordered men to retrieve the bones of Saul and Jonathan, along with the bodies of these seven descendants, for proper burial in their homeland (vv. 12-14). After that, God graciously brought an end to the famine.

LIFE STEP

God wants His people to keep their promises. Keep the principles of Scripture in your heart as you commit yourself to a specific action or promise (1 Peter 2:12). It's more than just a matter of integrity. It's bigger than simply proving yourself reliable and trustworthy. It's about honoring God by obeying His Word and representing Him well in a world that desperately needs a Savior.

What is the writer saying?

How can I apply this to my life?

PRAY   Poland – For the continued education and development of future church leadership.

It is believed that David wrote this song early in his flight from King Saul. It was included here as some of David's final words and is repeated almost word for word in Psalm 18 as a thanksgiving hymn. David drew from his many personal experiences as God's blessed servant, using multiple colorful titles for God as a way of praising Him for His mighty hand of blessing. Notice verse 2, for example, where he refers to God as *my rock, my fortress,* and *my deliverer.* Such metaphors provide a sense of strength, power, and protection--traits of God that certainly came to David's mind as he escaped from Saul's grasp on many occasions.

The use of the word, *horn,* in verse 3 is common for *strength,* found often in Hebrew literature as an image of the power, as in the strength possessed by bulls and oxen. David's trials and travails were, to him, like being enveloped in the raging seas, nearly drowning. He portrayed those times as nearly too much to bear, until he called upon the Lord and was saved. Verse 6 speaks of the *sorrows of Sheol,* words that suggest the wrapping of the dead in strips of cloth. It is as if David were saying, "I was so close to death that I was already in the coffin." The *temple* mentioned in verse 7 is not in reference to the Temple in Jerusalem, since that was not built in David's lifetime. Rather, it referred to heaven, the place of God's dwelling. God heard David's cries and responded quickly, bringing to bear His majesty and power to rescue David from his distress (vv. 8-9). David's poetic imagery included God's involvement with man, even as he descended from the heavens (vv. 10-11).

LIFE STEP   *It is good and proper to praise the Lord for His power, provision, and protection. Do you stop to consider how blessed you have been? Yes, there are trials and difficulties in everyone's life. But give God the glory for being the God who never leaves you. Express your thankfulness to God right now in a prayer of praise.*

What is the writer saying?

How can I apply this to my life?

PRAY Papua New Guinea – For the unity found in Christ to transcend ethnic differences among believers.

These are David's "last words" (v. 1), not necessarily in the sense of the words before his last breath, but last things he would publish. The psalm's header in verse 1 sees David as just an ordinary man, the son of Jesse, yet chosen *(anointed)* by God. David realized that his progression from shepherd boy to the sweet *psalmist of Israel* was God's doing and not attributable to anything of his own doing. In verses 2-3, David acknowledged that God gave him inspired words to utter. The essence of this inspiration is the same as described by the apostles Paul and Peter when referring to the inspiration of Scripture—that it is "breathed out" by God and written down by men (see 2 Timothy 3:16 and 2 Peter 1:21). The purpose of God's divine words to David was to guide him as a ruler over men (v. 4), a ruler whose justice is just as glorious as the sun rising to turn away the works of darkness.

Verse 5 is sometimes interpreted as a declarative statement and by others as a question, as if David were lamenting his own shortcomings in leadership. In either case, despite his failures, he rejoices in the benefits of the covenant relationship that God initiated with him—a covenant that remained firm and secure. Verses 6-7 speak of the downside of godless government, characterized by infliction of pain and worthy only to be chopped down and destroyed. Clearly, David recognized how God had blessed him by guiding him throughout his days as king over Israel.

LIFE STEP

David relied upon God's words to guide him. Do you? Will you? You will find all sorts of information from sources like online media or friends. The problem is that you can't trust everything you hear or read online, or what your friends may tell you. Remember to square your sources with the unchanging, uncompromising, Word of God. His Word is trustworthy—all the time.

What is the writer saying?

How can I apply this to my life?

PRAY   Czech Republic – Pray for young people to serve the Lord even in the face of serious opposition from family and friends.

Though the passage indicates that God (*He*, in 2 Samuel 24:1) motivated David to order a census, it is best to interpret this passage in the light of 1 Chronicles 21:1, which is a parallel account of this event. In that text, we read that Satan influenced David to do so. In either case, God allowed the king to order an accounting of all men of Israel of fighting age and readiness. Why? Some speculate that David was preparing for the transfer of power to Solomon, since the account in 1 Chronicles 21 is recorded just before David gave instructions to Solomon about building the temple. The request may also be viewed as David's attempt to assess the vast power of his kingdom, a signal that he had grown pridefully self-sufficient rather than relying on the Lord. Whatever the reason, David's commander, Joab, questioned the wisdom of this census (2 Samuel 24:3), but the demands of the king prevailed, and Joab ultimately came back with the number of war-ready men of Judah and Israel (vv. 8-9). David's conscience became sensitive to his sin almost immediately, and he prayed an honest prayer of confession to the Lord (v. 10). The sin he confessed was that of pride and self-sufficiency, and though he confessed it, the consequences would fall very soon. God sent the prophet, Gad, to deliver to David a choice of three consequences for David's transgression. David would choose between:

- Three years of famine in the land, or
- Three months of flight from pursuing enemies, or
- Three days of deadly plague upon the people.

David dreaded being chased by enemies again and chose the plague, knowing that the Lord is merciful. Still, 70,000 men died of the plague! As the angel prepared to bring the deadly plague into Jerusalem, the Lord restrained his hand and stopped the plague's progress. David saw what was happening and pleaded with God to spare the people and to lay the sin against him, as the people were innocent (v. 17).

LIFE STEP   *The sinfulness of national leaders often leads to deadly consequences for the innocent people of that nation. There is no better time than right now to pray for your leaders who govern your nation. Their choices may be good, bad, or neutral. The best hope you have is for them to pursue a pathway of God's design, rather than their own. Ask God to use these leaders for His glory.*

What is the writer saying?

How can I apply this to my life?

PRAY   Portugal – For the many counties that still have no evangelical congregations.

The location where David encountered the destroying angel was the threshing floor of Araunah, situated on the mountain identified in 2 Chronicles 3:1 as Mount Moriah, the same mountain upon which Abraham offered up Isaac as a sacrifice (Genesis 22:2). Solomon later chose this same site as the location of the magnificent Temple, known as Solomon's Temple (1 Chronicles 21:28-22:5).

As God's appointed messenger, the prophet Gad came to David and directed him to erect an altar to the Lord on this location, an act of atonement for his transgression (2 Samuel 24:18). David obediently approached the owner, Araunah, and offered to purchase the threshing floor for the purpose of making it a sacred place of worship. Demonstrating a sense of loyalty to the king and great respect for his mission, Araunah offered to give the property to David, along with his oxen for a sacrificial offering and the wooden threshing tools to build a fire (vv. 22-23). Then David uttered sweet words of wisdom that reflected his true heart for God (v. 24). *No, but I will surely buy it from you for a price; nor will I offer burnt offerings to the Lord my God with that which costs me nothing.* David's heartfelt desire was to honor God and make a sacrifice that would satisfy God's demand for righteousness, leading to forgiveness of sins. He knew that there is no sacrifice where there is no cost.

Once David built the altar on the site, having purchased it and the oxen at a price, he offered the sacrificial gift to the Lord and the Lord accepted David's prayer. The plague was withdrawn from Israel (v. 25).

LIFE STEP

"If you wish to gain, you must give something up." Maybe you've heard this as a truth statement from someone trying to encourage you to make sacrifices necessary to get ahead in a specific goal. Maybe it's attaining a new position or achieving a new level of expertise or knowledge. But in the spiritual sense, it's all about what you offer to God. Your devotion to God will cost you. Your maturity in Christ will cost you. Are you willing to pay the price? Don't offer to God that which costs you nothing. Whether time, money, or social acceptance, make yours a meaningful sacrifice.

What is the writer saying?

How can I apply this to my life?

PRAY South Africa – For national churches to commit financial aid to those seeking to attend Bible school.

Even those who serve the Lord faithfully may struggle with comparisons between the wicked, who seem to prosper, and God's faithful, who face struggles and trials. That is what Asaph, the writer of Psalm 73, is going through. He gets very personal and transparent in verse 2 by admitting that he almost stumbled because of his envy of the prosperity of the wicked people he observed around him.

What caused Asaph to voice his frustrations in such a way? His use of hyperbole (exaggeration for the sake of illustration) is obvious to most readers, since some wicked people do, in fact, suffer from their wickedness. But his lament to God is typical of Christians who become fixated with what is "fair" in this life. What he noticed is this:

- The wicked prosper and seem to get away with their wickedness (v. 4).
- They seem to be free from the troubles of other men (v. 5)

- They walk about all puffed up and proud, as if they are immune from God's judgment; they have full confidence in themselves (v. 6).
- They have more than their hearts could wish for (v. 7).
- They make fun of and ridicule the godly, even going so far as to question openly God's ability to judge them (vv. 8-9).
- They cause others to doubt God, as if God does not take notice of or bring consequences on the wicked (vv. 10-11).
- Their lives seem to be filled with riches and ease (v. 12).

Asaph wonders whether his dedication to cultivate a clean and pure heart has been in vain, since he feels the trials of life in a very real way. Interestingly, verse 1 is his "truth statement" that brings him back to the reality that living a godly life brings eternal rewards. God's goodness is measured in more than material prosperity.

LIFE STEP

Comparisons can lead Christians down a dangerous path, creating feelings of discontent and distress when our eyes shift away from God's goodness to the goodness enjoyed by others. When you find yourself looking around and comparing with others the level of "things" you possess, think of Hebrews 13:5. Contentment is a good thing. Talk to God in prayer today, acknowledging His goodness. Even when things don't go as you would like, trust Him to meet your needs. Stop making comparisons.

What is the writer saying?

How can I apply this to my life?

Asaph realized his thinking was all wrong. What about his obligation to the generation to come (v. 15)? Someone must stay true to God for their sake. How else will they know God's way? Notice what brought him around in his thinking—he went into God's Sancturary, the temple (v. 17). There, in quiet reflection and personal time with the Lord, his thoughts came around to God's truth.

Throughout the remainder of the psalm, he declares God's justice in bringing the wicked to judgment (vv. 18-20, 27). He acknowledges his foolishness in questioning God (vv. 21-22) and professes his unwavering confidence in God's presence and provision in the present day and in the life to come (vv. 23-24).

Asaph closes this psalm with a beautiful declaration of his hope in God (vv. 25-28). The eternal, all-knowing, all-powerful God is his greatest hope, his strength and his portion (provision). Nothing he might wish for in earth or in heaven compares to the care he receives from Almighty God! Therefore, he concludes that drawing near to God is good; it reminds him to trust in the Lord exclusively; it motivates him to serve as a messenger of God's goodness.

LIFE STEP

Oh, the importance and value of getting alone with God to gain or regain your eternal perspective! In everyday life, you may have neglected those quiet moments when you talk with God—really seeking His answer to your probing questions. Trust Him. Search Him out. Look to His Word for truth, mindful that the answers you seek are in His Word (2 Peter 1:3). Carve out time to be alone with God today and every day. Make a commitment to get God's perspective on your questions.

What is the writer saying?

How can I apply this to my life?

In these eight verses, the psalmist acknowledges with gratitude the goodness God has shown him, linking these blessings to God's Word (v. 65). He then prays for wisdom, evidenced by good judgment and knowledge of God's Word, expressing his belief in God's commandments. In truth, apart from God's Word our knowledge may be wasted, and the psalmist seems to have strayed in the past (v. 67). But now he keeps God's Word and seeks to learn more of God's truth and wisdom as he faces enemies who try to smear his good name with lies (vv. 68-70).

The picture painted with these words is of a man who has learned by experience the value of an undivided heart (v. 69); the benefits of observing and doing (*keep*) God's commands; and the pure joy (*delight*) he finds in discovering the truths of God's law (v. 70). The writer is able to see God's goodness even through the afflictions he has suffered, since they drove him to God's statutes (v. 71). Thus, he values God's law more than the wealth offered by gold and silver (v. 72).

LIFE STEP

Do you find that trials and difficulties drive you away from God, or toward God? It is said that the worst affliction of all is wasted affliction—wasted because we gained nothing from it by turning to God. Don't let your trials make you bitter. Like the psalmist, turn to God, who deals well with His servants. If you struggle with trusting the Lord in times of difficulty, why not give God that struggle. Like the psalmist, pray: "Teach me good judgment and knowledge; for I believe in your commandments."

What is the writer saying?

How can I apply this to my life?

PRAY El Salvador – For sound, Bible-believing churches to be planted among the Amerindian people.

The psalmist feels a sense of desperation because of the persecution of his enemies, yet his struggles do not stop him from expressing confidence in God's Word. His words describe a man whose life is genuinely in danger, and he has no difficulty taking to God his requests for deliverance. Notice that in three of the descriptions of his current physical/emotional state, he follows immediately with a statement of confidence and hope in God's Word (vv. 81, 83, 87).

He has been diligent to study God's Word, so much so that his eyes are weary (v. 82). This is the key to his confidence and hope—rather than abandoning God's precepts during his distress, he runs to them. He has made it his habit to look to God's law for answers and guidance.

We also learn from his questions and prayer requests precisely what he wants from God. He seeks:

- God's comfort in time of distress (v. 82)
- God's judgment on his persecutors (v. 84)
- God's deliverance (help!) (v. 86)
- God's revival (v. 88), not according to anything he deserves or has earned, but according to God's lovingkindness

We do not know precisely how he was being persecuted, but verse 87 indicates that he felt his physical death was almost a reality. Yet, in all that he faced he remained faithful. And he continued his commitment to give testimony of God's faithfulness (v. 88).

LIFE STEP

When you are feeling the weight of distress in your life, is your reaction to whine about it, cry about it, and get angry with God? That might be the reaction of one who isn't in a personal relationship with our all-knowing, all-powerful God, but for the Christian, the psalmist's example should be our reaction. We have the Word to guide us and help us. We have God on our side. Even when circumstances are against us, remember that God is for us. Take a few minutes to read Romans 8:31-39 and close with a time of prayer, thanking God for the truths in that passage.

What is the writer saying?

How can I apply this to my life?

PRAY Pray that the married couples of your church will nurture and protect their relationships by a dependence upon God's Word.

The writer starts this passage with a heartfelt, passionate expression of his love for God's law, coupled with a declaration that it (God's law) is the subject of his meditation all day long (v. 97). Is this the cause of his love or the result of his love for God's law? Either way, his life is wrapped up in the study of God's Word, and by it he has the confidence to claim:

- Wisdom greater than his enemies (v. 98)
- Understanding more than his teachers (v. 99)
- Understanding greater even than the aged and experienced (*the ancients*) (v. 100)

In verses 101-102, the writer speaks of two strategies he has maintained as priorities in his life to keep him in obedience to God's law. He has kept (*restrained*) himself from evil and remained faithful to (*not departed from*) God's judgments and laws. His was not just an intellectual pursuit of God's law for the sake of knowledge, but an experiential exercise that he trusted to keep him on the right path. Nor was his time in the Word a dull duty that he felt compelled to perform. Rather, to him, studying the Word was a sweet delight, sweeter even than honey (v. 103)! Because of the understanding he gained, he had learned to love what God loves and hate what God hates (v. 104).

LIFE STEP

Imagine how your life would change if you could honestly say, like the psalmist, "Oh, how I love Your law!" Sadly, many Christians cannot say this with honesty. Their intake of the Bible is minimal, at best, and they look at it as a dull duty. You can't make yourself love the Bible, but you can cultivate that love until it grows into full bloom. Make your daily intake of the Bible a priority, starting with your Quiet Time every day. Consider getting on a plan to read through the Bible in a year. Cultivate your love for God's Word.

FRIDAY - WEEK 31

What is the writer saying?

How can I apply this to my life?

PRAY Belarus – Pray for the evangelical Christians who are growing in number despite increasing opposition and persecution.

Make note of the personal, present-tense declarations from the psalmist when he speaks of himself with the pronoun, "I."

- *I hate the double-minded* (v. 113). *Double-minded* in this context refers to people who know about God but lack the determination to serve and worship Him only.
- *I love Your law* (v. 113) *and Your testimonies* (v. 119).
- *I hope in Your word* (v. 114).
- *I fear Your judgments* (v. 120). In other words, a reverential respect for the holiness and righteousness of God, coupled with the realization that he falls short of that standard.

Next, observe the verses in which the writer makes a statement about God:

- *You are my hiding place and my shield* (v. 114). The writer wasn't moved to love God's Word because of curiosity or a desire for intellectual knowledge. Rather,

he had experienced God's security! He knew he could trust God.

- *You reject those who stray from Your statutes* (v. 118). God's judgment is sure.
- *You put away all the wicked of the earth* (v. 119). God's judgment has a purifying effect in accordance with His will.

Finally, notice the requests he makes of God:

- *Uphold me* (v. 116) *according to Your Word.* He knew he could not stand against his enemies without God supporting him.
- *Do not let me be ashamed of my hope* (v. 116). He could pray this way because of where he placed his hope!
- *Hold me up* (v. 117). His dependence, stated again, is upon God.

Verse 115 stands alone as a statement directed not to God or about the writer's commitments or requests. It is a word to the wicked, whom he counts as his enemies as well as God's enemies. He wanted nothing to do with those who hated God's Word.

LIFE STEP

Try your hand at writing your own personal statements of commitment concerning God's Word. If you feel uncomfortable in boldly claiming the present situation, write what you would like to be said of you in the future. This is not an exercise to encourage bragging or the development of spiritual arrogance. Look at it as a way to chart your future growth—to put you on a path toward spiritual maturity by envisioning what could be and should be. Rehearse these statements regularly to help you stay focused.

What is the writer saying?

How can I apply this to my life?

Several themes are repeated in this stanza of the longest psalm in the Bible, giving greater weight to the writer's heartfelt commitment to God's Word. Notice that four of the eight verses address the writer's persecution or persecutors. Clearly, his life included experiences of the "regular guy" rather than those of an overprotected child. He mentions:

- *His affliction,* seeking God's deliverance (v. 153).
- *His "cause,"* begging God to intervene for him because only God could redeem him (v. 154).
- *The number of his enemies*—they are many (v. 157).
- T*he disgusting treachery of those who reject God's Word* (v. 158).

Three times in this passage we see again the writer asking God to "revive me"

- "... according to Your word" (v. 154)
- "... according to Your judgments" (v. 156)
- "... according to Your lovingkindness" (v. 159).

In total, there are seven instances in Psalm 119 in which the writer makes such a request for revival (See also Psalm 119:25, 40, 88, and 107.) Clearly, the psalmist was not seeking simply a feeling of renewal in his spirit or his physical body during a time of despair. He recognized that the best sense of renewal was in accord with God's Word, love, and mercy. Such genuine renewal serves to honor God and His Word. Though many people have adopted portions of the Bible as truth, the psalmist wrote an affirmation of his personal conviction that all of God's Word is infallible and eternal (v. 160). This is the reason he knew he could trust God's Word in every circumstance.

LIFE STEP

Memorize Psalm 119:160 and make it one of your foundational verses to remind you that all of God's Word is infallible (true) and accurate. After all, if you struggle with the truth of God's Word in one area (a specific miracle, perhaps), how can you place your faith in the One who came up out of the grave? God's Word is true. You can trust it. And, like the psalmist, you can experience its truth for yourself. Write Psalm 119:160 as your first step toward memorizing this awesome verse!

239

What is the writer saying?

How can I apply this to my life?

Trials! Can there be anything more common to everyone? There may be more sermons, songs, and study materials tied to this subject than any other. That's because trials prompt so many desperate questions. If anyone was qualified to speak to the issue, Paul was. In these opening verses he describes their affliction in Asia. Though he doesn't specify what it was, he says that it was so far beyond their ability to bear that they were certain it was "game over" for them (vv. 8-9)! Later in this epistle (11:24-28), he lists other things he had endured: whippings, beatings, stoning, shipwrecks, and many other physical extremes.

In today's verses, Paul provides us with two helpful insights about the purpose of trials. First, he reminds us that God is able and willing to adequately comfort us in our trials (vv. 3-4). That's wonderful! But why does God comfort us? So that we can then dispense the same comfort to others facing similar circumstances. Trials deepen our understanding, broaden our awareness, raise our level of compassion, and thus equip us to minister to others in ways known only to those who've "been there." Secondly, trials push us beyond our means so that we're forced to trust in God instead of in ourselves (v. 9)! Most of us believe that we can find a way out of every predicament. Then God allows us to be boxed into a situation we can't resolve. Frustrated and perhaps even angered, we desperately look for a way out and find none. It is only then that we can begin to learn how to really trust in Him alone. Only then do we consciously experience His enabling strength.

Notice, too, that Paul readily acknowledged the part the Corinthians played in helping him and his companions through their trials. Their prayers made a difference (v. 11).

What is the writer saying?

How can I apply this to my life?

PRAY Moldova - Pray for bearers of the Gospel to be trained and sent to the hundreds of villages with no witness.

One of Paul's purposes in this epistle was to defend himself against several false accusations. Here he addresses the charge that he could not be trusted because he had not honored his travel plans! He had spoken of visiting them a second time! (1 Corinthians 16:5), but this intention had not yet been fulfilled (v. 15). Was this proof that Paul was carnal and that he made decisions on a whim and was not to be trusted? Absolutely not. Paul affirmed that he had conducted himself in all good conscience and godly sincerity rather than worldly wisdom (v. 12). He affirmed that even as the original intention was pure, the change of plans was also out of a pure motive. He had chosen to delay his visit in order to "*spare them*" (v. 23). The context suggests that he wished to avoid having to apply further painful discipline, preferring to give them more time to resolve issues and to make needed changes themselves before he came to them a second time.

To strengthen his defense against accusations of being two-faced or untrustworthy, Paul appealed to their common bond in Jesus Christ. Starting in verse 18, he firmly proclaims that, as God keeps His word, so he and his companions kept their word. The same indwelling Spirit and anointing of God that sealed the Corinthians for eternity had anointed and sealed Paul, Silvanus (Silas), and Timothy (vv. 19; 21-22). Possibly responding to critics who accused the apostles of approaching the Corinthians as intellectual or spiritual superiors (*not that we lord it over your faith*), Paul spoke of working with them (v. 24). He saw their relationship as that of co-laborers in the faith.

LIFE STEP

When conflict arises between fellow believers, wouldn't it be great if everyone could be guided to consider their common bond in Christ rather than focusing on their differences. Maybe you need that word of reminder in a conflict you're dealing with right now. It might be that you could help settle a dispute between Christian friends by helping them see Paul's emphasis on common ground with the Corinthians. All Christians are sealed with the same Holy Spirit. We share a common future in Christ and a common goal in this world—to lead others to faith in Him.

What is the writer saying?

How can I apply this to my life?

PRAY

Rwanda – Pray for committed believers to stand firm in the face of cultural and tribal pressures.

Two things had occurred that supply the context for today's verses. The first was a painful visit (v. 1) followed by a painful letter (vv. 3-4). We have no record of either one of these (see the introduction for further details). Both were apparently prompted by the sinful actions of a believer at Corinth. We do not know if he was the incestuous man referenced in 1 Corinthians 5:1-5, but we do know that whatever this person had done, he had sinned both against Paul and against the Corinthian believers, which is why they both ultimately needed to forgive him (vv. 7,10). The most likely possibility is that he had challenged Paul's authority and sown much painful discord in the church. Whatever it was, the anguish and grief that Paul experienced in dealing with this (v. 4) hint at the seriousness of the offense. Paul had called for him to be put under discipline and most of the congregation had done so. We don't know what form this took but it was clearly severe (vv. 6-7). Thankfully, the discipline had produced its intended effect, and the brother had repented. Paul now calls for them to promptly discontinue the discipline, comfort him, reaffirm their love for him, and fully forgive him. If not, they would hand Satan an opportunity to take advantage of the situation

LIFE STEP

One of the key lessons we learn from Paul's second letter to the Corinthians is the importance of forgiveness. Even though he and the church were wronged in some way, the one responsible had been disciplined and was now, in Paul's view, in need of loving acceptance and restoration through heartfelt forgiveness. Who do you know who needs to be forgiven in a demonstration of Christian love? Will you take the step to help restore the one who may have sinned against you? Reach out to them in love today.

What is the writer saying?

How can I apply this to my life?

Up to this point, Paul had been recounting his journey beginning with his trials in Asia, his decision to delay his planned visit, the painful letter that he had sent to them by Titus, and how he had cut short his ministry in Troas and headed to Macedonia because Titus had failed to return as expected. These were spiritually and emotionally disturbing times for Paul! This helps explain why he now breaks off his narrative (which he will not resume until 7:5) in order to speak of other things. Why the sudden shift? Because discouraging circumstances always call for a reaffirmation of truth! Paul was so unsettled in his spirit due to the events surrounding the problems in Corinth that he found himself unable to preach the Gospel in Troas even though God Himself had opened a door for him to do so (2:12-13)! He clearly sensed his utter helplessness and insufficiency. He was a failure, unfit for the ministry, right? Wrong! It might have appeared that way to Paul's critics and perhaps even to Paul himself, but the truth was that God always leads His children in triumph; not because of who they are in themselves but because of their position in Christ the Victor (2:14-16).

Paul made the distinction in verse 17 between himself and his companions (*who preached in sincerity*) and the false apostles who were preaching to the Corinthians out of self-interest (*peddling the Word of God*). Neither Paul nor anyone else needed human affirmation to know that God was at work. The progress in the lives of the Corinthians was proof enough (3:1-3). Though he knew he was insufficient (v. 16), Paul took heart in the fact that his sufficiency came from God and not from himself (v. 5). When it comes to spiritual growth and impact, self-sufficiency is a myth. God-sufficiency is a certainty.

LIFE STEP

When you sense that you are getting nowhere in your God-given goals or efforts, step back a moment and determine who you're relying on. Is it evident that you've been trying too hard to "help God," as if it all depended on you? Your sufficiency is in Christ! When you learn to rest and trust in His sufficiency, you'll release the reins a bit more easily, and He will guide your steps. Write out three ways you can complete this sentence: "Because of who I am in Christ, I am/can..."

243

What is the writer saying?

How can I apply this to my life?

PRAY
Morocco – Pray for those troubled by increasing tensions between Islamists and moderates to be open to the Good News.

In the face of fearful and discouraging circumstances, Paul continued to press boldly forward because he knew that his sufficiency did not lie in himself but in God (vv. 5-6). Having affirmed this, he continues in the same line of thought by reminding his readers that the dynamic which brings about transformation into the image of Christ is not human effort or ability but rather the power of the indwelling Holy Spirit. He does this by contrasting the effects of the Old and New Covenants. When Moses received the Ten Commandments from God, his face glowed for awhile. Paul argued that if the Law written on stones which required human effort produced such a temporary effect, then the New Covenant which depends on Christ's finished work can be expected to produce a far more glorious and permanent result!

The phrase "*beholding as in a mirror*" (v. 18) is an attempt to translate one difficult Greek word. It has a two-way sense to it: contemplating and reflecting. It's like what happens when you stand in front of a mirror. As the mirror beholds you, it reflects you. Similarly, as a piece of film is exposed to a subject, it takes on the image of the subject. That's how the believer is changed. Transformation comes through contemplation, not imitation. As we contemplate Christ by spending time with Him, deepening our understanding of who He is and what He's done for us, we find ourselves reflecting Him more and more. This is the work of the Spirit changing us from within. The result is genuine, lasting spiritual transformation! It is this very transformation that Paul described in verse 16, the moment when one turns to Christ in faith and the spiritual veil is removed, giving light and life to those who believe. He describes the ongoing (*are being transformed*) transformation that follows in verse 18.

LIFE STEP

Today's passage offers an excellent contrast between the futility of the Law for salvation and removal of spiritual blinders that comes from faith in Jesus Christ. Read verses 14-16 again. Now consider how the message of hope in the Gospel may be what your lost friend or family member needs to hear. Write down in your own words a paraphrase of these verses and rehearse them till you feel comfortable sharing the truth of the Gospel message with your friends.

What is the writer saying?

How can I apply this to my life?

These verses are part of a larger section (2:14 – 7:15) which forms a break in Paul's account of the difficulties he had been experiencing. Throughout, he is seeking to explain what keeps him going despite tough circumstances (3:12; 4:1, 8-9,16), while providing a defense of his ministry to those who were questioning its authenticity. First, he was very much aware that God hadn't given him the ministry He had because he'd earned it (v. 1). That kept him from losing heart! When we believe the lie that God will only use us when we deserve it, discouragement is inevitable. Ministry is a merciful gift, not an earned privilege. Secondly, Paul knew that his responsibility was to simply proclaim the Word of God and to preach Christ. It wasn't to force people to change. When we believe the lie that it's our job to change people, it won't be long before we distort the message and try to manipulate and coerce them (v. 2). Many false teachers were doing just that. Many still do. What a relief to realize that our task is to clearly hold the truth up in front of people's consciences so that the Holy Spirit can bring conviction. Though Satan causes spiritual blindness in the minds of the lost (v. 4), you can count on the fact that the most hardened person still has a God-given conscience that may respond to truth as the Spirit prompts them. You see that Paul viewed himself as nothing more than a jar of clay (*earthen vessel*) that God could use to manifest His excellent power (v .7). When we believe the lie that we're something more than that, it won't be long before we lose heart because jars can't produce anything. They can only hold what someone else produces.

LIFE STEP

Take a hard look at what you believe about yourself as a servant of the Lord. Do you feel unworthy, unconvincing, and weak? You are correct on all three counts! That's why Christ has taken your place and is now all you could never be. He is worthy, convincing, and powerful. Ask God to teach you to consciously shift your dependence from yourself to Him. Remind yourself often that the power is of God, not of you.

245

What is the writer saying?

How can I apply this to my life?

One of the hardest things to overcome is the belief that God is asking too much of us. We can become convinced that we're the victims of unbearable burdens. Today's passage reminds us that, for the believer who is walking with God, the problem is never too much external pressure but rather too little dependence on internal support. In these verses, Paul shares the basic secret of his endurance. He talks about being afflicted, crushed, persecuted, and constantly delivered over to death (vv. 8-11). Anyone observing all that he endured would have to wonder how he could possibly put up with it all! The first part of the answer is to notice that Paul saw his burdens as being something that he carried around in his body (v. 10). In other words, he realized that the burdens were tied to what is temporary and external. With that as a backdrop, he unveiled his real secret in verses 14 and 16. How did he keep from caving in on the outside? First, he relied on the reality of the future resurrection from the dead for those who are in Christ (v. 14). Whatever his body may go through—even if death itself—he knew he could count on a glorified resurrected body. Secondly, he was being renewed every single day on the inside! By whom? By the Holy Spirit who releases God's strength in the inner person (Ephesians 3:16) as we respond to His promptings and ask for His strength. Paul was also aware that his burdens were light and momentary compared to the eternal weight of glory they were producing (v. 17). Focusing on what we'll experience in heaven is essential to being able to endure the burdens and disappointments we experience here.

LIFE STEP

Where are you looking to find the support needed to bear the burdens God has permitted in your life? Yourself? Others? Entertainment? Substances of some kind? None of these will ever be enough because they don't address the real need. Remember, the problem is never too much external pressure but too little dependence on God's inner strength. Today, when feeling weighed down, before doing anything else or turning to anyone else, first meaningfully ask the Lord to strengthen you. Then repeat this the next day, and the next, and the next…

What is the writer saying?

How can I apply this to my life?

PRAY   Costa Rica – For the growth and strengthening of Bible schools that train leadership.

Today's text addresses the way Paul handled fears about persecution, suffering, and the certainty of death. He continued to share what motivated him and kept him from losing heart in the face of these fears. He explained that our earthly body is like a tent that will wear out if it's not prematurely destroyed. But when that happens, it will not be a loss since we will immediately enter the Lord's presence. But there's more! In the coming resurrection, we will receive a new body that is so far superior to the one we now have that it's as though we're currently naked by comparison! It will be like Jesus' resurrected body: tangible, yet capable of supernatural things (Philippians 3:20-21; Acts 1:9-11). So, death is not the end for the believer but rather the beginning of real life (v. 4). To Paul, this was no "hope so" future benefit for the believer, but a sure promise from God that gives us confidence because we have the sealing of the Holy Spirit as our guarantee, our down payment for things to come (vv. 5-6).

But if it's far better to be with Christ, why continue in this life? The answer is this: because of the awesome potential to gain an eternal weight of glory in exchange for the light and momentary afflictions in this life! The doctrine of eternal rewards is sorely lacking in today's evangelical mindset, but it was highly motivating for Paul. He knew that one day we will all stand before Jesus and be judged for the deeds done in the body (v. 10). This judgement isn't to condemn us for our sins (He took our condemnation) but to reward us for what we did that was pleasing to Him. These incredible truths are what drove Paul and determined his earthly priorities (v. 9).

LIFE STEP

Can you honestly say, like Paul, that you make it your ambition—your aim—to be well-pleasing to the Lord? It's a big question, but if you're a sincere follower of Christ you'll want to answer, "yes," or at least, "I'm trying." What you focus on in this life will make or break your commitment to be well-pleasing to Him. If you were perfectly honest with God and yourself right now, what change (or changes) would you need to make to show that your ambition is to please Him? 247

What is the writer saying?

How can I apply this to my life?

Paul was a focused missionary whose primary reason for breathing and living was to draw people to the knowledge of the Savior through faith in Him. When he considered the righteous judgment (*the terror of the Lord*) that will come upon the unredeemed, Paul sought to persuade men everywhere to repent and believe (v. 11). Though the Corinthians in their spiritual immaturity were often attracted to those who had the appearance of God's anointing (v. 12), Paul and his co-laborers were more interested in what was going on within their hearts. What was the difference? Christ's love! They were compelled (*pulled along*) by the love of Christ to share the hope of salvation and the reality of the resurrection with all who were lost (vv. 14-15). Their hope was to bring to God (*reconcile*) those who were yet unreconciled, as representatives (*ambassadors*) for Christ (vv. 19-20). This was their ministry—the ministry of bringing people to God through faith in Jesus Christ (v. 18). At the cross, Christ was made to be what we were so that we could become what He is (v. 21). As a result, all those who place their faith in Christ experience a transformation in kind, not just in appearance. They become new creations (v. 17), capable of bearing genuine fruit.

LIFE STEP

If you have eternal life through faith in Jesus Christ, you are called to no longer live for yourself but for Him who died for you and rose again (2 Corinthians 5:15). How would you assess your life considering this truth? Talk to God about what needs to change in your life for you to truly live for Him. What do you need to put off or lay aside, and what do you need to take up or put on? Read Colossians 3:5-15 as you close and prepare to talk to God.

What is the writer saying?

How can I apply this to my life?

PRAY Sudan – Pray for the church to grow spiritually strong despite intense suffering and persecution.

This chapter opens with a great statement: "*workers together with Him*." That's a good summary of how Paul functioned as an ambassador of Christ. He was not out to establish his own ministry or to achieve notoriety as a self-styled religious worker. Instead, He worked together with God. In contrast to this, it could be said of his detractors that they worked alone without God. They did what they did in order to be seen, acknowledged, and praised by men. They lived for themselves rather than for the One who died and rose again on their behalf (5:15). If asked for credentials to authenticate their "ministry," they would point to their own strengths and visible accomplishments (5:12).

In today's text, Paul points to his credentials as a true ambassador of Christ. It's written as a series of twenty-seven things laid out in three sets of nine. The first is a list of nine trials which he patiently endured (vv. 4-5). Those who serve with God persevere even when it's costly, whereas those who serve themselves always stay in comfort zones. Then Paul lists nine qualities which marked his ministry and his methods (vv. 6-7). Finally, he lists nine seeming contradictions (vv. 8-10) about his ministry. These highlight the fact that God's ways transcend human methods and defy human logic. God's wisdom appears to be foolishness. His strength works in weakness. His joy is experienced in sorrow. His agenda moves forward despite "insurmountable" odds. His truth penetrates all error, and His riches appear as poverty to those who love this world's wealth.

LIFE STEP *It should be obvious that the life Paul and his companions experienced was filled with trials and suffering. Yet, they persevered even in the face of persecution. Don't let fear of rejection stop you from ministering to the lost people around you. Ask God to give you boldness to speak to others about your faith in Jesus.*

What is the writer saying?

How can I apply this to my life?

PRAY
Ukraine – Christian Camps. For God to give youth a passion to live for Him and reach their land.

Heart to heart. That's the essence of effective influence. If you want to speak to people in a way that reaches their hearts, you must do more than open your mouth and speak your mind; you must open your heart and share your affection. That's what Paul does: "*O Corinthians!... our heart is wide open.*" Only rarely did he address his readers by their collective name as he does here (see Galatians 3:1; Philippians 4:15). Their allegiance to him had been drawn away by false apostles (11:13-15) who had been steadily eroding their confidence in him and leading their hearts away from Christ (11:3). Paul urges them to fully renew their affection for him and to cut their ties with the false teachers. Verses 14-18 are often used to urge believers to isolate themselves from unbelievers. It's true we should be careful in our relationships with unbelievers, but how far does this go? After all, Jesus was separate from sinners (Hebrews 7:26), and yet He was called the friend of sinners (Luke 7:34). Paul can't be urging them to cut all ties with unbelievers (see also 1 Corinthians 5:9-11). In context, he is urging them to break ties with those who claimed to be apostles but who were actually unbelievers. To carry on heart relationships with them was to try to join things together that have nothing essential in common since they were different in kind, not just in name. It could only result in compromising their own fellowship with God (vv. 16-18). In the same way, we ought to avoid relationships with unbelievers that attempt to blend the holy with the unholy. Marriage and other close partnerships are obvious examples.

LIFE STEP

250

In your efforts to influence others to receive Christ as Savior, you cannot isolate yourself or just meet up with Christians. Right? There must be contact with unsaved people if you ever hope to be an ambassador for Christ, urging the unreconciled to be reconciled to God. Ask the Lord to give you wisdom in finding ways to influence unbelievers to know Jesus as Savior while, at the same time, guarding against becoming "unequally yoked" with unbelievers.

What is the writer saying?

How can I apply this to my life?

As Paul picks up the retelling of his experiences which he'd left off at 2 Corinthians 2:13, he explains how encouraged he was when Titus brought him news that most of them had changed their mind and renewed their affection for him (vv. 6-7). That's the core meaning of repentance: to change one's mind. When we continually repeat the same sins, it is evidence that we've not changed our mind about it. Here, Paul explains the change in a person that triggers genuine repentance and leads us away from sin: the right kind of sorrow. There are in fact two types of sorrow, as he points out. One is worldly, and the other is godly (v. 10). The first never leads to lasting change because it's focused on what sin has cost us (what we have lost) such as health, friendships, money, reputation, or privilege. It's simply vain regret. If nothing appears to have been lost, why change? Godly sorrow on the other hand is driven by what my sin cost others and especially, Christ Himself. Like the sorrow felt by someone whose actions have severely injured another, we begin to really turn from sin when we contemplate Christ enduring God's terrible wrath because of it. It's hard to take my sin lightly when I stand at the foot of the cross and see Him being crushed because of it. That's why Paul was able to say he rejoiced in their sorrow—because it led to their repentance and put them back on the right path (vv. 9-11). Seeing his beloved Corinthians back on that path encouraged Paul and renewed his confidence in them (vv. 13-16).

LIFE STEP

As you consider the sin you struggle with, you probably can identify with Paul's distinction between sorrow that leads to true repentance and that which equates to mere "regret." If you want to get past the destructive effects of sin, learn what it means to confess your sins in godly sorrow. Be specific in naming your sin. See your sin as against God and seek forgiveness through heartfelt confession (1 John 1:9)

What is the writer saying?

How can I apply this to my life?

PRAY Dominican Republic – For church leaders and their congregation to be good witnesses in tense and inequitable situations.

Ask anybody what topic draws the most criticism from the average church attender and you will most likely hear, "money." It seems that the preacher must urge people to give without being too pushy, while the people in the pews tend to think it's an off-limits subject and an infringement on their private affairs. Few topics are as sensitive as money because it touches on one of our most difficult struggles: selfishness. It's very easy to become protective of the resources we steward and to justify keeping most of them while forgetting that the love of money is the root of much sin (1 Timothy 6:10). Today's verses contain some helpful principles. For one, we shouldn't wait to have much before we give. Note how the Macedonians gave despite their deep poverty (vv. 1-3). If we don't give when we have little, it is unlikely we will give when we have much! Furthermore, we must perceive giving not as an expense but for what it really is: an awesome privilege to invest in the advancement of the Gospel--an investment with indescribable eternal dividends! To ask someone to give to God's cause is not to beg, it's to invite them to seize a great opportunity. If there's any begging to be done, it should be for the chance to give. That's what the Macedonians did (v. 4)! Reluctant asking and reluctant giving are both proof that we're only seeing earth, not envisioning heaven! Most importantly, selfless giving as described here will only happen when we first give ourselves to God (v. 5). If we've not surrendered the illusion that we belong to ourselves rather than to Him, we'll not surrender what we have to advance His cause rather than our own.

LIFE STEP

It has been said that one way to determine where your priorities lie is to analyze where you spend your resources like money and time. Why not settle the issue now about your giving to the work of the Kingdom of God? Don't think about how little you have but give freely and generously from what God has allowed into your hands—whether that is much or little. Talk to God about your giving and determine to honor Him in your stewardship.

SATURDAY - WEEK 33

What is the writer saying?

How can I apply this to my life?

PRAY Belgium – Pray for revival in this materially-prosperous but spiritually-poor land.

"I'm living with my boyfriend but it's OK because God knows we're not sleeping together!" "It doesn't really matter what others think about this, God knows my heart." Have you ever heard or said something similar? Such statements are based on the idea that the only important thing is what God sees (1 Samuel 16:7), and therefore we don't need to be concerned about what man sees. Though there's some truth to this, Paul would not agree that external appearance is of no consequence. In today's text, he highlights the importance of our public testimony, which is what people perceive as they watch what we do and how we live. Note how Paul gave careful attention to this and went out of his way to remain above reproach in the eyes of BOTH God and man (vv. 20-21). Here the issue was the handling of a collection of money destined for the saints in Jerusalem. Rather than simply sending it with Titus alone, he assigned this task to three men so as to avoid any possibility that someone could accuse them of mishandling the funds. It's not that Paul didn't trust Titus; it's that he didn't trust the enemy! He knew that the devil is always looking for an opportunity to accuse the saints and to discredit the Lord's work and His people. Being right in the eyes of God and doing right in the eyes of men are equally important. It's true that man only looks on the outward appearance and cannot see the heart. But that's precisely why we need to ensure that what they can see is beyond reproach.

LIFE STEP

As Christ's representatives, we should do what we can to avoid giving others an opportunity to level an accusation we can't disprove. At times this will mean giving up some liberty that we have (1 Corinthians 8). Other times it will mean going above and beyond to avoid needlessly offending people (Matthew 17:24-27). Give some thought to how people perceive your choices and actions. Are you taking pains to do what is right in the eyes of BOTH God and man? If not, what will you change?

What is the writer saying?

How can I apply this to my life?

Starting something is easy and most people manage that part of a project just fine. However, finishing well is the more challenging but far more important responsibility. Anyone can commit to doing something, but it takes a committed person to get it done. In these verses, Paul urges the Corinthians to finish what they had promised to do, namely to provide a generous offering for the saints in Jerusalem. They had eagerly committed to do so a year earlier (8:10-11). Paul had even used their example to prompt the Macedonians to do the same (v. 2) but apparently, he was concerned that when he arrived in Corinth, he would discover that they hadn't followed through on their good intentions. So, he sent Titus and the others ahead to ensure that their offering would be ready when he arrived. What could possibly intervene to prevent them from fulfilling their enthusiastic commitment? The same thing that easily sidetracks our good intentions to support God's work: covetousness. This is the meaning of the Greek word which is translated "*grudging obligation*" or "*exaction*" (v. 5). Covetousness is the desire to have what belongs to another. It amounts to idolatry (Colossians 3:5). It's easy to have all the right intentions as it relates to being generous and giving to the Lord and to His people. But our good intentions can easily be short-circuited by our idolatrous flesh that urges us to hang on to what we have even though it belongs to God. Today's text reminds us that, though God wants us to give out of a joyful heart rather than by compulsion, it is not unbiblical for others to urge us to honor a commitment to give generously to the Lord as He so generously gave to us (v. 15)!

LIFE STEP

Faithfulness can't be measured at the starting line but it's obvious to all at the finish line. On the day you give an account to the Lord for the use of your earthly resources, will you be able to point to more than good intentions? Replace good intentions with meaningful action today. If you've not yet started the habit of giving generously, consider the words of Paul to the Corinthians as God's message to you. Pray about it and respond obediently to God's direction.

What is the writer saying?

How can I apply this to my life?

There was much to be thankful for at Corinth, but there remained a few who continued to oppose Paul and denied that he was an apostle. This was serious because true apostles were Christ's chosen spokesmen. So, in this final section, Paul mounts a defense of his apostleship. He feels compelled to do so even though he compares it to foolish boasting. The false teachers were claiming that he was bold and firm when writing but cowardly when present in person (vv. 1,10). Paul affirmed meekness and gentleness (v. 1) but also stated that he was prepared to be very firm with them when he arrived (v. 2). He based his confidence on the weaponry he deployed in the spiritual warfare in which he was engaged. His were not fleshly (*carnal*) weapons (v. 4) such as swords and spears, but the divinely inspired weapons of prayer and the Word of God (see Ephesians 6:11-

18). Such weapons are powerful enough to destroy every false argument or human philosophy (*pulling down strongholds*) that mankind may set up as an alternative to God's ways. They are torn down by bringing every thought captive to the obedience of Christ (v. 5). Spiritual warfare is primarily waged in the mind. That's where Satan launches attacks and tries to wreak havoc. God wants to transform by truth (Romans 12:2), so Satan tries to conform by error.

Paul's overriding goal in defending his ministry was to affirm in the minds of the Corinthians that his motives were pure. He was called by God to present the Gospel message everywhere he could, and his strong desire was to spread that message beyond Corinth into other regions where it had not yet been heard (vv. 13-16). Only in this noble effort would he be found boasting—all to the glory of God (v. 17)!

LIFE STEP

We live in a day when nearly all of society and popular culture denies the existence of unchanging truths found in the Bible. Absolutes are being pushed aside and what was wrong is now "right" in the eyes of many, even among those who claim Jesus as their Savior. Don't let these worldly arguments gain a stronghold in your mind. Fight error with the unchanging truth of God's Word. Renew your commitment to His truth by memorizing Psalm 119:160. "The sum of your word is truth, and every one of your righteous rules endures forever."

What is the writer saying?

How can I apply this to my life?

PRAY

Jordan – Pray for Christianity to be held in high regard so that God's work in this strategic part of the Middle East would not be thwarted.

Paul seems like a fearless man willing to proclaim the truth and face the consequences. But it turns out that there were indeed some things that he was afraid of. One of them was that Satan would lead the minds of the Corinthians astray just as he had done with Eve (v. 3). The craftiness of Satan is often highlighted in this epistle. Earlier, Paul noted how the devil is a schemer who takes advantage of every opportunity to advance his cause (2:10-11). He clearly possesses a powerful intellect and a will that is deliberately set against Christ and His followers. Later, Paul noted how Satan blinds the minds of unbelievers so that they are unable to see the light of the Gospel (4:3-4). Yesterday we saw how he seeks to erect fortresses made up of false ways of reasoning that hold people in bondage to lies. Now Paul shares his fear that Satan will gradually draw their minds away from the simplicity of their faith in Christ (vv. 3-4). Satan will do anything to sabotage the Gospel and the assurance of those who have trusted in Christ for salvation. He confuses through complication, and it's happening all around us. Rather than preaching a salvation through childlike faith in Christ alone, many "gospel preachers" are front-loading the message with all sorts of conditions and expectations which rob people of any assurance of their salvation. This ought not to surprise us because Satan is a master of disguise who can actually appear to be an angel of light (vv.14-15). Those who are serving his cause will not appear to be doing so! When it comes to the Gospel, beware of complication! It's about trust in Him and what He did for us. Period!

LIFE STEP

Do you really believe that you could be led astray from your simple faith in Christ? To deny this is to underestimate Satan's genius at deception. Take a moment right now to read John 3:14-16. How hard is it to "look and live"? Perhaps you need to come back to that today and to recover the peace and assurance that come from simply trusting Him alone.

What is the writer saying?

How can I apply this to my life?

PRAY Ecuador – Praise, back in 1967 only 120 Quichua people were believers and today there are over 200,000!

Have you ever wondered about apparent contradictions in the Bible? Take Proverbs 26:4-5 for example. One verse says not to answer a fool lest you be like him and the other says to answer a fool so that he'll not be wise in his own eyes. So, which is it? Either approach can be the right course of action depending on the situation. There are times when it's best not to answer the ramblings of a fool, but then there are other times when it becomes necessary to counter his claims. This was one of those times for Paul. Although he didn't like to parade his qualifications as an apostle, he felt it necessary to do so to silence the false apostles who were masquerading as servants of righteousness (v. 15) and drawing people away from Christ. You can sense his reluctance in doing this as he compares it to foolish and insane boasting. Since the false teachers gloried in external appearances, Paul first showed that he could outdo them all on those grounds (v. 18). While doing so, he told of experiences that we know nothing about, including multiple beatings and shipwrecks. But then he did something that the false apostles would never do: he boasted in his weakness (v. 30)! He first shared the story of how he was run out of town in a basket through a window. Think of it! There hung the great apostle Paul, a basket case, at the mercy of those who were holding the ropes (Acts 9:19-25)! It's not exactly the kind of success story to which false teachers would want to draw attention. False teachers never highlight their weaknesses. In fact, they take pleasure in pointing out weaknesses in others in order to appear more impressive.

LIFE STEP *Do you often find yourself drawing attention to your accomplishments while highlighting the shortcomings of others? When we do this, it's a sign that we are glorying in the wrong thing. Take a few moments to consider how you might be doing this and to identify at least one specific way that you can put Christ on display today instead of yourself.*

What is the writer saying?

How can I apply this to my life?

PRAY   France – For believers to be evangelizing six million French Muslims.

As Paul continued to defend his apostleship, he revealed a stunning experience in which he was taken up into the very dwelling place of God. At first, it seems as though he was talking about someone else, but verse 7 makes it clear that he was referring to himself. His desire to avoid any credit for it is the most likely explanation for the way he talks about it. It was such a surreal experience that he couldn't tell if it happened while in his body or out of it. It may have occurred when he was stoned and left for dead outside of Lystra (Acts 14:19-20). In any event, the revelations were epic; so great in fact that he was not allowed to describe them. But even if he could, he probably would not have been able to do so any more than a person born blind could describe the colors of a sunset. Heaven's glories defy description. Because of the greatness of the revelations, the potential for pride was huge, so he was given a "thorn in the flesh" to keep him humble. Satan would never pursue such a result, so the thorn was clearly given by God. Yet the text refers to it as a messenger of Satan. This may mean that a demon was tasked with this specific assignment (see also 1 Samuel 16:14). If so, the demon must have complied reluctantly! Whatever the thorn was, the result was a profound sense of weakness and unworthiness which caused Paul to plead with the Lord to remove it. God answered his prayer, not by granting his request but by assuring him that His grace could handle the full extent of his weakness and unworthiness. God's grace is best seen and welcomed against the backdrop of our utter helplessness.

LIFE STEP

Do you struggle with thoughts of inadequacy or weakness in your service to God? Paul had a weakness that he labeled a thorn in the flesh. Those thorns that bring us to the end of our self-reliance are actually blessings, as they remind us to lean on God's grace, power, and strength. The key is to not allow our weakness to drive us away from God. Take time to thank the Lord for specific areas of weakness and to welcome His grace in your life.

What is the writer saying?

How can I apply this to my life?

Here is where Paul ends his boasting about his apostolic credentials. He had been reluctant to parade them but circumstances in Corinth had compelled him to do so (v. 11). Why? Because apostleship was no small matter. Apostles were personally chosen by Christ to serve as His spokesmen and appointed to lay the doctrinal foundation of the Church (Ephesians 2:20). They spoke with divine authority (see 13:10 and 1 Corinthians 14:37) and were authenticated by supernatural signs and wonders (v. 12). Luke recorded how God had performed particularly unusual miracles through Paul (Acts 19:11-12), lending to this former persecutor of Christians certain credibility as God's chosen messenger. There could be no mistaking the fact that he was indeed an apostle, and so, to discredit his teaching was to reject Christ's teaching! In today's verses we see how Paul further appealed to the selfless way in which he had conducted himself among them. Whereas he had every right to receive financial support from them, he had not exercised this right so that he would not burden them (v. 13). His tone is somewhat sarcastic at this point, no doubt because he was attempting to shock them into realizing that the claims of the false apostles were preposterous. Paul had acted in a way that was beyond any conceivable reproach. It had involved relinquishing a right, but the value of doing so was now completely obvious. What he hoped for in the present context is that he would find them in a state of repentance when he made his next visit and that their mutual fellowship would be fully restored (vv. 20-21).

LIFE STEP

Paul was willing to set aside his rights to receive financial support from the Corinthians so that he could minister more effectively. Are you willing to forego some of your own rights in order to advance the Gospel? This calls for a sense of mission above all else, requiring you to put God's agenda ahead of your own. How would you rate yourself in this area? Ask God to reveal to you anything you may need to yield or give up for the sake of the Gospel. Then, respond in obedience.

What is the writer saying?

How can I apply this to my life?

PRAY   South Korea – Complete renewing of the mind for South Koreans saved out of Buddhism and Confucianism.

Paul was preparing to visit the Corinthians for the third time, and he intended to deal very harshly with those who were still holding out against him. He had issued just such a warning on his second visit referred to in chapter 2. Notice how he affirms the biblical principle that the guilt of anyone should not be assumed but should be established on the testimony of two or three witnesses (v. 1). We ought not to move hastily to judge until we have sufficient evidence in hand. It is far too easy to jump to conclusions based on what one person has said rather than reserving judgment until we've had a chance to hear from others. Paul challenged them to test themselves to see if they are "*in the faith*" (v .5). This is usually taken to mean that he wanted them to verify if they were saved. This seems unlikely for two reasons. First, throughout the entire epistle, he spoke to them as saints and affirmed the genuineness of their salvation (1:8, 24; 3:1-3; 6:14-15; 7:1,11; 8:7; 11:2-3). Second, the immediate context is one of judging behavior, not salvation. Paul is warning that he will deal harshly with those among them whose behavior is not in keeping with the truth (v .8). In view of this, he calls upon his readers to make sure that their conduct is "*in the faith,*" in other words, that it is consistent with the fact that Christ is indeed in them.

LIFE STEP

Truth cannot be successfully sidestepped (v. 8). If our conduct doesn't match our position in Christ, it will not change the truth about anything. We will ultimately experience heartache and loss in this life. However, if our conduct matches who we are in Christ, we cannot fail to reap the benefits of such alignment. So, examine yourself today to see if you are "in the faith." Are you living in a way that matches who you now are in Christ (2 Corinthians 5:17)? If you fail that test, it's time to stop denying by your actions that Christ lives in you and to begin living for the one who died and rose again on your behalf.

What is the writer saying?

How can I apply this to my life?

The Book of Esther is a record of God's rescue of the Jewish people who were living in exile in Persia under king Xerxes, also known as Ahasuerus. Xerxes had taken over the vast Persian empire from his father, Darius, the same Darius who played a major role in the history of Israel as recorded in the Books of Ezra, Daniel, and Haggai. Though the account we read in Esther highlights God's sovereignty, it is also the only book in the Bible in which the name of God is not mentioned.

Today's reading sets the time and place for the rest of the record and introduces us to the location where Ahasuerus held a huge feast that lasted 180 days, to which he invited all his royal court and nobles of the land. Keep in mind that the Persian empire at this time spanned so much territory that it was considered the largest the world had ever seen. The occasion for this feast, historical records tell us, was the war council which occupied Ahasuerus' ambitions to attack the rival nation of Greece. Following this 180-day feast, Ahasuerus held another lavish banquet, this time a seven-day affair for the citizens of the capital city, Shushan. On the final day of this banquet, when the king was intoxicated, he ordered his attendants to bring Queen Vashti out to display her beauty. She refused, most likely because fulfilling the king's command would expose her to immodesty in some fashion. This sets the stage for the rest of the story and the introduction of Esther and Mordecai in the narrative.

LIFE STEP   *Xerxes named himself Ahasuerus, which means "king of kings." Although many world leaders have exalted themselves in their places of prominence, there is only one true King of kings—Jesus Christ. If you've placed your faith in Jesus, you are already a child of the one true King of kings! Praise the Lord for your salvation! If you've never made the decision to trust Jesus, now is a good time to do that.*

What is the writer saying?

How can I apply this to my life?

PRAY Ecuador – For an end to anti-missionary propaganda from anthropologists, traders, jungle exploiters, and those with a political agenda.

Queen Vashti's stand for her own dignity and moral decency certainly could have cost her life for rejecting the king's command. The records of the Persian empire under king Ahasuerus provide enough vivid detail to paint a picture of a man who could be brutal as well as foolish, and disobeying the king was on the short list of capital offenses. (See Esther 4:11) In this case, however, the queen's life was spared. In consultation with his so-called "wise men," the king settled on a plan to respond to Vashti's actions. Based on their fear that other women in the kingdom would hear of Vashti's disobedience and become emboldened to disobey their own husbands, the king chose to banish her from his royal court and select another woman to be queen.

A royal decree would be distributed throughout the provinces of the expansive Persian empire, requiring all women to honor their husbands. This decree was to be recorded in the *law of the Persians and the Medes*, an action which rendered such laws irrevocable (v. 19).

Historical evidence paints a picture of ancient Persia as a male-dominated society in which women were treated as mere possessions. Modern readers may be perplexed by such archaic and foolish decrees by government officials whose success in other areas of leadership was well documented. Yet, as we will see, God used this setting and these circumstances to bring Esther into the king's court for the good of His people.

LIFE STEP

When you read of heroes or heroines in the Bible, you will quickly discover that they often were used by God in the midst of their difficult circumstances, rather than being rescued out of those circumstances. Such is Esther's story. Take to heart this truth: God wants to use you right where you are. Yes, it may be that, in God's grand plan, you will be removed from your difficulty and will be greatly used. But don't wait for that day. Commit yourself to God wherever you are, no matter what the circumstances.

What is the writer saying?

How can I apply this to my life?

According to verse 16, this chapter begins four years after the events of chapter 1. The Greek historian Herodotus tells us that despite Ahasuerus' planning, massive army, and great potential, the Greeks beat him soundly. Herodotus reported that the king returned to his palace and "was comforted by his harem." The court officials wanted to get Ahasuerus' mind off his defeat. A massive beauty pageant was held with the goal of finding a suitable replacement for Queen Vashti (2:1-4). "Hegai" is the name given to the keeper of the harem. It may be a name, but it means *eunuch* and describes the type of man placed in this kind of position. We are also introduced to Mordecai, a descendant of the Jewish tribe of Benjamin, whose station was *in the citadel* (v. 5), another name for "the palace." This suggests that

he may have been a high official with some access to the king's officers and the politics of the day. Mordecai also had raised up his niece, Hadassah *(her Jewish name, meaning "myrtle")*, whose Persian name was Esther (meaning, star). Because she stood out as a beautiful woman (v. 7), Esther was picked as one of many young maidens who would now enter the care of the king's eunuch, to receive beauty treatments and food in preparation for the day when the king would choose his new queen (v. 8). In God's divine providence, she won favor with Hegai, who gave her special treatment above that received by other women (v. 9). Meanwhile, as Mordecai paced in front of the harem's quarters to determine how Esther was getting along, she kept her Jewish identity a secret (vv. 10-11).

LIFE STEP

A quick review of Bible history reveals that the greed and ambition of Judas, the weakness of Pilate, and the evil advice of Caiphas were instruments that led to Jesus' death, burial, and resurrection—making possible our salvation. We learn from this that God is perfectly capable of overcoming evil plots and actions. Think of Esther's plight in this way. To be lifted out of one's home and forced to serve as a concubine for the king—not good! But God will use this for His purposes. Remember Esther's story when you see evil and injustice around you. God is able to make something good out of evil.

What is the writer saying?

How can I apply this to my life?

PRAY   Cuba – Fruitfulness and a greater area of outreach for the Christian radio feeds out of Latin America.

It is difficult to read the Book of Esther without considering some obvious spiritual deficiencies in both Mordecai and Esther. Both bore names honoring pagan gods. They and their fellow Jewish countrymen were still living in Persia, having failed to return to Judea along with Zerubbabel and the fifty thousand who returned to their homeland (see the Book of Ezra). In today's passage, the young Jewish virgin, Esther, will sleep with a pagan king and then become his queen, with no protest from her guardian, Mordecai.

But God works in mysterious ways, and it is His choice to used flawed, imperfect vessels. Think of King David, who committed adultery and murder (2 Samuel 11). Consider the pridefulness of the two apostles who asked for prominent places in the heavenly kingdom (Mark 10:37). Considering these and many other examples, it would be best to think of Esther as an illustration of how God can turn any circumstance into a picture of grace and deliverance. More importantly, He does not require that all the people He uses live perfect lives. He may choose to use anyone. Esther was favored by all those who saw her and dealt with her in preparation for her assigned time to be with the king. When she appeared before the king, he also considered her most favorably (vv. 16-17). In fact, he made her queen, replacing Vashti. Both Mordecai and Esther demonstrated wisdom and courage in the difficult and demanding setting they found themselves in. In verses 21-23, we learn of Mordecai's intervention in an assassination plot involving two of the king's servants. Hearing of this conspiracy that threatened the king's life, Mordecai told Esther, who reported it to the king. The plot was thwarted, and the two would-be assassins were executed. God will use this incident to save the Jewish people in Persia.

LIFE STEP

Take heart that God uses flawed people, since we are all flawed in one way or another. In light of this truth, don't minimize what God may elect to do with you. Trust Him with all your heart. Acknowledge Him in all your ways, and He will direct your paths (Proverbs 3:5-6). Pray right now that God will use you to maximize your impact for the Gospel. Then, focus on how you can become better equipped to be used by Him.

What is the writer saying?

How can I apply this to my life?

At the conclusion of Chapter 2 (vv. 21-23), Mordecai distinguished himself by reporting to king Ahasuerus, through Esther, an assassination plot against the king. This good deed was promptly published in the governmental records and forgotten. Now, with Chapter 3, we are introduced to the final major character in this narrative—a man named Haman, identified as an "Agagite." Though there is some evidence to suggest that this identifier refers to a Persian province called Agag, many scholars link Haman to king Agag, the Amalekite king whom Saul failed to execute (1 Samuel 15:8) and the same Amalekites who were archenemies of Israel since Moses' days (Exodus 17:8-13). Such connections to the Amalekites may explain Haman's deep hatred for the Jews which becomes evident in today's reading. King Ahasuerus promoted Haman above all the princes of Persia, thus obligating all the king's servants to bow in homage as he passed by. Mordecai, however, refused to bow to Haman. When this became a daily occurrence and Haman was made aware of it, his anger grew hot. However, rather than approach Mordecai to demand respect, Haman began to plot ways to rid the Persian empire of all the Jews (vv. 5-6). Verse 7 describes an evil planning session involving the casting of lots *(think, rolling the dice)* solely for the purpose of choosing the day when Haman's destruction of the Jews in Persia would commence. In God's providence, the lot fell on the twelfth month—a full eleven months away. This gave Mordecai and Esther a chance to intervene. Amazingly, when Haman proposed that all the Jews be killed on a particular day, the king asked no questions. He allowed Haman to do as he wished (v. 10). Meanwhile, at least some of the citizens of the city were puzzled by this strange decree (v. 15).

LIFE STEP

Proverbs 16:33 tells us, The lot is cast into the lap, but its every decision is from the Lord. Do you get the meaning? When things happen by mere "chance," you may think of the words "luck," or "fate." For us as believers, there's no such thing. God's divine hand causes or allows things to occur. He controls the details of life and death. You may not like some of the things that happen in your life, but that doesn't change the reality of God's sovereign choice to either cause or allow it. Embrace this truth and trust Him.

What is the writer saying?

How can I apply this to my life?

PRAY Bangladesh – Pray for God to raise up spiritually mature leaders in the church who are committed to authentic discipleship.

The crisis at hand involved consequences of eternal significance if Haman's decree was played out to its intended conclusion. Not only would millions of innocent Jews die, but the very line of the Messiah and all the prophecies of salvation and blessing through Him were at stake. "Sackcloth and ashes" are a typical expression of extreme sorrow (vv. 1-3). Notice that at no time do we read that Mordecai or his fellow Jews prayed. It may be that the narrative was written to minimize any religious offense to Persian readers, or that as a literary device God is missing from the story to underscore that only He could have produced the results. While these are possible explanations, the sad conclusion is that these people were so spiritually dead that they progressed through the ancient trappings of intercessory prayer without really praying. The only ray of hope for Mordecai's spiritual discernment is that he does demonstrate a conviction that *fate* would protect the Jews from annihilation (v. 14). Esther was ignorant of the decree until Mordecai explained it through the intermediary, Hathach. She initially refused to talk to the king because even as his wife and the queen of the kingdom, she was not allowed to approach the king unbidden. To make matters worse, she had not been called to be in his presence for a whole month. Mordecai pushed back on Esther's hesitancy, reminding her that her place in the king's household may have been established *for such a time as this* (v. 14). Her request for fasting (v. 16) on her behalf may have included the expectation of prayer too. It is difficult to know, since her final statement (*If I perish, I perish.*) seems to preclude consideration of God's will and more like resignation to mere "fate."

Our response to a crisis should be different from the response of a person who believes merely in "fate" or "chance." As a believer in Jesus Christ, our hope is rooted in faith, and that faith is firm determination that God's Word is true and He will do what He says He will do. Settle the issue right now that you will navigate through life's troubles with eyes of faith. Pray to God for direction. Seek deliverance from your trials as you acknowledge His sovereignty over all things. Then, trust Him for the outcome.

What is the writer saying?

How can I apply this to my life?

Imagine what must have gone through Esther's mind as she prepared herself to appear before the king, unannounced and uninvited. Would he invite her to his side by extending his royal scepter? She wisely positioned herself in the inner palace, some distance from his throne, and faced the throne where he sat. Seeing her there, Ahasuerus favored her and extended to her his scepter. He apparently sensed that her appearance signaled that she had a request, so he asked what it was she desired. She asked that Haman be invited to a banquet that she would host. Amazingly, the king didn't ask questions. He simply gave the orders and Haman appeared (vv. 4-5)

At this banquet, the king again sought to know what Esther desired. Whether at this point she had lost her courage or her plan all along was to extend the meeting for maximum effect, Esther asked that the king and Haman attend a second banquet the next day. Haman assumed he was being honored because of his glory and status in the eyes of the queen and king. As he left the palace and saw Mordecai at the king's gate, he became enraged again, since Mordecai continually refused to acknowledge Haman by standing (*or trembling*). When he arrived at his home, Haman called his friends and family together and rehearsed with them his successes and frustrations (vv. 10-13). His wife suggested an easy solution to his frustration—simply kill Mordecai and wipe away the "problem (v. 14)." The gallows she envisioned would flatter his ego. He ordered the construction of the gallows reaching a height of seventy-five feet!

LIFE STEP

There should be no difficulty in seeing negative examples in Haman's character. The pride he exhibited in today's text cannot be missed. He assumed he was the object of Esther's interest; he allowed hatred to fester simply because Mordecai refused to stand and honor him; he bragged openly about all his accomplishments. Don't be like that. Let another main praise you, and not your own mouth; a stranger, and not your own lips (Proverbs 27:2). Put your pride, like every other sinful attitude, under the blood of Jesus. Pray for God's grace and help to replace pride with humility.

267

What is the writer saying?

How can I apply this to my life?

PRAY	Pray that the Lord will give you the strength to overcome temptation (Matthew 26:41).

God sovereignly intervened on several occasions in the story of Esther, but His intervention is never more evident than in this chapter. He used the sleepless night of the king to alert the king to an oversight that had occurred five years before. In the middle of a sleepless night, the king asked that the historical records be read to him. Can you guess where the servants started their reading? God's supernatural intervention directed them to read from the very spot that described an assassination plot five years earlier—a plot that Mordecai unveiled, leading to the arrest and execution of the perpetrators and the saving of the king from harm (see Esther 2:21-23). Imagine how surprised (*and possibly embarrassed*) the king was when he learned that nothing had been done to repay Mordecai for intervening and potentially saving the king's life! Again, we see the Lord's intervention at play. Unbelievable as it sounds, Haman had decided to pay a visit to the king (*presumably in the early morning*) the next day to proceed with the execution of Mordecai (v. 4). In an ironic twist of "fate," (*God's sovereignty, again*) the king asked Haman to suggest "*What should be done for the man whom the king delights to honor.*" Suspecting that the king was talking about him, Haman proposed that such a man should be honored with royal attire and a special parade through the streets, mounted on a royal steed (vv. 8-9). Imagine Haman's horror when the king responded favorably to his suggestion and told him, "*Do so for Mordecai the Jew!*" After suffering the indignity of leading the royal horse, bearing Mordecai, through the city streets (v. 11), Haman returned to his home. While his advisors and wife predicted disaster for Haman, the king's messengers arrived to hasten him to Esther's banquet.

LIFE STEP

It's difficult to imagine a turn of events so profoundly ironic as these. Haman thought he was at the top of his career and his future was about to get even brighter, while Mordecai, the man Haman hated, was just hours away from the gallows. But God intervened. He put just the right circumstances in place to make happen what He wanted to happen. Use this account to refresh your memory—that God is sovereign, and He cares about your concerns. Maybe He won't intervene miraculously in your case like He did in Mordecai's case, but He is able. Cast your cares on Him (1 Peter 5:6-7).

What is the writer saying?

How can I apply this to my life?

PRAY

Algeria – Pray for faith-filled, bold believers to persevere despite intensifying persecution by Muslims.

If king Ahasuerus had been attentive to the details of his administration, he would surely have noticed that the Jews in his kingdom were being targeted by Haman for destruction. The fact that he knew Mordecai was a Jew (Esther 6:10) and still did not realize Haman's intentions were to kill thousands, if not millions of his subjects, suggests his ignorance. So it is that Esther's second feast brought shocking news to the king (vv. 1-5). When he once more asked what it was that she desired, she told of the plot against her and her people—*to be destroyed, killed, and to be annihilated.* Hearing that someone he favored as he did Esther was being threatened with her life, the king sought to know who would dare to propose such action (v. 5). Esther wasted no words in identifying the evil Haman, naming him as *the adversary and enemy*, and *this wicked man*!

In his anger, the king removed himself from the presence of Esther and Haman, perhaps to determine what to do about this news. During his absence, Haman begged for his life before Queen Esther. As he threw himself before her on the couch where she was seated, the king returned and immediately deduced that Haman was attempting to assault the queen physically (v. 8). Haman's fate was sealed! The servants witnessing this confrontation didn't even wait for orders. They covered Haman's head with a cloth in preparation for his punishment they knew would soon come. When Harbonah, one of the king's attendants, pointed out that Haman had constructed the gallows for Mordecai, the king ordered, "*Hang him* (Haman) on it!" The wicked Haman was promptly executed.

LIFE STEP

"Be sure, your sin will find you out (Numbers 32:23)." How vividly this passage became real in Haman's wicked plot to destroy the Jews in Persia. If you are a believer, you must be honest about your sins and confess them to God. It is true that confessing your sins will not insulate you from all of sin's consequences. But your honesty with God will restore your fellowship with Him and bring you back to a proper walk with Him. Keep close accounts of your sins.

What is the writer saying?

How can I apply this to my life?

Recall that Haman's wife and his advisors had predicted the downfall of Haman and his household (Esther 6:13). Haman's death was just the beginning. What follows in today's reading brought to pass the rest of their predictions. The king awarded Esther the house of Haman and elevated Mordecai to replace Haman as his prime minister. Esther then placed Mordecai in charge of Haman's estate (vv. 1-2). Then Esther again fell at the king's feet and, in a tearful plea, begged the king to counteract the decree that Haman had initiated against the Jews. Notice how carefully and respectfully Esther put her appeal to the king (v. 5), not once presuming upon his favor or grace. She also knew that the decree would not be ignored or canceled under Persian law, but an additional (*new*) decree could be published that would alter the impact of the original decree. Thus, Esther asked *let it be written* to revoke the decree written by Haman. The king gave this privilege to Esther and Mordecai—to write whatever they pleased, and to seal it with the king's signet to assure its validity through his kingdom. Mordecai dictated the letter and the king's scribes copied it into every language spoken throughout the 127 provinces that made up the Persian Empire. The decree gave authority for the Jews to take whatever action necessary to defend themselves against attack. The details are gruesome--including the death of women and babies (v. 11). In the ensuing nine months, not only would the decree make it to every corner of the Persian Empire, but the people also had ample time to consider whose side the king most likely was on. Seeing the favor granted to the Jews, many Gentiles converted to Judaism as they contemplated the changing loyalties in the kingdom (v. 17).

LIFE STEP

Notice that the Gentiles who converted to Judaism (v. 17) were driven to do so when the favor enjoyed by the Jews became obvious. They wanted to be on the "winning side." Take this example to motivate yourself toward godliness, hospitality, kindness, and love. As a representative of the Lord Jesus (an ambassador – 2 Corinthians 5:20), you're much more likely to move people toward a decision for Christ by behaving like the winner that you already are! Remember—you have eternal life; you are a child of the King of kings (John 1:12; Romans 8:17).

What is the writer saying?

How can I apply this to my life?

PRAY South Africa – Pray for missionaries who invite those living in slums to become sons and daughters of the King.

Amazingly, despite the latest decree that authorized the Jews to defend themselves against any attackers (Esther 8:11), there were still men who hated the Jews enough to try to touch God's people. The appointed day arrived (as given in Haman's decree—the 13th day of the twelfth month) and the enemies of the Jews attacked them. However, rather than killing the Jews, the Jews overpowered their haters with a great slaughter (v. 1). Also, because so many of the subjects of the kingdom respected Mordecai's place of power as the king's prime minister, the Jews were helped in their defenses by the officials and leaders of all the Persian provinces (v. 3). In Shushan, the capital, five hundred men were killed on the first day. Haman's ten sons, who had lived the previous nine months with the shadow of their father's actions hovering over their heads, were also killed.

When the report of the first day of killing reached the king, he sought out Esther and asked her what more she may desire (v. 12). Her answer sounds to modern readers like a heartless, cruel request. However, it may be better to view her in the same light as Joshua's conquest over the Canaanites. Just as he would settle for nothing less than complete victory, so Esther seemed dedicated to ridding the Jews of all threats that may remain. So, she requested one more day to complete the job. Further, she asked that the dead bodies of Haman's ten sons be hung upon the gallows up for all to see (v. 13). The king agreed to her request. More killing ensued on the following day. The total killed in all the provinces was seventy-five thousand of the enemies of the Jews. After the killing, they held a day of rest and feasting.

LIFE STEP *The victory of the Jews over their enemies has characteristics of a supernatural empowerment for a specific crisis. God did not work behind the scenes only to arrange for the Jews' protection, He also arranged for a complete victory. This is our God. He intervenes in ways that we can't even imagine or recognize. Read Romans 8:28 and write a note to God expressing your gratitude for His intervention in your life.*

What is the writer saying?

How can I apply this to my life?

To memorialize the deliverance of the Jews out of the hands of the enemies led by Haman, the Jews in the Persian Empire began to celebrate as a holiday the thirteenth day of the twelfth month, as well as the fourteenth day. They feasted and sent gifts to one another (vv. 18-19) throughout the kingdom under the orders of Mordecai, who sent letters to all the Jews in the provinces in King Ahasuerus' kingdom (v. 20). This celebration became a yearly festival among the Jews, gladly accepted as a fitting remembrance of God's intervention and the turning of sorrow to joy (v. 22). Verse 26 tells the reader that these days of celebration became known as "Purim," after the name *pur*, which in the Hebrew language means "lots." This commemorates the casting of lots (*pur*) by Haman to determine the date on which to bring destruction to the Jews he hated so vigorously (Esther 3:7).

To this day, many Jewish people fast on the thirteenth day of the twelfth month in the Jewish calendar. On the evening of the thirteenth, the entire book of Esther is read in the synagogue. It is read in a dramatic/comic fashion with different voices speaking the dialogue. Verses 1:7, 3:15 and 7:4 are sung and 2:5, 8:16 are recited by the congregation. When the name "Haman" is read, the congregation cries, "Let his name be blotted out" and "The wicked shall rot." Children make noise with noisemakers, boo, and stamp their feet. The Rabbi reads the names of Haman's ten sons with one breath to symbolize their simultaneous hanging. It is to this day primarily a joyous holiday in traditional Jewish communities.

LIFE STEP

Too often we fail to recognize the true significance of our holiday celebrations, whether they have religious significance or not. Check your heart attitude the next time you find yourself in a holiday celebration like Christmas or Easter. Don't celebrate as one who simply has a day off from school or work. Celebrate as one who has been delivered from eternal separation from God through the perfect life, death, burial, and resurrection of Jesus.

FRIDAY - WEEK 36

What is the writer saying?

How can I apply this to my life?

The first three verses of the Book of Philemon are the greeting of the letter in the standard format that Paul used frequently. Paul states he is in prison (v. 1) and with Timothy, which fits the end of Acts (see Acts 23 and 24). While we don't know for certain Philemon's relationship to Apphia (v. 2) and Archippus, the standard suggestion is that Apphia was his wife and Archippus was his son. Note that this is not simply a private letter since the entire church, which met in Philemon's home, is being addressed. *Grace* and *peace* are the typical greeting of Paul, with the first being a normal Greek greeting and the second a normal Hebrew greeting.

Paul then commended Philemon for his love and faith (v. 5). Paul had been praying that Philemon would continue to share his faith (v. 6, the common idea behind *fellowship*). Additionally, Paul was thankful (v. 7) that Philemon displayed Christian love by caring for other believers—which would have direct bearing on the appeal Paul will make on behalf of a new Christian who escaped as a slave from Philemon's house (v. 10, tomorrow's reading). Paul elected to write this letter with the tone of a good friend, rather than to command Philemon to act in some way out of respect to Paul's apostleship (vv. 8-9). Therefore, he makes his appeal as a request rooted in love, rather than in authority.

LIFE STEP

Friends who share a common bond in Christ have something special as part of their relationship. Think about who you count as your closest Christian friends and offer a prayer of thanksgiving for their friendship. Perhaps now would be an appropriate time to jot a note or a text to that friend, encouraging them in their faithfulness and letting them know you are praying for them.

What is the writer saying?

How can I apply this to my life?

PRAY Praise God for sending His Son to be our Savior.

Onesimus, the slave who ran away from Philemon, had come to faith in Christ through his interaction with Paul while visiting Paul in prison. Notice that Paul referred to him as *my son, Onesimus*, and indicated he (*Onesimus*) made this transition to Christ-follower while Paul was *in chains* (v. 10). As a result of this transformation, Onesimus was now much more than a runaway slave—he was of profit to both Philemon and to Paul as a brother in Christ (v. 11). To head off any potential argument from Philemon about his former slave as a profitable friend, Paul suggested that Onesimus' flight from Philemon was orchestrated by the divine hand of God (v. 15), and he should be treated as a beloved brother—no longer a slave. Still, Paul did not want to coerce Philemon to act out of a sense of obligation, but rather to voluntarily receive Onesimus back into his house without the punishment a runaway slave might expect.

Therefore, Paul felt comfortable sending Onesimus back and urging Philemon to receive him in love.

Paul continued to justify his request by pledging to pay out of his own resources anything owed by Onesimus to Philemon, a signal that Onesimus may also have stolen from his master in addition to running away (v. 18). Then, in a subtle way appealing to Philemon's sense of love and gratitude, Paul hinted that Onesimus may have come to faith through his (Paul's) ministry, and therefore owed a great debt to Paul. Note that Paul used his own handwriting at this point, to help demonstrate the authenticity of the letter. He delivered one final appeal to Philemon to act in accordance with his wishes (v. 20) and expressed his confidence that Philemon will do as Paul asked (v. 21). Paul hoped to visit Philemon, apparently expecting to be released from prison soon (v. 22).

LIFE STEP

The way we treat fellow believers should be motivated out of our love for one another and God's Word, which consistently encourages love and kindness between believers (see Ephesians 4:32). Make that your goal today and every day as you interact with your Christian friends. Love them. Be kind to them. Treat them as family members, all related to the same Father. Remember, all who have believed in Jesus Christ are the children of God (1 John 3:1).

What is the writer saying?

How can I apply this to my life?

The first account referred to in verse 1 is the Gospel of Luke (see Luke 1:1-4). As the author of both this book and of the Gospel that bears his name, Luke sought to arrange his material in as orderly a fashion as possible (Luke 1:3). Theophilus, whose name means friend of God, was more than likely a wealthy Gentile who may have financed all of Luke's research, writing, and distribution costs.

This first section introduces the major themes that will be developed throughout the book. Luke's selection of the question asked by the disciples (v. 6) was not a random choice. It was intended to alert the reader to his primary purpose. The Book of Acts answers this simple question: "Since the Messiah has come, how can the kingdom still remain imminent?" Answer: The Church Age and its imminent conclusion via the Rapture allow the kingdom to be an about-to-happen event even though a new and unexpected worship system has emerged.

Jesus told the disciples that there would be some momentous changes coming. The pouring out of the Holy Spirit was the first major event of this new age, but in Joel it was also associated with the launch of the kingdom. In effect, Jesus told them that they didn't need to know what was about to happen. The kingdom could begin, but an equally momentous yet unrevealed event could also begin, which would require similar signs to authenticate its divine origins. The Holy Spirit would come as prophesied, but the direction of human history in the immediate future would be determined by something else. Jesus clearly left the impression that the coming of the kingdom was still a real possibility for the disciples to experience, but that this was not a necessity. In God's unfolding plan, it would depend on the response of the generation that had witnessed Christ's greatest sign: His bodily resurrection!

LIFE STEP *We live in a world of instant gratification where waiting has become a lost art. If we are ever going to experience everything God has for us, we need to learn to patiently wait on the Lord. What is God asking you to wait on Him for? Commit yourself once again to trust His timing.*

What is the writer saying?

How can I apply this to my life?

PRAY | Italy – Pray for the power of God to be revealed and to set free those lost in the darkness of occult, pagan, and New Age practices.

The events recounted in Acts 1:12-26 are a clear indication of the disciples' attitude about the future. They were not planning for the start of a new worship system (which we call "the Church"); they were busy preparing for the kingdom promised to Israel. Twelve was not an arbitrary choice for the number of disciples that were needed. Jesus had told them that they would sit on twelve thrones and rule the twelve tribes of Israel. So, the first "act" of these apostles was to replace Judas, whose behavior disqualified him from that position, so that this number could be maintained.

The methods that Peter used to make this decision may seem a little unusual to Church Age believers. We do not cast lots to choose pastors or deacons! This was a reminder to the readers that the Church Age had not yet begun. These men were using the methods revealed to Israel to resolve such matters. Peter, who was appointed second-in-command by Jesus in Matthew 16, took his responsibility seriously and, in Jesus' absence, used one of the options available to Old Testament leaders for such situations. When the king needed an answer from God, he could use the Urim and Thummim (part of the High Priest's garments), or he could cast lots. The former were no longer available in Israel; therefore, Peter used the lots and Matthias was selected as Judas' replacement.

This event is important. It shows that there did not appear to be any doubt in the minds of these men that Jesus was about to return, and that the kingdom was going to be set up soon. Accordingly, they did their duty to ensure that twelve qualified men were ready to rule with Him.

LIFE STEP

Any confusion about how events recorded in Acts apply to the Church today is a result of misunderstanding Luke's purpose in writing. The initial acts of the Apostles were in keeping with the expected launch of the kingdom promised to Israel. These included miraculous authenticating signs that God never intended to be repeated in every generation of the church. Even as we do not use lots today to discern God's leading, we should not expect that God is performing stupendous signs and wonders through chosen apostles on a massive scale such as we see in the very early years of the Church Age (Acts 2:43; 5:15-16). Our calling is to walk by faith and not by sight (2 Corinthians 5:7).

What is the writer saying?

How can I apply this to my life?

PRAY Kenya – Pray for foreign agencies and missionaries to transition from leadership to consulting for growing national organizations.

As one travels along any highway, there are places where two or more routes join for some distance before parting ways. While driving on that road, there is no way to know which route each car will finally take. We are entering just such a period in the Book of Acts. We know which road was eventually taken, but other drivers had different agendas. We know that the Church started in Acts 2 (Acts 11:15), but for the persons living then, this had not yet been revealed. And so, the apostles were about to offer the kingdom to Israel just as Jesus had.

For this offer to be legitimate, all the criteria set down by the Old Testament had to be met. One of the signs that the prophets foretold concerning the coming of the kingdom was a general outpouring of the Spirit (Isaiah 32:15; 44:3; Ezekiel 39:29; Joel 2:28; Zechariah 12:10). The Spirit had been poured out before upon certain individuals, but never in such a widespread and indiscriminate way. This was always intended by God to be a sign of the approaching kingdom, but in this case, it took place in a "transition zone" with two possible outcomes. One of them, the kingdom, had already been revealed; the other, the Church, was only a potential future that had not yet been revealed. It was still a mystery to the apostles at that point in time (Ephesians 3:1-11).

LIFE STEP

The miracles recorded in the New Testament functioned as signs. In fact, this is what John always called them in his Gospel account (2:11, 23; 4:54; 12:18, 37; 20:30). Just as signs announce or point to something, miracles served to authenticate Christ, His apostles, their offer of the kingdom to Israel, and the launch of the Church. We are now called to walk by faith, not by sight, and to live in the power of the Holy Spirit while we await the coming of Christ to take us to be with Himself (the Rapture). Rather than seeking signs and wonders, we are called to know Christ and to make Him known (1 Corinthians 1:22-24). Make that your focus today.

What is the writer saying?

How can I apply this to my life?

Peter could have chosen any number of passages from the Old Testament to explain this event. The crowd standing before him knew the Old Testament and that the pouring out of the Spirit was a sign of the coming kingdom. They may not have been willing to accept it, but they were aware of the concept. Peter chose to quote from the Book of Joel because it was one of the earliest prophetic writings that referred to the coming of the Spirit as a sign associated with the time of Israel's national salvation. The Old Testament did not say that this would be the only time that the Spirit would be poured out, only that this event would be a necessary first step at that specific time. In this moment, two potential futures merged in the same way that two routes may be temporarily merged as a part of one highway.

The uncertainty was real. Israel faced a very important choice. Would she repent and accept Jesus as her Messiah, or would she continue on a path of rebellion and rejection? Just as the historical nation of Israel stood on the border of the Promised Land and listened to the report of the twelve spies, the people now stood on the edge of the messianic kingdom and listened to the twelve men who had followed Jesus for the previous three and a half years. This was a choice that the nation had to make. Would they step up and claim what God had promised or fall back into the hardship of Gentile oppression? Israel felt that she was indispensable to God because of her part in the kingdom. It was about to become clear that men should never use prophecy to manipulate God.

LIFE STEP

The generation that left Egypt with Moses did not enter the place of promise. They looked at events through the eyes of facts, figures, and physical realities. History was now repeating itself and God was about to implement another waiting period for His chosen people, the nation of Israel. How are you evaluating your current circumstances? Through the eyes of human logic or by faith in the living God and the knowledge that He is working out all things for good?

What is the writer saying?

How can I apply this to my life?

Having explained the significance of the immediate miracle (tongues), Peter began to tie this to the recent events that had taken place in Jerusalem: the trial and crucifixion of Jesus Christ. Peter started his presentation with Scripture. The first pillar in his argument was that God had always intended for the Messiah to be put to death and resurrected from the grave. This was the truth that the disciples themselves had found difficult to grasp (Luke 18:31-34). Throughout Christ's ministry, they had resisted this idea. They thought that it would disqualify Jesus as their Messiah. But now, Peter understood the Old Testament Scriptures and he began to minister to the crowd in the same way that Jesus had ministered to His disciples. He opened the Scriptures and showed them that the crucifixion was not a detour or misstep in the messianic mission. If the Messiah was to provide a new kind of life, the old life would have to be discarded. Later, the Apostle Paul would explain more fully that to live with Christ, one first needs to die with Him. David understood something of this when he penned Psalm 16, the text which Peter quoted. He knew that he could not defeat the grave, but he also knew that Another would come Who would shatter the bonds of death and set the captives free. Jesus led the way through death and back again. David was not just speaking of a resurrection; he was speaking of a rescue. Jesus entered the grave to rescue those who had no hope in their own strength.

LIFE STEP *Some commentators resist the idea that Psalm 16 is speaking about Christ. They imply that Peter was misusing this passage, but this cannot be the case. To defeat death, the Messiah had to die—to experience it Himself—and to come back victorious over death. It was the only way and He did it. How can this encourage you today?*

279

What is the writer saying?

How can I apply this to my life?

PRAY   Greece – Pray for a clear presentation of the Gospel to reach a nation where very few have heard the Truth.

The reaction to Peter's sermon was marvelous. In the same way that this message had opened the disciples' hearts, it now pierced the hearts of the assembled crowd. They called out to Peter and asked what they should do. Peter told them to repent and be baptized. This verse has caused a lot of controversy among believers. On the surface, at least to modern readers, it seems to imply that one must be baptized in order to be saved. But the modern reader is not the intended reader. If a modern believer were to hear in a sermon that one must die daily or be crucified with Christ, he or she would immediately put that into a proper context. We understand such metaphors. A Jewish person living in the first century would understand baptism terminology in the context of John the Baptizer. Baptism was simply an outward confession of an inward reality. It was part and parcel of the message that Peter had just preached. Unless we identify ourselves with the death, burial, and resurrection of Jesus Christ, there is no hope to defeat death. Baptism illustrates that. It is a confession that the person being baptized is renouncing self-righteousness and choosing to be resurrected in newness of life with Jesus' righteousness. Baptism is an act of faith and as such, is no different than words of faith. Paul tells us in Romans 10:9 that we must confess with our mouth and believe in our heart. Confessing with the mouth simply means to openly agree with what someone else has said, in this case, with what God has said about Jesus Christ. Baptism is a way of demonstrating that one accepts the death, burial, and resurrection of Jesus Christ as my own.

LIFE STEP

God has always designed outward acts of faith to be informative. Baptism is a highly visible and very memorable way of affirming that we have been crucified and buried with Christ in order to be raised in newness of life. Take some time to read and reflect on Romans 6:1-14. It is a profound passage about what took place when we trusted Christ to save us. He didn't merely provide forgiveness for the sins that we do, He fundamentally changed who we are.

What is the writer saying?

How can I apply this to my life?

PRAY   Fiji – Pray for salvation and discipleship for Fijian university students representing every island territory.

The narrative immediately jumps to an incident that took place shortly after the sermon on the Day of Pentecost. Peter and John were heading to the temple when they encountered a man who was lame from birth. This is the first miracle recounted since the Holy Spirit came upon the apostles at Pentecost. The fact that Luke spends so much time recording this event indicates that it's especially significant. The fact that it created such a stir among the patrons of the temple would clearly indicate that this type of thing had not been happening regularly in Jerusalem, even though the Spirit had been poured out. The apostles, led by Peter, were about to embark on a journey filled with wondrous signs and irrational responses. These signs did not randomly occur within the believing community of that day. They were always linked to the apostles. How, and why, they were linked to the apostles is what Luke was about to reveal in the coming chapters.

It is also significant that this miracle occurred on the very doorstep of the political body (the Sanhedrin) which had illegally tried Jesus and condemned Him to death. It is an open proclamation that the apostles were no longer hiding and that the Good News would continue to be preached publicly and in the power of the Spirit at the very seat of resistance. The Great Light that came out of Galilee was about to turn the ancient world upside down, and at the middle of this storm were twelve ordinary men who had literally walked with an awesome God.

LIFE STEP   *We sometimes get so enamored with the miraculous that we forget that such power is always secondary in importance. It is the message that saves. Make this your focus today.*

What is the writer saying?

How can I apply this to my life?

PRAY

Pray for the many staff and workers at Word of Life. They are the "behind-the-scenes" people that help keep things going.

As a crowd began to materialize and try to figure out what was going on, Peter seized the moment and began to give an explanation. He did not talk about himself and his part in what had just taken place. Instead, he talked about Jesus' death, burial, and resurrection. He kept it simple and yet there was a kind of oddness to his sermon. Consider verses 19-21. Peter was telling this crowd that if they would repent, Jesus would come back and bring "times of refreshing" from heaven (v. 19). What did he mean by this term? Verse 21 provides the answer. It was a reference to the "restoration of all things" that had been predicted by the holy prophets. This was a kingdom message, the message that Jesus had been preaching for the previous three and a half years!

This is how we know that the Book of Acts is about transitions. Here, at the beginning of the book, the apostles were still preaching the Gospel of the kingdom. They were still convinced that the seventieth week of Daniel 9:24-27 would soon begin. The nation of Israel was being given one more opportunity before God formally instituted a new worship system, the Church. There is no question that the Church began at Pentecost (Acts 11:15). But there is uncertainty about when believers realized that the Church began at Pentecost. God's knowledge of events is outside of time, and this allows Him to set events in motion before outcomes are revealed in time and space. The disciples were operating by kingdom principles because they still hoped that Israel would accept her Messiah. Until the Church was unveiled, there was still a real decision to be made in time by the nation of Israel. What God knows never invalidates what God offers.

LIFE STEP

We sometimes belittle the importance of our decisions simply because God knows the outcome. Human responsibility is not diminished by divine sovereignty. We know this because God says so, not because it is logical to the human mind.

What is the writer saying?

How can I apply this to my life?

One cannot help but be impressed with the transformation that had taken place in Peter's life. Not long before, he had hidden in the shadows and denied that he even knew Jesus. The rest of the disciples had also melted away in fear. But now these men stood fearless before the very authorities that had previously intimidated them.

Luke made it a point to list the dignitaries that were present (vv. 5-6). This was not a minor gathering. These were the most important and powerful religious leaders in Israel, the very same men who had conspired to have Jesus crucified. Luke made it very clear that the religious establishment in Jerusalem was given every possible opportunity to repent and to recognize Jesus as the Messiah. The Gospel did not formally go to the Gentiles until God had exhausted every possibility with respect to Israel. Note Peter's statement in verse 11. Jesus had become the stone which Israel rejected, and which caused her to stumble.

Verse 12 indicates exactly why these men would not accept their Messiah. They wanted a salvation that was under their control. They did not want Jesus to be the sole mediator between God and man. They wanted their names to be up in lights. But salvation comes from God and on His terms, not from man. It can never be designed or administered by any human authority.

LIFE STEP

One of the most difficult things for men to do is to give up all control of their destiny. We always want to have a security blanket. Unfortunately, the only thing that can come between us and God is us. What is God asking you to surrender to His control today? Are you trusting in Christ alone to save you, or are you counting on being able to do that yourself?

283

What is the writer saying?

How can I apply this to my life?

PRAY

Azerbaijan – Pray for God's love to be proclaimed in the dozens of towns and villages which have never heard the Gospel.

The confrontation which began in yesterday's passage continues in today's verses. The spiritual leaders of Israel realized that they were at a great disadvantage. The fact that a forty-year-old man who had been lame for many years was now healed and standing before them was quite intimidating! But rather than believing the message that was authenticated by this sign miracle, their concern was to ensure that news of the miracle would not spread!

Compare this mindset with that of the apostles. While it is true that Peter rejected their order to stop preaching in the name of Jesus, he did not do so in a disrespectful way. Even though Peter could have felt justified in giving these men an earful, he did not. He honored these authorities in the same way that he would have had they not crucified

Christ. When Peter proclaimed that men ought to obey God rather than men, he was not suggesting that believers have no obligation to worldly powers. The only time that it is appropriate for believers to resist earthly powers is on those rare occasions when the earthly power commands a believer to do something that is the exact opposite of what God has commanded.

On those rare occasions, the believer ought to follow Peter's example. He was never disrespectful or confrontational. He showed deference to these men and only objected when they directly forbade the preaching of the Gospel. At that point, Peter explained his predicament. He did not say one thing and then go out and do another. All his dealings with these authorities were totally transparent.

LIFE STEP

Whether at home, at school, or at work, we all have authorities in our lives. Even in difficult times, we must honor them while maintaining our allegiance to our highest authority, God Himself.

What is the writer saying?

How can I apply this to my life?

PRAY — Bahamas – Nearly a third of the population are Bible-believing Christians. Pray that these communities would grow in their love for each other and the lost.

James captured the spirit of today's passage when he wrote, "My brethren, count it all joy when you fall into various trials." (James 1:2). The apostles were not unaffected by the threats that they had just received. They returned to the larger group of believers and recounted all that had been said. Notice all the positive blessings that flowed out of what many might consider a major setback. The immediate response was prayer. This put the trial into the right perspective. They did not call upon the Lord to remove the threat; rather they asked that they might have the courage to carry on with this important work.

Additionally, the whole body of believers became united. They were together with "one heart and one soul" (v. 32). This kind of unity is an awesome demonstration of the Spirit's work. Too often, we want the power of the Holy Spirit to make us special. It is natural for humans to want to stand out, to be cool, and to do their own thing. What takes a miracle is when a diverse group of believers becomes united in their hearts and minds.

Finally, we see the love of the Spirit shed abroad in the hearts of these people. They truly loved one another in deeds, not just words. They willingly sold their possessions in order to support the community. If the religious leaders had realized how their actions would unite the believers in such a powerful way, they might have thought twice about threatening them!

LIFE STEP — *Too often when we pray, we ask God to change others. We should never ask God to do such a thing unless we have asked God to change us first. Often, when we change, we're not as concerned about seeing others change.*

285

What is the writer saying?

How can I apply this to my life?

The narrative concerning Ananias and Sapphira can be a very chilling one. There does not appear to be any similarity between this event and what one commonly experiences in churches today. Once again, this is evidence that these events occurred during a transition period between kingdom expectations and the Church Age. The apostles were still preaching the kingdom of God and expecting Jesus to return to set it up at any moment. Several similar incidents took place in the Old Testament. Achan was destroyed because he stole some merchandise from Jericho. Uzzah was killed because he touched the ark of the covenant. Elisha's servant contracted leprosy because he took payment from Naaman. Uzziah was afflicted with leprosy when he entered the temple and offered a sacrifice. During that dispensation (Law), different rules applied which do not govern the Church Age. The events that we read of today are stern reminders that Peter and the rest of the apostles are high-ranking officials in the coming kingdom.

There are significant differences between the theocratic kingdom that existed in the Old Testament and the Church Age. If we do not keep these in mind, we can be misled by some of the occurrences in Acts. Many of the uncomfortable events in Acts would be very normal under the Mosaic system. We need to be careful that we do not use the early part of Acts as a pattern for church administration. The Holy Spirit did not intend it to be used that way. Later, Paul would give instruction specifically for the church (1 Timothy 3:14-15).

LIFE STEP

Giving honor to whom honor is due is not just a matter of politeness. It is an obligation. Peter showed respect even to the evil authorities that arrested him. In contrast to this, Ananias and Sapphira failed to respect God's appointed representatives, the apostles, and paid a very heavy earthly price.

What is the writer saying?

How can I apply this to my life?

For just a moment it appeared that the message of the kingdom was beginning to win the day in Jerusalem. The sick were being healed simply by having Peter's shadow fall on them, and yet Israel would soon snatch defeat out of the jaws of victory! Behind the scenes, the same religious leaders who had orchestrated the crucifixion of their Messiah were now busy plotting how they would crush this revival. The evil in this world never sleeps. While it was specifically the leaders of Israel that were to blame for this rejection, it should not be overlooked that the population in general went along with them. No matter how many signs and wonders the apostles did, when the time came to choose sides, the people went along with their leaders. Sin damages the heart. People will generally choose that which is in their own self-interest. However, when the matter involves God, people will often choose to die rather than accept a helping hand.

It seems logical that if God opened the doors of the prison to set the apostles free, it would be evidence that God was working through these men. But when people do not want to believe, no amount of evidence is going to change their minds. In Luke 16:31, Jesus said that if someone would not believe the Scriptures, they wouldn't believe even if someone came back from the grave. This is precisely what happened in Jerusalem. All the wondrous events that transpired had little effect except to enrage the religious establishment.

LIFE STEP

Jealousy is a cruel master. One would think that everyone would be encouraged when needs were met, and lives were rescued. But it was not so. People, like the leaders of Israel, usually care more about who gets the credit than they do about the suffering of the people. We must beware of the same tendency.

What is the writer saying?

How can I apply this to my life?

It is not hard to sense the desperation of the religious leaders. They thought this matter would be done with once they had taken Jesus out of the mix. Apparently, they did not think that the disciples had what it would take to carry on the mission. They were shocked that these twelve uneducated Galileans were somehow turning Jerusalem upside down with their teaching. As on the previous occasion (4:19), Peter was very respectful in dealing with these rulers. He did not rail against them but simply stated that whenever he was forced to make a choice between obeying God and obeying man, he would always choose God. This was not a slap in their face because they all would at least technically agree with this statement.

In effect, Peter was tying their hands. He went one step further this time and made reference to the resurrection and to the Holy Spirit who was coming upon new believers all around Jerusalem. These things were not rumors from a distant land but real events that were happening right under their noses and which could not be ignored. But as it was with Pharaoh, these signs only served to harden the hearts of these men. The more love God shows, the more men seem to reject Him. The reason that God did not set up the kingdom in the first century is because His people did not want Him. They wanted a kingdom that was run by their rules and not by God's. They wanted the kingdom, but they did not want the King.

LIFE STEP — *Willfulness can have tragic results. We often fight for our own way to our own detriment. It is too easy to get so focused on how we want things to be that we miss all the good things that are happening all around us. Take time to appreciate God's goodness in your life.*

What is the writer saying?

How can I apply this to my life?

PRAY Venezuela – For the defeat of any legal proposal to end or restrict evangelism in any way.

The disciples were found innocent but nonetheless were beaten mercilessly before being released with a stern warning. This only emphasizes the irrational behavior of the members of the Council. They were so frustrated because every step they took to crush this new "religion" only seemed to breathe additional life into the cause.

Gamaliel is mentioned only a couple of times in Scripture, here and in Acts 22:3 where we are told that he was the Apostle Paul's teacher. The Talmud (Jewish theology book) teaches that he was the grandson of Hillel. If that is true, then he was likely an important member of the Sanhedrin. The fact that he is not mentioned in the trials of Jesus is a bit of a mystery, but he could have been away at the time. Since he seemed to be less emotionally caught up in the situation, this may indicate that he did not participate in the events surrounding Jesus' death.

Whatever the case, he made a very good point: If something is not of God, it can't prosper, but if it is of God, it can't be stopped! The Council was persuaded to follow his advice. There is an ancient church tradition that Gamaliel converted to Christianity and was baptized by Peter and John together with his son and Nicodemus.

As with the first encounter, these events only served to encourage the disciples and they continued to preach daily all over Jerusalem. The passage doesn't give us a detailed description of the content of their message, but it's worth noting that it included the fact that Jesus was the Messiah (Christ). Once again, this is in keeping with a kingdom focus.

LIFE STEP

Gamaliel's advice is worth taking to heart. We can be discouraged to watch plans and projects that do not honor the Lord experience success, while churches close their doors and ministries struggle to survive. Make no mistake; what is not of God can't ultimately succeed and what is of Him cannot ultimately fail. It's impossible! Let's not be weary in doing God's work.

What is the writer saying?

How can I apply this to my life?

PRAY   Haiti – Pray for a spiritual outpouring of faith in God in this poverty-stricken nation.

A growing ministry is a recruiting ministry. Leadership is essential for many reasons. In chapter 6, we are introduced to the second wave of early leadership. While this passage is often referenced in discussions about deacons in the church, it is unlikely to be referring to the office of deacon as described by Paul much later. These men were not initially called to a teaching/preaching ministry, but some of them quickly developed into gifted preachers. The immediate need had to do with the serving of food. The rapidly expanding number of believers led to the problem of some of the needy being overlooked during the daily distribution of food. The apostles immediately arranged for seven men to be responsible for this area of service. Two of these men,

Stephen and Phillip, quickly became a part of the preaching team and had an almost immediate impact.

The text first focuses on Stephen. It is not clear why the Sanhedrin chose to single him out, but it seems likely that they were trying to avoid the public outcry that might have resulted if they took one of the Twelve. The text is clear that Stephen was performing many signs and wonders and that people were beginning to recognize his leadership abilities. The Council made its first move against Stephen in order to see how such an act would be perceived by the general population. As with Jesus, they put forward false witnesses who claimed that Stephen was speaking out against the temple and the Law.

LIFE STEP

Serving the Lord in small matters is the training ground for future leadership. Never despise those who serve tables. This is where God looks when the big shoes need to be filled. Be willing to serve at any level when the Lord calls you.

What is the writer saying?

How can I apply this to my life?

PRAY Indonesia – Pray for Christians to boldly demonstrate and proclaim the grace and salvation of Jesus Christ.

Stephen's appearance in the text seems so short, and yet it was so meaningful. He went from serving tables to standing before the Sanhedrin in just a short period of time. This is the longest recorded sermon in Acts and one of the longest in the Bible. In it, Stephen demonstrated an incredible understanding of the Old Testament. He wove together old truth with new truth that had been revealed in Jesus Christ in such a way that the crowd was incensed.

The message began with a quiet tone and a soothing quality that drew the hearers in. Stephen made those who had gathered feel comfortable, at least it first. He spoke of Abraham, Isaac, and Jacob. He traced the working of God from Abraham's call in Mesopotamia to his sojourn in Egypt. Stephen rehearsed the promises of a son (seed) and of the land in which they were now living. He then reviewed the deliverance from famine through Joseph and the sojourn in Egypt.

The main point of Stephen's message would come later in verse 51 when he accused them, saying, "You are doing just as your fathers did." Earlier, Jesus had made the same criticism of that generation (Matthew 23:31-32). Stephen's message highlighted a history of hard-heartedness and rebellion against God's guidance. One cannot but be amazed at how God used this relatively new leader.

LIFE STEP

There is a gap between the objective and the personal. Many of us have a clear and clinical understanding of the Gospel and of the Savior, but it has never become personal. What Stephen does in this sermon is make the Gospel a personal matter. Is it for you?

What is the writer saying?

How can I apply this to my life?

PRAY Papua New Guinea – Increased provision of aircraft and staff for missions reaching into remote areas.

One of the charges against Stephen was that he rejected the Law of Moses. We notice in today's passage that Moses was not immediately accepted by the children of Israel. In fact, while Moses was on the mountain, the crowd below forged an idol from silver and gold and danced before that idol as they had done in Egypt. In his message, Stephen made the point that Israel never really changed. He implied that by failing to accept Jesus, the Council was siding with the crowd that had rejected Moses in the first place. The members of the Council knew all these narratives and many of them were experts in the Law. They had always pictured themselves as the true heirs of Moses and the guardians of his Law. Stephen was suggesting that they were actually the spiritual children of those ancient ancestors who rejected Moses and caused him to flee into the wilderness of Midian where he would live for the next forty years (Exodus 2:11-15).

Human nature is rather adept at this very thing. We have no problem seeing the effects of sin in the lives of others, but when the finger of Scripture begins to point our way, we often become blind to the very same danger. Stephen's audience was still calm, but the storm was brewing and was about to erupt.

LIFE STEP

Our towns and cities are filled with churches that no longer preach or teach the Gospel as it is revealed in Scripture. We look around with complacent expressions never thinking that this could happen to us. Peter warned that we must take heed because, when we think we stand, we are often just about to fall.

What is the writer saying?

How can I apply this to my life?

PRAY Thailand – For believers to stand strong in a land where more people earn their living through crime than honest labor.

Stephen continued with the account of Moses' life. God had spoken to Moses through the burning bush and had sent him to deliver the Israelites from bondage. Through Moses, God showed His power to Pharaoh by great signs and wonders. God parted the Red Sea for Israel and caused the same water to drown the Egyptian army. But while Moses was on Mount Sinai receiving the Law, the people's hearts turned back to the evil they had learned in Egypt.

Stephen made one especially important point in these verses. He reminded them that God promised Moses that He would raise up another prophet like Moses from among the people. This introduced the main point of the sermon toward which Stephen was heading: Israel had a history of rejecting God despite His miraculous signs, and they were doing the same. If Israel would not accept Moses with all the wonders and signs they'd seen, why would the present generation welcome another like him with open arms?

Jesus was the "new Moses" who brought new revelation from God. He came to His own people with many signs and wonders, but His own people received Him not. They claimed to be followers of Moses, but they really were followers of the people who had rejected Moses. Stephen was making the point that this was not unusual; it was the way it had always been with Israel.

LIFE STEP

If we do not take great care, we too can drift away from the Lord despite all that He has done to show us His greatness and His faithfulness. It may be time to rehearse all that the Lord has done for you and ask Him to warm your heart to His goodness.

What is the writer saying?

How can I apply this to my life?

PRAY Argentina – Pray that the church will have a vision to impact their communities and do more to address the enormous poverty in the city.

As we come to the end of Stephen's sermon, we need to ask why Luke spent so much time on it. This is especially true since, other than this sermon, Stephen did not play a very large role in Acts. There are two important elements within Luke's central message that hinge on the events surrounding Stephen's death.

First, Stephen's sermon explained why Jesus did not return from heaven and set up the physical kingdom right then and there. Had God been willing for Israel to enter the Promised Land? Yes, He had been. So why did Israel wander in the wilderness instead of entering it? Because they had rejected God's leadership through Moses. A similar situation prevailed in Stephen's day. Was God willing to set up the kingdom promised to David right then and there?

Yes, He was. So why did it not happen? Because they rejected God's leadership through the "new Moses."

Just as He had done in the past, God gave Israel more than one chance. They had rejected God (the Father) the first time when they refused the testimony of the forerunner, John the Baptist, and what took place at Jesus' baptism (Luke 3:21-22). They had rejected God (the Son) the second time when they crucified Him. Now they rejected God (the Spirit) for the third and final time by picking up stones and murdering Stephen, a man filled with the Holy Spirit. It is as though they had rejected each member of the Trinity. The second element of Luke's message that would hinge on Stephen's death will be seen tomorrow.

LIFE STEP *God's grace is marvelous, but He will never force anyone to accept a Savior they do not want. God's love and offer of salvation must be accepted; it will never be forced on anyone.*

What is the writer saying?

How can I apply this to my life?

PRAY   Costa Rica – For a new generation of godly, effective leaders for the churches that will commend the Gospel.

As mentioned yesterday, the stoning of Stephen was a pivotal moment in Acts. We all recognize such moments when they occur in modern literature. A new person is introduced into a storyline in such a way that everyone knows that it is significant to the development of the plot. That is the case here. Just as Stephen was being stoned, Luke introduced Saul who, though not throwing stones, was sitting off to the side watching over the outer garments of those who were (Acts 22:20).

From this point on the storyline changes. For the next five chapters the story goes back and forth between the Twelve and Saul/Paul. The emphasis on the kingdom diminishes while talk of the Church begins to take center stage. The kingdom had been offered to that generation for the final time. God's temporary replacement was now beginning to emerge more clearly from the shadows. The man that God used to reveal and explain this new age would be the Apostle Paul.

There is a sense in which Paul's life corresponded perfectly with what was happening in the churches. Those who had once been considered enemies and afar off (the Gentiles), were now to be welcomed into the new worship system without any formal restriction such as circumcision. Similarly, Paul, whom we first met as an avowed enemy of the Gospel and the last person anyone would expect to be saved, would become the primary spokesperson for this new era.

LIFE STEP   *God's ways are definitely not our ways! We are left to marvel at many of God's choices. If you ever feel that you have nothing to offer, just remember Saul. Who could have guessed what great things God would accomplish through this persecutor of the early believers?!*

What is the writer saying?

How can I apply this to my life?

PRAY

Cyprus – Pray for discipleship, spiritual maturity, and bold witnesses among ethnic minority believers.

Philip's ministry in the city of Samaria follows quickly on the heels of the introduction of Saul/Paul. This brought the focus back to the Twelve and their ministry, but it also marked the beginning of a shift away from Jerusalem and its Jewish audience to other regions, in this case Samaria, an area normally avoided by Jews. Once again, it was becoming increasingly obvious that things were shifting and new, unexpected things were happening.

Luke also began to clarify the purpose of the outpouring of the Holy Spirit and of the signs and wonders which had been taking place all over Jerusalem. Remember, God never acts without purpose. In Samaria, Philip led many people to the Lord, but Luke focused on the conversion of one very prominent magician named Simon. This individual had mastered the fine art of illusion. He immediately understood that Phillip was doing something that he had never seen before. Simon was even more impressed when Peter and John came from Jerusalem and bestowed the Holy Spirit on these new believers by laying hands on them. This is a very significant point! Only an apostle could do this (Romans 1:11; 2 Timothy 1:6). In fact, such power was one form of evidence that they were genuine apostles (2 Corinthians 12:12). Other people like Philip could perform sign miracles, but they could never distribute such power to another person. Nowhere in the Acts of the Apostles or in the remainder of the New Testament did a person perform sign miracles without being an apostle or having direct contact with an apostle. We know from 1 Corinthians 12-14 that sign gifts such as tongues did not come without complications. They could be used inappropriately for selfish reasons. Despite this danger, God continued to use sign gifts in the early years of the Church Age. This emphasizes how important these gifts were in authenticating the identity of the apostles who were called to lay the foundation of the Church (Ephesians 2:20; 3:5). Without such signs, anyone could have claimed apostolic authority. In fact, many did who were but messengers of Satan (2 Corinthians 11:13-15)!.

LIFE STEP

It's easy to understand how someone could become enamored with sign gifts and the supernatural power behind them. Simon certainly was and wanted to have this power for selfish reasons. He was soundly rebuked because his heart and affections were in the wrong place. What are we looking for? God desires our affections to be set on Him, not on whatever gifts He chooses to give us.

What is the writer saying?

How can I apply this to my life?

The storyline immediately shifts from Samaria to an Ethiopian eunuch. Keep in mind that Samaritans were genetically connected to Abraham and thus were, in a sense, half-Jewish. But this person was a non-Jewish proselyte, a Gentile who was following all the requirements of the Law (especially circumcision). Step by step, Luke was recording how the Gospel expanded from being exclusively Jewish to include an ever-expanding cross section of humanity. He traced the spread of the Gospel from Jerusalem to Samaria, and then to the uttermost parts of the earth. The Ethiopian eunuch marked another step in this process. His baptism was important because it demonstrated that he was fully accepted into this new worship system and would not have to endure "partial membership" anymore.

For the modern believer, none of this appears unusual, but it was not only revolutionary in that day, it was also considered heresy by most! God was introducing a new way to worship and fellowship with Him: an assembly without walls. It was new and shocking to those who had been raised under the Mosaic Law, but it was clearly a work of God and not of man. The miraculous signs were proof of that!

We sometimes miss so much because we ask the text to meet us where we are. We try to uncover some morsel that we can relate to our present experience. Try seeing the text the way the original readers experienced it. There is both excitement and consternation.

LIFE STEP   *Is God doing something new in your life that you never expected? Don't dismiss what He may be trying to accomplish. Ask Him to help you to be open and to recognize new directions in which He may be leading you.*

What is the writer saying?

How can I apply this to my life?

PRAY Romania – For building materials and skilled laborers to meet the demand for new church construction.

Chapter 9 refocuses our attention on Saul who had been commissioned by the Council in Jerusalem to search out and arrest members of the followers of Jesus in Damascus. The text describes Saul as "breathing threats and murder against the disciples of the Lord." This does not sound like someone who would listen to a Gospel presentation!

Saul's encounter on the road to Damascus was spectacular and supernatural. Christ Himself visibly appeared to Saul in such a glorious way that he was blinded by it. Christ even audibly spoke to him. Why such a stunning and personal intervention? Because Saul was not going to be an *ordinary* convert. He would be the last apostle to be personally appointed by Christ with all the power and authority that accompanied such a calling

(1 Corinthians 15:1-11). Each of the other apostles had also been directly chosen and personally taught by Jesus Christ. In Galatians 1-2, Paul was adamant that the Gospel he preached, even though the same as what the other apostles proclaimed, had been communicated to him directly by Jesus, just as the other apostles had received it.

It should be noted that although Saul was persecuting Christians, he was doing so for theological reasons and not from jealousy. He genuinely believed that Jesus was a false Messiah and that he was serving the one true God of the Old Testament Scriptures. This is not to excuse what Saul was doing, but it shows that it's possible to be sincerely wrong. Many have done great evil in God's name. Such evil cannot be excused.

LIFE STEP

The epistles written by the apostles have divine authority because they were penned by divinely appointed apostles. The teaching found in them is therefore authoritative and provides us with the doctrinal foundation of the Church Age by divine intent. They are not man's suggestions but God's directives for us. The Old Testament and the Gospel accounts are extremely important but be sure to include the epistles in your reading and reflection. That's where we find the primary teaching for our time.

What is the writer saying?

How can I apply this to my life?

PRAY   Pray for the faithfulness of those who evangelize and minister to those in your local prisons.

Yesterday we saw how Galatians 1-2 related to Luke's account of Paul's conversion. Galatians was Paul's first epistle and the very first issue he dealt with was his own independent status as an apostle. We recall from Acts 1:21-22 that the primary apostles were only chosen from among those who were with Jesus from the very beginning of His ministry and who were taught by Him. Paul claimed to be an equal with these pillars of the Church because he had seen Christ and had been directly taught by Him in the same way as the original Twelve.

What Paul says in Galatians is confirmed here in Acts. We might expect that if Paul were such an important addition to the early church, God would have sent Peter to give him back his sight, but this was not the case. Instead, He sent Ananias, a disciple living in Damascus. God was intentionally taking Paul down a path that would demonstrate to all that this man, who had once persecuted believers, was now to be accepted as an apostle of equal standing as the Twelve. There is something else worth noting. Only the apostles could grant the power to perform sign miracles and anoint others with the Holy Spirit. But in this case, no other apostle was present when Paul was healed and received the Holy Spirit. This was kept distinct in every way possible from the other apostles, not merely to affirm his equal standing with them but possibly because he was being uniquely commissioned to go to the Gentiles (v. 15).

LIFE STEP

People sometimes say that "the devil is in the details," a colorful way of saying that keeping track of all the details is essential to a successful outcome. Thankfully, Luke did a masterful job investigating and reporting all the details. God orchestrated every aspect of what was happening in the early church so that His purposes would be absolutely clear. We must always pay attention to the details in Scripture. They are there for a reason.

What is the writer saying?

How can I apply this to my life?

PRAY   Malawi – Pray for Bibles and theological instruction for under-resourced believers.

Saul had an immediate impact in the synagogues, no doubt because he still had "status" and could speak freely. It is difficult to determine the precise timeline here in Acts 9, but according to Galatians 1:15-18, Saul spent as much as three years in Arabia. Given what he says in the surrounding verses, it seems most probable that this is when he was taught by Christ. It's interesting that the Twelve had also spent about the same amount of time with Christ.

As best we can understand, this would seem to have taken place between verses 22 and 23 of Acts 9. What might appear to be happening rather quickly was likely spread over several years. This fits with verse 23 which makes it clear that quite a bit of time had passed. The first twelve chapters of Acts stretch over fifteen years. By the time Paul visited the apostles in Jerusalem (v. 26), more than five years had passed since the Day of Pentecost (Acts 2). The conversion of Cornelius (Acts 10) occurred about five years after that.

Paul's time in Arabia would have allowed rumors of his conversion to diminish so that when he went up to Jerusalem, there was still a lot of fear that he might still be on a mission to destroy believers. The fact that the disciples were being very careful in this matter (v. 26) suggests that they had not yet met Paul face-to-face. It is interesting to note that the persecution of the church eased up for a few years around this time. It is also interesting to see that it had been ten years since Christ's resurrection, and yet the Gospel had not yet formally gone to the Gentiles.

LIFE STEP

The experience of being let down through the wall of Damascus in a basket (vv. 23-25) was one that Paul never forgot. He would later refer to it as an example of the kind of humiliating experience which he welcomed rather than boasting in what God was doing through him (2 Corinthians 11:30-33). Are you experiencing a humiliating circumstance that has turned you into a "basket case," entirely dependent on others for your well-being? Choose humility and joy over pride and bitterness. God is at work to protect you in ways you may not be able to envision.

What is the writer saying?

How can I apply this to my life?

PRAY   Bulgaria – For believers to have the wisdom and discernment to avoid doctrinal error.

Jumping ahead five years, the storyline once again reverts to Peter. The churches in and around Judea and Galilee had been enjoying a time of peace and expansion. It appears that everyone was comfortable with this arrangement. However, Jesus had told His disciples that they were to go to the uttermost parts of the earth. It was time for the next move.

Peter had been traveling throughout the region. Lydda was a town not too far from Joppa on the coast. It was a little more than halfway on the road from Jerusalem to Joppa. Luke recounts a healing that happened at Lydda and how Peter was then summoned to Joppa where he raised Dorcas from the dead. The fact that the saints called Peter when Dorcas died would seem to imply that Peter had done this sort of thing in other locations. There were incredible miracles happening throughout the region, but it was still basically a Jewish church. Samaritans (half-Jews) and a proselyte (a convert to Judaism) had been welcomed into the church, but the big barrier had yet to be breached. Ten years had elapsed since the Day of Pentecost and yet there is no record of a single Gentile convert to Christ. We may assume that many of the believers were still offering sacrifices and attending services at the temple. But all of this was about to change. The events in today's passage set the stage for an important turning point in chapter 10.

LIFE STEP   *So many things that we take for granted in our relationship with Jesus Christ were astonishing developments to those who first experienced them. What is happening here in the Acts of the Apostles shook the early church to its very foundation. How do we respond when God does the unexpected in our lives?*

What is the writer saying?

How can I apply this to my life?

PRAY Venezuela – Perseverance and patience for those discipling believers from dysfunctional backgrounds.

To this point all conversions in Acts have been either Jews, half-Jews (Samaritans), or Jewish proselytes (the Ethiopian eunuch). Cornelius is the first recorded instance of a Gentile being converted directly to Christianity. The amount of space given by Luke to the account of his conversion highlights its importance.

Today we are introduced to Cornelius and the events that led up to Peter's visit to his home. It would be hard to imagine a less likely Gentile candidate to have any interest in God, let alone come to faith in Jesus Christ. Cornelius wasn't just a Gentile; he was a Roman! Not only that, but he was also a professional officer in the Roman army stationed in the luxurious city of Caesarea, the Roman capital of Judea, which boasted a stunning artificial harbor built by Herod the Great. As a centurion, he commanded at least one hundred men, but it may have been far more if he had oversight of the entire Italian cohort (v. 1).

As unlikely as it might seem, we read that Cornelius was seeking after God and that he was "one who feared God." This designation was used by Jews to refer to a Gentile who was unwilling to fully convert to Judaism but who was committed to both monotheism and to the Jewish ethic. For the most part, Cornelius would likely have followed Jewish practices but without being circumcised. He was a devout man who gave alms to the Jewish people and was continually reaching out to God in prayer. The greatest surprise of all was that God took note of his alms and responded to his prayers. Something was about to happen that would shake the early church and shift a long-standing paradigm.

LIFE STEP

If you've ever wondered if God hears and responds to the prayers of unsaved people, the story of Cornelius is your answer. Clearly his heart was being drawn to the Lord and God was preparing something very special for him and his entire family. Let's not give up hope as we pray for unsaved family members and friends. God can do amazing work in the hearts of those who appear least likely to ever be saved!

What is the writer saying?

How can I apply this to my life?

The paradigm shift that was about to happen pushed the early church out of a long-standing comfort zone. The power of the Gospel was going to save even Gentiles, and they would even receive the Holy Spirit, starting with a Roman officer and his family, no less!

God chose the Apostle Peter to witness and authenticate this pivotal moment, but his heart would need to be prepared. In a vision, Peter was instructed to eat animals that were designated unclean and forbidden by the Mosaic dietary laws (Leviticus 11), something he had never done. It was a scandalous suggestion to which Peter objected. But God wanted him to realize that He had the right to change His way of administering His rule over mankind. While Peter was trying to understand all of it, the delegation from Cornelius arrived and the Spirit instructed Peter that their arrival was connected to the vision. The words "doubting nothing" in verse 20 are very instructive. Under normal circumstances Peter would have had serious misgivings about taking the Gospel to a Roman centurion. He was still in the "go-only-to-the-lost-sheep-of-the-house-of-Israel" mode. Had he not received clear direction from God, he would have no doubt dismissed Cornelius' vision. God didn't talk to Gentiles through angels! But now, through the eyes of faith, Peter was catching a glimpse of what Jesus meant when He said to go "to the end of the earth." (Acts 1:8)

Throughout the Gospels and the Book of Acts, the apostles clearly underestimated the breadth of God's program. Up to this point, Peter probably thought this command was referring to the Jews who were scattered throughout the Roman Empire. He could not envision that God was about to turn the whole Gentile world upside-down. The Gospel was about to make an incredible leap; so much so, that in a few short years, the Church would become almost entirely Gentile.

LIFE STEP — *In a similar fashion to Peter, we sometimes underestimate the extent to which God wants to work in our lives. We are happy with the portion we have. Let us pray that God will enlarge our vision in order that we might endeavor to do the great work to which He has called us.*

What is the writer saying?

How can I apply this to my life?

PRAY Hungary – Effective outreach and godly teachers in public schools where Christianity is welcome.

It should be noted that Peter did not enter Cornelius' home without some trepidation. He clearly had misgivings about a Gentile becoming a part of the family of God without first going through some initiation into the nation of Israel. Peter was still under the impression that salvation was primarily a Jewish thing. One can almost feel the awkwardness as Peter and Cornelius met for the first time. Peter was struggling with a lifetime of teaching that told him that everything about this situation was wrong. For his part, Cornelius was overwhelmed with the possibility that he could be accepted into the family of God as a full partner and no longer needed to worship as a second-class citizen.

The contrast between the two could not have been greater. One was a Roman officer and, though he clearly had a place in his heart for the Jewish people and their God, he lived among men who despised religious Jews. The other was a Galilean fisherman, a man that most Roman soldiers would consider on a social level not much higher than a slave. Despite this, God had brought them together to participate in one of the greatest peace accords ever witnessed in human history. A wall that had existed for generations was about to begin tumbling down (Ephesians 2:11-16). It was an event that shaped all the centuries of church history to come.

LIFE STEP

As we read the Book of Acts, we can become preoccupied with the miracles that Peter and the other apostles performed. But don't overlook the spectacular change that the signs were pointing to. God was doing something totally unexpected. Could it be that we fail to notice God working around us because we're not expecting Him to "show up" where He does?

What is the writer saying?

How can I apply this to my life?

Peter's message was short and to the point. He opened with a very important statement, one that would be debated throughout most of the rest of the Book of Acts. The issue had to do with the Gospel and the Gentiles. In verses 34-35, Peter set forth a revolutionary idea: Salvation was not limited to the Jews but available to all, regardless of nationality. Furthermore, a person did not need to become a Law-abiding Jew or be connected to a Jew in any way to be saved. Notice the elements contained in this message. These are the same components that would become the essentials of Paul's Gospel. Peter first established the deity of Jesus Christ, calling him "Lord of all." (v. 36) Then Peter emphasized Jesus' humanity; how He came from Nazareth and was empowered by the Holy Spirit (v. 38). He then described Christ's death and resurrection (vv. 39-41) and declared that,

as a result, salvation from sin was available to all men by faith (v. 43). Note the opening phrase of verse 43: "To Him all the prophets witness." All these things were according to the Scriptures. This simple Gospel message marked the first time that all references to the nation of Israel were removed. Peter, to whom Jesus had given the keys of the kingdom (Matthew 16:17-19), had opened the door for a truly international offer of salvation by grace through faith in Christ.

In times of great change, God had always validated the changes using signs and wonders. So it was that when Cornelius and his family responded in faith to Peter's message, they received the Holy Spirit and began speaking in tongues. It was a miniature version of the Day of Pentecost all over again. Peter recognized this as the divine seal of approval on this stunning, unprecedented event.

LIFE STEP

Peter had witnessed a stunning demonstration of the fact that "God shows no partiality." (v. 34). Salvation is equally available to all. Though we may not often think about this, partiality is something that we can struggle with. James had a lot to say about this matter as well (James 2:1-13). Examine your own heart on this issue and ask the Lord to reveal any traces of favoritism or prejudice that may be preventing you from desiring to see everyone receive the gift of eternal life through faith in Jesus Christ.

What is the writer saying?

How can I apply this to my life?

It is in our nature to resist change. But our God is not a dead or stationary piece of gold or silver. He is a God who has instituted many dramatic changes in His dealings with mankind. When Peter returned to Jerusalem with his account of Gentile conversions in Caesarea, there was a great stir among the Jewish believers. They immediately reacted negatively to the very idea that a Gentile could be saved without first converting to the Jewish faith. Peter was very forceful in his retelling of the events that led him to share the Gospel with Cornelius. He made it very clear that it was God who had initiated this change and not him.

It's important to note that this change was only instituted based on clear, authenticated revelation from God. It was not just a response to changing culture and moral values. Truth is eternal but programs can change. These changes were always made in a way that made it clear Who had initiated them. In this case, Peter had not only seen a vision three times, but his actions had been verified by an outpouring of the Holy Spirit at Cornelius's conversion. This outpouring of the Spirit resulted in the distribution of a sign gift (tongues). These gifts only had value when there was a divine event or messenger that needed to be authenticated. Signs without someone or something to be authenticated only lead to confusion.

LIFE STEP

Notice Peter's question in verse 17: "Who was I that I could stand in God's way?" It's an excellent reminder that if God is behind something, no matter how unexpected, we cannot successfully resist Him. Our pride can sometimes pit us against God in such a way that we resist any new directions that He wants to lead us in. Consider how He may be at work in new ways in your own life. Are you open to that?

What is the writer saying?

How can I apply this to my life?

PRAY

Bolivia – For missionaries willing to serve in the remote villages of the Quechua and Aymara people.

Even though Cornelius, his family, and close friends had already become Spirit-indwelt believers, there was still no large-scale, concerted effort to reach out to the Gentiles (see v. 19). The exception was in Antioch where a few believers began sharing Christ with some Greeks and many were saved. Barnabas (his name means comforter) was sent by the church in Jerusalem to evaluate what was happening. He rejoiced to see God's grace at work and then went to Tarsus to look for Saul and bring him to Antioch where they ministered together for an entire year. They did not realize it at the time, but the foundations were being laid for the first missionary outreach to the Gentile world.

The gift of prophecy (a sign gift) was very important to the early church. It not only served to authenticate the apostolic ministry, but it also provided much needed direction in the absence of the apostolic writings we now know as the New Testament. Both these needs have since disappeared with the completion of the New Testament and the passing of the apostles. One such prophet was Agabus. His prophecy concerned a famine that would affect the whole Roman Empire. This famine took place during the reign of Claudius (41-54 A.D.). The prophecy had a profound effect on the church, and they immediately sent a contribution to help their fellow believers in Judea.

LIFE STEP

Barnabas' response to what God was doing in Antioch is a great example. When he saw the evidence of God's grace being poured out on Gentiles, he rejoiced (v. 23)! It's easy to welcome the grace of God when it's poured out in our own lives, but do we rejoice when we see God grant unmerited favor to others? We might object that they don't deserve it. But that's precisely why it's grace! How can you rejoice in God's abundant grace in the lives of others today?

What is the writer saying?

How can I apply this to my life?

PRAY   Cayman Islands – For Christians to continue to hold fast to their Christian values in the midst of wealth and materialism.

The Herod mentioned in this chapter is Herod Agrippa II, a grandson of Herod the Great. Under his persecution, James, the brother of John, became the first apostle to be martyred. The response of the unsaved Jewish community shows their opposition to Christianity (v. 3). The reason Peter was not immediately executed was because of the Feast of Unleavened Bread. This took place during the seven days following the day of Passover. Today the two holidays are combined into Passover week. Because these were holy days, the Jews would not look favorably on any execution during this celebration.

The story of Peter's miraculous "jail break" is one of the most dramatic events in the whole of the Book of Acts. He wasn't merely locked in a cell; he was chained between two soldiers while other guards watched over the entrance. Perhaps the Romans remembered how Jesus had mysteriously disappeared from a sealed tomb and wanted to avoid a similar incident. Despite all this, Peter was sleeping soundly when an angel woke him up, released his chains, and brought him safely out of the prison. Peter's response is very revealing. He could not believe that it was really happening and thought instead that it was just a vision. This shows us that even though God was doing unusual signs and wonders in those days, they were not so frequent as to be considered the norm. It was not until Peter was standing alone on the street that he realized that a remarkable miracle had occurred. Such rescues from danger were the exception, not the norm.

LIFE STEP

Peter's deliverance from prison begs the question: Why did God engineer such a miraculous escape for him while allowing James to be killed? Though we cannot know the answer, it does show that God's plan for each person is unique and accomplishes God's purpose for His glory and our ultimate good. Is the Lord allowing things in your life that He has seen fit to spare others? You can trust Him!

What is the writer saying?

How can I apply this to my life?

PRAY For the many summer children's camp leadership staff, as they share the Gospel with hundreds of children.

In today's passage Luke describes the reaction of the believing community that had been praying for Peter's release. A prayer meeting was taking place at the home of Mary, John Mark's mother. A young girl, Rhoda, responded to Peter's knock at the door but was so excited to tell the others that she forgot to open the door. Peter was left standing outside while Rhoda tried to convince them that their prayers had been answered, quite literally! They were shocked when the door was opened and Peter stood before them, in person!

Unable to accept the possibility of the supernatural, Herod assumed that this was an "inside job" and had the jailers executed. His failure to get rid of Peter so shamed him that he left Jerusalem and went down to Caesarea, where he met a rather gruesome end. Josephus, a well-known Jewish historian of the day, added further details to the biblical account of Herod's demise. He wrote, "At the same time he was seized by a severe pain in his belly which began with a most violent attack... He was carried quickly into the palace... and when he had suffered continually for five days from the pain in his belly, he died in the fifty-fourth year of his age and the seventh of his reign." Herod's power to hurt the Church had been taken from him, and the ministry of the Gospel, which he had attempted to stifle, continued to flourish.

LIFE STEP

Do we pray with such faith that when God answers, we are not surprised? Herod's power was formidable and seemed insurmountable. Even the praying believers did not expect such a clear victory in the face of such persecution. But Herod's audacity only served to embolden and empower the spread of the Gospel. We too can expect resistance, but we must not be discouraged. God is still in control, and He can thwart the power of the enemy in remarkable ways.

What is the writer saying?

How can I apply this to my life?

The church at Antioch must have been quite a place. Verse 1 gives a list of some of the prominent men who ministered there. Barnabas and Saul (Paul) are well-known characters in the New Testament, Simeon and Lucius, not so much. Some have suggested that Simeon is Simon of Cyrene, who carried the cross of Christ. In Mark 15:21, we are told that he had two sons, Alexander and Rufus. The fact that Mark mentions them is a clear indication that they were known to the Roman churches (Mark's Gospel was written for Roman Gentiles). In Romans 16:13, Paul referred to a Rufus and his mother. It is possible that Paul considered the mother of Rufus as a mother because he stayed with them while he was in Antioch.

Note how sensitive the leaders of the church were to the guidance of the Holy Spirit as they fasted and prayed (v. 2). Even after the Spirit had given them clear direction regarding the ministry that God was calling Barnabas and Saul to, they kept on fasting and praying, no doubt out of a desire to ensure that they would continue to do God's will. They did this even though they had prophets in their midst. And so, Paul, Barnabas, and John Mark set out on the first of three great missionary journeys recounted in the Book of Acts and immediately encountered opposition. Herod may have been removed, but Satan has many ways to resist God's work and His people!

LIFE STEP

Prayer can easily be put on the back burner. When we are looking for direction, we find it easier to make it a priority. But once we receive that direction, we often charge into the fray and leave prayer behind. Has this happened in your life? We must beware of this tendency.

What is the writer saying?

How can I apply this to my life?

A group of three set out from Antioch on this first missionary journey. Paul and Barnabas are well-known, but in today's passage we focus on John Mark. It was at his mother's house that the church had prayed for Peter. Their journey brought them first to the island of Cyprus. They traveled the island from east to west, starting out in the capital of eastern Cyprus, Salamis. They then traveled to Asia Minor (modern Turkey), where John Mark abruptly left the group. The reasons for his departure are not mentioned here, but Paul and Barnabas would later part company over the issue of Mark's worthiness for service because of this incident (Acts 15:36-41).

As Paul entered the city of Antioch in Pisidia, he first announced the Gospel in the synagogue. This established a pattern that he followed throughout his missionary journeys. Why Paul chose to do this likely had more to do with practical than theological matters. Members of the synagogue would have known much of the background material necessary to give the Gospel a context. Furthermore, the God-fearing Gentiles associated with the synagogue gave Paul an open door into the non-Jewish community. The phrase, "you who fear God" (v. 16) would have been a direct reference to those God-fearing Gentiles present in the synagogue. In a small way, this reflects the greater commission given to the Twelve in Acts 1:8—Jerusalem (Jews), Samaria (half-Jews and proselytes), and to the end of the earth (God-fearing Gentiles).

LIFE STEP *Paul always followed the path of least resistance when bringing the Gospel to a new location. He never compromised the message, but he always sought the best way to gain a foothold and to secure a hearing. He maximized the opportunities at hand to the best of his ability. We should do the same.*

What is the writer saying?

How can I apply this to my life?

PRAY   Germany – For new and effective ways of reaching the youth for Christ.

Today's passage contains the heart of the Good News that these early missionaries preached. Paul's message was clearly geared toward a predominantly Jewish audience but contained the essentials of the Gospel: the death, burial, and resurrection of Jesus Christ (see also 1 Corinthians 15:1-4). Three times Paul emphasized that what happened to Christ was not a failure in God's plan (vv. 27, 29, 33). Rather, all these things happened according to God's predetermined plan. This was an important point to Paul and ought to be for us as well. God always intended that Jesus should die, be buried, and rise again as He did. There is clear continuity between the Old and New Testaments. The Jewish religious leaders had opposed Christ and had Him crucified, in part because they had misinterpreted the Old Testament. But even their resistance had been part of God's sovereign plan.

In the same way, the opposition that we encounter as we share the Gospel is a part of God's sovereign plan. Paul never even considered the possibility that the things he suffered were unusual or that they somehow lay outside of God's will. Peter would later point out that opposition and suffering are part of the calling that we have received as we follow Christ's example (1 Peter 2:19-21).

LIFE STEP

Have you been facing opposition and even suffering as a result of your faithfulness to God's Word and the sharing of the Gospel? Take some time to read Paul's summary of the opposition he encountered in his ministry found in 2 Corinthians 11:22-33. Then, ask the Lord to encourage your heart with the fact that you are following in the footsteps of the apostles and that your Heavenly Father is fully in control of all things, even the opposition we encounter.

What is the writer saying?

How can I apply this to my life?

Spiritual blindness is a cruel master. It not only blinds a person's heart and mind, but it seeks to impose this blindness on others as well. So, it was with the Jews in Antioch of Pisidia. They not only rejected the Gospel themselves; they also conspired to keep anyone else from accepting it. The same is true today. In a society which accepts all manner of immoral behavior and protects it under the banner of diversity and tolerance; there is only one group which will not be tolerated, those who stand for God's Truth. They are labeled fanatics and enemies of freedom.

These Jews, as had been done in Jesus' case, stirred up the members of high society and the civil authorities to oppose Paul and Barnabas. This radical idea that salvation was free and available to all shook them to the core. When they saw people leaving their assembly and converting to Christianity, they became envious. The act of shaking the dust off their feet as they left Antioch mirrored what Christ had told His disciples to do (Matthew 10:14; Luke 9:5). The act was specifically directed toward the Jewish community rather than the city as a whole and was a symbol of excommunication, tantamount to calling someone a heathen. The believers were not discouraged by this turn of events but were filled with joy and the Holy Spirit.

LIFE STEP

Though we are to always pursue peace, we must realize that the Gospel can bring as much division as it does unity. To those who believe, it is the tie that binds our hearts together in Christian love; to those who reject it, it is a stumbling stone. This is what we should expect.

313

What is the writer saying?

How can I apply this to my life?

PRAY   Bermuda – For teens to mature and develop godly leadership skills through Bible Clubs.

Paul and Barnabas proceeded to Iconium, where once again they began their ministry in the Jewish synagogue. As in Antioch of Pisidia, there was an immediate and sizable response to the Gospel among both the Jews and Gentiles. But once again, opposition originated with unbelieving Jews who launched a propaganda campaign to poison the minds of the Gentiles and of the civic leaders, forcing the apostles to flee to Lystra. It seemed that Satan had scored another victory, but this was not the case. The only thing the opposition succeeded in accomplishing was to further spread the Gospel to other locations. In fact, in the grand scheme of things, God providentially used the persecution experienced in the days of the early church to keep His messengers on the move.

As Paul preached in Lystra, a man born crippled was in the audience. Paul perceived that he had faith to be healed. We're not told how Paul perceived this, but something about the man's demeanor indicated that he believed what Paul was sharing. Faith is not something invisible that cannot be seen. Faith manifests itself outwardly in the way we take God's Word seriously and move to act on it.

LIFE STEP   *Faith is not intended to merely be a private matter; it should be visible to others. Do you live in such a way that people can perceive your faith? If not, what do you need to do to change this?*

What is the writer saying?

How can I apply this to my life?

PRAY   Spain – Wisdom for pastors ministering in a society staggering under drug abuse, unemployment, and gambling addiction.

After Paul healed the crippled man, the crowd jumped to the wrong conclusion and assumed that the apostles were Greek/Roman gods. The reaction of the apostles could not have been stronger. They vehemently denied it and refused to take any credit for what had been accomplished. Notice how determined the multitude was in their desire to venerate the apostles as divine beings and yet how quickly they were persuaded to violently turn against them! This tendency to quickly change their minds was characteristic of the people of this region called *Galatia*. Julius Caesar even said, "The infirmity of the Gauls is that they are fickle in their resolves, fond of change, and not to be trusted." Paul later noted this as well in his epistle to the Galatians (1:6; 3:1; 5:7-8).

The crowd ended up stoning Paul and leaving him for dead. But he revived shortly afterwards, went back into the city, and moved on to Derbe the next day. This may have been when the events of 2 Corinthians 12:2-4 took place. Paul may have actually died and been taken up to the third heaven before coming back to life to resume his ministry. It can't be known for sure, but it is interesting to note that even Paul was not certain whether his journey to heaven was in or out of the body.

From Derbe, the apostles backtracked through the cities they had already visited and appointed elders in every church (v. 23). This makes it clear that churches were to function under local leadership rather than being governed by some central body.

LIFE STEP   *Local churches were planted by the apostles, but they were not controlled by them. Each church was ruled by men chosen from their own midst. This is one of our most important responsibilities as believers: to appoint leadership within our churches that will honor God and allow the church to flourish in its unique setting.*

What is the writer saying?

How can I apply this to my life?

PRAY Afghanistan – Pray for the many Afghans who are uncomfortable with terrorist actions in Islam's name, but are interested in discovering more about Jesus Christ.

As the Gospel spread to the Gentiles, an inevitable controversy began to arise. Did Gentile believers need to be circumcised? In the very early years, when believers were mostly Jewish, this had not been an issue. But as more and more Gentiles were added to the church, there arose a group of believing Pharisees who were having a hard time letting go of their ceremonial past and who insisted that Gentile believers had to be circumcised and to follow the Law of Moses (v. 5). The discussions became so intense that it was decided to send a delegation to Jerusalem led by Paul and Barnabas to meet with the apostles and the elders to resolve the matter.

The first to speak was Peter, the one who had witnessed the conversion of the Roman centurion Cornelius and how the Holy Spirit had come upon him and many other Gentiles with him (Acts 10). He noted that this had happened quite apart from the Law and circumcision. If God had not required it, who were they to insist on it? Peter's characterization of the Law as a *yoke* (v. 10) was very appropriate. It seems that the more legalistic believers were arguing that the Law should be used at least as a means of sanctification (spiritual growth), perhaps even justification (salvation)! The Book of Galatians was written around this time. In it, Paul seemed to indicate that the biggest issue within the early churches was whether sanctification was by faith or by works.

LIFE STEP

Rules and regulations, whether in the Old Testament or the New, were always meant to be a diagnostic tool. God never suggested that they could make anyone righteous (Romans 3:20). Laws can demonstrate that we are sinners, but they cannot do anything to set us free from sin (Colossians 2:20-23). For that, we need faith in God and His provision for spiritual growth through dependence on the power of the Holy Spirit.

What is the writer saying?

How can I apply this to my life?

After Paul and Barnabas had shared testimonies of God's saving work among the Gentiles, James addressed the assembly. This James is not the brother of John but rather the half-brother of Jesus and the author of the Book of James. The fact that he made the final judgment call, which was then affirmed by the others, suggests that he was the primary leader of the Jerusalem church (see also Galatians 2:12).

The decision that was made amounted to an all-out victory for Paul and Barnabas and the Gospel they had been preaching: that salvation was entirely by faith without the works of the Law.

Nevertheless, the Holy Spirit led the apostles and elders to impose four restrictions on the Gentile believers of the day. One was a clear biblical mandate to avoid sexual immorality (1 Thessalonians 4:3), while the other three addressed matters of personal conviction. If there was to be harmony in the church, Gentile believers needed to be sensitive and respectful of the personal convictions of Jewish believers regarding food offered to idols and the consumption of animal blood. Paul later addressed these matters in greater detail in Romans 14 and 1 Corinthians 8.

LIFE STEP

The fact that we are under grace and not under Law does not mean that we can never be compelled to live under any restrictions whatsoever. The call to love God and to love our fellow believers is a continual obligation and privilege (Romans 13:8). To flaunt our Christian liberties in the face of those who have convictions that differ from our own is as wrong as requiring circumcision to be saved. Review Romans 14 and 1 Corinthians 8. How do these apply to your situation?

What is the writer saying?

How can I apply this to my life?

PRAY   Nicaragua – God's guidance for pastors counseling the many people devastated by death, poverty, and divorce.

Even spiritual leaders can have legitimate disagreements. Paul and Barnabas were both filled with the Holy Spirit and yet they disagreed about taking John Mark on their second missionary journey. Paul objected to the idea because Mark had quit the team in Pamphylia on the first missionary journey (Acts 13:13). His desertion had probably caused them some hardships. Though we don't know precisely what Paul's concern was, he clearly considered Mark unfit for this type of ministry.

Barnabas, on the other hand, was John Mark's cousin (Colossians 4:10) and saw qualities in the young man that Paul did not. Both men stuck to their positions and the result was a parting of the ways. Now, instead of one missionary team, there were two! To his credit, Paul later commended Mark in his epistles (Colossians 4:10; Philemon 24; 2 Timothy 4:11). God used this circumstance to double the missionary impact of the church in Antioch. Was Mark ready to go with Paul at that time? Probably not. Did he need the discipleship and encouragement that Barnabas was known for? Probably. In the final analysis, the disagreement resulted in a greater benefit for all. Silas was chosen as Paul's new partner. He had been part of the delegation sent to Antioch by the Jerusalem church (Acts 15:22). Like Paul, he was a Roman citizen, a fact that provided much legal protection and could open many doors.

LIFE STEP

As believers, it should be our policy to avoid conflict as much as possible. There are times, however, when we must remain true to our convictions. If we do so in the right spirit, as Paul and Barnabas did, such confrontations can result in positive consequences.

What is the writer saying?

How can I apply this to my life?

PRAY For the perseverance of fellow believers and unashamed boldness for those who preach the Gospel (Ephesians 6:18–19).

Paul and Silas recruited Timothy, a young man who was probably saved during Paul's first visit to the city of Lystra. They were planning to continue their work in Asia Minor. The churches were young, and the needs were great. The fields were truly ripe for the harvest (John 4:35). Twice they attempted to enter regions that they had not formerly visited, and both times the Holy Spirit prevented them from doing so. The exact manner by which God communicated this to them is not stated. It may have been by prophecy or by direct revelation, but it resulted in the missionary team being pushed to the west and to the north, where they ended up in the port city of Troas.

There Paul received a vision which is often referred to as the "Macedonian Call." They immediately made plans to cross over to Macedonia and, with that, the Gospel officially entered Europe for the first time! Luke's use of the word *we* in verse 10 indicates that he had joined them by this point. This is the first of several sections in the book in which the use of the word *we* seems to indicate that Luke joined the missionary team from time to time. Paul immediately headed to the major city in that part of Macedonia, Philippi. It was a colony started by the Romans for military purposes. It would, therefore, be very familiar with Roman law. This fact would come into play when Paul revealed his Roman citizenship to the magistrate.

LIFE STEP

Clearly Macedonia was not Paul's first or second choice for missionary service, but God had other plans. Always remember that God leads as much by closing doors as He does by opening them. Are you being prevented from pursuing a ministry that you would like to be involved with? Have you considered that the closed door may be God's way of directing you elsewhere?

What is the writer saying?

How can I apply this to my life?

Luke chose to record three conversions that occurred in Philippi. The first was Lydia, a God-fearer (v. 14). It would appear that there was no formal place of worship, such as a synagogue, in this city. The Jewish community was either too small or nonexistent. In such cases Jewish people typically worshiped near a body of flowing water. Therefore, Paul went to the riverside on the Sabbath where Jews, proselytes, and God-fearers might worship. It was one of these God-fearers who responded to the Gospel and offered her home as a center for Christian worship.

The second convert was entirely different from the first. A young slave girl who was "possessed with a spirit of divination" took it upon herself to advertise for the apostle. Her ability to tell the future was a very marketable commodity in that city. The word translated "spirit" is literally *pythoness*. Clearly, her supernatural ability derived from demonic powers. Even though her actions seemed to support their ministry, Paul rejected this woman's endorsement and cast out the demon that had been afflicting her. Ends do not justify means,

The matter with the fortune-teller created enough of a stir that Paul and Silas were brought before the magistrate who ordered them beaten and cast into prison. From a human perspective, things did not look very promising. But the story was not yet over. God's ways are not our ways.

LIFE STEP　*Many who labor in the field of Christian service become discouraged when the opposition seems to be winning. We can often feel that the good guys always finish last. But the truth is exactly the opposite.*

What is the writer saying?

How can I apply this to my life?

PRAY   Honduras – Pray for salvation decisions to result from radio broadcasts.

Paul and Silas could not have been very comfortable as they sat in the dark and gloomy dungeon at Philippi. Their backs were raw from the beating they had just endured, and the stocks made getting into a comfortable position impossible. The fact that they could not sleep did not discourage them. At midnight they were singing praises to God. At that point, an earthquake rattled the prison, every door was flung open, and restraining devices came off all the prisoners.

The jailer is the third Philippian convert recorded by Luke. Thinking that the prisoners had all escaped, he was preparing to commit suicide when Paul called out from his cell. Not only were Paul and Silas still there, but all the other prisoners were as well. The jailer reacted in a totally different way to his circumstances than did the missionaries. He didn't know the God who ruled the universe. So, rather than trusting in the Lord, he panicked. The difference between the two was the hope that believers have in their Lord.

LIFE STEP

The Word of God exhorts us to rejoice, no matter how difficult our trials may be (Romans 5:3; James 1:2). We often dismiss this as some sort of deep, inner joy that we force ourselves to embrace while we continue to agonize and complain on the outside. This is not what Paul and Silas modeled; they sang! Theirs was not a manufactured emotion. It sprang from a deep conviction that whatever happened to them was under God's control and, therefore, the best thing possible. We need to be reminded that God is the God of the prison cell just as much as He is the God of the winner's circle. Wherever He leads, we can totally trust Him, and rejoice on the outside as well as on the inside.

What is the writer saying?

How can I apply this to my life?

PRAY South Africa – For loving outreach by those in youth ministry to a very vulnerable generation.

The next major city that Paul and Silas visited was Thessalonica, the capital city of Macedonia. As usual, Paul began by going to the synagogue where he ministered for three Sabbaths, showing from the Old Testament Scriptures that Jesus was the Messiah. At that point, it seems that they were prohibited from continuing to speak in the synagogue, but they may have ministered in the city for several more weeks or months. The text does indicate that a man named Jason had welcomed them to his home (v. 7). Only a few Jews were convinced by Paul's teaching, but a very large number of Gentiles believed and turned to Christ. This brought a strong reaction from the unbelieving Jews. Overcome by jealousy, they enlisted the help of some unsavory characters and started a riot which ended up at Jason's house, where the missionaries were staying and where they may have been holding meetings. Since Paul and Silas were not present, Jason was dragged before the courts and forced to hand over something valuable, which he would lose if the trouble continued. This resulted in the missionaries being sent off by night to Berea.

LIFE STEP *While the Gospel brought peace and joy to the lives of individuals who believed, it brought turmoil to the whole city of Thessalonica and was turning the world upside down (v. 6). Is our witness producing similar results, or are we afraid of upsetting anyone with the Gospel?*

What is the writer saying?

How can I apply this to my life?

The Bereans received one of the greatest compliments given to any of the cities that Paul visited. We are told that they were more noble than the Thessalonians because they searched the Scriptures to see whether Paul's Gospel was accurate. The written Word of God was clearly their final and ultimate authority.

Even with this positive reception, trouble still emerged in Berea. The members of the synagogue in Thessalonica, upon hearing that Paul was preaching in Berea, sent representatives to agitate the community against Paul and Silas. One may wonder how a few people from another city could exert such a powerful influence. In the Roman Empire, all religions had to be approved by the government. If anyone belonged to an illegal religion, they were considered criminals. As such, they could be arrested, and all their property confiscated. If the Jews from Thessalonica could convince the authorities that a new and illegal religion was being promoted by some members of the synagogue, there could have been some very severe sanctions that might have benefited the accusers themselves. From Berea, Paul headed to Athens where he found a very different kind of opportunity to address the citizenry.

LIFE STEP

The Bereans may have heard of the miraculous powers that Paul had demonstrated or of the supernatural jailbreak that he and Silas had experienced in Philippi. Even so, they were not prepared to believe what these men said without verifying it against the Scriptures that they already had. Their final authority was the written Word of God. No matter how impressive an experience may be or how strongly we may feel about something, our authority must be the written Word of God. Do we believe any so-called "spiritual teaching" that comes our way, or do we examine it in the light of Scripture? We need to be Berean Christians.

What is the writer saying?

How can I apply this to my life?

PRAY   Congo, Democratic Republic of Congo – Pray for revival among believers in this war-torn, nominally Christian nation.

Paul's sermon before this group of philosophers in Athens was much different than the ones he had preached in the synagogues. The central content remained the same, but it was packaged in a way that would attract and retain the interest of the crowd. His opening remarks were a classic example of the approach that should be taken when presenting the Gospel: he started where his audience was. The altar dedicated "TO THE UNKNOWN GOD" presented a golden opportunity to speak about the one true God. His listeners would not be able to reject Paul's teaching out of hand because they themselves, by erecting this very altar, had affirmed their belief that there was at least one god that they did not know. If this was true, then it would be irrational not to listen to what Paul had to say and to give it fair consideration! Throughout the sermon, rather than quoting the Old Testament, Paul quoted Greek philosophers (v. 28). By using thoughts and concepts that were known to them, Paul was able to unlock and illustrate new truths which they did not know. The Gospel itself will never change, but the way in which we present it must be adapted to the circumstances in which we find ourselves. If Paul had spoken to these men in the same way he did to Jewish audiences in synagogues, they would not have understood the message. Paul did not modify or leave out any essential truth. He was as transparent as ever, but he used different illustrations to keep the message as clear as possible.

LIFE STEP

Truth is fragile. Sometimes believers think we must use human logic to win people to Christ. Notice that Paul did not use Greek philosophy to replace the Gospel but to illustrate and explain the Gospel. The Gospel is the power of God, not human logic.

What is the writer saying?

How can I apply this to my life?

PRAY Australia – Godly workers to reach youth through religious instruction classes offered in public schools.

From Athens, Paul moved southward to Corinth. This city was famous for its depravity and rampant sexual immorality. Located on a narrow neck of land between northern and southern Greece, it was both a seaport and a land route. This meant that thousands of travelers passed through this city each year. With this volume of visitors, it is easy to see why prostitution and other such activities abounded. But just as it was an ideal location for Satan to market his poison, it was also an ideal location for Paul to maximize the impact of the Gospel. The crowds were coming to him and moving on to other locations.

Notice two of the men mentioned in this passage: Titus Justus who lived next door to the synagogue, and Crispus who was the ruler of the synagogue (vv. 7-8). Their names are forever engraved in Scripture because they were willing to help the Apostle Paul as he ministered in Corinth. Too often, acts of kindness and support go unnoticed by men but never by the Lord (Hebrews 6:10).

Paul's stay in Corinth lasted a year and a half but was not without incident. God had promised that no harm would come to him, but He did not promise freedom from opposition. Sure enough, the unbelieving Jewish population of the city rose up against Paul and tried to enlist the aid of civil authorities to stop the spread of the Gospel. They dragged him before Gallio, a man whose reputation for fairness and wit are well attested in secular literature. Not only did Gallio dismiss the charges as frivolous, but he paid no attention while the Greeks beat Sosthenes, the new ruler of the Jewish synagogue.

LIFE STEP

Today's text shows just how quickly the tables can be turned. Paul the accused was left unharmed to continue his ministry in Corinth for quite some time (v. 18) while Sosthenes, no doubt one of Paul's main accusers, ended up being beaten. On a grander scale, the tables will ultimately be turned in favor of the Lord's people and against those who do not obey the truth. On which side will you find yourself in the end?

What is the writer saying?

How can I apply this to my life?

PRAY

Bangladesh – Pray for the 240 million Bengali (the largest group of unreached people) both in Bangladesh and scattered around the world.

Very few people apart from the apostles were singled out for special attention in the Book of Acts. One such person is introduced in today's text, a man named Apollos, who became very influential in the early church. Paul made multiple references to him in the Book of 1 Corinthians, listing him alongside himself, Peter, and Christ as someone with whom people wanted to be identified (1 Corinthians 1:12).

Apollos was an Alexandrian Jew who had already received instruction regarding Jesus Christ and was accurately teaching what he had learned up to that point. But he still had a lot more to learn. Enter Aquila and Priscilla. They had been Paul's first converts in Corinth (Acts 18:2) and

were tentmakers by trade, as was the apostle. They had then accompanied Paul when he left Corinth and traveled with him to Ephesus, where the events of today's passage occurred.

After hearing Apollos' accurate teaching about Christ, they took him aside and instructed him more fully so that his teaching could be even more complete. What had he been missing? Apparently, he was only aware of what John the Baptist had taught regarding Christ. Aquila and Priscilla taught him more fully the truths of Christ's death, burial, and resurrection. Baptism into Christ was what Apollos needed to understand. This made him even mightier in the Scriptures, as he then departed Ephesus for Corinth.

LIFE STEP

It's refreshing to see Apollos' teachability. He was already an eloquent orator with an outstanding knowledge of the Scriptures. But when he recognized that he had more to learn, he humbly accepted this and became even more effective in his communication of the Word of God. Be open to what God wants to teach you through others who have a deeper experience of the Lord than you do. Fools despise learning, but wise people are happy to receive instruction from qualified sources (Proverbs 9:9; 12:15).

What is the writer saying?

How can I apply this to my life?

PRAY | Sudan – Pray that the great hunger for Christian and educational reading materials might be met.

The chapter break at this point is rather unfortunate because Luke was trying to set two narratives side-by-side just as he had done with Peter and Philip in chapter 8. In that case, Philip had a great ministry in Samaria, but no one received the empowerments of the Spirit until Peter and John came and laid hands on them. In a similar fashion, the end of chapter 18 tells the story of Apollos' "faith update," but there had been no mention of the Holy Spirit. In today's passage, Paul meets others who needed a similar "faith update." They had been followers of John the Baptist but had not heard the teaching about being baptized into Christ, likely because they had left Israel before Jesus' ministry.

So, Paul informed them of all that had happened since they had been under John's ministry. They welcomed the good news of the Gospel and were baptized. Paul then laid his hands on them, and they received the Holy Spirit and began speaking in tongues and prophesying. Once again, we note how the apostles had the unique ability to distribute sign gifts to others (see also Acts 8:17; Romans 1:11; 2 Timothy 1:6). If everyone could do this, then such gifts could not function as signs.

LIFE STEP

Sign gifts may seem to be blessings that we miss out on because there are no apostles today. But we must remember that the greater blessing is to have in our possession the written Word of God left to us by the apostles. Like the Bereans in Acts 17, we need to keep our focus on studying the truth that God has revealed to us in their writings.

What is the writer saying?

How can I apply this to my life?

PRAY   Costa Rica – For God to keep the school doors open for the Gospel to be preached.

Following on the heels of Paul's encounter with the twelve disciples of John, this passage is an example of someone attempting to use authority that does not belong to them. It is dangerous (and forbidden) to dabble in the spirit world. Demons exist and are powerful. The gift of exorcism is one of the sign gifts. It is always listed with such gifts as healing the sick and raising the dead. Unless we have been authorized by Jesus Christ to cast out demons, we should not claim to have the power to cast out demons. Praying for those we suspect to be controlled by demons is the appropriate course of action today. Likewise, we are authorized to pray for healing but not to heal the sick.

Satan is a very real and present danger but only in clearly defined ways. Christians can be externally influenced and oppressed by Satan and his forces, but demons cannot possess the believer and control him against his will from the inside. James is clear about this when he says that sin occurs when we are drawn away by our *own* lusts (James 1:14). Believers are indwelt by the Holy Spirit and thus cannot be indwelt by an evil spirit at the same time, any more than light and darkness can exist in the same place at once (2 Corinthians 6:14-18). The believer can never say, "Satan (or a demon) made me do it!"

These Jewish exorcists had apparently been casting out demons previously. But had they really been successful in doing so? When they tried to do it in the name of Jesus, they were confronted by the evil spirit and attacked by the man who the spirit was possessing! So, it would seem that their "exorcisms" were only apparent and not genuine. Demons clearly play games with those who are supposedly casting them out. Think of the advantages that Satan can gain by "authenticating" false teachers in this way (2 Corinthians 11:13-14).

LIFE STEP   *Notice how the demons knew Jesus and Paul but did not know the Jewish exorcists. May we live in such a way that we might have a reputation among demons as godly men and women!*

What is the writer saying?

How can I apply this to my life?

PRAY   Mozambique – Pray that religious freedom might continue and that true Christian faith and love might be expressed throughout society.

Paul had a profitable stay in Ephesus, but soon his preaching began to adversely affect a highly influential segment of the community, the silversmiths. The practice of biblical Christianity will always generate opposition from the world. Benign Christianity is a lifeless Christianity. This, however, does not justify going out of our way to cause a conflict. Paul himself commanded that we should live at peace, if possible, with all men (Romans 12:18).

The opposition we read about here was spearheaded by Demetrius. There is no doubt that his major concern was financial, but he wrapped his greed in the guise of religious commitment. It is sad to see to what extent people can become committed to false gods and develop false religious systems. Unfortunately, their commitment can often exceed the commitment which believers demonstrate toward the Lord.

In this passage we see a good example of what Paul meant when he wrote, "For rulers are not a terror to good works, but to evil" (Romans 13:3). If we behave in a peaceable and responsible way, civil authorities can often become our friends. That is exactly what happened in Ephesus. It's an example of what it means to be in the world but not of the world (John 17:14-16). Once Demetrius had stirred things up, they soon spun out of control, and no one could speak for two hours because of the noisy crowd filling the theater. This event marked the end of Paul's stay in Ephesus.

LIFE STEP   *We sometimes assume that ministers of government are going to resist us without reason. Though that is possible in some circumstances, we need to recognize and take advantage of the positive opportunities that they may provide and avoid unnecessarily antagonizing them.*

What is the writer saying?

How can I apply this to my life?

Returning from Greece to Asia Minor, Paul stopped for seven days at Troas, a port city on the northeast corner of the Aegean Sea. It is here that he performed the greatest sign miracle of all. When a young man named Eutychus dozed off and fell from the window to his death, Paul raised him from the dead and carried on his sermon!

This is a far cry from the so-called faith healers today, who never deal with the kind of traumatic injuries that must have occurred in this story, let alone actually raise people from the dead. They do not frequent hospitals and morgues to exercise their healing powers in favor of those who could desperately use their ministry. Rather than going to the sick, they ask the sick to come to them and then perform their "miracles" in tightly controlled environments, much like professional magicians. This is no small matter. If it is claimed that these things are happening today just as they did in the Book of Acts, then they ought to happen just as they did in the Book of Acts, spontaneously out in public and not in managed environments. Paul held no healing services, but when a need arose, he met it in the power of the Holy Spirit. Note also how this stunning miracle was handled by Paul. He did not treat it as a big deal which needed to be trumpeted far and wide. He simply went back to his message. The preaching and practice of the Word are much more important even than resurrections (see Luke 16:29-31).

LIFE STEP

There are some today who claim the office of apostle, but anyone making such a claim must be able to perform the sign gifts that the apostles did. Raising someone from the dead is a hard act to follow! Stay focused on the preaching and practice of the Word.

What is the writer saying?

How can I apply this to my life?

Japan – For the believers to have a joyful heart in all circumstances.

From Troas Paul proceeded to Miletus, a seaport to the south of Ephesus. Rather than going into the city, he summoned the elders to join him in Miletus. Paul had spent almost two and a half years with these men. They were dear friends with whom he had shared good and bad times. His farewell speech was charged with emotion. He asked them to remember his ministry among them, a ministry fraught with danger and hard work, and yet the apostle had labored with patience and love. Notice that Paul had not skipped over anything that would have been of benefit to the Ephesian believers.

We get a little glimpse into Paul's mindset in verses 22-24. When he said that he was "bound in the spirit," he meant that he was functioning out of a deep inner conviction that he must go to Jerusalem. He was uncertain about what the future held, but the Holy Spirit had made it clear to him that some very difficult trials lay in store for him there. Paul's situation was a good news/bad news dilemma. The good news was that Jerusalem held a new opportunity for him to serve the Lord. The bad news was the increased opposition he would experience.

Some have wondered if the Holy Spirit was telling Paul that he should not go to Jerusalem. It is best to give the apostle the benefit of the doubt in this matter. He was not going to let anything stop him from completing the ministry that Jesus Christ had given him to do (v. 24).

LIFE STEP

Do we have this kind of determination in serving the Lord? What would it take to stop us from witnessing to a family member, friend, or neighbor? What would it take to get us to witness to them?

What is the writer saying?

How can I apply this to my life?

PRAY For many to accept Christ at summer camps around the world.

Paul, in dramatic fashion, declared that he had met his entire duty to the people of Ephesus. He knew that there would be no more missionary journeys. He was going to Jerusalem, heading for an unknown future. But if there was one thing he did know, it was that he had done his best.

Paul also knew that wolves are ever vigilant, and that no weakness escapes their notice. The wolves he was speaking of were false teachers who were experts at corrupting and misrepresenting God's truth. No effective work for the Lord Jesus Christ will go unchallenged by Satan and his ministers. The wolves have no concern for the flock of God; they are only out for personal advantage. Therefore, every church and ministry must be on their guard. Now Paul turned this responsibility over to the Ephesian elders. What a bittersweet time this must have been for the apostle: bitter because he had to tear himself away from a group of believers whom he loved dearly, sweet because he was embarking on God's will for the rest of his life. Before he left, however, he shared with them a few things that they needed to know. Notice verse 33. It perfectly describes the motivation of false teachers both then and now. Paul had not taken anyone's money while in Ephesus but had worked to support himself. He taught elsewhere that God's workers are worthy of financial support (1 Corinthians 9:9-14), but in this case, Paul had chosen not to use that right.

LIFE STEP

When we take the Gospel to another people group, we should always be sure that the Gospel is preached free of charge to them. It is not only the church's responsibility to care for its own ministers but also to provide for the taking of the Gospel to the "end of the earth." How should you be involved in supporting God's work around the world?

What is the writer saying?

How can I apply this to my life?

When Paul arrived in the port city of Caesarea, he stayed at the house of Philip, the one who had led the Ethiopian eunuch to the Lord (Acts 8:26-40). Philip was now married with four single daughters who had the gift of prophecy. There's no mention of any specific prophecies which they made. However, when another prophet named Agabus had come from Judea, he predicted that Paul would be bound and delivered over to the Gentiles. This shows us that prophecy was not a spontaneous occurrence that overtook the prophet. Instead, the prophet retained a measure of control over when he would prophesy. Paul later taught this very thing and insisted on its importance in maintaining order in church meetings (1 Corinthians 14:29-33).

Agabus' prophecy was of grave concern to everyone but Paul. He was already aware that troubles lay ahead and had settled in his own mind what he must do. God's will is not altered by the circumstances of life. It remains constant in the midst of a constantly changing environment. Paul's comment in verse 13 is classic. It was not the future danger that most concerned Paul; it was the tears of his friends which were breaking his heart. Those who suffer most in a time of testing are not always the ones who are directly involved. Sometimes it is those who look on, unable to help, who suffer greater frustration. But eventually, even those who were arguing that Paul should not go to Jerusalem acknowledged that God's will needed to be done.

LIFE STEP   *We can't say why God chose to reveal these prophecies if He wanted Paul to go to Jerusalem. However, just because danger may lie ahead, we should not allow that to stop us from doing what we know God wants us to do.*

What is the writer saying?

How can I apply this to my life?

PRAY Chile – Reconciliation among believers who have been deeply divided by past political problems.

Today's passage is one that many interpreters have puzzled over. Why did Paul give in to the pressure of James and the other leaders of the Jerusalem church and take this vow? The answer lies in 1 Corinthians 9:20-22: "And to the Jews I became as a Jew, that I might win Jews; to those who are under the law, as under the law, that I might win those who are under the law; to those who are without law, as without law (not being without law toward God, but under law toward Christ), that I might win those who are without law; to the weak I became as weak, that I might win the weak. I have become all things to all men, that I might by all means save some." To Paul, outward actions were less important than maintaining every possible opportunity to present the Gospel, as long as those actions did not violate truth. Just as he could refrain from eating meat offered to idols even though it was not required to do so (1 Corinthians 8:13), Paul did not see any intrinsic evil in taking this vow.

At this point, it appears that Jewish believers in Jerusalem were still involved in many of the ceremonies of the Mosaic Law, not as a means of salvation or sanctification, but out of respect for the civil laws within the Mosaic code. We must always remember that the Law of Moses was both a political and a religious document. While Christ ended the ceremonial aspects of the Law, there were still civil laws that needed to be respected in Israel. It is also important to realize that the epistle to the Hebrews, in which temple worship would be discouraged (if not forbidden), had yet to be written. As far as Luke was concerned, even at this later stage in the history of the early church, Jewish believers were still transitioning from the temple worship system to the church worship system.

LIFE STEP *The Book of Acts describes a period of transition. Paul was right to participate in practices that had not yet been terminated by God's revelation. That does not give us the right to do the same since we live after the later revelation was given.*

What is the writer saying?

How can I apply this to my life?

Despite Paul's attempts to meet the expectations associated with entering the temple, when he was recognized by the people, they were outraged, not because of anything he had done, but because they thought he had broken the Law and brought Gentiles into the temple. Like what had happened in Ephesus (Acts 8:29-34), a mob quickly formed, intent on killing Paul. Once again, the authorities came to his rescue. The Roman commander was shocked to hear Paul speaking Greek and even more startled to know that he was a Roman citizen. It was the military's responsibility to protect all citizens of the realm. Allies of God's work often come from unexpected sources.

Paul's response was amazing. Amid all the chaos, he looked for an opportunity to address the crowd. Paul never saw a crowd that he did not want to preach to. Some may have been discouraged that so many people wanted to kill him, but Paul saw beyond the danger to the opportunity that was being presented to him. Where else would these people ever get the chance to hear the Gospel? This approach to life is one that characterized Paul. He saw every tribulation as a cause for rejoicing because of the opportunities it provided. Anxiety accomplishes nothing. Paul got his wish, and for a few moments, the angry mob quieted down and listened to what he had to say. Paul spoke to them in Hebrew to remove every barrier to the Gospel.

LIFE STEP

What is our perspective on life and ministry? Do we only see the potential dangers, or do we perceive the opportunities? Paul saw life from a different angle than most people do. He always looked for an opportunity in every situation and invariably found one.

What is the writer saying?

How can I apply this to my life?

PRAY　　Australia – For churches to have strong, sound leadership that produces committed believers.

Having been granted permission by the Roman commander, Paul began to speak to the crowd in Hebrew. This immediately caught the attention of the Jews and piqued their interest in what he had to say. He mentioned that he knew the high priest and the elders of Israel. He also mentioned Gamaliel, the well-known Jewish teacher under whom he had studied. He shared how he had been a persecutor of the Christians and had tried to wipe them out. All of this would have grabbed the attention of his audience. Paul was building bridges to them.

Having gained their attention, Paul began to set the stage to share the Gospel. He told them about his encounter with Jesus Christ on the road to Damascus. One of the great things about this sermon is that the audience could easily check Paul's facts. Many of them no doubt had known him for many years and could verify what he was saying. The lives we live and the circumstances that we go through are all used of God to prepare us for opportunities that will come our way in the future. Paul continued to hold their interest by unfolding events from his old life little by little while at the same time weaving elements of the Gospel into his message (v. 16).

LIFE STEP　　*Paul was given the opportunity to defend himself. But rather than doing that, he jumped at the chance to preach Christ. If we are prayerfully looking for opportunities to witness, opportunities will arise. But they may not come in the way that we are expecting or even desiring.*

What is the writer saying?

How can I apply this to my life?

When Paul referenced the stoning of Stephen (v. 20), it is likely that many in the audience remembered it and may have even been personally involved. Stoning would not have been a very common occurrence in Jerusalem since the Jewish Council did not possess the authority to carry them out.

Paul made the most of his opportunity to preach, but the response was anything but positive. The enraged crowd demanded that he be put to death. The soldiers, not ready to kill Paul, decided to scourge him. At that point, Paul appealed to his civil rights as a Roman citizen. In those days, Roman citizenship was a privilege not an entitlement, one that very few people enjoyed. The Roman commander had paid a large sum of money to obtain his citizenship, whereas Paul had received it by birth. When the soldiers heard this, they immediately withdrew, and the commander convened the chief priests and the Council.

This Council was the Sanhedrin, the highest Jewish court allowed by Roman law. The Council had tried Jesus and stoned Stephen. Though some of its members had undoubtedly changed, it is very likely that some of the same eyes that Jesus looked into were now staring at Paul. For Paul, this was just another opportunity to share the Gospel. When Stephen had appeared before this group twenty years before, he'd had no protection, whereas Paul enjoyed protection as a Roman citizen. It was no act of cowardice to use this privilege, but a wise use of a divine provision.

LIFE STEP   *There were many occasions when Paul chose not to use a legitimate right, but in this case he did. It is not wrong to appeal to our civil rights, but we need discernment and the direction of the Holy Spirit to know when it is appropriate to do so and when we should let them go for the sake of the Gospel (1 Corinthians 6:1-7; 9:1-12).*

What is the writer saying?

How can I apply this to my life?

PRAY   Nicaragua – Praise the Lord that the church has doubled in the last 10 years!

As Paul stood before the Sanhedrin, his greatest desire was to have an opportunity to clearly present the Gospel. He wanted to ensure that the men present would be listening attentively, but the trial didn't start well. Paul entered a plea of not guilty and was immediately slapped in the face by command of the high priest. This was in clear violation of the Law. Deuteronomy 25:2 stated that a man could only be struck if found guilty. The Council had not been convened to determine whether Paul was guilty; they had simply determined in their own minds that he was and then illegally skipped to the sentencing phase.

Knowing that the Sanhedrin was composed of both Pharisees and Sadducees, Paul saw an opportunity to either secure a more meaningful hearing or to quickly bring the proceedings to an impasse. One of the bitterest disagreements between both groups was over the issue of the resurrection. The Pharisees taught that there was a future resurrection, while the Sadducees denied it. When Paul claimed that he was being called into question because of his stand regarding the resurrection of the dead, he was effectively backing the Pharisees into a corner. If they did not give Paul a fair hearing, it would be like admitting that the Sadducees were right. Unfortunately, this is not what happened. Instead, the two groups launched into an argument, which became so bitter that the commander had to escort Paul out of the building!

LIFE STEP

Earlier, Paul had used his Roman citizenship to help escape a beating. Now he used his knowledge of theological controversies between the Pharisees and Sadducees to his advantage. There's nothing wrong with being shrewd when dealing with opposition. Jesus Himself encouraged it (Matthew 10:16).

What is the writer saying?

How can I apply this to my life?

PRAY Cuba – For a greater influx of resource materials and more educational opportunities for pastors.

It seems reasonable to conclude that things were not going exactly the way Paul had imagined they would. He surely had hoped that the Gospel would have touched a few of the many who had heard him speak. As far as we know, no one responded in faith to the message. So, the Lord encouraged Paul (v. 11) and made it clear that Rome, not Jerusalem, was where he would end up. Rome had always been the destination God had in mind. Luke wanted it to be clearly understood that God had not abandoned Israel but that Israel had abandoned God. Paul had been called to serve as the apostle to the Gentiles (Acts 9:15; 22:21), but he had also been given many opportunities to preach to his own people, the nation of Israel. Now they wanted him dead. The people who were trying to accuse Paul of breaking the Law were themselves breaking the Law by trying to take his life. The Jews were destroying the very thing they were claiming to protect because of an almost insane hatred for Jesus and His messenger, Paul. The Sanhedrin itself was conspiring with criminals in an attempt to have Paul murdered. None of it made sense, but sin never does. At every turn, it seemed that the Jewish authorities were resisting God, just as Stephen had said (Acts 7:51-52). Their hearts were blind, cold, and treacherous. But there was good news: Paul was spending a lot of time with Gentile soldiers!

LIFE STEP

Opportunity ignored is opportunity squandered, whether it is an opportunity to trust Christ or to preach Christ. For Israel, it would be an opportunity lost, but for the Gentiles, it would be an open door. Has God placed an opportunity before you that you are ignoring? Don't mistakenly imagine that because it's there now it always will be. Seize it today!

What is the writer saying?

How can I apply this to my life?

Paul was beginning to be a problem for Claudius Lysias, the Roman commander in Jerusalem. A plot to kill Paul was uncovered, so it was decided to send him away from Jerusalem to Caesarea, where the governor of Judea lived. This would reduce the investment of time and personnel needed to protect the prisoner. The commander sent along a letter describing the events surrounding the arrest and mock trial.

When Paul arrived, he was immediately granted a brief audience with the governor. Following the reading of the letter and a few moments of questioning, Paul was dismissed and sent to the official residence of the governor, Herod's Praetorium. Paul's trials were expanding the opportunity to reach people who would otherwise be inaccessible to him. The actions of those who were trying to kill Paul had expanded the potential reach of the Gospel once again. Paul was being continually brought into contact with individuals who had most likely never heard the Good News. Paul could have easily complained about the unfairness of his situation. He could have grumbled about the lies that were being spread about him. But Paul saw the big picture. God was providing an armed escort and free transportation to Rome.

LIFE STEP

Luke was an excellent historian. Here we see how he even included the text of a Roman commander's letter in his account (vv. 25-30)! We may wonder why the Holy Spirit prompted him to include so many details. Not only do they help to validate the accuracy of his writing, but each small detail shows how God was providentially orchestrating events to get Paul to Rome. Paul was not a victim at the mercy of ruthless opponents. He was God's messenger being presented with opportunities to preach the Gospel to many more people who would otherwise never have had the chance to hear it. We can be encouraged to know that the Lord is ultimately in control of our circumstances as well.

What is the writer saying?

How can I apply this to my life?

Notice how the lawyer for the Sanhedrin tried to flatter Felix, the governor of Judea, while twisting the facts to his own advantage. He even accused the commander in Jerusalem of misbehavior, raising the specter of unlawful Roman violence. Perhaps this was an attempt to get the governor to turn Paul over to him. No attempt was made to bring in any neutral observers. Instead, those who accused Paul were willing to use any means to discredit and destroy him.

Paul pointed out the inconsistencies in the prosecution's account of events and focused on what had really started the trouble in the Sanhedrin, the controversy about the resurrection of the dead. His purpose in doing this was to point out that the issue was a religious, not a political one. He knew that Felix would not try him for a religious squabble. The authorities were wise enough not to involve themselves with internal religious disputes.

By bringing up the resurrection, Paul did more than simply shift the focus toward religion; he opened the door to highlight the very heart of the Gospel message. The Sanhedrin had rejected the Gospel, but Paul hoped that some in Felix's court might take an interest in the subject.

LIFE STEP   *Starting a Gospel presentation with the concept of the resurrection and life after death can be a great way to begin. A simple opening question might be, "What do you think happens after we die?"*

What is the writer saying?

How can I apply this to my life?

PRAY Japan – For God to reveal Himself in this land where only 10% believe in the existence of a personal God.

Today's passage is a continuation of Paul's defense before Felix, the governor of Judea. While summarizing what had happened, it is worth noting that Paul did not say anything about having offered a sacrifice when he was in the temple. When he talked about being purified (v. 18), he was referring to an aspect of the ceremony that he had been involved in while accompanying the four men who were completing a vow and having their heads shaved (Acts 21:23-26). Though he was willing to comply with temple rituals to a point, he did not yield in any area that would contradict or hinder the Gospel.

It's interesting to note that Felix was very familiar with Christianity, what was here called "the Way." At the conclusion, he decided that he needed to hear more evidence before making a final decision and placed Paul under light arrest. Paul was given plenty of liberty, which enabled him to carry on a productive ministry. As difficult and unfair as the situation seemed, it was still a part of God's plan for the apostle. God's will is always good, acceptable, and perfect (Romans 12:2), even though not always pleasant.

Sometime later, Felix and his wife listened to Paul make a more complete presentation of faith in Christ. Even though Felix came under great conviction (v. 25), there is no indication that he was ever saved. In fact, he was secretly hoping to get some money out of the whole affair. Paul ended up spending the last two years of Felix's governorship under guard. Felix could have let Paul go at any point during this time but was more concerned about keeping the Jews happy than he was about treating Paul fairly.

LIFE STEP

Every person who heard the Apostle Paul did not get saved. Felix came close but ended up putting it off as so many do (v. 25). In the same way, we will not see everyone to whom we witness get saved, but this should not discourage us. Each opportunity should be taken full advantage of.

What is the writer saying?

How can I apply this to my life?

PRAY For wisdom and guidance from the Holy Spirit for Dr. Don Lough, Jr., the President and CEO of Word of Life Fellowship, Inc.

Even though two years had passed, the high priest and Sanhedrin in Jerusalem had not forgotten about Paul. As soon as Festus was installed as the new governor of Judea, they immediately began plotting Paul's murder all over again. They presented Festus with their charges against Paul and asked that he be brought to Jerusalem. As before, their plan was to ambush the party along the road and kill him. Festus declined and invited them to come to Caesarea instead to present their case. Paul would once again be given an opportunity to defend himself and to present the Gospel to another strategic audience. The more the Sanhedrin tried to keep Paul from preaching, the more opportunities they created for him to do exactly that! As had been the case two years before, their charges could not be proven. However, this time Festus appeared to be leaning in favor of turning Paul over to them out of a desire to please them; it would be a way of gaining points with his new subjects. Seeing this, Paul used the last defense at his disposal and appealed to Caesar, a right of any Roman citizen. This appeal option had originally been designed to protect the inhabitants of the city of Rome from being mistreated by the courts of a foreign country. But the right was eventually extended to all citizens, even to those who had not been born in Rome. Paul would finally have the opportunity to make the journey that he had long hoped for. He was headed to Rome, where so many needed to hear the Gospel.

LIFE STEP

Paul was always willing to wait upon the Lord's timing. He did not appeal to Caesar the moment he was arrested. He waited until his hand was forced. There is no need to rush God. Paul was under arrest for over two years, but he knew that God would work out His plan in His time. We must also learn to wait upon the Lord.

What is the writer saying?

How can I apply this to my life?

While Paul was imprisoned at Caesarea, awaiting his trip to Rome, Herod Agrippa II (the grandson of Herod the Great and son of Herod Agrippa I, who had James killed in Acts 12) came for a visit, perhaps to welcome the new governor. While he was there, Festus thought it would be great entertainment to have the king hear what Paul had to say. King Agrippa had no authority over Festus but was an expert in Jewish affairs and had wanted to hear Paul for some time (v. 22). He may have been looking for some advice, but more likely he was just looking for a good way to pass a few hours.

Whatever the case, Paul was once again given a great opportunity to present the Gospel to people who would never hear it under normal circumstances. In fact, these folks were not the type to "darken a church door." Bernice was Agrippa's sister, not his wife (their other sister was Drusilla), and they were involved in an incestuous relationship together. For a time, Bernice was also the mistress of Emperor Vespasian and then of his son, Titus. However, she always eventually returned to her brother. Governor Festus began by sharing with his guests the events that had led up to the present moment, including the way Paul had appealed to Caesar. This seemed to present a problem for Festus, who did not have any formal charges to send to Rome that would make any sense.

LIFE STEP

Once again, we see that every situation in which we find ourselves presents an opportunity to honor God and to advance His cause. That was Paul's perspective. Make it yours today.

What is the writer saying?

How can I apply this to my life?

When he was permitted to speak, Paul stretched forth his hand, a common way of beginning speeches in those days. Agrippa was very familiar with Jewish customs, having grown up in the area. As Paul started to talk about the resurrection of Jesus, the intensity in the room must have gone up several notches. The topic had no doubt been the subject of much conversation and of some embarrassment to local authorities. It had only been about twenty-two years since the crucifixion and resurrection of Christ.

Against this controversial backdrop, Paul once again began rehearsing his testimony. While doing so, he appealed to Agrippa's knowledge of, and expertise in, Jewish customs. It must be remembered that Paul wasn't formally on trial at this moment. Instead, he had been handed yet another golden opportunity to share his story and was clearly hoping that Agrippa and others would come to faith in Christ (vv. 28-29). Paul recounted his life prior to his conversion, his upbringing, and the fact that he had lived as a strict Pharisee. He spoke of the hope of the promised Messiah and of the resurrection, and how he had zealously persecuted followers of Jesus of Nazareth, convinced that they were in the wrong.

He then described his personal encounter with Christ and the commission that he had received from Him to take the Gospel to the Gentiles. It could not have been lost on Paul that the very center of Gentile power was Rome. Paul was not hoping to be released; he was anxious to continue his mission to Rome.

It can be easy to miss the forest for the trees. We can get caught up in the immediate challenge of the moment and fail to consider the bigger picture. What situation has you out of your comfort zone right now? Ask God to help you to place that into the broader perspective of what He is doing in your life right now.

What is the writer saying?

How can I apply this to my life?

PRAY Lithuania – Pray for discernment as believers are increasingly confronted with numerous opposing theologies.

Paul continued telling his story to King Agrippa and Bernice. Governor Festus suddenly interrupted Paul, loudly proclaiming that he was going mad. Denying it, Paul turned to Agrippa and pressed his points home. As a young man, Agrippa had probably heard of the slaughter of the infants in Bethlehem. He had likely been alive when James had been killed and when Peter had been miraculously rescued from prison. Furthermore, the crucifixion of Christ and the accounts of His resurrection were known throughout the land. As Paul said, "this thing was not done in a corner" (v. 26).

Maybe it was Agrippa's curiosity that kept him listening. Perhaps, he was sincerely searching for the truth, or maybe it was just for the amusement of it all, but Agrippa listened! By the time Paul was done, Agrippa was ready to acquit him of all charges. We might be tempted to think that it might have been better for Paul not to have appealed to Caesar at all. But we must remember that if Paul had not appealed to Caesar, he would not have been around to speak to Agrippa at all!

Some of the saddest words in the history of the world occur in today's passage: "You almost persuade me to become a Christian" (v. 28). Agrippa came so close! Salvation was within his grasp, but he let it slip away. No one ever knows how long the Lord will continue to speak to one's heart.

LIFE STEP

It is always the right time to respond to God's promptings because tomorrow can never be counted on. Make the most of what God brings into your life today. Redeem the time because the days are evil. Eternity stretches like an infinite road ahead of us. But the present is most precious because it is the only time when we can make a decision that will determine what our forever will be like.

What is the writer saying?

How can I apply this to my life?

PRAY Madagascar – Pray for well-trained Christian workers willing to serve in isolated areas with difficult living conditions.

Notice that the text uses the pronoun *we*, indicating that Luke had once again joined the delegation. This likely accounts for the numerous details which are included, details which could be of great value. The people whose names are mentioned would be in Rome when Luke's manuscript was completed, and thus readers would be able to verify the details of his account.

There were other prisoners on the ship, but as to their identity, we can only speculate. Luke probably did not name them because they would not be considered reliable witnesses in the court of public opinion. Paul would have been treated far better than any other prisoner who did not have Roman citizenship. When they stopped at Sidon, he was even given the freedom to visit his friends and benefit from their care. What a meeting that must have been!

Much of today's passage is taken up with a detailed description of the route that the ship traveled. Such details may have been of special interest to Luke, or they may have been more significant to the ancient readers. Paul did warn the centurion that danger lay ahead, but given the circumstances, it's not surprising that he was totally ignored. At first, it seemed as though all was well and was working out the way they wanted, but disaster was just around corner.

LIFE STEP

How easy it is to ignore wise counsel and then to feel that we've chosen the better path because we're getting exactly what we want (v. 13). However, notice the first words of the very next verse: "But not long after, a tempestuous head wind arose ..." (v. 14). The same thing had happened to Jonah. He was happily asleep running from God's will, but then "the LORD sent out a great wind ..." (Jonah 1:4). Present peace of mind does not guarantee that we're in the right path. We can only be sure that we are when we're paying close attention to God's commands and direction.

347

What is the writer saying?

How can I apply this to my life?

PRAY Bolivia – For a caring youth ministry in a land where 80% of children are living in extreme poverty.

Today, we find Paul aboard a ship on his way to Rome. Bad weather had trapped them as the sailors valiantly attempted to make the dangerous voyage around the southern tip of Italy. The vessels of that day were much smaller than today's ships. The situation became so critical that the crew had to throw all the cargo overboard. Even the essential ropes and tackles for sailing were thrown away. But still the vessel was in distress.

After many days of not seeing the sun or the stars, they had no idea where they were. When they had lost all hope, Paul stood up to speak. He had received a vision from God affirming that he would stand before Caesar just as He had said (Acts 23:11) and that the lives of all who remained on board would be spared. But in the process, they were going to lose the ship. Paul could have been frustrated by yet another delay in his journey to Rome, but instead, he became a source of strength and of comfort. Paul had been ignored before, but there's something about being in a desperate situation that causes people to pay attention to someone claiming to speak on behalf of God.

One of the most difficult circumstances to accept is when we find ourselves in trouble because someone ignored the wise counsel that we had given them. It can lead to a lot of anger, bitterness, and broken relationships. Not so with Paul. Even though his warnings had been dismissed, he was resting in God's sovereign purposes. There were 275 other people on the ship (v. 37) and they were about to witness the power of the living God. Knowing Paul, every one of them was also going to hear the Gospel!

What is the writer saying?

How can I apply this to my life?

PRAY Japan – Praise the Lord for the new openness caused by economic, social, and natural disasters.

In Paul's vision, the angel had promised that every person would be saved if they stayed on board. The sailors began measuring the depth of the water and realized that they were getting close to land. Some tried to escape using a lifeboat, claiming that they were intending to lower anchors. This time the centurion listened to Paul and had the lifeboat cut loose so no one could get away.

Paul then encouraged all the men to get some nourishment since they'd hardly eaten anything for several days. This seems to have revived their strength a bit, and they prepared to attempt to beach the ship on land, which they spotted in the morning. But the ship ran aground on a reef and began to break apart in the pounding surf. Before jumping overboard, the soldiers were planning to kill all the prisoners for fear of their own lives. Under Roman law, any soldier who lost his prisoner would either forfeit his own life or face the same punishment intended for his prisoner. Fortunately, Julius opposed the plan, and everyone ended up escaping safely to land, just as the angel had said.

LIFE STEP

The way we respond under stress is a testimony to others of our trust in the Lord. Not one of these men would ever forget Paul, his faith in God, and the way he handled the situation with calm and confidence. They also would never forget the Gospel he most certainly shared with them. How do others around us see us handle the difficulties that come our way? Are we showing that God can be trusted, or are we setting an example of unbelief?

What is the writer saying?

How can I apply this to my life?

PRAY Jamaica – Leadership within the government and churches to be untainted by corruption or compromise.

Exactly as the angel had said, the ship was lost, but everyone on board had been saved. They now found themselves on the island of Melita, known today as Malta. The people who lived there were very friendly and prepared a fire for the castaways. As the people gathered around, God's purpose for the events of the last few days began to unfold. Two things happened that drew everyone's attention to the Apostle Paul. First, a poisonous snake bit him but failed to harm him. Second, Paul miraculously healed the father of the leading citizen of the island. These events no doubt led to many opportunities to share the Gospel.

At last, after a long and perilous journey, Paul finally arrived in Rome. As he drew closer to the city, word of his arrival spread, and excitement began to build among the believers. He had written them a letter at least two years earlier, and they had looked forward with great anticipation to his visit ever since. Paul must have wept for joy as he was welcomed once again into the Gentile world. He would always be a Hebrew of the tribe of Benjamin, but his heart was forever tied to those whom Christ had especially called him to reach, the Gentiles.

LIFE STEP

The progress of our lives often seems to drift along by means of a random chain of chance events and encounters. The little island of Malta was not a scheduled stop on Paul's itinerary. If it had been, he likely would not have been heard by as many people as he was. Are you struggling with delays and unexpected detours in your life? Reaffirm your trust in the Lord as your Good Shepherd. He always leads us well.

What is the writer saying?

How can I apply this to my life?

Even though the Book of Acts ends at this point (around A.D. 60), Paul's life and ministry would go on for many more years. During this first time in Rome, Paul was under house arrest. He wrote the Books of Ephesians, Philippians, Colossians, and Philemon. He also enjoyed a productive ministry in the lives of believers in and around Rome.

Paul was released after two years and, over the next five years, he visited several locations, including Ephesus, Macedonia, Crete, Nicopolis, and Troas. We learn much of this from his later letters. In A.D. 67, he was once again arrested and taken to Rome. This imprisonment was much different than the first. Instead of house arrest, he was placed in a traditional dungeon with none of the comforts he

had enjoyed during his first stay. From there, he wrote his final epistle to his son in the faith, Timothy. The following year, Paul was beheaded. The same human authorities whom God had used to protect and transport Paul for so much of his trip to Rome were now used of God to usher him into glory. Absent from the body, our dear brother Paul is now with the Lord.

The book closes with a brief reference to the kingdom which ties the reader back to the bigger picture. Yes, Paul was the apostle to the Gentiles, but he never relinquished his conviction that God would one day reestablish His relationship with Israel and inaugurate the kingdom that He had promised to Abraham and to his descendants.

LIFE STEP

If you had met Saul in A.D. 35, you could never have imagined what God would do through his life. Even less could Saul have envisioned it. It is not the man or woman who makes the difference; it is the God Who lives within the man or woman. Put your life entirely in His hands without reservation and follow hard after Him. If you do, you will be amazed looking back over the years, to see what He will have done in and through your life as well.

What is the writer saying?

How can I apply this to my life?

PRAY

Czech Republic – Crime, sexual immorality, substance abuse, and suicide are prevalent. Pray that people would turn to God during these dark times.

In today's passage, the writer dispenses words of wisdom on a variety of topics in no apparent order of importance. It is helpful to remember that Solomon's writings are often classified as "Wisdom Literature" in the Bible. We see here the outflow of a wise man's thoughts directed toward his family. In God's providence and under His inspiration, modern readers have Solomon's wisdom to help guide them, as well. Common themes found in this passage are found in many of Solomon's other proverbs—like the contrast between the wicked and the righteous in their thoughts (v. 5), words (v. 6), and heart attitudes (v. 8).

As if laying the foundation for all wisdom, Solomon chose to begin by linking instruction and knowledge as assets to be sought (v. 1) and contrasting those who love knowledge with the "stupid" person, who hates correction. We see this contrast played out today when we consider people who are "unteachable," whose normal reaction to any form of instruction or correction is resistance. In addition to the themes previously mentioned, Solomon contrasted the virtuous (*excellent*) wife with the wife whose actions bring shame to her husband (v. 4), like rottenness to his bones. Verse 9 contrasts the proud man who exalts himself but has nothing to eat versus the man who is slighted (*suffers an insult*) but has more than enough. This contrast supports the reality that looks can be deceiving, and that people are not always what they claim to be. Finally, in verse 10, a person's character is demonstrated even in the way he treats animals.

LIFE STEP

Laying a solid foundation for life starts with gaining wisdom and knowledge (v. 1). There is no source of wisdom better for you than the Word of God. The question is not whether you believe it, but rather, whether your belief is demonstrated in your actions. Do you behave as one who has gained the wisdom offered in God's Word, or are your actions more like those attributed to the "stupid," the wicked, and the perverse man? Choose wisdom. Choose to learn from God's Word.

What is the writer saying?

How can I apply this to my life?

PRAY   Cambodia – Pray for a display of God's power and continued unprecedented growth within the Cambodian Church.

When reading Proverbs, it is often helpful to take note of repetition and common themes addressed by the writer. Solomon often repeated his thoughts that addressed the fool and the wise, or the wicked and the righteous. Today's reading contains some of these common themes but also brings out new themes, such as the impact of one's words (vv. 13-14, 17-19). Solomon's treatment of this topic is instructive for us today in many situations:

- The evil person is trapped (*ensnared*) by his words; what he says often gets him into trouble (v. 13).
- A good man's words bring good things to him and to others because they are encouraging and kind (v. 14).

- The speech of a righteous person can be trusted, especially in the legal setting requiring testimony; the words of the false witness can never be trusted (v. 17).
- Some people can bring healing and life through their words, while others' words are like the wounds of the sword (v. 18).
- Truthfulness leads to a lasting impact, while the impact of falsehood and deceit is fleeting; the term *but for a moment* may be interpreted literally "in the blinking of the eyes" (v. 19).

LIFE STEP

When you listen to other people talk, you can discern quickly whether they are wise or foolish. The same could be said of what people learn about you when you speak. Don't be foolish in the way you speak. Listen to sound wisdom from others. Let your words demonstrate to people around you that you are controlled by an inner source of wisdom—the Holy Spirit within you. Write the words of Psalm 19:14 and commit that verse to memory. Carry it with you every day as your goal for your speech.

What is the writer saying?

How can I apply this to my life?

PRAY

Ecuador – A spiritual maturity in the church that roots out false teaching and embraces a heart for the less evangelized.

Just for fun, read each of the verses in today's passage and write down one word or phrase that speaks to the traits and characteristics Solomon promoted, as well as the traits he disdained in his writing. What you will see is a sort of index of topics that could be useful for your future growth and development as a believer. For example, some of the traits and characteristics to be avoided are deceit (v. 20), lying lips (v. 22), and laziness (vv. 24 and 27). In these same verses, Solomon commended to the reader two desirable traits: truth and diligence in one's work.

A close look at his contrast between the lazy man and the diligent worker provides timely insight into the future of those who neglect their work. A lazy person cannot expect to become a leader of the team; instead, he will be the "hired hand" during his working life because of his laziness (v. 24). Though he might be assertive enough to hunt down wild game for a meal, he is too lazy to even cook it for himself (v. 27) and therefore, goes hungry. "Lying" occurs eight times in Proverbs, "lips" or "tongue" sixty-one times, and "truth," "true," and "truly" eleven times. We can safely conclude that our speech and our integrity are important issues to God. In contrast to these negative elements of man's speech, Solomon also wrote of the value of good words. Verse 25 identifies a "good word" as an antidote for anxiety. This is a simple truth that is supported even by research in today's world. An anxious heart can be encouraged and calmed by a good word.

LIFE STEP

Many people in our post-pandemic world report that they are suffering from anxiety. As you relate to others, think about how you can be a part of the problem or part of the solution—based solely on how you talk. As a child of the King, consider each interaction with other people as a way to spread joy and encouragement. Take Ephesians 4:29 as your guide for speaking to others. Choose to speak words that build up, not tear down. Look for ways to encourage someone today with a "good word."

What is the writer saying?

How can I apply this to my life?

PRAY Nicaragua – For a mighty work of salvation to occur among this country's military forces.

Here we have more of Solomon's catalog of wise sayings and advice for his son(s). First, he urged his son to listen, as a good son should (v. 1). Then, he began to address issues that come to his mind—issues that serve to help the listener stay clear of trouble. Verse 13 returns to the value of heeding the word—a reference generally thought to speak of God's instructions but also including the advice of the father.

- Speaking positively to others brings prosperity and favor, but the reverse is true of the one whose speech is unfaithful (treacherous) (v. 2).
- The lazy man is again the subject in verse 4. Though he may boast of great ambition, his lazy habits yield an empty basket, whereas the diligent plodder in life accumulates wealth over a long period.
- Righteousness stands as a guard and protector of a person who seeks to walk blamelessly, while sinners find themselves overcome by their wicked ways (v. 6).

- Riches without righteousness lead to an empty life, while the faithful who may be poor enjoy God's blessings that transcend material wealth (v. 7). In a very practical way, the poor man is unencumbered with the hazards associated with the wealthy. He doesn't have to hire guards for his many possessions or worry about losses. Not so the rich man, whose wealth can enslave him to worry and fear of loss (v. 8). Solomon came back to the topic of wealth in verse 11, this time contrasting the wealth gained dishonestly (diminished) with that gained by honest work (labor), which increases.
- Solomon contrasted the light enjoyed by the righteous and godly, against the darkness that spreads over the wicked. This may be a suggestion that the righteous enjoy long life, while the wicked die early (v. 9).

LIFE STEP *Take Solomon's advice to his son about laziness and hard work. Do not let yourself fall into lazy habits by looking for the quick and easy way out. Our Creator gave man a beautiful world and commanded man to work it (see Genesis 2:15). Perhaps now is the time you need to step out of lazy habits and pursue honest work. Honest, hard work is a blessing with its own rewards.*

355

What is the writer saying?

How can I apply this to my life?

PRAY Mexico – Effective ministry to youth through Christian camping, outreach activities, and social aid.

Wisdom has many rewards. Solomon called it a fountain of life and portrayed it as a shield against premature death that so often comes to the foolish (v. 14). He chose a snare as his word picture to depict how foolish living can entangle its victims like an animal caught in a trap. Following a word of encouragement to gain understanding (v. 15), he returned to the wise and prudent man whose actions are informed by his diligent search for knowledge (v. 16). The modern reader may be familiar with the saying, "Show me your friends, and I'll show you your future." Solomon believed that to be true in his day, as indicated in verse 20. Walking (friendship, fellowship) with the wise will mark your life and help you become wise, whereas those who consort with fools will face destruction and ruin.

Verse 21 paints a word picture of evil in pursuit of the sinner. The point is that the evil devised and perpetrated by sinful people falls back on them, as if they are in the very grasp of the evil they commit. They cannot get away from it. In contrast, the righteous reap goodness as a return on their investments in good deeds. Verse 22 advocates sound financial planning for the good (morally upright) man who is able and willing to leave to his grandchildren an inheritance. The unwise sinner, on the other hand, typically loses his wealth due to foolish financial practices. Sound parenting principles may be gained from adhering to verse 24. The "rod" need not be interpreted solely as a means of corporal punishment, but discipline in general. Taken as such, we conclude that proper discipline for a child is a demonstration of love, as it helps mold and shape the child for success in life.

LIFE STEP

Who are your friends? There is undeniable wisdom in Proverbs 13:20 that should motivate us to pick our friends carefully. Right now, take inventory of the habits and behaviors of your closest friends. Do you sense that they help you grow closer to God, or is it possible that they are more likely to draw you away from godly choices? The same question could be turned back to you. Are you the kind of friend who helps friends grow closer to God? Or are you an obstacle to their spiritual growth? Commit yourself to being a godly friend who seeks out godly friends.

What is the writer saying?

How can I apply this to my life?

PRAY Poland – Summer camp ministry safety, salvation decisions, and consecration commitments.

The opening verses introduce two big ideas that will shape the rest of the story recorded in this book: the sovereignty of God over Gentile world powers and the faithfulness of four young Jewish captives whose faith would put God on display in the mightiest empire on earth! The year is 605 B.C., and the world superpowers are Babylon and Egypt. The two face each other at the battle of Carchemish, and Egypt is defeated. Nebuchadnezzar now turns his attention to Jerusalem and besieges it. All hope for the Jews appears lost, but God, not Nebuchadnezzar, is in control (v. 2)! Though King Jehoiakim is delivered into Nebuchadnezzar's hands, it's not yet God's time for the city's destruction. News of the death of Nebuchadnezzar's father forces a hasty retreat. A few temple vessels are carried away (v. 2) along with some of the young men with outstanding leadership potential. Among them are Daniel and three of his friends. It's difficult to imagine how radically life changed for them. Their God-honoring Hebrew names were changed to ones that honored Babylonian gods, they were educated in all the ways of the Chaldeans (the elite class of Babylonian wise men), and they were offered the best food available! The only problem was that to eat it was to participate in Babylonian worship. Daniel and his friends were under tremendous pressure to conform. They faced the pressures of an unfamiliar environment, intimidation, and potential comfort. How could they possibly resist?! Daniel and his three friends had already made up their minds to stay pure (vv. 8, 14). Decisions are powerful when they're made before the pressure is on!

LIFE STEP

You have choices to make every day. We all do. But of all the decisions and choices you need to make, your stand for godliness is most important. What decision or decisions do you need to make right now so that you can stand firm when the pressure to conform or compromise comes your way? Don't wait until the temptation or pressure comes to make up your mind.

What is the writer saying?

How can I apply this to my life?

PRAY Austria – Each student receives their own free copy of the Bible at school. Pray that they would study it and accept its truths.

What do you do when you can't comply with the orders you've received from a supervisor? That's the situation in which Daniel and his friends found themselves. We can learn a lot from the way Daniel appealed to his authority. Note first his respectful tone. He did not grumble nor make demands. Instead, he made a request (v. 8) and addressed his superior politely (v. 12). When appealing, it's never a good idea to launch an offensive attack! Proverbs 15:1 says that a soft answer turns away wrath. Similarly, a gentle request usually preempts a harsh response! Secondly, he proposed a reasonable alternative that had been well thought through (vv. 12-13). Failure to do this only comes across as more trouble to a supervisor. Don't leave it up to them to figure out what to do! Thirdly, Daniel showed that he was sensitive to the concerns of his superior who was afraid of what would happen to him if they didn't eat the king's food. It's easy to forget that those in authority over us are held accountable as well. Helping them to fulfill their responsibilities can go a long way in making them favorable to our appeals. Finally, Daniel continued to demonstrate submission by suggesting that his supervisor could head in a different direction if the results were unfavorable (v. 13). Daniel's gracious approach resulted in his supervisor granting their request (v. 14). In the end, all four were ten times better than the rest. Notice how the Lord was moving His plan along through these young men (v. 17). God was sovereignly elevating them to positions of influence in the most powerful nation on earth. It's amazing how God has His way of putting His representatives in just the right place at just the right time!

LIFE STEP

Reflect on your relationship with someone in authority over you. Determine one specific way you can help them to carry out their responsibilities today. By doing so, you will help them to better lead you!

Dig into God's Word *every day* with Word of Life Quiet Times. There's something for everyone!

- Gopher Buddies Quiet Time Diary Daily Devotional – Ages 4 - 6
- Challenger Quiet Time Diary Daily Devotional – Grades 1 & 2
- Conqueror Quiet Time Diary Daily Devotional – Grades 3 & 4
- Champion Quiet Time Diary Daily Devotional – Grades 5 & 6
- Interactive Quiet Time Diary Daily Devotional – Teens
- Quiet Time Diary Daily Devotional with Commentary – Teens & Adults
- Online Quiet Time App – Teens & Adults

Word of Life Short-Term Trips: Missions for Every Believer

With over 30 options for people of all ages, we guarantee there's an opportunity for you to serve on a Word of Life Short-Term Missions Trip, no matter what stage of life you're in.

Not sure about your next steps?

Lay the foundation for a faith-filled life at Word of Life Bible Institut

Word of Life.
Bible Institute

Word of Life Camps

Connect with family and
experience the best week of
your summer! Whether you're
6 or 96, there's a place for you
to deepen your faith at Word
of Life Camps this summer.

A **Word** of **Life** Camp

A **Word** of **Life** Camp

A **Word** of **Life** Camp

A **Word** of **Life** Camp

A **Word** of **Life** Camp

What is the writer saying?

How can I apply this to my life?

PRAY United Kingdom – For many teens to be saved through Christian camping and outreach events.

This chapter contains the first prophetic vision in the book, and it was given to a Gentile king! We can conclude from verse 1 that Daniel and his friends were in the second year of their three-year training period (1:5). They had already distinguished themselves in wisdom and understanding and were numbered among the wise men of Babylon (1:20). God's time had now come for Daniel to be elevated above all of the wise men of Babylon. Nebuchadnezzar had a troubling dream. It appears that he was so disturbed by it that he wanted to be absolutely certain to understand what it meant. One can conclude from the way he approached his wise men that he did not fully trust them to give him an accurate answer. So, rather than tell them the dream and ask for an interpretation, he tested their abilities by demanding that they describe the dream themselves – something which would clearly require supernatural abilities. Of course, none of them could do it.

The stage was being set for Daniel's God-given abilities to surface. True wisdom is more than knowledge and common sense. It's the ability to see things the way God sees them. Even the wisest of Nebuchadnezzar's men recognized that no man on earth could be expected to discern another man's private thoughts or dreams and render an accurate interpretation (vv. 10-11). They thought the "gods" had the answer but lacked the wisdom to know that only Daniel's God—the one true God—was the proper source for the king's answer.

LIFE STEP *Do you need wisdom for some decision today? Why seek it anywhere else? Ask God for it. He has promised to give it (James 1:5)!*

What is the writer saying?

How can I apply this to my life?

Imminent danger reveals a person's true source of confidence. Never is this truer than when a person's very life is threatened. Today we observe how Daniel responded to the news that he was to be killed along with his three friends. Rather than panic and fight, his response revealed a profound and confident trust in God and left us an example to follow when we receive threatening news. Notice his calm response. Rather than replying in fear or anger, he responded with "counsel and wisdom." (v. 14) The Hebrew word translated "counsel" is used only here in the Bible and expresses the idea of speaking with prudence and restraint. The point is that Daniel responded calmly rather than escalating an already tense situation with inflammatory words. Then he respectfully requested clarification as to why the order had been given. He may have already known the reason; in which case his question was a way of creating an opportunity to request a stay of execution so that he could seek an interpretation of the dream from God. He then went to his friends and asked them to pray that God would reveal the king's dream to him. God answered their request and Daniel's prayer of thanksgiving shows us that his trust had been in the Lord all along. What a great example to follow when we're faced with threatening news: respond calmly, obtain whatever clarification you can on the issue, and ask close friends for prayer while trusting in the Lord all the way through.

LIFE STEP   *Are you faced with a threatening situation that's robbing you of peace? Perhaps it's related to family, friends, finances, or your future. Choose one specific issue and ask three people to pray with you today for God's peace and His clear direction in that area.*

What is the writer saying?

How can I apply this to my life?

PRAY Canada – For outreach into the Asian, Indian, Chinese, and Arabic-speaking immigrant communities.

Have you ever dreamed of being a hero whose exploits save many lives? Or maybe you just like to be the bearer of some exclusive news that you know is going to radically change people's future. In either case, it's easy to take the credit in subtle (or not so subtle) ways. Daniel had just received the revelation of the king's dream in answer to prayer. He was sitting on some news that was going to result in many lives being spared. As soon as he informed the king's commander, he was taken before the king who asked him a tantalizing question: "Are you able to make known to me the dream?" (v. 26) What a perfect opportunity to become a hero. All he had to do was answer, "Yes, I can, O king, and here it is!" Instead, Daniel immediately set the record straight. No man could possibly do this but God in heaven could (v. 28), and He had revealed it to Daniel. This was in no way a product of any wisdom that he had within himself nor because he was any better than anyone else (v. 30). This kind of self-effacing, God-exalting attitude is so rare in our world today. Instead, most people go overboard to advance their own name and to ensure that they are noticed, appreciated, and praised. In God's economy, down is up and up is down. The one who exalts himself will be humbled, and the one who humbles himself will be exalted (Matthew 23:12). We see a perfect example of godly humility in the life of John the Baptist. Like Daniel, who deflected all praise away from himself and onto God, John said, "He must increase, and I must decrease" (John 3:30).

LIFE STEP

Are you always maneuvering to be noticed, appreciated and praised? If so, you have signed up for one of life's most stressful assignments. Pride101 is a brutal curriculum because it requires you to constantly pursue the limelight to get the credit. Why not sign up for a different course and learn meekness and humility from Jesus Christ? In doing so, you will find rest for your soul (Matthew 11:28-30). Choose to affirm three people today for something they have done, and make sure you don't expect any compliments in return!

What is the writer saying?

How can I apply this to my life?

Daniel began describing in detail the dream that had haunted Nebuchadnezzar. It was of a massive image constructed of different materials, the worth of each descending in value from top to bottom, with the gold head at the top and iron mixed with clay at the feet (bottom). This magnificent image was shattered into pieces by a stone that was cut out without hands. What remained of the image was blown away like chaff in the wind, while the stone became a great mountain that filled the whole earth (vv. 31-35).

Then Daniel gave the meaning behind the dream, first giving honor to Nebuchadnezzar as "a king of kings" (v. 36). This is precisely what the king thought of himself, but his dream made it clear that God is the one who sovereignly raises up and puts down kings and their kingdoms. This great statue with its metal parts clearly refers to a succession of kingdoms (the word kingdom appears ten times) that would rule the world (v. 39). It is a description of the Gentile world powers which would dominate the holy city of Jerusalem in the absence of their legitimate King, God Himself. Jesus referred to this period as the Times of the Gentiles (Luke 21:24). The head of gold is clearly Babylon, which was the first nation to rule over Jerusalem (v. 38). It would be followed by four others. Though the dream did not specifically identify these nations, we can identify the first three in retrospect since they've obviously come and gone: chest and arms of silver (Medo-Persia), belly and thighs of bronze (Greece), legs of iron (ancient Rome). Though the metals decrease in value, they increase in strength. The last Gentile world power will be described in greater detail tomorrow.

LIFE STEP

The wealth and power of this world's nations may appear to be determining the course of events on earth. But make no mistake. It is God who is the ultimate sovereign of the universe, and His Kingdom will one day replace them all (Revelation 11:15). Spend a few minutes reflecting on the fact that God will have the last word in human history. Identify one way in which this reality should change your outlook and priorities today!

What is the writer saying?

How can I apply this to my life?

PRAY   Czech Republic – For Czech citizens to turn to Christ to fill the void left by years of Communism.

Daniel continued his interpretation of Nebuchadnezzar's dream, pointing to the days of those kings (the kings and kingdoms referenced in 2:41-43) which we believe will be an alliance of ten kingdoms symbolized by the ten toes of the feet of the great image. Verse 44, then, refers to a yet future event in which God sets up an everlasting kingdom headed up by Jesus Christ. The fact the worldly kingdom of verse 44 is of iron (vv. 41 and 45) suggests a link with the legs of iron (ancient Rome), though it is clearly different in substance and strength. The ten toes are said to be ten kings (v. 44; 7:24). The fact that iron does not mix with clay suggests instability. We conclude that it will be a world power brought about by the fragile union of ten nations that have some link to ancient Rome, perhaps by virtue of their history and geography. The dream then described a stone cut without hands (not of human origin) which struck the feet of the statue, destroyed it, and filled the earth (v. 35). This refers to God's indestructible kingdom which will one day rule the earth (v. 44; Revelation 11:15). The Times of the Gentiles will have come to an end, and God will once again reign from Jerusalem. He is truly sovereign over Gentile world powers. Nebuchadnezzar reacted by showering Daniel with gifts and elevating him to a position of power over all the other wise men. Most people who experience such a promotion leave their friends and even their families in the dust, but not Daniel. He petitioned the king on behalf of his friends and set them over the affairs of the province of Babylon (v. 49).

LIFE STEP

Are you quick to share God's blessings with others, or do you tend to "hoard" His many blessings? It's so easy to assume that we're being blessed by God for our own sake, when in fact it is often for the benefit of others. Follow Daniel's example. Maybe it's a material blessing. Or it may be something more hidden, like peace of mind, or real joy. Choose one specific way to share God's blessings with someone else. Then do it!

What is the writer saying?

How can I apply this to my life?

PRAY

Peru – For churches as they seek to meet the needs of their congregations in which many attendees are unemployed.

This chapter records Nebuchadnezzar's reaction to the interpretation of his dream. Through Daniel, God told him that the great statue made of different metals represented a succession of kingdoms which would rule the world prior to the establishment of God's kingdom. He learned that he and his kingdom were the head of gold but that he was not the ultimate world ruler. Other kingdoms would follow his (2:38-39). Instead of being grateful for the privileged position he was in and acknowledging God's sovereignty, Nebuchadnezzar defied the Lord and built a ninety-foot statue made entirely of gold, as if to say that his kingdom would never end! Even worse, he essentially claimed deity by ordering everyone to fall down and worship the golden statue when the music started playing. Sure enough, as soon as the band struck up its tune, the masses fell down like pawns and worshiped a lifeless hunk of metal! It was the politically correct thing to do. Why stand out, look foolish, and risk one's own life? Pride and selfishness were doing their deadly work in everyone's heart; everyone that is except for three brave young men. Power has a blinding effect that can lead to folly. When you're "on top" looking down, it's easy to think that you're responsible for the position you are in and act as though you're God. When you're on "the bottom" looking up, you can easily be intimidated into compromise.

LIFE STEP

Ask God to search your heart and to show you where pride is leading you to act foolishly. Write down one specific area that comes to mind and ask God every day this week for help in acting wisely in this area.

What is the writer saying?

How can I apply this to my life?

PRAY

Romania – For Romanians who will go as missionaries to countries inaccessible to other foreigners.

We've already seen how Daniel and his three friends had been elevated to positions of power without compromising their faith in the living God. We now see the first hints that there were others in high places who were not happy about this. They seemed very eager to draw to the king's attention the fact that Shadrach, Meshach and Abed-nego had failed to worship the golden statue. Interestingly, Daniel is not mentioned in this passage. Had he worshiped the statue?! That seems highly unlikely given his faithfulness to this point and in subsequent events. We conclude that he must have been away at the time.

The three men were brought before the king who threatened them with certain death in a fiery furnace and taunted them with the arrogant question, "who is the god who will deliver you from my hands?" (v. 15) The men's confident response demonstrated the depth of their trust in God. Rather than arguing the point with the king, they simply stated their conviction that their God was able to deliver them, and that even if He chose not to, they would not deny Him by worshiping anyone or anything else (vv. 16-18). When your trust is placed entirely in God, you cannot be disturbed by what others may say or threaten to do to you. You don't need to defend God or even know what the earthly outcome of some trial may be. Instead, you can rest in the knowledge that God is in control and that He will do nothing that is not ultimately for your own good.

LIFE STEP

The three Hebrew men in our text faced a real crisis of faith. Some might even say they would have been justified for caving to the pressure and bowing down to Nebuchadnezzar's golden image. After all, their lives were on the line! In your crisis of faith, praise God for their example of faith! It is not likely that your life will be on the line because of your stand for God, but maybe your social standing or your popularity will be. Write out any area(s) in which you need to trust God more. Then, ask Him to increase your faith and to help you to stand on your faith, just as these three men did (Mark 9:24).

367

What is the writer saying?

How can I apply this to my life?

PRAY   France – For an impact to be made on the core French population.

Today we read how God walks with His children through the hottest of circumstances! The fiery furnace may have been an industrial pottery kiln of which several remains have been unearthed in that part of the world. Shaped like a beehive with an opening at the top, these could be heated up by using giant bellows to blow air through an opening in the side. The temperature must have been incredibly hot to take the lives of the men who threw Shadrach, Meshach, and Abed-nego into the flames! The fact that these three even made it into the flames without dying, let alone survived it once they got in, is testimony to God's protection through the entire experience. The fire immediately consumed whatever had been used to bind them, and they began walking around in the flames.

They were joined by a fourth person with a supernatural appearance. This may have been what is referred to as a theophany, a preincarnate appearance of Christ. Nebuchadnezzar was shocked by what he saw and immediately called them out of the flames. God's glory was put on display as they were scrutinized by all of the government officials who were amazed that they didn't even smell of smoke! Notice that the three Hebrew men who went through the fire were rewarded for their faith. Nebuchadnezzar, recognizing the surpassing greatness of their God (because there is no other God who can deliver like this), promoted them to higher positions (v. 29). It's interesting to note how the king made proclamations to honor God but did not claim Him as his own. Sadly, many do the same today.

LIFE STEP

God walks with His children through fire and deep waters (Isaiah 43:2), through deserts (Deuteronomy 8:2), and even through the valley of the shadow of death (Psalm 23:4). He has promised never to leave us nor forsake us (Hebrews 13:5). Are you aware of His presence in your current circumstances? Find a way to remind yourself of this at multiple points throughout your day today and let that truth encourage you. His presence makes all the difference!

What is the writer saying?

How can I apply this to my life?

PRAY Bermuda – Pray that Christians in Bermuda would get more involved financially and spiritually to support missions.

This chapter records one of the most remarkable conversion testimonies in the Bible, that of Nebuchadnezzar, king of Babylon! In it he records how he was humbled and came to understand that God, not himself, was sovereign over the nations of the world. It began with another dream which he could not understand. Verse 5 suggests that it may have been a recurring dream that bothered him over a period of time. Once again, his best wise men could not provide an interpretation, so Daniel was finally called in (v. 8). You would think the king would have immediately called for Daniel, given Daniel's reputation and success in interpreting the king's previous dream (2:24-49). The fact that he did not suggests that Nebuchadnezzar may have suspected what his dream meant and was reluctant to have it confirmed by God through Daniel. We are often quick to listen to those who will tell us what we want to hear rather than what we need to hear.

Nebuchadnezzar called Daniel by the Babylonian name he had been given, Belteshazzar, which means Bel protect his life (a reference to the Babylonian god, Bel). He described how he had seen a great, flourishing tree that was cut down on the orders of a "watcher," leaving only the stump in the ground. The "watcher" most likely was an angelic messenger sent to reveal to Nebuchadnezzar what was going to happen. The tree clearly represented a person (v. 16) who would become like an animal for seven periods of time. The purpose of this would be to demonstrate that the Most High God is the ultimate sovereign over world events (v. 17). Nebuchadnezzar was going to learn it the hard way.

LIFE STEP *How does God speak to you? While it is true that God can and does reveal His will in various ways, you will discover that you hear from God most clearly through your prayers and your intake of His Word, the Bible. Write out the various ways you see God speaking to you through the words of Scripture found in 2 Timothy 3:16-17. Write out the benefits of communicating with God through prayer after reading James 4:2-3.*

What is the writer saying?

How can I apply this to my life?

After Nebuchadnezzar finished describing his dream, God revealed its meaning to Daniel. Rather than rejoicing over the fact that his captor would face terrible humiliation, Daniel was appalled and hesitated to share the news with the king (v. 19). God had elevated Nebuchadnezzar to his lofty position, but the king had become proud and would now face a humiliating experience. He would be driven from his throne and become like an animal for what is generally thought to be seven years. However, just as the stump had been left in the ground to flourish once again, the king would be restored after he had truly recognized God's sovereignty (v. 25). Daniel earnestly called the king to repent in the hopes that God might relent and prolong his prosperity. In all of this, Daniel demonstrated an attitude that was the exact opposite of that of the prophet Jonah. Jonah hated his enemies and wished that they would be destroyed, which is why he initially refused to go to Nineveh to call them to repentance. Then, when they did repent and God relented, he was angered by God's show of mercy (Jonah 4:1-3). Daniel, on the other hand, truly desired that Nebuchadnezzar be saved from judgment.

LIFE STEP

How do we react when God is merciful to someone we do not like? Is God's grace just as amazing to us then as it was when He poured it out on us? Do we earnestly desire the salvation of all, or would we rather see some face hell for what they've done? Such an attitude betrays our own pride, for it reveals the fact that we consider ourselves more worthy than others to receive God's blessings. Take a look at yourself in the spiritual mirror. Ask God to give you a merciful spirit in the same way you've been granted mercy. Read Luke 6:36 and meditate on what God desires of you.

What is the writer saying?

How can I apply this to my life?

PRAY   Paraguay – For God to call laborers to the more than 400 interior villages that remain unreached.

Pride is a terrible thing. It deceives you into overconfidence, distances you from others, and ultimately sets you up for disaster. Proverbs 16:18-19 reminds us that "Pride goes before destruction and a haughty spirit before a fall. Better to be of a humble spirit with the lowly than to divide the spoil with the proud."

In today's passage, we learn that God can humble those who walk in pride, but He would prefer that we humble ourselves! We see this reflected in the fact that God waited an entire year before carrying out the judgment described in Nebuchadnezzar's dream (v. 29). The king was given plenty of time to reform his ways, but he did not. Instead, he continued in his arrogance until God had no choice but to bring him down. The condition which afflicted Nebuchadnezzar may have been some form of lycanthropy, a mental illness that causes the victim to think that they are an animal and to begin acting like one (v. 33). Daniel himself may have cared for the king during this time. Thankfully the experience produced the desired result. At the end of the prescribed period, the king repented and recognized God's sovereign authority in a beautiful statement of His unmatched power and majesty (v. 35). Based on his own testimony, it appears likely that he came to know, trust, and honor the Lord, which means that we may very well meet Nebuchadnezzar in heaven some day! Arguments for Nebuchadnezzar's saving faith focus on the fact that he humbled himself by acknowledging his pride, praised God for His sovereignty over all, and worshipped God with praise as the Most High God (v. 37). What a testament to God's ability to deal with the most hardened, arrogant heart.

LIFE STEP

Genuine humility is impossible to generate on our own. It's like a bar of wet soap. The moment you think you have it firmly in your grasp, you lose it! It's encouraging to know that God can break our pride and produce authentic humility. Invite Him to do this in your own life. The result will be rest for your soul (Matthew 11:29) instead of the stress that comes from always having to appear better than others!

What is the writer saying?

How can I apply this to my life?

PRAY Bolivia – For the Holy Spirit to bring about maturity in the lives of those studying for the ministry.

Approximately twenty-three years have passed since the end of chapter four. Nebuchadnezzar had been gone for at least twenty years, and Belshazzar was reigning as king. For many years, this was touted as an example of a historical error in the Bible since no mention of Belshazzar had ever been found in any ancient records. Then in the 1850s, four clay cylinders were unearthed which revealed that he was the son of Nabonidus, king of Babylon. Nabonidus was away for several years and had appointed Belshazzar co-regent in his absence. This explains why he offered the position of third ruler in the kingdom to whoever could interpret the handwriting on the wall (vv. 7, 16).

The feast which he organized was a deliberate act in defiance of God. Belshazzar almost certainly knew of God's revelations to Nebuchadnezzar concerning Babylon's fall (v. 22). Historically, we know that the Medo-Persians had already taken everything but the city itself, which may explain why so many officials were tucked away behind its thick walls. In this setting, they deliberately chose to drink out of the temple vessels which had been taken from Jerusalem years before (1:2). Belshazzar was essentially challenging God to go ahead and try to bring him down. His audacious confidence was soon replaced with stark terror as he saw the handwriting on the wall!

LIFE STEP

Never treat as common what God has consecrated or set aside for His purposes. This includes how you treat yourself, since God has called you out as a member of a royal priesthood, so that you may proclaim the excellencies of Him who called you out of darkness into His marvelous light (1 Peter 2:9). Honor God by keeping your body pure and holy before Him. Write down two ways you can honor God by taking care of yourself.

What is the writer saying?

How can I apply this to my life?

PRAY Pray for summer camp counselors, supervisors, and teen staff to serve Christ wholeheartedly.

The handwriting on the wall had been seen by all but understood by none, so Daniel was summoned to give the interpretation. This shows that he had not been attending the feast. Belshazzar clearly did not know him although he admitted to having heard of him (vv. 13-14). This suggests that Daniel was no longer serving in a prominent government position. When offered riches and power, Daniel declined the reward but agreed to interpret the writing (v. 17). He began by reminding Belshazzar of Nebuchadnezzar's pride in years past and how he had been humbled by God. He then rebuked the king for his own arrogant defiance of the Most High God and his failure to recognize His sovereignty. The heart of Daniel's rebuke is found in verse 23: "the God who holds your breath in His hand and owns all your ways you have not glorified." The handwriting on the wall, ordained supernaturally by God, made it clear that Belshazzar's kingdom had come to an end and would be replaced by Medo-Persia. The head of gold would give way to the chest and arms of silver (see Daniel 2:32). Incredibly, Belshazzar responded with a "business as usual" approach and called for the reward to be given to Daniel! But time had run out. That very night, the Medes and the Persians who were camped outside the city diverted the river which ran under its walls, entered the city, and Babylon fell. Belshazzar the king was killed.

LIFE STEP

How easy it is to forget that we are not self-sustaining. God holds our very breath in His hands. If we are alive, it is because He wills it and desires that we should glorify Him. Spend a few moments reflecting on specific ways you can put God on display today rather than living for yourself. This is clearly how Daniel had been living, and it's the only path to true fulfillment.

What is the writer saying?

How can I apply this to my life?

We come now to what is likely the most famous account in the book: Daniel in the lions' den! In Sunday school lessons, Daniel is often portrayed as a young man, but he was actually at least eighty years of age when these events took place. A new day had dawned in the world with the fall of Babylon to the Medes and the Persians. Daniel quickly rose to prominence under a new administration and was appointed one of three governors who oversaw the kingdom. His effectiveness resulted in the king planning to establish him over the entire realm. Once again, this drew out the worst in other leaders with hidden agendas. What follows stands in stark contrast to what we generally see today in the world of politics. As hard as they tried, "they could find no charge or fault because he was faithful nor was there any error or fault found in him" (6:4).

What an amazing testimony! It's one thing to appear to be above reproach but it's another to actually be above reproach even under the microscope of hostile scrutiny. They finally concluded that the only way to bring Daniel down would be with regard to his faithfulness to the Lord. Sure enough, as soon as Daniel heard of the prohibition against petitioning anyone but the king, he proceeded to pray as usual to God with thanksgiving and with windows wide open toward Jerusalem (v. 10). Now that's integrity! Those familiar with the Apostle Paul's writings may point to Romans 13:1, which encourages obedience to the laws of governing officials. But taken as a whole, the Scriptures always give priority to obedience to God rather than men when a conflict exists between God's Word and man's laws (see Acts 5:29)

LIFE STEP

If someone wanted to discredit you, how hard would it be for them to find some "dirt"? The concept of integrity is the idea that we are whole, rather than two or three sided. What we are in public is what we are in private. Ask the Lord to help you to act in such a way today that if all you did and said were known to everyone, you would have no reason to be ashamed. In any case, nothing we do is done in secret, since God sees and hears it all (Hebrews 4:13)!

What is the writer saying?

How can I apply this to my life?

PRAY   Mozambique – Pray for the development of projects that build biblical knowledge among oral learners, who constitute the majority of the population.

The Medes and the Persians had a governing principle which stated that any injunction signed into law by the king could not be revoked, not even by the king himself. Daniel's enemies were counting on this unchanging law as well as on Daniel's unchanging life to achieve their sinister plans. They had essentially manipulated and maneuvered the king into a corner. Darius had come to love and appreciate Daniel, but his hands were now tied. Try as he may, he could not revoke the injunction he had signed (v. 14). Daniel would have to be thrown to the lions. Daniel's testimony had already impacted the king to such an extent that Darius himself affirmed his belief that the God whom Daniel served would deliver him (v. 16). Despite his statement of confidence in Daniel's God, he spent a sleepless night fasting and worrying about it! But let's not come down too hard on Darius, since we frequently behave the same way. We also worry about many things while simultaneously affirming our belief that God is in control! One wonders if the king prayed to the God of Daniel during the night. In the end, Daniel experienced God's divine protection, and his manipulating enemies lost their lives by the very means they had intended for Daniel's harm (v. 24). The irony of it reminds us of Haman who was hung on the very gallows he had built for Mordecai (Esther 7:10)! You can sometimes manipulate men, but God cannot be outmaneuvered.

LIFE STEP

Just as God was able to stop the mouths of hungry lions to save Daniel, His power is sufficient to stop any obstacle you may face. When you find yourself fixating on the obstacle or the giant challenge before you, remind yourself of God's unmatched power and His love for His children. Then give your fears and anxieties to Him and let Him do what He does (Philippians 4:6-7). You may not be miraculously delivered as Daniel was, but you can certainly trust Him for what is best.

What is the writer saying?

How can I apply this to my life?

PRAY   China – Special need for study Bibles, children's Bibles, and safety for those transporting them.

While in a season of prayer, Daniel received a visit from the angel, Gabriel, who came forth to give him skill to understand (v. 23). What follows in verses 24-27 is an explanation of end times prophetic events as these events relate to Israel. Daniel knew that Israel's exile in Babylon, as predicted by Jeremiah, was to last seventy years (see Jeremiah 25:11-12). Therefore, his search for understanding (9:1-2) became the context for Gabriel's expansive explanation not of seventy years, but of seventy weeks of years (70 X 7), or a 490-year period. Within Gabriel's message, we learn that:

- The seventy weeks are focused on the Jewish people, Daniel's people (v. 24).
- The culmination of the prophecy, when Israel's sin will be brought to an end, is the end of human history and the beginning of the Messiah's reign (seal up the vision and anoint the Most Holy).
- The starting point, the first of the seventy weeks, is Artaxerxes' decree in Nehemiah's day to restore and rebuild Jerusalem and its walls (v. 25).

- Sixty-two weeks of years later, the Messiah will be cut off (v. 26). This prediction is, we believe, fulfilled by the triumphal entry of Jesus (Matthew 21) and His crucifixion.
- The horrific events of the final days before God's judgment show up in verse 26, as well, including wars, destruction of the city, and the "prince who is to come" (Antichrist).
- Scholars suggest that we are now in a "gap period" between the sixty-ninth and seventieth weeks, a time known as the Church Age, awaiting the Rapture of the church.
- The seventieth week, the final period of seven years, is the tribulation period that comes after the Rapture of the church (v. 27). Note the half-way point of that period, when great abominations occur and one who makes desolations is at work. This is believed to describe the Great Tribulation, the final three and one-half years of tribulation.

LIFE STEP

While it may be difficult to discern with certainty the timing of Christ's return and the final judgment of God upon the unbelieving world, the fact remains that He is coming again. Make your eternal destiny certain. Settle that issue once and for all by placing your faith in Jesus and what He did on the cross to offer you salvation and redemption. If you're certain that you've been redeemed, praise the Lord!

What is the writer saying?

How can I apply this to my life?

PRAY   Equatorial Guinea – Pray for nominalism and animistic traditions to die as Christ is revealed.

Imagine being part of a church that lacked organization and leadership, one that struggled with the day-to-day challenges of ministry and the care of the church's members. This would frustrate you, as it should. That is the setting for Paul's letter to Titus, a man whom Paul called a true son in our common faith (v. 4). Though very little is known about Titus, we know from Paul's writings elsewhere that he considered Titus a genuine brother (2 Corinthians 2:13), a partner and fellow worker (2 Corinthians 8:23), and a man who walked in the same spirit as Paul (2 Corinthians 12:18). Paul trusted Titus for the task at hand—to bring order to the church by selecting Spirit-filled leaders who would serve the church well. In his greeting (vv. 1-4), Paul mentioned his own credentials as a bondservant of God and an apostle of Jesus Christ. The word Paul chose for bondservant speaks of his willing enslavement to God. He also identified himself as a steward of the Gospel, called by God to preach the words of life transformation (v. 3).

Having started a church on the island of Crete, Paul deliberately left Titus behind for two specific purposes identified in verse 5.

- Titus was to set in order the things that are lacking. This phrase is a medical term suggesting the setting of a crooked limb or a broken bone to bring healing. Apparently, there was a sense that the church was not a healthy church.
- He was to appoint elders in every city to lead the church. The balance of our reading today provides specific qualities Titus was to look for in making these selections. Notice that these qualities (vv. 6-8) are similar to those Paul identified in 1 Timothy 3:2-3.

LIFE STEP   *Take a close look at the qualifications of elders that Paul mentioned in his letter to Titus. Do you see anything in that list that isn't true of you as a follower of Jesus? Pick out one or two qualities from this list that you, with God's help, want to improve or enhance. Close your quiet time by asking God to help you meet these qualifications for His glory and for the good of others.*

What is the writer saying?

How can I apply this to my life?

PRAY For professors and staff at Word of Life Bible Institutes as they prepare for a new school year.

The latter part of verse 9 gives a hint of some of the problems Paul hoped to have Titus address in the church at Crete. Some in the church were contradicting sound doctrine. The "for" that begins verse 10 is to be taken as a continuation of that concern, or the rationale for Paul's admonition to Titus to seek out leaders who were committed to sound teaching. What were the types of "contradictors" they needed to correct? Three negative traits are identified in verse 10: they were insubordinate, meaning that they refused to submit to God's order of authority; they were idle talkers, indicating that their talkativeness did nothing to draw people to God or toward moral excellence; and they were deceivers—their words could not be trusted. Paul pointed out for special concern those who were of the circumcision, a reference to Jewish converts who continued to insist that followers of Christ keep the Law of Moses—that faith in Jesus was not sufficient for salvation. The seriousness of their error was such that Paul wanted their voices silenced (v. 11), lest they continue undermining entire families of the church. To make matters worse, these false teachers brazenly sought to advance themselves financially at the expense of the church. Even their own citizens understood the ungodly nature of these Cretans (v. 12). Paul urged Titus to rebuke them sharply (v. 13) in hopes that they may be turned back to sound doctrine. Until that happened, however, Paul concluded that their Christianity was a sham. They professed to know God, but their works denied Him (v. 16).

LIFE STEP

If people watched you closely in your private world, would they see consistency in the way you talk and the way you live? That was the problem with the false teachers in Crete. Don't be like those who claim to know God but whose works deny that relationship. Ask the Lord to search your heart and reveal to you any area of your life that is inconsistent with your identity as a believer (Psalm 139:23-24). If you know you're just masquerading as a follower of Jesus, confess that sin right now and receive Him as your personal Savior.

What is the writer saying?

How can I apply this to my life?

PRAY   Chad – Pray for pioneer missionaries to persevere in difficult places in order to reach the unreached.

It may be helpful to summarize this passage in the context of the previous reading in Titus 1:10-16, where Paul categorized the heresies and ungodliness of the false teachers. Think of this as the other side of the coin—the contrasting view of those who are masquerading as authentic Christians. Paul began with the older men in the church, urging Titus to instruct them in right conduct as men of God (v. 2). Many of the qualities Paul mentioned are among the qualities to be found in candidates for the eldership of the church (see Titus 1:6-9). He then turned his attention to the older women in the church and identified three specific qualities they should demonstrate in their lives (v. 3) as well as their responsibility to teach younger women in the context of marriage, family, and domestic life (vv. 4-5). Interestingly, in verse 6, Paul addressed the young men in the congregation with just one quality for

Titus to teach and encourage—to be sober-minded (self-controlled). Paul then stepped back from his pattern of addressing the needs of various groups within the church and began to address Titus personally (vv. 7-8). Probably because Titus was, himself, a younger man, Paul urged him to be consistent in all things, showing a pattern of good works, sound doctrine, sound speech, and a host of other qualities that would lead any observer—even an opponent— to declare Titus above reproach. Finally, Paul called on Titus to address the bondservants who were in their Christian community—to be obedient, and to exemplify godly character in their role as bondservants (vv. 9-10). Notice that the intent of Paul's instruction, as stated in verse 1, was for Titus to speak these things to his congregation(s). It was Paul's desire that Titus preach these topics consistently.

LIFE STEP

Fill in the blank in this sentence: "When I read the positive qualities Titus was to teach the Cretans, I sense that the trait I need to work on most is _____." Next, write down one way you will commit to growing more like the Christian who displays that positive quality. Acknowledge right up front that the power to change is only through Jesus Christ.

What is the writer saying?

How can I apply this to my life?

PRAY

Bulgaria – That Christians would be protected from the violent attacks of neo-Nazi groups.

The conjunction "for" that starts out verse 11 is Paul's way of explaining the "how" of the previous verses. Think of how it is even possible for bondslaves, older men and women, and young men and women to be transformed in their conduct. It is through the grace of God! Paul is talking about the saving grace that turns sinners from darkness to light and from the power of Satan to God. Verse 14 points to the fact of their transformation, made possible only through the redemption (purchased with a price) offered through the sacrifice of Jesus. This makes the Christians at Crete (and all believers) a special people whose lives should be marked by good works. Verses 12-13 define the habits and traits to be denied as well as those we are to adopt as part of our new identity in Christ, linked directly to our expectation of Christ's imminent return. Paul urged Titus to conduct his teaching and preaching ministry with encouragement, correction, and boldness (v. 15). As is often the case with Christians, the Cretan believers needed to be reminded of truths they already knew. That was Titus' job as pastor, and Paul wanted him to teach them (remind them) to be model citizens, obeying the governmental authorities willingly and showing a lifestyle of good works (Titus 3:1). To be sure their obedience was not merely passive assent to the ruling authorities, Paul also charged Titus with encouraging the Cretans to assertively model behaviors that were distinctively Christian, such as kind speech, peacefulness, gentleness, and humility (v. 2). What a powerful display of grace and redemption these Christians would present in their communities by conducting themselves like this, especially considering what they all (and we) once were as unredeemed sinners (v. 3).

LIFE STEP

Do you find yourself sometimes just "going along" with a set of expectations or rules that you've been taught? Why not make it a point to look for ways to represent Jesus Christ as His ambassador (2 Corinthians 5:20)? Be a positive influence among your friends and family. Focus today on how you might encourage others through your speech, your peaceful spirit, and your gentleness. Pray right now for God's help in demonstrating how you've been changed by the Gospel.

What is the writer saying?

How can I apply this to my life?

PRAY Bahrain – Pray for courage for Bahraini believers to be lights in the darkness despite daily hostility.

Paul's final words to Titus appear here in three parts. First, in verses 4-7, he reminded Titus of the power of the Gospel to transform believers from what they once were (Titus 3:3) to what they now are as redeemed sinners. He spoke of God's initiative in reaching out to sinful man as an outpouring of His abundant mercy and grace. It was not at all because of man's worthiness that we are saved, but according to His mercy (vv. 3-5) that He saved us! Notice Paul's references to the washing and renewing that brings about this change (v. 5), all through the Holy Spirit. Through this process of new life, we are declared justified (just as if we had never sinned) before God and now enjoy the promise (hope based on certainty) of eternal life (v. 7).

Paul then offered specific, detailed instructions to Titus concerning what he was to preach and teach and what he was to avoid (vv. 8-11). He is told to affirm constantly the all-important truths of the Cretan Christians' transformation as believers in the Lord Jesus Christ (mentioned in vv. 4-7), and by this affirmation to spur everyone toward good works (v. 8). Paul's concern here seems to be with the witness of the Cretans among others who are not yet converted to Christ. He warned that some arguments and disputes were a waste of time and should be avoided, and that those who persisted in such senseless arguments should be rejected. Paul closed his letter with personal instructions and greetings. His final encouragement to Titus was yet another reminder of the importance of authentic Christian conduct, telling Titus to teach his congregation to be fruitful in good works and meeting the needs of others (v. 14).

LIFE STEP

If you claim to be a Christian, your conduct ought to match your claim. That was Paul's consistent concern when instructing Titus, and it is still a relevant message for today. Be intentional today about showing yourself faithful as a "fruit-producer." Reach out to someone in need. Look for some way to do a good deed in the name of Jesus Christ. Refuse to get involved in disputes that are of no importance and focus on what God has called you to as His representative in this world.

What is the writer saying?

How can I apply this to my life?

PRAY Czech Republic – For the young people to search for answers in the Word.

Most scholars agree that Paul wrote this letter to the Thessalonian believers while in Corinth, along with Silas (Paul used the Latin version of the name, *Silvanus*, here) and Timothy (see Acts 18:5). He greeted the Thessalonians in the name of himself and these co-laborers to affirm their role in helping move the ministry along where they were located. Thus, the collective "we" is Paul's pronoun of choice to address these Christians throughout this letter.

Following a traditional greeting of grace and peace, Paul praised the Thessalonians for their great faith and love, emphasizing the magnitude of these Christian qualities they demonstrated through terms like *exceedingly* and *abounds* (v. 3). So exemplary were the Thessalonians in living out these qualities that Paul reported boasting to the other churches in the region regarding their great faith and patient endurance, even in the face of persecution (v. 4). This, it seems, is one of Paul's major purposes in writing to the Thessalonians. He had apparently been alerted to the growing trials and persecutions suffered by the Thessalonians at the hands of both Jewish and Gentile enemies of the Gospel. Considering their perseverance and steadfast faith, Paul therefore considered it a binding obligation (*bound*, in v. 3) to boast of the Thessalonians among other churches. His praise for these stalwart believers continued in verse 5, as Paul reminded them of the privilege of being counted worthy to suffer for the sake of God's kingdom.

LIFE STEP

If anyone were to boast about you, let it be about the way you honor the Lord Jesus with your faithful and loving service. Don't focus on gaining the praise of men, but simply be faithful in loving others and serving them in the name of Jesus.

What is the writer saying?

How can I apply this to my life?

PRAY   Uruguay – For the spiritual awakening of a country that is disillusioned by secularism.

"Tribulation" refers to the persecution of believers in many passages (see v. 4), but it also refers to God's judgment on unbelieving sinners, as in verse 6. These are the enemies of the Gospel who were "troubling" the Thessalonians and for whom God will bring a special tribulation period, when He will pour out His wrath on sinful mankind. Verse 7 speaks of Christ's second coming at the Battle of Armageddon to carry out this judgment against all unbelieving mankind. Their punishment, termed *everlasting destruction* (v. 9), is not annihilation, for other passages speak of eternal conscious punishment in Hell. It speaks of the horrors of eternal separation from the only One who can make life worthwhile—the Lord God.

Verse 10 says that Christ will be glorified "in" (not by) His saints. In our glorified state, we will reflect His glory at His return. Paul prayed that the Thessalonians would remain faithful and not crack under the immediate pressure of the persecution (vv. 11-12). This prayer was intended to empower them for further service and was especially important to the Thessalonians who were confused about the timing of Christ's return. Some had even stopped working for a living because they expected His return at any moment. (More on that in tomorrow's passage.) God desires to be glorified through our lives and accomplishments, and to mirror His glory by displaying His goodness to others. For a third time in chapter 1, God the Father and God the Son are mentioned on equal terms (v. 12).

LIFE STEP   *There is coming a day when all of humanity will give an account of what they did with Jesus. Considering this, make the best use of your time today and every day by living with purpose—to magnify the Lord Jesus Christ and point others to Him! What will you do differently today that will help you live with eternity in mind?*

What is the writer saying?

How can I apply this to my life?

PRAY   China – For the 44,000,000 members of unregistered house churches, persecuted by officials.

Recall that Paul had, in his first letter to the Thessalonians, instructed the Thessalonians about the Rapture of the church (1 Thessalonians 4:16-18). In the present letter, Paul felt the need to clarify and correct the Thessalonian believers who had misunderstood the timing of those events. First, he wanted them to calm down (*not be too soon shaken*) and consider what he truly meant to communicate (v. 2). He also wanted to stop the gullibility that had been their habit, having been easily deceived into believing that Christ's return (*that Day*) had already occurred, and they were now in the period of the Great Tribulation. Specific signs were yet to be fulfilled, such as the *falling away* (apostasy), and the revealing of the *man of sin*, also called *the son of perdition*. This is a reference to the colossal departure from the faith by organized Christianity in accepting the Man of Lawlessness (the Antichrist).

Verse 4 explains further how this individual (*man of sin, son of perdition*) will distinguish himself as a tool of Satan and opponent of God. In that day of rebellion, he will demand to be worshiped as God, even setting himself up as God in the Jerusalem temple. This is the only reference in Paul's church epistles to a temple during the tribulation period and therefore indicates the restoration of temple worship during that time of great trials. This demand for worship is also explained in Revelation 13:1-6 as a reference to the Antichrist. What seems to bother Paul about having to clarify himself in these matters is clear in verse 5. He told the Thessalonians these very things when he was last with them!

LIFE STEP

Fear of being left behind haunted some of the Christians in Thessalonica, and it impacted their lives. You need not have such fears! Praise God for the anticipation of His return and the reality of your security as a believer. Based on His Word, you can trust Him to spare you from the wrath to come if you have placed your faith in Christ (1 Thessalonians 1:10). Now, whom do you know who needs to be brought into God's family so they, too, will be spared God's coming judgment against unbelieving sinners?

What is the writer saying?

How can I apply this to my life?

PRAY   New Zealand – Bold and vibrant witness of those ministering in secondary schools and universities.

In his attempts to turn the Thessalonians back to truth about the coming of the Lord, Paul reminded them that they know what is the restraining power that is holding back the lawless one (vv. 6-8). Clearly, this is the Holy Spirit. How can they know? Because Paul had taught them these things (v. 5), and the evidence of Satan's work was in the present very active, even though the identity of the Man of Lawlessness was still hidden. Paul contends that "He" who restrains this individual and the full impact of Satan's deceptions will do so until He is taken away. Since the Book of Revelation describes people coming to the Lord during the tribulation period, we conclude that the Holy Spirit is not permanently removed from the earth when the church is raptured. It is best to consider the Rapture as simply a reversal of Pentecost, with the Holy Spirit removing the church from the earth at that moment. The Spirit will remain to affect the salvation of those who will believe in Christ after the church is removed.

Paul assured his readers of two facts regarding the lawless one (also called *Man of Sin*): he will be revealed when the Holy Spirit removes His restraint, and he will be destroyed by the mere brightness of Jesus' coming (v. 8). When he is fully active, this Antichrist will mimic the miracles performed by Jesus (*power, signs, and lying wonders*) to deceive those who refuse to believe in Jesus Christ (vv. 9-10). "Those who perish" (v. 10) reads in the original language, "those who are in the process of perishing." They are walking dead men! These unbelievers will believe the lies of the Antichrist and face condemnation by our Holy God, since they turned their backs on the truth and reveled in unrighteousness (v. 12).

LIFE STEP

As modern readers of this passage, it may be best to simply acknowledge how comforting it is to know that "God's got this!" Though Satan's deceptions have plagued mankind since the days of Adam and Eve, he is already a defeated foe (Genesis 3:15). Praise God for His plan of redemption for those who believe. Pray earnestly for the Gospel to reach the lost. Pay attention today to opportunities to share what you know of God's redemption.

What is the writer saying?

How can I apply this to my life?

Pray for your pastor and the leadership of your local church.

In this passage, Paul stepped away from correcting the Thessalonians in their understanding of the end times and began again to praise them and encourage them in their walk with the Lord. He felt compelled (*bound*) to offer thanksgiving to God for their salvation, acknowledging God's sovereign choice in bringing them to salvation (v. 13). Notice here that Paul mentions both God's initiative (*from the beginning chose you*) and man's responsibility (*belief in the truth*). Notice also that salvation is *by our gospel* (v. 14). Paul consistently affirmed in his writings that faith comes by hearing and hearing by the Word of God (Romans 10:17).

The "therefore" that begins verse 15 points to the previously stated truths. Considering their salvation and the glory which is theirs through Christ, Paul urged the Thessalonians to *stand fast*. This phrase is common in Paul's epistles (see 1 Corinthians 16:13; Philippians 1:27; 4:1) and implies a firm commitment to something. Here, they are told to remain firmly committed to (*hold to*) the traditions they were taught (v. 13). These *traditions* are not man-made teachings or religious dogma separated from the Word of God, but truths based on the messages proclaimed by Christ and the apostles and handed down orally from one man to another. Paul had in mind the apostolic traditions that were being preserved for us in the record of the New Testament. Paul recognized that the errors in doctrine that had crept into the Thessalonians could be corrected by knowing and heeding these teachings. He closed this thought with a prayer of comfort and peace for the Thessalonians, that their good works would continue (vv. 16-17).

LIFE STEP

Paul's advice to the Thessalonians is good advice for us today. We all need to stand firm on biblical teaching. What changes do you need in your habits to demonstrate your full commitment to the Word of God? Since you're reading this, it is evident that you have at least some sense that God's Word is important. Think of at least one step you could take in your daily activities that would enable you to be firmly committed to biblical truths. Write it down, then make it happen.

What is the writer saying?

How can I apply this to my life?

PRAY

Honduras – For godly, moral leaders to be elected to positions within the government.

Paul introduced the last major part of his letter with the word *Finally*, signaling again a change in topic. His topic was prayer—specifically, prayer for himself, Silas, and Timothy, that the Gospel they preached (*the word of the Lord*) would spread like wildfire (*run swiftly*), just as it had with the Thessalonians (v. 1). He also desired their prayers of protection and deliverance from enemies of the Gospel who would attempt to stop the spread of their message. This request surely resonated in the hearts of the Thessalonians, since they had experience with unbelievers who wanted to thwart the spread of the Gospel (2 Thessalonians 1:4-6).

Paul was careful to leave his believing friends in Thessalonica on a positive note, and in that effort, he expressed supreme confidence in God's faithfulness to *establish* and *guard* the Thessalonians from their enemies who were tools of Satan (v. 3). Considering Paul's other writings, this confidence stands out as a consistent theme to provide hope to Christians of all generations. God has Satan on a leash and will not allow him unrestrained freedom to afflict God's people (see 1 Corinthians 10:13 and Luke 22:31-32). Paul's confidence also rested in the Lord's continued influence within the Thessalonians to bring about their obedience (v. 4). The conviction here is that what God had started in them would be carried on through the power of Christ and the Spirit of God who dwells in them (Philippians 1:6).

LIFE STEP

Do you notice how prayer is integrated into Paul's life and ministry? We can never pray too much or too often. Use Paul's prayers as an example. Ask for prayer for your effectiveness in sharing the good news of salvation with others. Pray to God for the boldness and opportunity to minister today to someone in Jesus' name. Pray for others, that they will be drawn to the Gospel and that needs will be met according to God's perfect will.

What is the writer saying?

How can I apply this to my life?

PRAY Korea – For seminary graduates to humbly commit themselves to less prominent, rural pastorates.

Despite his clarifications and reminders, Paul knew that the church at Thessalonica included some who were unwilling to change their ways. Some had stopped working and were relying on handouts from the church members (v. 11). Paul urged the church to withdraw from such people (v. 6), pointing to himself and his companions as examples. When they were with the Thessalonians, they pulled their own weight and worked for their food so that they would not be a burden to the church (vv. 7-9). Even then, their message was clear: "If anyone will not work, neither shall he eat." Modern readers may struggle with such a concept, but it is worth noting that Paul's guidance was toward those who refused to work, rather than those who could not work. There's a big difference! Nothing in the teachings of Jesus or the apostles advocated ignoring real needs or refusing to help needy people. The antidote for a hungry busybody who had simply stopped working? Verse 12 is Paul's answer: they were to *work in quietness* and *eat their own bread.* The idea of *quietness* is simply to stay out of other people's business. Meanwhile, the actively engaged Christians in Thessalonica were encouraged to keep doing what they were doing to remain faithful, not growing weary in doing good (v. 13). As was his custom when suggesting discipline among church members, Paul reminded them to discipline (in this case, withdrawing from the disobedient) in love, with an eye toward restoring the erring brother (see Galatians 6:1). In bringing his letter to a close, Paul pointed out that his own handwriting was used to bring this message to the Thessalonians. This was Paul's consistent habit, most likely to affirm his personal feelings of love and to authenticate his message (v. 17).

LIFE STEP

The work ethic Paul called for in this passage is still God's ideal for man. Do your best to contribute to your own welfare as fits your situation. Maybe you're still in school and don't have a "real job." Find ways to contribute to your keep at home by helping out without being told to do so. If you're in the working world, be the best representative of Jesus Christ you can be. Work hard to earn your wage or salary. Don't be a busybody looking for others to take care of you!

MOBILIZE
OR THE CAUSE

GUIDE TO SHARE
ND GROW YOUR FAITH

TABLE OF CONTENTS

LIFE WITH JESUS LASTS FOREVER

List a few things that don't last.

1._____

2._____

3._____

4._____

Most everything in our world wears out and needs to be replaced. We get new clothes, new phones, and sometimes new friends. When we are really pressed to think about it, we realize not much lasts forever. That is what makes God's promise of eternal life, life with Jesus forever, so amazing.

Read Romans 6:23

According to this verse, what has God given to us as a gift?

▢ A better attitude

▢ Eternal life

▢ The ability to do good works

Notice that the verse says eternal life is a gift. If something is a gift, all you need to do is receive it and it is yours; there is no work involved!

Read Romans 3:23

According to this verse, what is it that we all do?

▢ Seek God

▢ Try to do good

▢ Sin

If eternal life, life with Jesus forever, depended on you and me being good enough to deserve it, it would be a lost cause because we all come far short of God's standard of sinless perfection. We all think, say and do things that disobey God; we all have sin as a part of our "DNA." We were born with a natural propensity to sin. Think about it: no one had to teach you how to lie, you just did it instinctively.

Read John 3:16

This verse says God gives eternal life to everyone who believes. That is so simple. Anyone who believes in God's one and only Son (Jesus) can have eternal life, life with Jesus forever. Jesus is God. He was born of a virgin and lived a perfect life without sin. Jesus took the punishment for our sins. He died and rose again, proving He is God and has the power to forgive our sins and give us eternal life. By believing in Jesus, we receive the forgiveness of sins and eternal life that lasts forever.

Read John 10:28

What promises do you see in this verse? (Check all that apply.)

☐ I will never perish.

☐ If I am a good person, I receive eternal life.

☐ Jesus gives me eternal life.

☐ No one will take me out of God's hand.

This verse teaches that eternal life is *given*, it's not something you work for or something you have to work to maintain. **ETERNAL LIFE IS A GIFT THAT LASTS FOREVER!**

We can have confidence that eternal life is a gift from the loving and never-changing God of the universe. The next time you are thinking about those things that DON'T last forever, let it remind you of the one thing that *does* last forever, eternal life. Remember, eternal life started the day you believed in Jesus and will last forever.

ACTION STEPS

☐ As you wake up each day this week, take a few minutes to thank Jesus for giving you eternal life that lasts forever.

☐ Write out a prayer to God thanking Him for the forgiveness of sins.

MY STORY

THE GOSPEL CHANGES EVERYTHING
Watch the Gospel Changes Everything video (Scan the QR code)

All followers of Jesus have a story to tell. It is the story of their life without Jesus, how they came into a relationship with Jesus, and how knowing Him has changed their life. One of the best ways to share the Gospel is to simply share the story of your personal journey to Jesus. To do this, you share what changed your mind about Christ and what has happened to you since. Here is what makes your personal journey to Jesus so powerful:

1. It is intensely personal.

2. It brings the power of the Gospel to life through your story.

3. It's REAL! It is hard to argue with a transformed life.

Read Mark 5:2-5, 8, 14-20

The man in this story receives deliverance from the possession of evil spirits. When Jesus set him free, and he was back to normal, the man wanted to go wherever Jesus went. The man was grateful for his healing and wanted to be with the person who had changed his life. Jesus had a different plan. He challenged this new believer to go home and tell his story. There were friends, neighbors and family who knew about his awful condition, and now he could share how Jesus changed his life. Jesus said to him, "Go home and tell them all the good things I did and how I saved your life." Keep in mind that this man was a new believer with no formal training in how to tell others about the change in his life. While we may not have all the answers for a skeptic, our story is real, even if it is not accepted or believed.

Even in the most intimidating situations, the story of how you came to faith in Jesus is simply you telling your personal story.

SHARE YOUR STORY

Think through the story of your journey to Jesus. To tell it well, it is good to write it down. This will help you focus on the main parts. As you are preparing, think about sharing three key things:

1. BEFORE: What you were like before Jesus

Maybe you were wild and crazy, or a partier, maybe life was dark and full of pain, maybe you were a cutter. Maybe you had a fear of dying because you saw a movie about hell. Whatever it was, just tell about life before Jesus. Go to the **My Story Worksheet** on the next page to outline **your life BEFORE Jesus**.

2. THEN: The turning point

What was it that helped convince you to believe in Jesus? Were you looking for something more because life seemed empty or hopeless? Was it a Christian friend who had something you didn't? Was it the feeling of guilt after doing something you knew you shouldn't? Was it the fear of death or hell?

Remember, your turning point was sent from God to help turn you toward Him, and it may do the same for others as well! On the **My Story Worksheet**, outline **what THEN was your turning point**.

3. AFTER: What your life is like now with Jesus

The third component should be a brief description of how your life is different since you put your trust in Christ. Maybe you feel unconditionally loved, or the nagging guilt is gone because your sins are forgiven. Whatever it is, share it from your heart, with grit and raw honesty. On the **My Story Worksheet**, outline **what your life has been like AFTER trusting in Jesus**.

MY STORY WORKSHEET

Use the following space to write out the story of your journey to Jesus. You can get started with the friend who is going through this lesson with you. Get the basic outline written and then work to complete it by the next time you meet so you can share it and make adjustments.

1. BEFORE: What were you like before you believed in Jesus?

2. THEN: What was the turning point for you?

3. AFTER: How is your life different since you put your trust in Jesus?

ACTION STEPS

◻ Ask the person doing this lesson with you to share their story with you.

◻ In the coming week, complete your story so you can share what you have written.

LIFE IN 6 WORDS

Read 2 Corinthians 5:20

From this verse, what can you learn about God's plan to get the message of the GOSPEL to people who do not know Jesus?

- God Himself will speak to each person.
- God's plan is to work through me.
- God has no plan to reach people who do not know Jesus.

One thing you need to learn is the "big-picture" theme of the Bible so you can explain it to others. There is a simple acrostic that will guide you in explaining the gospel to those unfamiliar with the Bible so they will understand. The acrostic spells the word "GOSPEL" and shares six key truths.

Learning these truths is like putting in the prep work needed to play a guitar. First, you learn the chords. Chords give you the basics, and as you master them, you can begin to play a simple song that others are willing to listen to! As your musical abilities continue to improve with practice and experience, you'll progressively improve until you reach the point where you're able to improvise, be creative, and make your own beautiful music. Mastering these six key truths will prepare you to be used by God to get the Gospel to your friends.

THE G.O.S.P.E.L. ACROSTIC

God created us to be with Him.
Read Psalm 100:3

God's original plan was that all humanity would be happy and in a perfect relationship with Him. God designed us to be in perfect harmony with Him. We were made to fit together like peanut butter and jelly.

Our sins separate us from God.
Read Romans 3:23

God's plan for us to live in a perfect relationship with Him was disrupted by an evil act thousands of years ago when Adam and Eve sinned in the Garden of Eden. This verse says that every human falls short and cannot keep the perfect standard of God. It's like having a contest to throw a rock to the moon. No one can actually do it. Some throw it further than others, but everyone falls short of this impossible goal. God is holy and His perfect standard has been violated by everyone, even the best of us. Every person has sinned because sin was passed on to us, it is a part of us, and we cannot change that.

Sins cannot be removed by good deeds.
Read Isaiah 64:6

Many people try to remove their sin by doing good things, but good works don't work! This verse says that God sees all our attempts to be good as filthy rags. When we do good works to try to make up for our sins, it is like putting white frosting on burnt cake. It puts a covering over something that is bad, but it does not remove the problem.

Paying the price for sin, Jesus died and rose again.
Read Romans 5:8

Jesus rescued us from our sins by being judged by God as if He had committed our sins. He took the full force of the wrath of God for our sins by dying on the cross. Jesus took our place! It is like Jesus pushing us out of the way of an oncoming bus and taking the hit Himself. Jesus was buried and then three days later, He rose from the dead.

Everyone who trusts in Him alone has eternal life.
Read John 3:16

Eternal life is a gift given by God. Jesus paid the price so you don't have to! Eternal life is free! You do not need to try or cry, you just need to trust in Jesus alone. Like putting your full weight in a chair you sit in, you put your full trust in what Jesus did for you on the cross, not in your own good works.

Life with Jesus starts now and lasts forever.
Read John 10:28

Eternal life starts as soon as you believe in Jesus, when you receive the free gift of eternal life from God.

ACTION STEPS

- Over the next week review the GOSPEL acrostic until you have it memorized.
- Download the Life in 6 Words App on your device.
- In the App, watch one video a day for the next few days until you have viewed them all.

 Scan the QR code to download the Life in 6 Words App.

ASK, ADMIRE, ADMIT

One of the biggest roadblocks to sharing the Gospel with people who are not Christians is knowing how to bring up the Gospel. Using the Ask, Admire, Admit method makes it easy to turn a secular conversation into a spiritual conversation.

Watch the Ask, Admire, Admit video
(Scan the QR code)

ASK

People generally like to talk about themselves, so by asking questions, you are engaging the person in a conversation about themselves. As they are sharing, pray that God will show you ways you can turn the conversation toward spiritual things. The reason to ask good questions is not to trip them up but to show you care about them and want to get to know them on a deeper level. You can ask great questions like...

- Where are you from?
- What sports do you play?
- What do you do for fun?
- What hobbies do you like?
- What is your favorite TV show?

Try to find things you have in common with them. If they are a close friend, you may already know this. The goal is to move toward questions about their faith, like:

- Do you have any spiritual beliefs or belief in the supernatural?
- What do you think about God or do you believe in God?
- Do you go to church anywhere or do you ever think about religion?

No matter how they might answer your question, you can ask them to explain to you what they believe. Remember, we want to ENGAGE people not ENRAGE them. With good questions it is possible. Remember, you are not out to win an argument. The goal is to have a Gospel conversation in which you share the Gospel.

ADMIRE

Once you have gained more understanding of their spiritual beliefs, look for ways you can admire what they believe. Find something to admire about their faith system and thank them for sharing.

Read Acts 17:22-23

How do you see the Apostle Paul admiring the Athenians' spirituality in these verses? (Check all that apply.)

- [ ] He called them very religious people.
- [ ] He condemned their idol worship.
- [ ] He noticed all their altars.

Once you have admired what you can about their beliefs, ask them if you can share your spiritual beliefs.

ADMIT

Now you simply admit how messed up your life was and how Jesus radically changed you! This is the perfect place to share your story, the story of how you came to put your trust in Jesus to forgive your sins and receive eternal life. This is where you share what you developed in the "My Story" lesson. Remember to keep your story brief, about 3-5 minutes. As you are telling your story, you will be sharing God's story, the GOSPEL!

After you finish sharing the GOSPEL just ask two more questions:

- "Does that make sense to you?"
- "Do you have any questions?"

If they have questions, keep talking with them. If they do not, ask if they would like to put their faith in Jesus Christ right now!

ACTION STEPS

- [ ] I will ask God to give me an opportunity to share the Gospel this week.
- [ ] When God gives me the opportunity, I will use the *Ask, Admire, Admit* method to share the Gospel.

THE CAUSE CIRCLE

Watch the Cause Circle video
(Scan the QR code)

The Cause Circle is a simple tool that will help you be more intentional about sharing the Gospel with your friends. It is built around three simple priorities: **prayer, care, and share.**

PRAYER!

Jesus knew how important it was to talk to God about people before He talked to people about God. The same is true for us. When we start by praying for the people we are seeking to reach with the Gospel, it prepares them to hear the Good News of Jesus Christ.

The first focus of our prayer should be to ask God to give us a great concern for the souls of the people around us: our friends, family, and neighbors. When we do this, we are asking God to let us join Him in what He's already doing! As He brings to our mind the names of people He wants to use us to reach, it helps us create our Cause Circle. We must not only pray for our lost friends to be reached, but also for God's Holy Spirit to give us the courage to do whatever it takes to reach them, even if sharing our faith with our friends feels a little scary because we might be risking our popularity.

CARE!

Jesus often healed the sick, fed the hungry, and helped the hurting. In the same way, we must show love to those we are trying to reach. We do this by listening to them and caring for them. It could be simply saying something nice, inviting them to sit at your lunch table or helping them with homework. Ask God for some creative ways you can show them the love of Christ!

SHARE!
Read 2 Corinthians 5:20

Notice in this verse it says that God is making his appeal through us! Remember, God wants to use you to share the GOSPEL with the people in your Cause Circle. Share the Gospel with them out loud with words as the Holy Spirit leads. A great way to do this is to use the Triple A method (Ask, Admire, Admit). We must lovingly share the Gospel message clearly and confidently. A restored relationship with God is the absolute best news on the planet, so don't be afraid to ask them to put their trust in Jesus!

ACTION STEP: BUILD YOUR CAUSE CIRCLE

Use the Cause Circle below to think through who you will pray for, care for, and share the Gospel with. Under PRAYER, write the names of people you know who need to begin a relationship with Jesus. Use this every day as a reminder of the friends you are asking God to bring to Jesus. In the CARE section, think of ways you could show Christ's love to your lost friends or family members. Take time and write a few creative ways you could do this. Ask God to help you think of specific, creative ways you can show care for each person. When you are ready to share the Gospel with someone, think through how you will do this. Then write the details of where, when, and how in the space provided in the SHARE section.

PRAYER!

_____
_____
_____
_____
_____

CARE!

_____
_____
_____
_____
_____

SHARE!

_____
_____
_____
_____
_____

QUIET TIME

Now that you have begun a relationship with the Best Friend you will ever have, you will want to spend time with Him every day; this is called a quiet time. Quiet time is all about spending time with God, learning how to listen to Him (by reading the Bible) and learning how to talk to Him (through prayer).

Read Psalm 42:1-2

What words do you see in this verse that show the writer's desire to spend time with God? (Check all that apply.)

 THIRST   LOOK   LONG   PANTS

In the following paragraph, put a box around "Word of God," circle "the Bible," and highlight "Best Friend."

The Word of God, the Bible, changes us as we read it, think about it, and do what it says. God's Holy Spirit, Who lives inside every believer, also uses the Bible to speak to us. He takes the words written in the Bible and tells us what God wants us to know for our lives. Investing time to read the Bible, trying to understand it, and then applying it in your life, will have an incredible effect on you!

YOUR QUIET TIME PLAN

Think through your typical day and decide what time you will set aside for your quiet time. Select a time that you can make consistent each day, when things are quiet, and you can really think. Choose a place that is quiet and has no distractions. Put a reminder somewhere, like on your phone, to help you build the habit. Plan to share what you learn each day with a friend, youth leader, or parent. The more detailed you are about the plan, the more likely you will be to follow through with it.

YOUR TIME WITH GOD

Pray

Before you start reading, take some time to talk with God by asking Him to speak to you through His word. Ask Him to help you understand what you read and also to help you do whatever He tells you.

Peruse: "to examine with attention"

Go to the Quiet Time page and look up the Bible verses. If you aren't sure where the verses are, use the index in the front of your Bible, do a Google search, or use a Bible app. Read the verses and answer the questions. Your Word of Life Quiet Time will help you think about the meaning of the verses and how they can apply directly to your own life. You can use some of the following questions to help you with this:

- What does this passage teach me about God, others, myself, or life?
- Is there a command to obey?
- Is there a promise from God that applies to me?
- Is there a warning for me to pay attention to?
- Is there an example to follow or avoid?

If you have any questions, get stuck or have a hard time understanding something, feel free to ask for help from the person going through this lesson with you.

Practice

The last step is to apply God's Word. This is when you take what you read and do something about it. Ask yourself, "If I were to take action on what I have learned, what would I do?" These questions can help you think through your application:

- Is there sin in my life I need to stop?
- Is there a way of thinking or an attitude that needs adjustment?
- Is there something I can celebrate and thank God for?
- Is there an action I need to take or a conversation I need to have?
- How will I live this out in my life today or this week?

You can reinforce what you learn by:

- Posting what God shows you to your favorite social media platform.
- Make a note about what you learned somewhere and read it a couple of times a day.
- Text what you learned to your parents, a friend, youth leader, or pastor and ask them what they learned from their quiet time with God.

ACTION STEPS

☐ Get your own Quiet Time this week at wol.is/Quiettime. If needed, have the friend going through this lesson help you. Once you have your Quiet Time, use the information in this lesson to set up your plan. (Scan the QR code)

- When - I will do it: ☐ morning ☐ afternoon ☐ evening.
- Where - I plan to do it at this location: _____
- Who - I will daily share what I learn with: _____

☐ Do at least one day of Quiet Time before your next meeting.

TALKING TO GOD

Which statement(s) do you think best describes what prayer is? (Check all that apply.)

☐ the words I use to talk to God

☐ my lifeline to Jesus

☐ when I bring praises, requests, and confess sins to God

☐ a way to show how much I need God

Be real when you pray

When we pray, the important thing to remember is that God already knows our deepest thoughts and feelings. We might think we need to present a version of ourselves that is neat and well-kept. The problem with this is we are not showing the version of us that God wants! He wants you to come to Him as you are, the real you - broken, messy, emotional, insecure, and yes, even at times explosive. He wants us to come to Him in our weakness and trust Him with our deepest fears, pains, and questions.

Read Psalm 6:2-3, 6-7

Below, list the words you see in these verses that show emotion.

_____

A Pattern for Prayer

You can use the acrostic A.C.T.S. for an easy pattern to follow as you think through how you talk to God when you pray.

"A" is for adoration.

Read Matthew 6:9-10

Adoration means "to have strong feelings of love or admiration." To put it simply, just tell God how awesome He is! In Matthew 6:9-10, it says, "Hallowed be your name. Your kingdom come, Your will be done on earth as it is in Heaven." When we tell the Lord that we want His will in our lives, we are saying that we accept that He knows what is best for us. As a believer, you can trust God because He loves you and wants the best for you.

Write one example of why God is awesome and why you choose to trust Him.

_____

"C" is for confession.

Read 1 John 1:9

Confess means "to admit our sins to God and ask for forgiveness." When we trusted Jesus, we received not only forgiveness of all our sins, but also eternal life that started immediately and will last forever. This does not mean we will never sin again. It is important when we sin as Christians to come to God and admit (confess) our sin and ask for His forgiveness.

Our unconfessed sins are obstacles to open communication with God. God *never* changes in His love and care for us when we sin. We are the ones who turn away from Him. When we confess our sin, we turn back to God who never changed in His love toward us. Confessing our sin restores our free and open communication with God again. We confess by admitting to God that we sinned and ask for forgiveness.

"T" is for thanksgiving.

Read 1 Thessalonians 5:18

According to this verse, in what circumstances should we give thanks? _____

Thanksgiving is "an expression of gratitude for a benefit received." Thanksgiving is simply telling God what you are grateful for. Most of the time we express gratitude when good things happen to us, but keep in mind that we can also be thankful for difficulties in our lives because God can use them to help us grow deeper in our relationship with Him.

What are three things you can thank God for right now?

1._____

2._____

3._____

"S" is for supplication.

Read Matthew 6:9-14

Supplication is "respectfully asking God for the needs and wants of others and myself." God cares about everything that is important to us. Things like food, clothing, and a place to live are examples of needs that we all have. Notice in verse 5 Jesus says, "When you pray." He is teaching us how to pray. As you read verses 9-14, what phrases did you see that reflected making a request? (Check all that apply.)

☐ show us ☐ give us ☐ help us ☐ forgive us ☐ lead us

ACTION STEPS

Take a few minutes to think through your plan for prayer. If you have a Word of Life Quiet Time, there is a prayer section you can use for this.

☐ **WHERE** I will pray here: _____.

☐ **WHEN** I will pray at this time: _____.

MY PLAN

☐ I will pray as soon as I wake up.

☐ I will set my phone alarm to remind me to pray.

☐ I will ask _____ to be my prayer partner.

☐ I will pray every time I _____.

☐ Other _____

Start your own prayer list by writing three things you can pray to God about:

1._____

2._____

3._____

THE BEST SOCIAL NETWORK

Social networks are designed to connect you with other people who have similar interests, to share ideas, and to hang out with people who like what you like. When you trusted Christ as your Savior, you were added to another "network" called the church, but we are not talking about a physical building. This network is the worldwide group of people who call themselves Christians.

You are probably more familiar with the local church, the buildings you drive by in your town. This is where youth groups and church services happen. Getting connected to a local church will give you some amazing benefits that will help you grow in your new relationship with God. You will also be able to contribute your unique gifts as you serve others.

There are many different types of churches and it can be confusing to determine which one would be best for you. As you are considering which church you should make *your* church, look for these three key characteristics:

1. The church teaches the Bible.

For you to grow in your new faith, good Bible teaching is vital. You will learn each week from a pastor who has spent years studying God's Word. To get the most out of your visit, seek to attend weekly, get a copy of the Bible (digital or book), go expecting to learn, take notes, and plan to put into practice what you learn. Also, find out when the church's youth group meets and make that meeting a priority as well. This meeting will be customized for you as a student.

Read Acts 2:42

What did the people referred to in this verse commit to? (Check all that apply.)

▢ They learned from the Apostles' teaching.

▢ They did group icebreakers.

▢ They prayed together.

2. The church helps people grow spiritually.

If you were on a team, you would expect each member to encourage one another in order to make the team the best it could be. The same is true of a church. Find a church where students and adults are serious about growing in their personal relationship with Jesus. A church youth group is a great place to interact with Christian students and adults who love Jesus, love students and what to encourage you to grow. Make weekly attendance at your church's Sunday service and youth group a priority in your schedule.

Read Hebrews 10:24-25

What are Christians encouraged to do in this verse? (Check all that apply.)

▢ Encourage each other to do good works.

▢ Continue to meet together.

▢ Make sure they give money to the church.

One way the church can help people grow is by encouraging each other. This is one of the key reasons we are encouraged to regularly attend a local church.

3. The church makes the Gospel a priority.

Find a church that is focused on getting the Gospel to others who do not know Jesus. Look for a church that regularly encourages members to share the Gospel. See if church leaders are setting the example in sharing the Gospel. Now that you are a follower of Jesus, God desires to use your words to share the Gospel with your friends. Being a part of a church that makes the Gospel a priority means you will be reminded about your need to get the Gospel to your friends.

Read Mark 1:17

What does this verse say Jesus would do for those who follow Him?

▢ He would make them a better person.

▢ He would protect them.

▢ He would make them into someone who shares the Gospel with others (fishers of men).

ACTION STEPS

Talk through the following questions to determine your plan to get connected to a great church.

Where do you currently attend church? _____

Are you free to attend another church if necessary? ▢ Yes ▢ No

Do you need transportation to get to youth group and Sunday worship service?
▢ Yes ▢ No

I IDENTIFY WITH JESUS

When you are excited about a sports team, you might wear things that show you are proud to be a fan. In a similar way, baptism is your way to say, "**I identify with Jesus**." In your baptism, you are preaching a message without using any words at all.

Baptism shows obedience.
Read Matthew 28:19-20

Notice the logical progression of this passage; go and spread the Gospel, then disciples are made, those disciples are to be baptized, and then taught to obey the words of Jesus. Notice the key part baptism has in this process. Baptism is a clear command of Jesus Christ. So, if you are a follower of Jesus, and you want to be obedient, you will be baptized.

Baptism identifies you with the death, burial, and resurrection of Jesus.
Read Romans 6:4-6

Being submerged in baptism is symbolic of dying to our old lives and being buried. Emerging up out of the waters of baptism is symbolic of being raised with Christ to a brand-new life. When you become a Christian, baptism is one of the ways you can show others that you have put your faith in Jesus Christ. You are saying, "**I identify with Jesus**." It shows you have a new life, the life Jesus gave you.

ILLUSTRATION

When a couple gets married, they begin to wear a wedding ring. The ring does not make them married. The wedding ring represents the commitment of the couple to faithfully love each other and is a public testimony to that commitment. The wedding ring identifies a wife with her husband and a husband with his wife, so the ring is an outward symbol of an inward commitment. In the same way, baptism is also an outward symbol of an inward commitment.

When should I be baptized?

A person should be baptized as soon as possible after putting their trust in Christ. Some people were baptized or sprinkled as infants. Being baptized as an infant is not the infant's decision but someone else's. If you have come to faith in Christ, baptism is a statement of your personal identification with Jesus Christ. You alone must make the decision to say, "**I identify with Jesus**" for yourself. No one can do that for you.

Should I invite my friends and family to my baptism?

Absolutely! Nothing could be more appropriate. Remember, baptism is a public testimony of your faith in Christ. It is also a visual re-enactment of the death, burial, and resurrection of Christ. At your baptism you are given an opportunity to share your story of how you came to put your faith in Jesus. This is a great way to get the gospel to non-Christian friends and family.

What if your parents/guardians don't want you to be baptized?

This is something that you should speak to a trusted pastor about. These situations can be complicated, but they are also important opportunities for you to grow. Sometimes following Jesus can be challenging, but in this challenge, He will give you wisdom. Talking to a pastor about your particular situation will help you as you seek to be obedient. At times what God asks of you as a believer might conflict with what your parents, teachers, or the government says. This is a place to learn when to "obey God rather than men" (Acts 5:29).

ACTION STEPS

Is baptism something that you would like to pursue?

   Yes

   Yes, but later

   No (If not, what is your hesitation?)

_____

When will you set a meeting with your pastor to talk about this?

Date _____

YOUR CONTROL CENTER

I know of no other single practice in the Christian life more rewarding, practically speaking, than memorizing Scripture. . . No other single exercise pays greater spiritual dividends! - Pastor Chuck Swindoll

Read Proverbs 4:23

What do you think the word "heart" means in this verse?

The physical organ

The inner person

The heart emoji

To understand this verse, you must have a biblical definition for the heart: the *control center* of man. This verse places a high value on what is going on in our heart, or control center. We could conclude from this verse that we are where we are in our lives today because of what is going on in our control center. If you think of the heart as your life's control center, that means that every thought you have originates there. So, what you think about will ultimately shape your life since your thoughts drive your control center.

Read Joshua 1:8

Check the statement below that you think is best reflected in this verse.

God promises that I will always be happy.

Meditation on God's Word will give success in life.

Meditation of any kind is needed.

God gave Joshua instructions to follow and promised that if he followed them, he would have success in life. The instructions and promises found throughout the Bible, when followed, will make you successful as a Christian. The success we are talking about here is skill in living, not necessarily making tons of money or getting your way. The key to this success comes when we meditate on and live out God's Word. The best way to meditate on Scripture is to memorize it.

Read Hebrews 4:12

A good paraphrase of this verse would be *God's Word is alive and powerful, it exposes our deepest thoughts, motives and desires.* The Scripture has the power to expose our thoughts. This means Scripture can show us where our thinking and actions are off and can help us to get back on the right path. Memorizing Scripture is a great way to put the power of the Word of God in our thoughts so God can use it to change our thinking to be in line with His.

Committing Scripture to memory is not just a good idea, it is essential for us if we are to grow in our relationship with Jesus Christ and have the successful life He desires for us.

YOUR SCRIPTURE MEMORY PLAN

The Bible has thousands of verses so you might be thinking, "Where do I start?" Word of Life has put together verses on topics designed for today's student. There is no cost for these and you can access them through the free Quizlet app. Once you have the Quizlet app, click on the magnifying glass and search for "WOLLCM-student." Scroll to the topic you desire and tap the translation you want (ESV, NASB, NIV, NKJ, or KJV).

As you begin to memorize, make sure you also learn the meaning of the verse. Look up the words in an online Bible tool, in a study Bible, or simply ask your youth leader or pastor. Learning the meaning of the verse will allow you to live it, which is the goal.

Many people think they don't have the ability to memorize verses, but we memorize things all the time: locker combinations, class schedules, and information for tests. It comes down to this: "How much do you want your life to change?" If you really want to memorize something, you can do it because your mind is powerful.

Give the following plan a try. You will be amazed by how much you can learn. You will not only be able to learn, but you will also be able to remember verses for years.

LEARNING
From Monday through Friday, say the verse out loud 10 times each day.

DAILY
Then for the next 3 weeks just say the verse once a day. At this point you know the verse and need little help to recall it.

WEEKLY
After this, commit to reviewing and saying the verse once a week for two months. Now the verse is locked into your mind.

MONTHLY
Now you could review the verse just once a month to keep it fresh for the rest of your life.

ACTION STEPS

I choose to take the challenge to memorize a few verses this year!
☐ Yes, starting this week.

The topic I will begin to memorize is _____.

My first verse to memorize is _____.

I will have this verse memorized by _____.

☐ Yes, but later. ☐ No.

YOUR IDENTITY: NEW LIFE

Have you ever secretly wished that you could start your life all over again? The good news is that spiritually, it already happened--when you put your faith in Christ!

Read 2 Corinthians 5:17

According to this verse, what is said to be new?
▢ the day ▢ someone in or belonging to Christ ▢ the Word of God, the Bible

One of the most powerful statements in Scripture about our identity after we begin our journey of following Jesus is found in this verse. Though you might not feel like it, God says that every person who puts their faith in Jesus has become a *new creation*. This verse states that Jesus has given us a completely new identity. It's true, you really do have a new life!

You have been raised to a new life!

Read Romans 6:5–12

The Bible also uses the word picture of dying and being resurrected with Christ to show we have a new life. In the following verses, put a downward arrow (↓) next to words that relate to death and dying and put an upward arrow (↑) next to the words that relate to life or living.

> *For if we have been united with him in a death like his, we will certainly also be united with him in a resurrection like his. For we know that our old self was crucified with him so that the body ruled by sin might be done away with, that we should no longer be slaves to sin—because anyone who has died has been set free from sin. Now if we died with Christ, we believe that we will also live with him. For we know that since Christ was raised from the dead, he cannot die again; death no longer has mastery over him. The death he died, he died to sin once for all; but the life he lives, he lives to God. In the same way, count yourselves dead to sin but alive to God in Christ Jesus. Therefore do not let sin reign in your mortal body so that you obey its evil desires.*

Notice that we become a completely different person after we put our trust in Jesus. This isn't speaking of an upgrade or improvement, but it is talking about the death of one person and the creation of a completely new person. This new life is one that is free from slavery to sin. It's a life of being connected to, accepted by, and adopted by God! It's a life of freedom from sin and the death and destruction it brings!

Now the challenge is, you must believe and live out this new identity. Notice that the Scriptures tell us to "count ourselves dead to sin."

[Find and underline "count yourselves dead to sin" in the verse above.]

The word *count* means "to keep a mental record, or to hold in regard." Because of this new life you have in Christ, you are told to regularly rehearse that this is true for you. This new identity will have its greatest impact as you choose daily to meditate on it, believe it, and act on it. This is something you can do every morning when you wake up and every night before you go to bed.

ACTION STEPS

Invest 5 minutes to review the identity statements below every morning when you wake up and every night before you go to bed.

God loves me more than I can ever understand. He even loved me when I was not loveable, when I was a sinner.

Romans 5:8, But God demonstrates His own love toward us, in that while we were still sinners, Christ died for us.

In Christ, there is nothing I can do that would make God love me more and nothing I have done that would make God love me less.

Romans 8:1, There is therefore now no condemnation to those who are in Christ Jesus, who do not walk according to the flesh, but according to the Spirit.

YOUR IDENTITY: ADOPTED

Adoption is a wonderful part of our society. It is hard to imagine a more loving act than parents welcoming a child into their family. There is a special love that these parents have for the child even before the adoption takes place.

Just as an adopted child had a need for a physical home, every person has a spiritual need to be adopted. Before we put our faith in Jesus, we were lost in our sin and on a path of physical and spiritual destruction. Even in that condition, God loved us. Jesus died to rescue us from our sin and give us a new life. This new life in Christ is completely opposite of the old one. We are no longer controlled by the bondage of sin. We have been adopted by God and are now His children through spiritual adoption. This means we are dearly loved children with an intimate and personal relationship with God, once broken but now restored.

YOU ARE ADOPTED BY GOD!

Read Galatians 4:5–7

In these verses, what words or phrases did you see related to being free? (Check all that apply.)
- [ ] Freedom
- [ ] Kindness
- [ ] No longer a slave

What phrase did you see related to an intimate relationship? (Check all that apply.)
- [ ] Adopted
- [ ] Love
- [ ] Abba Father

Do you see the words "Abba, Father" in these verses? *Abba* means "daddy." It is very personal and intimate. Jesus used this word when pouring His heart out to God (His Father) in prayer. This shows us that because of our faith in Jesus we are brought into the same father-child relationship that Jesus shares with God. If your relationship with your parents is not great, this might not bring the best thoughts to mind, but keep in mind we are talking about God as our father, the perfect and holy one who rescued us from sin.

Check the boxes below that might make up an ideal relationship:

- [ ] Joy when you are with them
- [ ] Wanting the best for them
- [ ] Selfless love
- [ ] Seeking our own desires
- [ ] Complete trust
- [ ] A listening ear
- [ ] Disinterest

The characteristics that make up an ideal relationship are true of your relationship with God. This is possible NOT because you are so loveable, but because God is so loving. We have been brought into an intimate relationship with God through Jesus' death on the cross!

Now, through Jesus, we are true sons and daughters of God! Unlike our human parents, God is the perfect father. God will never get angry or annoyed with you. He will never make mistakes as He cares for you. God always wants to hear from you, whatever is on your mind, and He will never give up on you. This is an amazing truth. You have been adopted by God, you are now His dearly loved child, and He will never leave you or forsake you.

ACTION STEP

After reading the verses below, write a prayer to God expressing your gratitude for adopting you as His dearly loved child.

Read Ephesians 1:5–8

God decided in advance to adopt us into his own family by bringing us to himself through Jesus Christ. This is what he wanted to do, and it gave him great pleasure. So we praise God for the glorious grace he has poured out on us who belong to his dear Son. He is so rich in kindness and grace that he purchased our freedom with the blood of his Son and forgave our sins. He has showered his kindness on us, along with all wisdom and understanding.

_____

_____

_____

_____

Scan the QR code to listen to the song Jesus, Thank You.

QUIET TIME
SCHEDULE OPTIONS

The following chart displays the Bible books and chapters for this year's quiet times. All quiet times cover the same passages each day so the whole family can stay connected to God's Word. Two schedules have been included or you can create your own for your group or family.

WEEK #	BOOKS (CHAPTERS)	2023-24 ACADEMIC SCHEDULE	2024 CALENDAR SCHEDULE
WEEK 1	Colossians 1-2	Aug 27 - Sep 2	Dec 31 - Jan 6
WEEK 2	Colossians 2-4	Sep 3 - Sep 9	Jan 7 - Jan 13
WEEK 3	Ruth 1-4	Sep 10 - Sep 16	Jan 14 - Jan 20
WEEK 4	1 John 1-2	Sep 17 - Sep 23	Jan 21 - Jan 27
WEEK 5	1 John 2-4	Sep 24 - Sep 30	Jan 28 - Feb 3
WEEK 6	1 John 5, 2 John, 3 John	Oct 1 - Oct 7	Feb 4 - Feb 10
WEEK 7	Joshua 1-5	Oct 8 - Oct 14	Feb 11 - Feb 17
WEEK 8	Joshua 6-14	Oct 15 - Oct 21	Feb 18 - Feb 24
WEEK 9	Joshua 20-24	Oct 22 - Oct 28	Feb 25 - Mar 2
WEEK 10	1 Peter 1-3	Oct 29 - Nov 4	Mar 3 - Mar 9
WEEK 11	1 Peter 3-5	Nov 5 - Nov 11	Mar 10 - Mar 16
WEEK 12	Jonah 1-4, Haggai 1-2	Nov 12 - Nov 18	Mar 17 - Mar 23
WEEK 13	Luke 1-2	Nov 19 - Nov 25	Mar 24 - Mar 30
WEEK 14	Luke 2-4	Nov 26 - Dec 2	Mar 31 - Apr 6
WEEK 15	Luke 4-6	Dec 3 - Dec 9	Apr 7 - Apr 13
WEEK 16	Luke 6-8	Dec 10 - Dec 16	Apr 14 - Apr 20
WEEK 17	Luke 8-9	Dec 17 - Dec 23	Apr 21 - Apr 27
WEEK 18	Luke 9-11	Dec 24 - Dec 30	Apr 28 - May 4
WEEK 19	Luke 11-13	Dec 31 - Jan 6	May 5 - May 11
WEEK 20	Luke 13-15	Jan 7 - Jan 13	May 12 - May 18
WEEK 21	Luke 16-18	Jan 14 - Jan 20	May 19 - May 25
WEEK 22	Luke 19-20	Jan 21 - Jan 27	May 26 - Jun 1
WEEK 23	Luke 21-23	Jan 28 - Feb 3	Jun 2 - Jun 8
WEEK 24	Luke 23-24	Feb 4 - Feb 10	Jun 9 - Jun 15
WEEK 25	Proverbs 7, Psalm 119	Feb 11 - Feb 17	Jun 16 - Jun 22
WEEK 26	1 Samuel 1-9	Feb 18 - Feb 24	Jun 23 - Jun 29

QUIET TIME SCHEDULE OPTIONS

WEEK #	BOOKS (CHAPTERS)	2023-24 ACADEMIC SCHEDULE	2024 CALENDAR SCHEDULE
WEEK 27	1 Samuel 10-17	Feb 25 - Mar 2	Jun 30 - Jul 6
WEEK 28	1 Samuel 17-20	Mar 3 - Mar 9	Jul 7 - Jul 13
WEEK 29	2 Samuel 5-15	Mar 10 - Mar 16	Jul 14 - Jul 20
WEEK 30	2 Samuel 18-24	Mar 17 - Mar 23	Jul 21 - Jul 27
WEEK 31	Psalm 73, Psalm 119	Mar 24 - Mar 30	Jul 28 - Aug 3
WEEK 32	2 Corinthians 1-4	Mar 31 - Apr 6	Aug 4 - Aug 10
WEEK 33	2 Corinthians 5-8	Apr 7 - Apr 13	Aug 11 - Aug 17
WEEK 34	2 Corinthians 9-13	Apr 14 - Apr 20	Aug 18 - Aug 24
WEEK 35	Esther 1-5	Apr 21 - Apr 27	Aug 25 - Aug 31
WEEK 36	Esther 6-9, Philemon 1-10	Apr 28 - May 4	Sep 1 - Sep 7
WEEK 37	Acts 1-3	May 5 - May 11	Sep 8 - Sep 14
WEEK 38	Acts 3-5	May 12 - May 18	Sep 15 - Sep 21
WEEK 39	Acts 5-8	May 19 - May 25	Sep 22 - Sep 28
WEEK 40	Acts 8-10	May 26 - Jun 1	Sep 29 - Oct 5
WEEK 41	Acts 10-12	Jun 2 - Jun 8	Oct 6 - Oct 12
WEEK 42	Acts 13-15	Jun 9 - Jun 15	Oct 13 - Oct 19
WEEK 43	Acts 15-17	Jun 16 - Jun 22	Oct 20 - Oct 26
WEEK 44	Acts 17-20	Jun 23 - Jun 29	Oct 27 - Nov 2
WEEK 45	Acts 20-22	Jun 30 - Jul 6	Nov 3 - Nov 9
WEEK 46	Acts 23-25	Jul 7 - Jul 13	Nov 10 - Nov 16
WEEK 47	Acts 26-28	Jul 14 - Jul 20	Nov 17 - Nov 23
WEEK 48	Proverbs 12-13, Daniel 1	Jul 21 - Jul 27	Nov 24 - Nov 30
WEEK 49	Daniel 2-3	Jul 28 - Aug 3	Dec 1 - Dec 7
WEEK 50	Daniel 3-6	Aug 4 - Aug 10	Dec 8 - Dec 14
WEEK 51	Daniel 6-9, Titus 1-3	Aug 11 - Aug 17	Dec 15 - Dec 21
WEEK 52	2 Thessalonians 1-3	Aug 18 - Aug 24	Dec 22 - Dec 28

Word of **Life**®

Plan your free campus visit
in New York or Florida.

We would love to connect with you!

Join us for a free visit to experience our campus,
connect with an admissions counselor, and see
for yourself why Word of Life Bible Institute is
the perfect place to deepen your faith.

wol.is/visit

DEEPEN
YOUR FAITH